BRITISH CINEMA,
PAST AND PRESENT

British Cinema, Past and Present responds to the commercial and critical success of British film in the 1990s. Providing a historical perspective to the contemporary resurgence of British cinema, this unique anthology brings together both leading international scholars and new voices to investigate the rich diversity of British film production, from the 1930s to the present day.

The contributors address:

- British Cinema Studies and the concept of national cinema
- the distribution and reception of British films in the USA and Europe
- key genres, movements and cycles of British cinema past and present
- questions of authorship and agency, with case studies of individual studios, stars, producers and directors
- trends in British cinema, from popular and middlebrow cinema of the 1930s to propaganda films of the Second World War, and from the New Wave and the 'Swinging London' films of the 1960s to key developments in contemporary film-making
- the representation of marginalised communities in films such as *Trainspotting* and *The Full Monty*
- the evolution of social realism, from *Saturday Night and Sunday Morning* to *Nil By Mouth*
- changing approaches to Northern Ireland and the Troubles
- contemporary 'art' and 'quality' cinema, from heritage drama to the work of Peter Greenaway, Derek Jarman, Terence Davies and Patrick Keiller

Justine Ashby is Lecturer in Television and Film Studies at the University of East Anglia. **Andrew Higson** is Senior Lecturer in Film Studies at the University of East Anglia.

BRITISH CINEMA, PAST AND PRESENT

*Edited by Justine Ashby and
Andrew Higson*

London and New York

First published 2000
by Routledge
11 New Fetter Lane, London EC4P 4EE

Simultaneously published in the USA and Canada
by Routledge
29 West 35th Street, New York, NY 10001

Routledge is an imprint of the Taylor & Francis Group

Typeset in Garamond by Taylor & Francis Books Ltd
Printed and bound in Great Britain by Biddles Ltd, Guildford and King's Lynn

British Library Cataloguing in Publication Data
A catalogue record for this book is available from the British Library

Library of Congress Cataloging-in-Publication Data
British Cinema, Past and Present /
edited by Justine Ashby and Andrew Higson.
Includes bibliographical references and index.
1. Motion pictures – Great Britain.
I. Ashby, Justine. II. Higson, Andrew.
PN1993.5.G7 B695 2000 99-087256
791.43'0941–dc21

ISBN 0–415–22061–0 (hbk)
ISBN 0–415–22062–9 (pbk)

791.430941
B

FOR CHARLES BARR,
WHO SET THE BALL ROLLING

CONTENTS

CONTENTS

CONTENTS

CONTENTS

ILLUSTRATIONS

Plates

Table

CONTRIBUTORS

Justine Ashby is Lecturer in Television and Film Studies at the University of East Anglia. She has published essays on British cinema of the 1980s and 1990s and is a contributor to *Dissolving Views: Key Writings on British Cinema* (ed., A. Higson, 1996). She is currently working on a book for Manchester University Press, *Odd Women Out: Betty and Muriel Box.*

James Chapman is Lecturer in Film and Television History at The Open University. He is the author of *The British at War: Cinema, State and Propaganda, 1939–1945* (1998) and *Licence to Thrill: A Cultural History of the James Bond Films* (1999), and co-editor, with Anthony Aldgate and Arthur Marwick, of *Windows on the Sixties: Exploring Key Texts of Media and Culture* (2000). He is a member of the Management Committee of the Society for the Study of Popular British Cinema and of the editorial board of the *Journal of Popular British Cinema.*

Paul Dave lectures in film and visual theory in the Department of Art and Visual Theory at the University of East London. He has published work on contemporary British film in *New Left Review* and is currently researching British cinema culture (post-1945) and making a documentary film on class struggle in eighteenth-century London.

John Ellis is Professor of Moving Image Studies in the Bournemouth Media School at Bournemouth University, where he is head of research. He is the author of *Visible Fictions* (1982) and *Seeing Things* (1999). For many years he ran the independent production company Large Door Productions, making such television documentaries as *The Man Who Ruined the British Film Industry, French Cooking in Ten Minutes,* and the *Visions* series about world cinema.

Leo Enticknap is the technical manager of a repertory cinema and film education centre in York. He has an MA in film archiving from the University of East Anglia and a Ph.D. from the University of Exeter, on postwar newsreels and documentaries in Britain.

Julia Hallam lectures in Communication Studies at Liverpool University and researches and writes on aspects of cultural identity. She was Chair of Mersey Film and Video from 1993–1997 and is currently chair of the Policy Committee of North West Arts Board and and a member of the BFI National Forum. She is co-author (with Margaret Marshment) of *Realism and Popular Cinema* (2000) and author of *Nursing the Image: Media, Culture and Professional Identity* (2000).

Sue Harper is Reader in Film History at the University of Portsmouth. She has written widely on British cinema. She is the author of *Picturing the Past: The Rise and Fall of the British Costume Film* (1994) and *Women in British Cinema: Mad, Bad and Dangerous to Know* (forthcoming, 2000). She is currently working on a history of British cinema in the 1950s, with Vincent Porter.

Andrew Higson is Senior Lecturer in Film Studies and Deputy Dean of the School of English and American Studies at the University of East Anglia (UEA). He has written widely on British cinema, including *Waving the Flag: Constructing a National Cinema in Britain* (1995) and *English Heritage, English Cinema* (forthcoming). He is editor of *Dissolving Views: Key Writings on British Cinema* (1996) and co-editor, with Richard Maltby, of '*Film Europe*' and '*Film America*': *Cinema, Commerce and Cultural Exchange, 1920–1939* (1999), winner of the Prix Jean Mitry 2000. He was director of *Cinema, Identity, History: An International Conference on British Cinema*, held at UEA in July 1998.

John Hill is Professor of Media Studies at the University of Ulster. He is author of *Sex, Class and Realism: British Cinema 1956–1963* (1986) and *British Cinema in the 1980s: Issues and Themes* (1999), and co-author or co-editor of a number of books, including *The Oxford Guide to Film Studies* (1998).

Peter Hutchings lectures in film at Northumbria University. He is the author of *Hammer and Beyond: The British Horror Film* (1994) and a contributor to the *BFI Companion to Horror* (1996). He has published articles on horror, science fiction, the films of Alfred Hitchcock, British cinema and television, and genre theory and criticism. He is currently writing a book on the British film director Terence Fisher.

Marcia Landy is Distinguished Service Professor of English/Film Studies at the University of Pittsburgh. Her publications include *British Genres: Cinema and Society 1930–1960* (1991); *Film, Politics, and Gramsci* (1994); *Cinematic Uses of the Past* (1996); *Queen Cristina* (1995); *The Folklore of Consensus: Theatricality in the Italian Cinema 1930–1943* (1998); and *Italian Film* (forthcoming). Her articles have appeared in such journals as *Screen, Cinema Journal*, and *boundary 2*.

Adam Lowenstein is Assistant Professor of English and Film Studies at the University of Pittsburgh. His essays on cinema, history and culture have appeared in such places as *Cinema Journal* and *Post Script*. He is currently working on a book concerning historical trauma and the modern horror film in an international context.

Moya Luckett is Assistant Professor of Film Studies at the University of Pittsburgh. She is currently completing a book on cinema spectatorship, the city and modernity, focusing on Chicago from 1907–1917, and a volume on national identity and femininity in 1960s British and American film and television. She is the co-editor (with Hilary Radner) of *Swinging Single: Mediating Sexuality in the 1960s* (forthcoming), has published essays in *Screen* and several anthologies, and was formerly editor of the journal *The Velvet Light Trap*.

Claire Monk is a Lecturer in Media Studies at De Montfort University. As a critic, she has contributed to *Sight and Sound* since the early 1990s. She has also contributed to *British Cinema of the 90s* (ed., Robert Murphy, 2000), *British Crime Cinema* (eds, Steve Chibnall and Robert Murphy, 1999) and the *Journal of Popular British Cinema*. She is currently completing a doctorate on British heritage films and their reception, and collaborating with Amy Sargeant on an edited collection on representations of the past in British cinema.

Lawrence Napper is researching a Ph.D. at the University of East Anglia on British cinema and the middlebrow between the two world wars. He contributed a chapter on the 'quota quickies' of the 1930s to *The British Cinema Book* (ed., R. Murphy, 1997).

John Orr is Professor of Sociology at Edinburgh University where he teaches in film and contemporary culture. He has published widely on different aspects of twentieth-century culture and his recent film books include *Cinema and Modernity* (1993) and *Contemporary Cinema* (1998). *The Art and Politics of a Film* and a co-edited film reader, *Postwar Cinema and Modernity,* are due to be published in 2000.

Vincent Porter is Professor of Mass Communications and Director of the Centre for Communication and Information Studies at the University of Westminster. His many publications include *British Cinema History*, which he co-edited with James Curran (1983). Among his current projects is a history of British cinema in the 1950s, co-authored with Sue Harper.

Phil Powrie is Head of the School of Modern Languages and Director of the Centre for Research into Film at the University of Newcastle upon Tyne, where he is directing research projects on masculinities in European cinema and on film versions of *Carmen*. His books include *French Cinema* *in the 1980s: Nostalgia and the Crisis of Masculinity* (1997), and an edited volume of essays on French cinema in the 1990s (1999). He is currently writing a book on the films of Jean-Jacques Beineix for Manchester University Press, and co-authoring a student guide on French cinema for Arnold.

Jeffrey Richards is Professor of Cultural History at Lancaster University. He is general editor of the *Cinema and Society* series at I.B. Tauris, and the *Studies in Popular Culture* series at Manchester University Press. He has published widely on British cinema. Among his many books are *The Age of the Dream Palace: Cinema and Society in Britain, 1930–1939* (1984), *The Unknown 1930s* (1998) and *Films and British National Identity* (1997).

Amy Sargeant qualified as an architect and worked as a production designer. She now teaches Media Art at the University of Plymouth. She has published on British Cinema in *Moving Performance: British Stage and Screen, 1890–1920z* (eds, Sarah Street and Lorna Fitzsimmons, 2000) and *The Projected Image and Popular Entertainment in the Nineteenth Century* (eds, Simon Popple and Vanessa Toulmin, 2000) and in *Film Studies*, *The Journal of Popular British Cinema* and *The International Journal of Heritage Studies*. She is currently collaborating with Claire Monk on an edited collection on representations of the past in British cinema.

Pierre Sorlin is Professor of Sociology of the Audiovisual Media at the Université de la Sorbonne Nouvelle, Paris. He has published widely on European cinema. His most recent books include *European Cinemas, European Societies, 1939–1990* (1991), *Italian National Cinema* (1996), *Les fils de Nadar. Le siécle de l'image analogique* (1997) and *L'immagine e l'evento* (1999).

Jane Stokes is Senior Lecturer in Media and Society at South Bank University. She is the author of *On Screen Rivals: The Cinema and Television in Britain* (1999) and co-editor of *The Media in Britain* (1999).

Sarah Street is Senior Lecturer in the Department of Drama: Theatre, Film and Television at the University of Bristol. She is the author of *British National Cinema* (1997) and numerous articles on British cinema; she is co-author, with Margaret Dickinson, of *Cinema and State: The Film Industry and the British Government, 1927–84* (1985). She has also published on costume and Hitchcock and is currently completing a book on the distribution and exhibition of British films in the USA.

Michael Walsh was born in London of Irish parents. He is Associate Professor at the University of Hartford, where he was principally responsible for starting the new Cinema major. He is working on a book on British cinema of the 1980s and 1990s and has previously published essays on Peter Greenaway, on films that show Margaret Thatcher, and on the future of the Lacanian method in film studies.

ACKNOWLEDGEMENTS

The chapters in this book first saw light as papers delivered at *Cinema, Identity, History: An International Conference on British Cinema*, held at University of East Anglia (UEA) in July 1998. We would like to thank all the people who were involved in organising the conference, especially Jayne Morgan, Conference Administrator, Julia Albert, and Pam Cook, who was involved in the early stages of the conference planning. Our thanks too to all the contributors, who did such a good job of turning their conference papers into chapters, and all those other conference participants, both those who delivered papers and those who attended as delegates. The conference was made possible by support from UEA, the British Film Institute, Channel Four, British Pathé, Anglia Television, Norwich City Council, the British Academy, and Eastern Arts Board.

We were delighted when Routledge agreed to publish this volume and are grateful for the encouragement that we have received from Rebecca Barden and Alistair Daniel. Our colleagues in Film Studies at UEA, Charles Barr, Peter Krämer and Yvonne Tasker, have also been wonderfully supportive. There is no doubt that this book would not be what it is were it not for the strength of the Film Studies sector at the University of East Anglia, who hosted *Cinema, Identity, History*. This is the third general collection of writing on British cinema to be edited from UEA, following Charles Barr's *All Our Yesterdays* and Andrew Higson's *Dissolving Views*. Like its predecessors, this collection bears the marks of the thriving graduate Film Studies programme at UEA, with six of the contributors past or present graduates of that programme. Jane Bryan, yet another UEA graduate, did a splendid job of compiling the bibliography. We are also grateful to Alex Noel-Tod, Film Studies Librarian at UEA, for compiling the index. Andrew Higson was granted a sabbatical by UEA and a Research Leave Award by the Arts and Humanities Research Board, without which he would have been unable to complete his part of the editorial work for the book.

A special thank you from Justine to George for his love, patience and numerous dinners, to Lauren for her genuine appreciation of mermaids, and to Jayne. Val, Billie and Luisa generously put up with all the usual stuff from Andrew, as ever distracting him at all the right times and in all the right ways.

Film stills were provided by the British Film Institute, the Kobal Collection, Pictorial Press and Patrick Keiller. For granting permission to reproduce illustrative material, we would like to thank Carlton Television (Plates 3, 5, 6, 10–13, 15–18), FilmFour (Plates 1, 4, 21, 23), Christine Parry and FilmFour (Plate 2), Canal + Image UK, Ltd. (Plates 9, 14, 19, 20), Fox Searchlight, courtesy of the Kobal Collection (Plates 8, 22), Calender Productions, courtesy of the Kobal Collection (Plate 24), Mondial, courtesy of the Kobal Collection (Plate 29), the British Film Institute (Plate 28), Patrick Keiller and the British Film Institute (Plate 30), Nik Powell (Plate 7), Penguin Books, Ltd. (Plate 25), The National Trust (Plate 26), and Destination Sheffield/Tourist Information Centre, Sheffield (Plate 27). We would also like to thank Intellect for granting Amy Sargeant permission to re-use material from her article 'The Darcy Effect: regional tourism and costume drama', in *International Journal of Heritage Studies*, vol. 4, nos. 3–4, Autumn 1998, © Intellect Ltd (www.intellectbooks.com).

INTRODUCTION

Justine Ashby and Andrew Higson

A string of British films enjoyed considerable critical and box-office success in the 1990s, from *Four Weddings and a Funeral* (Mike Newell, 1994) to *Trainspotting* (Danny Boyle, 1996), from *The Full Monty* (Peter Cattaneo, 1997) to *Elizabeth* (Shekhar Kapur, 1998), from *Sliding Doors* (Peter Howitt, 1997) to *Lock, Stock and Two Smoking Barrels* (Guy Ritchie, 1998), from *Shakespeare in Love* (John Madden, 1998) to *Notting Hill* (Roger Michell, 1999). There is a similar vitality and energy to be found in the academic study of British cinema. New books appear by the shelf-full: from Sarah Street's *British National Cinema* to Robert Murphy's *The British Cinema Book*, from Pam Cook's *Fashioning the Nation* to Charles Barr's *English Hitchcock*, from Jeffrey Richards' *The Forgotten Thirties* to John Hill's *British Cinema in the 1980s*.[1] The *Journal of Popular British Cinema* has become an annual fixture. Universities, colleges and schools all over the United Kingdom, not to mention the United States, Australia and elsewhere, offer an increasingly diverse range of courses on British cinema. The conference that spawned this publication was a major event, attracting speakers from all over the world. British cinema, past and present, is now a well-established area of study.

The chapters that follow demonstrate the richness of both British cinema itself and the ways in which scholars are writing about it. They began as papers presented at *Cinema, Identity, History: An International Conference on British Cinema*, which was held at the University of East Anglia in 1998. Charlotte Brunsdon, one of the keynote speakers at the conference, described it as a landmark event in British Cinema Studies, a view with which others have concurred.[2] If it was a landmark event, this was due to the fact that it revealed the maturity of this area of study, the range, depth and professionalism of the work being done and the number of people doing it. It would surely have been a much more modest event had it been held even just a few years earlier.

A revisionist dialogue

Like the conference before it, this anthology brings together different

1

research agendas and voices – strands of work that in the past too frequently ran in parallel but rarely met. If they did meet, too often it was in a spirit of antagonism rather than dialogue. Like the conference, this volume finds scholars listening more carefully to each other's voices. Appearing in the year 2000, this book affords us the opportunity to take stock of these developments, to celebrate the vibrant state of British Cinema Studies, but also to make some suggestions about what still needs to be done.

Although the anthology has grown out of a conference, it is much more than merely the publication of the conference proceedings. For a start, we could not possibly have included the seventy-odd papers delivered at the conference. Instead, we have been selective and endeavoured to present work on a range of topics, written from diverse perspectives, by a mix of established scholars of British cinema and those who are newer to the field. We also wanted to include a substantial body of material on contemporary British cinema while at the same time ensuring good historical coverage. We have deliberately omitted work on the silent period, however, since this will be the subject of another collection with its roots in the same conference.[3]

Thus what follows is a general collection on British cinema in the sound period, from the 1930s to the present. It is not intended to be comprehensive: no book of this size could possibly hope to be so, unless it were to adopt a thoroughly impressionistic approach to its subject matter. Instead, the book is indicative: of the conference, but more important, of both current work on British cinema and key developments in the history of that cinema. We trust that this rationale will prove attractive both to students coming new to the study of British cinema, but also to those who have a longer standing professional investment in this subject area. Our goal has been to edit a book that is both accessible but challenging, that respects what has gone before but is not afraid to question received wisdom. The blend of the familiar and the orthodox with the unfamiliar and the unconventional is thus quite deliberate. We hope the inclusion of a select bibliography on British cinema will enable others to take this work further. The bibliography covers the period from 1930 to the end of the 1990s; for ease of reference, it is organised into thematic and chronological sections. While we were by no means expecting the bibliography to be exhaustive, we were pleasantly surprised at the extent of the material that demanded to be included. This surely once again demonstrates that research and publishing in the field of British Cinema Studies has come of age.

The twenty-four chapters that follow are also organised thematically and to some extent chronologically, in that the final two sections deal with contemporary cinema. The separate introductions to each section explain the rationale behind the grouping of chapters. The boundaries between sections are, of course, artificial and what we want to do in this main introduction is to draw out some of the connections between chapters in different sections and consider the various ways in which the book can be seen as distinctive.

We think it significant that our contributors attend to both popular and quality cinema, to fiction and non-fiction, to the mainstream as well as minority film cultures such as the avant-garde and art cinema, to the canonical and the critically celebrated but also those areas of British cinema that critical opinion has tended not to favour. We also think it notable that the book demonstrates a diversity of approaches to its subject matter. Thus film criticism, textual analysis and theoretical endeavour find a place alongside studies of cinema firmly situated in their cultural-historical context, the speculative is given voice alongside the empirically grounded, the survey and the overview co-exist with the detailed case study.

Some of the chapters explore questions of authorship and agency; others focus on particular genres, movements or production cycles. Some of the contributors are more concerned with the shape of things on the ground: the organisation of the industry, for instance, or of the market that it serves. Others are more interested in questions of representation, whether in terms of gender, class and taste, or regional, national and transnational identity. Some of the chapters are written from an avowedly feminist perspective, some from an explicitly left-wing position, others from the point of view of a knowing empiricism or a carefully theorised post-structuralism. Some espouse a populist stance, others are more attached to a middlebrow sensibility, to modernism, or to the high ground of intellectual endeavour.

Several of the contributors can be seen as revisionists. For some, it is a question of revisiting familiar territory but giving it a new spin. Thus James Chapman challenges some of the received wisdoms about government propaganda policy and British cinema during the Second World War. Adam Lowenstein offers a fresh take on Michael Powell's *cause célèbre*, *Peeping Tom* (Michael Powell, 1960). And Moya Luckett reconsiders the Swinging London films of the 1960s in terms of the theme of female mobility. Others bring to light little known aspects of British cinema history. This can be seen in Part II of the book exploring the export market, and specifically the distribution, exhibition and reception of British films in western Europe and the USA. It can also be seen in Leo Enticknap's investigation of the Rank Organisation's postwar series of short documentaries, *This Modern Age*; and in the chapters by Vincent Porter, Jane Stokes, Peter Hutchings and Justine Ashby, who begin to map a previously neglected decade, the 1950s. Yet other contributors propose new approaches, as in John Ellis's argument that films need to be understood as performances that engage their audiences in particular ways, or in Andrew Higson's suggestion that we need to rethink the boundaries of British cinema from a transnational perspective.

For those contributors dealing with contemporary cinema, because the lines are less well drawn, there is less to revise and more to do in the way of original mapping. John Hill explores some of the ways in which the 'gritty realism' of films by Ken Loach, Alan Clarke, Mike Leigh and others both draws on and diverges from earlier traditions of British realist cinema. Both

Plate 1   *Brassed Off* (Mark Herman, 1996): an unexpected box-office success story of
the 1990s that forms part of a recent cycle of popular films exploring
masculinity and class in contemporary Britain.

Julia Hallam and Claire Monk discuss a related cycle of more mainstream
films produced in the 1990s, including such major successes as *Trainspotting*,
Brassed Off (Mark Herman, 1996) and *The Full Monty*, which Monk terms
'underclass films'. John Orr, Phil Powrie and Paul Dave, on the other hand,
deal with films produced for the specialised, art-house end of the market.
While Orr is able to draw on a reasonable body of work about his chosen
film-makers, Peter Greenaway and Derek Jarman, Powrie's investigation of
films by Terence Davies and Gillies MacKinnon, and Dave's of Patrick
Keiller's films operate in less well charted waters. Like Orr, both Michael
Walsh and Amy Sargeant can engage in a dialogue with existing work.
Walsh throws new light on recent films about Ireland, and especially British
films that attempt to come to terms with the troubles in Northern Ireland.
Sargeant re-examines some of the key terms in the debates about heritage
cinema and television.

From representation to reception

Questions of representation figure strongly in most of the contributions on
contemporary cinema. Orr, Powrie and Dave look at the way their chosen

films construct images of the nation, class and cultural identity. This is writ large in the two films by Keiller that Dave discusses, which are more or less poetic treatises on the state of the nation. In the case of the films by Jarman, Greenaway, Davies and MacKinnon, the themes have to be teased out more speculatively. Monk and Hallam read the underclass films of the 1990s as expressing the prevalent ideologies of the period. Like Powrie, Hallam concentrates on discourses of regionalism and nationalism – including Scottish and Welsh nationalism. Unlike Powrie, she situates the films firmly in the context of political economy, linking them to local and national production initiatives and patterns of investment. Monk, on the other hand, deals primarily with class and gender, and specifically with the theme of working-class male disempowerment in these films. Monk suggests that the retrograde image of heritage Britain was largely replaced in the late 1990s by these contemporary dramas of everyday life among the dispossessed. Sargeant's analysis of 1990s film and television culture, however, suggests that heritage England remains a prominent image. But, like Hallam, they both agree that developments in contemporary British cinema can be linked to the culture of enterprise and regeneration.

The chapters by Moya Luckett, Justine Ashby, Marcia Landy and Sue Harper can be linked by their shared feminist concerns. Landy and Ashby touch on the appeal of, among other films, selected British woman's pictures of the 1940s and 1950s, while Luckett offers a feminist re-reading of the Swinging London films. Harper delineates a series of female star types in British cinema in the 1930s; in assigning actresses to these types, she explores their social function in the culture of the period. While all of these contributors have something to say about the representation of women on the screen, Ashby also looks at some of the circumstances in which such representations are produced, since her central concern is with Betty Box as a female producer in an otherwise male-dominated profession. Similarly, Harper explores the possibility for individual actresses to exercise autonomy within the rigid confines of a male-dominated industry, and shows how certain actresses' performative manoeuvres allowed for limited but significant forms of agency.

As this eclectic set of contributions demonstrates, much Film Studies remains focused on films as texts. The treatment of films as texts can be very productive in terms of understanding how they are put together as aesthetic works and the range of meanings they can generate. Most of the contributions to this anthology do much more than simply analyse films, however, since they also situate those films in broader historical contexts. Questions of representation are in this sense given some historical grounding. An increasingly prominent aspect of this historical turn in Film Studies is the growing body of work that addresses the performance of films in the marketplace. Ideological analyses of films have often speculated about how audiences might engage with those films, usually by identifying an ideal spectatorial response implied by the organisation of the films as texts – as here in the essays by Ellis, Monk, Powrie and others. But this is not the same as generating knowledge about actual audience behaviour or about how audiences interact with films. Nor can such analysis tell us very much about the conditions under which films circulate in the culture at large.

This is where studies of distribution and exhibition policy and practice can be instructive. These may take the form of industrial analysis, as in the chapters by Sarah Street on the distribution of British films in the USA or Pierre Sorlin on their distribution in western Europe. Neither chapter is devoted solely to industrial analysis however, since they both also look at promotional strategies, box-office records and critical reception as ways of understanding how films performed with audiences. The vagaries of critical reception also feature in the chapters by Chapman and Lowenstein. As Sorlin points out, however, such evidence is always limited in what it can tell us about actual audiences. It is in an effort to go beyond these limitations that some researchers have adopted an ethnographic approach, seeking to understand how audiences use films and cinema-going by carrying out detailed work with specific audience groups.

While none of our contributors take on ethnographic research, two of the chapters do draw on some of its insights. Thus Marcia Landy provides a wonderful anecdotal account of her own history as an American growing up watching British films (like Street and Sorlin, she supplements her personal account with quotations from contemporary film reviewers). Biography, autobiography and personal history have been vital sources for certain sorts of historical research on cinema and television. Ellis, too, draws on such sources in constructing a history of film exhibition as performance, making connections between the way audiences act in the cinema auditorium and the way certain types of films address them. In order to explore the latter issue, Ellis also draws on textual analysis, thus combining the empirical with the speculative. His insights about film presentation can also usefully be combined with a brief section at the beginning of Enticknap's chapter, which outlines the main ingredients and the shape of the typical film programme offered by British cinemas in the late 1940s.[4]

Landy, Sorlin and Street all deal with the mobility of films, their capacity to travel across national boundaries. One of the most revealing things to emerge from their analyses is the way in which films can be transformed in this movement. The way that the persona of Alec Guinness is understood in the USA or in France may thus be quite different to how it is generally understood in British writing about his films, as becomes clear from reading Sorlin's and Landy's chapters. Of course, critical writing will rarely equate with the range of audience responses a film will generate. As Ellis points out, a key factor here is the space of the cinema auditorium in which films are traditionally consumed. Ellis argues that it is not enough to view a film separate from the environment in which audiences take it up, hence his attempt to reconstruct the ambience of the auditorium in the 1930s and 1940s and the way that films worked in that context.

If Landy introduces the metaphor of travel as a way of understanding the circulation of British films in the American export market, Higson and Luckett re-work the same metaphor in reading a range of British films for what they might say about the formation of the nation and national culture. Higson links the themes of travel and mobility to the hybrid and frequently transnational identities he locates in an eclectic selection of British films from the 1930s to the 1990s. For him, these tendencies call into question the very idea of British cinema, or at least how British cinema has tradition-ally been understood as a national cinema. Luckett takes up the theme of travel between home and elsewhere in comparing the relative immobility of the male protagonists of the British New Wave with the relative mobility of the female protagonists of so many Swinging London films.

Authorship and agency

Another theme running through several of the contributions to the book is that of authorship. As Hutchings argues in his chapter, authorship is not a constant, unchanging factor. On the contrary, different models of authorship characterise different sectors of the industry and indeed may alter as indus-trial circumstances change. We might also note that each critical discourse operates with its own model of authorship. Thus in Orr's chapter on Greenaway and Jarman, authorship emerges as a form of individual self-expression. This model of authorship of course is central to the institution of art cinema and the critical discourses that espouse it. It is no surprise then to find Powrie and Dave working implicitly with the same model, describing the films of key directors whose films have circulated primarily in an art-house context. The authorial model holds less tightly with these two contributions, however. Thus Powrie initially situates the films of Terence Davies and Gillies MacKinnon in the broader generic context of a cycle of rite-of-passage films. Dave, on the other hand, discusses the films of Patrick Keiller in terms of what they say about the state of the nation rather than what they tell us about their creator.

Ashby, Porter and Hutchings also deal with questions of authorship and agency but they do so in the context of mainstream cinema of the 1950s and 1960s. In this context, authorship is understood much more in terms of a nego-tiation between different forces, where cinema is a form of cultural production rather than an artistic realm separate from the ravages of industry. For Ashby, the task is to explore what impact a female producer – Betty Box – might have had on the films she produced and the industrial and cultural context in which she operated. For Porter, the films produced by the Associated British Picture Corporation in the 1950s were shaped more by the studio line managers and the overall production regime than by the films' directors. For Hutchings, the object of study is the more conventional authorial figure of the director, in this case Roy Ward Baker. The argument, however, is less about delineating a consistent style and world view in Baker's films and more about understanding how those films were shaped by the circumstances in which Baker worked at different stages of his career.

Another director who receives attention from both Porter and Hutchings is J. Lee Thompson. Baker, Box, Thompson, Keiller, MacKinnon: this is hardly a familiar litany of the great *auteurs* of British cinema. None of our authors, however, make grand claims for their chosen figures: the point is not to celebrate hitherto forgotten or ignored *auteurs*, to write new *auteurs* into the history of British cinema. On the contrary, the point is to explore the idea and the reality of authorship, to understand the different modes of authorship that emerge under different institutional circumstances. Why, for instance, did such figures as Baker or Box emerge when they did, and what does it mean to describe them as authors?

Genres, cycles and cultural traditions

One of the main ways in which individual authorship is mediated in film is through the conventions of genre. Genres, movements and production cycles are also addressed in their own right in several of the contributions that follow. Chapman reconsiders the cycle of 'realist' feature films made during the Second World War for propaganda purposes. In looking in detail at a much more theatrical and spectacular propaganda film, *Henry V* (Laurence Olivier, 1944), he sets out to challenge the prominence of that cycle in critical discourses about film-making during the war. Enticknap's discussion of *This Modern Age* also revises the accepted view of the history of British documentary-realist film-making. Much less well-known than the films associated with the documentary movement of the 1930s and 1940s, he points out that this is precisely because the series was not much liked by the opinion leaders of that movement. The fact that *This Modern Age* was a carefully planned series of course gives the individual films a much greater institutional coherence than most genres, movements and cycles possess. The fact that they are documentaries concerned with information and education as much as entertainment also clearly situates them as part of the long and celebrated tradition of British documentary-realist film-making.

For Luckett and Lowenstein, the relative coherence of the New Wave cycle of the late 1950s and early 1960s becomes a standard against which other films can be compared. For Lowenstein, the question is why the surface realism and the class appeal of the cycle was acceptable to film critics of the period but why they were so offended by *Peeping Tom*. For Luckett, as we have seen, the stasis of the young male protagonists of the New Wave films is contrasted with the mobility of the young female protagonists of the Swinging London cycle of films. Both these chapters also chart much broader transformations in the British cultural formation. Lowenstein sees the outraged critical response to *Peeping Tom* as indicative of a prevailing moral panic about the emergence of a classless mass culture, a panic that is soothed by the New Wave films. In Luckett's case, the Swinging London films are depicted as a sign of a modernising, feminising trend in British culture, in which female travel challenges the apparent certainties of traditional working-class communities.

The concern with realism, class, gender, community and culture re-emerges, as we have seen, in the essays by Hill, Hallam and Monk on the realist and underclass cycles of the 1990s. While these authors are in part exploring films that draw on the rich legacy of the realist tradition in British cinema, films like *Trainspotting* obviously owe as much to the modernism of the Swinging London films and their fascination with a commercialised consumer culture. The realist tradition from the 1930s to the 1990s has always been promoted in terms of cultural value, pitting the authentic, indigenous culture of 'ordinary people' against the Americanised culture of glamour, spectacle, commercialism and 'mere entertainment'. There is another side to this debate about cultural value, tradition and indigeneity, however, and it is one that several of our contributors address. First, as Higson points out, what we think of as 'tradition' is always an ideological construction, while to call a cultural practice indigenous is always to some extent to engage in cultural cleansing, a means of creating a 'pure' national identity. Second, the realist tradition in British cinema, even when it deals with 'ordinary people', is often pitted against a critically denigrated working-class popular culture.

Several of our contributors delineate the terms of that popular culture without at the same time seeking to devalue it. Indeed, taking popular culture seriously, treating it with the respect and sympathetic analysis usually reserved for more elitist cultural practices, has been a defining mark of much recent writing about British cinema, as Jeffrey Richards makes clear in his chapter. Stokes taps this vein here in her examination of the comedy of popular entertainer Arthur Askey. In looking at two Askey films set in the world of television, *Band Waggon* (Marcel Varnel, 1940) and *Make Mine a Million* (Lance Comfort, 1959), she shows how his comedy was at odds with the anti-populist culture of the BBC, but also with the crass consumerism of commercial television. Ellis tackles another populist film with a very similar theme, *Radio Parade of 1935* (Arthur Woods, 1934). Here again, a 'genuine' popular culture is pitted against the staid and repressive 'official' culture of the BBC.

Lawrence Napper too explores the BBC's cultural role, but his argument is different in that he sees the BBC as performing a central role in establishing a middlebrow culture in Britain between the two world wars. He goes on to argue that, while apologists and practitioners of high culture may have despised middlebrow culture, it none the less formed the staple of popular British cinema in the 1930s when such films as *The Good Companions* (Victor Saville, 1933) espoused middlebrow sensibilities and national consensus. Central to this tradition of middlebrow cinema is the literary adaptation. Sargeant revisits middlebrow cinema and the literary adaptation in the 1990s in her investigation of filmed heritage drama. In addressing the relationship between 'quality', canonical texts and popular culture, she suggests that screen adaptations of classic literature have, to some extent, been popularised, even democratised, in their appropriation by the heritage industry.

Classicism, of course, has become a major term in Film Studies over the last two decades, not least because of the influence of David Bordwell, Janet Staiger and Kristin Thompson's magisterial *Classical Hollywood Cinema*.[5] Bordwell and his colleagues set out to define what they saw as the standard American film, routinely produced between the 1910s and the 1960s, and in many respects since. Ellis implicitly challenges their position in his comparative discussion of the energetic performativity of popular comedy and the much more culturally respectable and carefully honed classical narrativity of a quality film like *Brief Encounter* (David Lean, 1945). He argues that the performative cinema is in fact more popular than the classical narrative mode defined by Bordwell *et al*. Indeed, he suggests that the performative is not an aberrant mode of film-making, but the dominant mode. Classical narrative cinema, Ellis implies, is of only minority interest, and the institution of cinema must work hard to attune a majority audience to its sensibilities. Although he is writing about British cinema (in fact, responding to an argument advanced by Higson in *Waving the Flag*)[6] his argument would seem equally applicable to American cinema.

The art cinema discussed by Orr, Powrie and Dave, as well as one of the 'Irish' films Walsh discusses, *Elephant* (Alan Clarke, 1988), a short, highly stylised piece made for television, draw on all of these traditions in various ways. The films of Keiller, Davies, MacKinnon and Clarke call on aspects of both the documentary-realist tradition and classical narrative cinema (least so in the case of Keiller's work). The films of Jarman and Greenaway blend elements from performative and narrative cinema. But in each case there is also a modernist (postmodernist?) concern with narrative experimentation, which radically distinguishes these films from many others discussed in the book. On this evidence, one might speculate that the institution of cinema has given up the attempt to win a mass audience for the classical film and has instead created a specialised up-market product for minority audiences. It is as if the modest narrational experiments embodied in *Brief Encounter's* flashback structure have been allowed full rein.

Heritage films constituted one of the most prominent cycles in British cinema of the 1980s and 1990s, from *Chariots of Fire* (Hugh Hudson, 1981) to *Wings of the Dove* (Iain Softley, 1997), and from *A Room with a View* (James Ivory, 1986) to *Elizabeth*. The cycle has also attracted considerable attention from critics and scholars. Several of our contributors revisit the cycle. Sargeant does so the most thoroughly, exploring some of the interconnections between the heritage film, heritage drama on television, English literary culture and the tourism and heritage industries. Once again the issue of realism raises its head, this time in the guise of the debate about historical authenticity. Questions of national identity and tradition clearly figure strongly in discussions of heritage drama. Orr, Powrie and Dave – and the films they discuss – address these same questions of heritage and Englishness in very different ways. It is perhaps not surprising that Powrie suggests that films set in the past but dealing with 'ordinary people' rather than the upper middle classes, and with a strong regional sensibility far removed from the genteel southern England, should be called 'alternative heritage' films.

The links Sargeant draws between cinema and the heritage and tourism industries are typical of a thread running through many of the chapters in this book. For many of our contributors, to write about cinema is to engage in cultural history. But cultural history does not draw neat lines between different cultural practices. Cinema is not a discrete medium, a 'pure' art form. Rather it draws on a range of related cultural practices. Ellis, Napper and Stokes discuss cinema alongside radio and, with Sargeant, alongside television as well. Sargeant and Napper bring literature into the equation, Stokes music hall, Enticknap the press, Chapman the machinery of propaganda during wartime. More generally, as we have seen, cinema at times takes on a populist or middlebrow guise, at times a modernist or intellectual guise. In some circumstances it aligns itself with official culture; in others it struggles against it. Under some conditions, it takes on a strongly industrial complexion; under other conditions, it presents itself precisely as a distinct art form. Here we are entering the realm of the politics and economics of culture. While none of our contributors tackles such issues head on, they are addressed to some extent and in very different ways by Dave, Porter, Hallam, Monk and Walsh, among others.

The diversity of research methodologies

To write about British cinema from the perspective of cultural history is precisely to adopt a particular perspective, to research and present the topic in question in a particular way. It is, of course, by no means the only way of researching or writing about cinema in general or British cinema in particular. Indeed, as should already be clear, it is not the only perspective adopted in this book. British Cinema Studies is not a coherent, self-sufficient single-party state, and it is in our view all the better for that. Pluralism is to be welcomed. As Higson shows in his discussion of films made during the Second World War, different perspectives can yield different insights. We thus see the diversity of research methodologies adopted in the study of

British cinema as a positive factor, although we also recognise that diversity will be most productive if different research agendas and voices interact with each other. Without dialogue, without listening to each other, diversity becomes merely disparateness.

In his chapter 'Rethinking British cinema', Richards surveys the field of British Cinema Studies, summarising what has been achieved to date but also identifying what he believes still needs to be done.[7] He makes a broad distinction between Film Studies and Cinema History, the former growing out of the study of literature and focusing on films as texts, the latter growing out of the discipline of history and seeking to situate films in their historical context. Our own use of the term British Cinema Studies is intended to signal a conjoining of these different approaches. Like Richards, we are committed to historical investigation, but history is not a neutral or objective discipline. History is never simply the amassing of empirical facts, the accumulation of evidence. For a start, different historians identify different kinds of evidence as significant; then, once the evidence has been accumulated, the details must be mobilised into a story – and of course there is always more than one way of framing the facts or telling a story.

Chapman provides a useful illustration of this in his discussion of three 'schools' of writing about British cinema and the Second World War. The first school consists of those who played an active part in wartime film culture and whose subsequent histories drew on personal recollection and reproduced the dominant critical values of the 1940s. The second school Chapman calls the empiricists, by which he means historians who go back to primary sources, especially official documentation about the war period. The third school he identifies as theory-led, more concerned with reading the films of the period ideologically. Each school adopts an historical perspective, but each tells the story of British cinema during the Second World War in a different way. In effect, the empiricists aspire to what Richards calls Cinema History, the theory-led scholars to what he calls Film Studies. The implicit distinction between theory and history is an interesting one, not least because, as Richards points out, empiricism is itself a theory. Chapman notes that many of the empiricist historians of British cinema have strong links with the *Historical Journal of Film, Radio and Television*, whose output, he suggests, 'represents probably the most important development in the emergence of a new film historiography in the 1980s'. Yet it is notable that the *Historical Journal* has in fact rarely been concerned with questions of historiography as such. The material it publishes seldom exhibits a self-reflexivity about how one does history. Its writers prefer to get on with the job, rather than reflect on how the job should be done. In this respect, it is worth comparing the self-consciousness about historical investigation to be found in Robert C. Allen and Douglas Gomery's *Film History: Theory and Practice*, in a special issue of *Film History* or in Pam Cook's introduction to *Gainsborough Pictures*.[8]

Different types of historical investigation and reportage can be found in the chapters that follow. Several of our contributors have produced solidly researched empirical histories that attend carefully to primary sources, among them Chapman, Enticknap, Porter, Sorlin and Street. But if they have sought out official documents, contemporary trade publications, statistical information, company records and the like, they have not held back from interpreting the films they discuss. Indeed, it is important to remember, as any film archivist will remind us, that films themselves can constitute primary documents. But it is also important to remember, as Ellis points out, that films divorced from their historical contexts of exhibition can mislead the contemporary viewer or analyst. The balance between historically informed interpretations of films and the speculations of the present-day analyst is always therefore a precarious one.

That balance is negotiated in different ways by the other contributors to the book, almost all of whom adopt an historical perspective but who rely on different types of evidence, including secondary as well as primary sources, contemporary critical discourses and biography, autobiography and anecdote. Just as important is the fact that these writers are involved in producing cultural histories (in the case of Walsh and Dave, social and political histories) more than histories of the industry, government policy or the market. They are also more inclined towards the speculative and the interpretative than those in the first group. Indeed, if they have carefully historicised their subject matter, most of these writers also set out to test a particular theoretical model, a particular way of making sense of the cinematic development they focus on. One thing that emerges clearly from all these essays is that the empirical and the speculative are always interdependent: the one cannot exist without the other, however much some historians and theorists may believe otherwise.

Of all the contributions to the book, perhaps the least inclined to historicise the films and themes they work on are those by Orr and Powrie. Yet Orr's evaluative criticism and Powrie's cultural theorising open up fascinating interpretative possibilities in relation to the work of Jarman, Greenaway, Davies and MacKinnon. This question of interpretation, the question of where meaning resides, or how it is created, has of course become a central issue in Cinema Studies. If for some, the problem is tackled at the level of theoretical debate, for others the solution lies in the abandonment of textual analysis and the turn towards history, and especially towards reception studies in one form or another. We noted earlier that empiricist cinema historians have rarely debated the questions of historiography. This is perhaps true of scholars of British cinema more generally. We tend to operate pragmatically, rather than worrying over questions of methodology; we tend to get on with the research and the writing, rather than asking why, and how, we do what we do. There are big debates taking place in Film Studies at the moment, but they tend once more to be rehearsed using American cinema as the model.[9]

The one debate that we have developed, but which hasn't developed in the same way around American cinema, is the debate about national cinema. The question of how we should conceptualise British cinema, or what it means to talk about British cinema as a national cinema, is addressed by various contributors to this book, but especially by Higson. The attention to popular cinema as well as quality cinema, to routine fare as well as critical and box-office successes in the pages that follow is testament to the diversity of British cinema. Is it testament also to an overly parochial sensibility, an obsession with the accumulation of detail about even the most marginal elements of British film culture? If it is, that is because there is a concerted effort to map British cinema as thoroughly as possible, to understand the ways in which different cultural layers interact (or not, as the case may be), different audiences and tastes are formed and then served, and different industrial strategies are played out. It would be difficult to explore such issues without addressing local concerns and developments. Yet at the same time it is important not to blow the local or the mundane out of proportion. Equally, while taxonomy is important, it can't be the final result. Empirical detail only becomes meaningful through informed analysis.

Contemporary British cinema

Will British Cinema Studies one day be forced to become an entirely historical discipline because there is no contemporary British cinema to discuss? Certainly the death of British cinema has been feared for many years. On 6 March 1924, for instance, the *Bioscope*, one of the leading British film trade journals of the period, ran an ominously black cover with the caption 'Lights Out': no films had been in production that week in British studios and this seemed to be the end of the story. British cinema history is often characterised as a history of crises and revivals. As we noted earlier, it is currently enjoying one of its most vibrantly high-profile periods to date. In 1994, *Four Weddings and a Funeral* achieved what was, at the time, an unprecedented commercial success for British film. Its widespread popularity served as a proverbial shot in the arm for British cinema, boosting the confidence of those working in British film production and raising the profile and prestige of British films both at home and in the international marketplace.

Encouragingly, the success of *Four Weddings* has been followed by further successes, with each new year bringing a fresh crop of critical and box-office hits. The New Labour government elected in 1997 has been much more supportive of the British film industry than the Conservative governments that preceded it, although the injection of cash via various National Lottery-funded initiatives was already under way when it came into power. By the time this book is published, a new umbrella organisation for the industry, the Film Council, should be making its presence felt. There are then reasonable grounds for optimism as British cinema looks forward to the new millennium. Less encouragingly, it would be difficult to point to more than two or three genuine British film hits per year, while the capital available for film production in Britain in any one year might just about pay for the production of a single Hollywood blockbuster. Much of the capital invested in British film production today is in any case American. Scholarly debates about British cinema have questioned the concept of an indigenous, discrete national cinema, but as transnational funding becomes the norm, this argument may quickly be settled by trends in film production rather than by developments in film scholarship. Considering such factors, it is difficult to see the prevailing situation as indicative of a thriving national film industry.

A cinema is more than an industry, however, and the substantial space this book devotes to chapters on contemporary matters is intended to reflect and engage with the energy of British film culture and the renewed popularity of at least some British films in the 1990s. While we may have good reason to celebrate the apparent health of contemporary British film culture, we should not allow this to obscure critical judgement. Nor should we turn a blind eye to British cinema's continued weaknesses, its inconsistencies and its failures to provide equal opportunities for film-makers, regardless of ethnicity or gender, and to address comprehensively the range of ethnic and political communities who make up British society today.

While editing this anthology (and putting together the conference that preceded it), we were disappointed by the scarcity of scholarship discussing British cinema in terms of race, ethnicity and multiculturalism. The quality of work that has been produced in this field is generally impressive, but the quantity is far less so.[10] It is possible that the meagreness of debates about ethnicity in British Cinema Studies is in part caused by a corresponding marginalisation of black and Asian film-makers and films that take as their central theme issues of race and ethnicity. While films such as *My Beautiful Laundrette* (Stephen Frears, 1985), *Bhaji on the Beach* (Gurinder Chadha, 1993) and *Babymother* (Julian Henriques, 1998) (which was screened at *Cinema, Identity, History: An International Conference on British Cinema*) have made important contributions to contemporary British film culture, representations of multiculturalism or of ethnic minorities have all too often been seen as peripheral to mainstream British film production. It is certainly difficult to ignore the fact that of the films currently celebrated as instrumental in British cinema's most recent revival, none can be said to tackle questions of ethnicity with any conviction. Nowhere is this lack more blatantly illustrated than in the controversy that surrounded the success of *The Full Monty*. Allegedly based on an original story featuring five black male characters who turn to stripping to boost their finances, the film in the end found room for only one black stripper in the troupe, and even he was peripheral to the narrative.[11]

The big British hit at the time of writing this introduction is *Notting Hill*. In many ways, this film looks back to the middlebrow British cinema

Plate 2   Mixed relations: traditional ethnic and gender identities are explored and challenged in Gurinder Chadha's *Bhaji on the Beach* (1993).

of the 1930s and 1940s, with its collection of ordinary people from different backgrounds and walks of life, clearly situated within a thriving local community: here then is a metaphor for a consensual nation. *Notting Hill* also acknowledges the current vogue for heritage cinema, with Julia Roberts playing an American star who is at one point seen shooting a costume drama set in England. Yet, as in the middlebrow films of the 1930s and 1940s and the heritage drama of the 1980s and 1990s, the central characters remain overwhelmingly white, with Notting Hill's black community very much in the background. Even *Notting Hill*'s anxiety about the role of the media recalls the debates of the 1930s that Napper discusses in his chapter on the middlebrow and cinema.

How does Julia Roberts, the Hollywood film star, fit into this vision of the nation? On the one hand, she is simply the latest in the long line of American film stars who have been imported to beef up parochial British productions and add a touch of international marketability. On the other hand, the impact she has on the ordinary British people she meets in the film can be seen as a metaphor for British cinema's relation to Hollywood. By this account, British cinema has an enormous star-struck inferiority complex. It aspires to the glamour of Hollywood yet revels in its own mundane, underachieving domestic reality – like the characters at the dinner party in *Notting Hill* who compete for the title of most hopeless social failure. So long as British cinema remains in thrall to Hollywood, culturally and financially, it will continue to struggle. So long as it makes films that so entertainingly poke fun at this 'national malaise', it will continue to have a presence in international film culture. Whether British cinema has the long-term entrepreneurial energy to promote a film culture of diversity capable of speaking eloquently to diverse audiences is another matter. We hope the discussions that follow will go some way towards helping us to understand how we got where we are and how we can productively move on from here.

NOTES

1 S. Street, *British National Cinema*, London, Routledge, 1997; R. Murphy (ed.) *The British Cinema Book*, London, BFI, 1997; P. Cook, *Fashioning the Nation: Costume and Identity in British Cinema*, London, BFI, 1996; C. Barr, *English Hitchcock*, Moffat, Cameron and Hollis, 1999; J. Richards (ed.) *The Forgotten Thirties: An Alternative History of the British Cinema, 1929–1939*, London, I.B. Tauris, 1998; J. Hill, *British Cinema in the 1980s: Issues and Themes*, Oxford, Clarendon Press, 1999.

2 See, for example, M. Wood, 'Cinema, Identity, History: An International Conference on British Cinema', *Screen* ('Reports and Debates' section), Spring 1999, vol. 40, no. 1, pp. 94–6.

3 Andrew Higson (ed.) *Young and Innocent? Cinema and Britain, 1896–1930*, Exeter, University of Exeter Press, forthcoming.

4 For further material on audiences, exhibition and reception in Britain, see pp. 365–6 of the Select Bibliography, this volume.

5 D. Bordwell, J. Staiger and K. Thompson, *Classical Hollywood Cinema: Film Style and Mode of Production to 1960*, London, Routledge and Kegan Paul, 1985.

6 A. Higson, *Waving the Flag: Constructing a National Cinema in Britain*, Oxford, Clarendon Press, 1995, ch. 4.

7 For a similar overview, see A. Higson, 'British Cinema', in J. Hill and P. Church-Gibson (eds) *The Oxford Guide to Film Studies*, Oxford, Oxford University Press, 1998, pp. 501–9.

8 R.C. Allen and D. Gomery, *Film History: Theory and Practice*, New York, Knopf, 1985; *Film History*, Spring 1994, vol. 6, no. 1; P. Cook (ed.) *Gainsborough Pictures*, London, Cassell, 1997, pp. 5–9.

9 See, for instance, D. Bordwell and N. Carroll (eds) *Post-Theory: Reconstructing Film Studies*, Madison, University of Wisconsin Press, 1996; and E. Hanson (ed.) *Out Takes: Essays on Queer Theory and Film*, Durham/London, Duke University Press, 1999.

10 See, for example, S. Bourne, *Black in the British Frame: Black People in British Film and Television, 1896–1996*, London, Cassell, 1998; S. Malik, 'Beyond "the cinema of duty"? The pleasures of hybridity: black British film of the 1980s and 1990s', in A. Higson (ed.) *Dissolving Views: Key Writings on British Cinema*, London, Cassell, 1996, pp. 202–15; K. Mercer (ed.) *Black Film, British Cinema*, London, ICA, 1988; and J. Pines, 'British cinema and black representation', in R. Murphy (ed.) *The British Cinema Book*, London, BFI, 1997, pp. 207–16.

11 See P. George and P. Sawyers, '"*Full Monty*" stripped of its black inspiration', *Observer*, 7 September 1997, p. 31.

Part I

RE-FRAMING BRITISH CINEMA STUDIES

Introduction

The publication of *British Cinema, Past and Present* acknowledges that British Cinema Studies has come of age, and that it has reached its present maturity by drawing on a diversity of approaches and methodologies. In this first section, two writers instrumental in establishing historical and critical debates about British cinema offer fresh perspectives on some key developments in the field to date. Jeffrey Richards charts the different influences and agendas that have shaped writing about British cinema history and identifies several issues that he thinks deserve fuller investigation in the future. He mounts a persuasive defence of empiricist history, demonstrating how close attention to the specific social and industrial conditions in which a film is produced and received is an indispensable prerequisite of rigorous cultural history. At the same time, he warns against the antagonism that has sometimes surfaced between Cinema History and Film Studies and prescribes a more collaborative climate in which scholars of British cinema, whatever their creed, recognise their shared interests and investments.

Andrew Higson enters into a dialogue about how best to define and implement the boundaries of British cinema. He questions the validity of persevering with the critical concept of British national cinema, suggesting that it is – and perhaps always was – a tenuous idea as much the product of critical reading strategies as of the films themselves. In its place, Higson argues for a more pluralist and flexible term, 'post-national cinema', able to take account of the complexities of transnationalism and multiculturalism.

Richards and Higson use their chapters as an opportunity to take stock of the present state of British Cinema Studies. Both offer accessible and reflective overviews of significant trends in British Cinema Studies, reconsidering and revising their own established positions. But while they describe British cinema scholarship with broad brushstrokes, they also attend to detail, applying their arguments to specific historical periods, genres or cycles.

19

Thus Richards rethinks the 1930s from the perspective of a cultural historian. Similarly, Higson revisits some of the so-called consensus films of the 1930s and 1940s, showing how these texts are as susceptible to readings that emphasise themes of diaspora and liminality as the more explicitly 'post-national' films of the 1980s and 1990s.

1

RETHINKING BRITISH CINEMA

Jeffrey Richards

As we enter the twenty-first century, the study of the previous century's
distinctive art form – the cinema – seems to have come of age. On all sides
there are new journals, new book series, new courses, and path-breaking
conferences. There is an almost palpable sense of intellectual excitement in
the air – and at its heart lies the systematic and creative process of
rethinking British cinema.

As we engage in this process, we need to be aware that there are broadly
speaking two principal alternative approaches to the study of film in the
UK: Film Studies and Cinema History. They grew out of different disci-
plines, each with its own emphases, methodologies and approaches. Film
Studies developed out of English Literature and Cinema History out of
History. At the risk of oversimplifying, Film Studies has been centrally
concerned with the text, with minute visual and structural analysis of individual films, with the application of a variety of sometimes abstruse
theoretical approaches, with the eliciting of meanings that neither the film-
makers nor contemporary audiences and critics – so far as we can tell –
would have recognised. Cinema History has placed its highest priority on
context, on the locating of films securely in the setting of their makers'
attitudes, constraints and preoccupations, on audience reaction and contemporary understandings. Neither camp has an exclusive monopoly of wisdom.
Both are needed. Both are valuable. Recently there has been a rewarding
convergence between the two approaches, as cinema historians have taken on
board some of the more useful and illuminating of the theoretical developments, such as gender theory, and the Film Studies scholars have been
grounding their film analysis more securely in historical context. The result
has been that many scholars on both sides would now regard themselves
more broadly as cultural historians. But there remains an unproductive
hostility between some adherents of the alternative approaches. This has
taken the form of the cursory dismissal of works which deserve a more
serious engagement with their ideas and approaches.[1] Criticism is of course
inevitable and desirable, but it is best delivered in a spirit of gentleness and
good humour. For we are, when all is said and done, all colleagues in the

wider struggle against the enormous condescension of the likes of François Truffaut who famously declared the terms British and cinema to be incompatible.

Empirical cinema history

A regular criticism of Cinema History is that it is devoid of theory. As an empiricist of many years standing, I feel that it is worth pointing out to the proponents of that argument that empiricism is a theory and one that is longer established and more thoroughly tried and tested than some of the more fashionable but short-lived theories of recent years. The wholesale application to film criticism of the French linguistics theories associated with Saussure and the psychoanalytic ideas of Lacan, part of a bid to treat film analysis as a precise science, led for a while to the critical dominance of 'the sterile notion of the self-sufficient text', the idea that films possessed a meaning that was independent of the prevailing social, cultural, political and economic contexts.[2] That approach is now seen as both restrictive and ahistorical. The empirical cinema historian deals for the most part not in mere speculation but in solid archival research, the assembling, evaluation and interpretation of the facts about the production and reception of films. Particular emphasis is placed on establishing and exploring the context, social, cultural, political and economic, within which the film was produced. The empirical cinema historian has three main concerns. The first is to analyse the content of the individual film and ascertain how its themes and ideas are conveyed by script, *mise-en-scène*, acting, direction, editing, photography and music. The second is to understand how and why the film was made when it was made and how it related to the political, social and industrial situations in which it was produced. The third is to discover how the film was received by reference to box-office returns, newspaper reviews and audience reaction where it can be ascertained.[3]

It is a truism that films change their meaning with the passage of time, with changes in the nature and circumstances of the audience. A film produced in 1930 necessarily means something very different to an audience in 2000 from what it meant to an audience in 1930. But my primary interest as a cultural historian is to recover from films evidence about the contemporary values and attitudes, about the social and sexual roles of men and women, the concepts of work and leisure, class and race, peace and war at the time when the films were made. For me, therefore, films are one way of entering the mind of the 'silent majority'. What particular films come to mean to later generations, what they may mean now, is of much less interest to me than what they meant when they first appeared. Because this is the project, my concern is exclusively with cinema in the period from the 1920s to the 1960s when cinema-going was in the words of historian A.J.P. Taylor, 'the essential social habit of the age'.[4]

This empirical project and its contextual emphasis seem still not to be understood fully in some quarters. My recent book, *Films and British National Identity*, was castigated by some critics for failing to take much account of British cinema in the 1970s and 1980s.[5] But this criticism wholly failed to recognise that I was avowedly dealing with the cinema when it was a mass medium aiming to reach a cross-class, all-age audience. Since the 1970s the cinema has been a sectional medium, largely aimed at the under-thirties, and has been supplanted by television as the vehicle for the expression of a national identity. Cinema is therefore of much less value today for the contextual cinema historian as an indicator of the nation's preoccupations in the round than the popular television soaps, police thrillers or docudramas: hence my concentration on cinema pre-1970.

The empirical approach to British cinema history has not a founding father but a founding mother – Rachael Low, whose work has in my view been insufficiently acknowledged by students of film history. It would not be too much of an exaggeration to say that Low virtually invented the history of the British cinema. She was working for the British Film Institute (BFI) Information Department when it was decided that there should be some form of publication to mark the fiftieth anniversary in 1946 of the introduction of cinema into Britain. There existed at that time no systematic or authoritative history of the British cinema. The BFI set up a committee to plan and direct a programme of research into the history of the film industry and Rachael Low was commissioned to research and write what eventually ran to seven volumes covering the history of the British cinema from 1896 to 1939. She identified three sources of information. The surviving films of the period, which she systematically viewed; the reminiscences of pioneer film-makers, renters and exhibitors whom she interviewed; and documentary evidence both published and unpublished: catalogues, press books, contemporary reviews, letters, memoirs and above all the trade press, in particular complete runs of the *Bioscope* and the *Kinematograph Weekly*, which she patiently ploughed through, issue by issue, year by year.[6] The films, the written documents and oral history remain the principal sources of empirical histories, and in the end there is no substitute for immersing yourself in all three, steeping yourself in the images, ideas and words of the period, so that when you come to make sense of particular films and particular directors you can hear their voices in your head and see their world in your mind's eye.

British film culture

Rachael Low's volumes were the product of a particular moment in British film culture – a moment of confidence and belief, largely inspired by the cinema's wartime achievements. The general attitude of the intelligentsia to British cinema during the 1920s and 1930s had been one of despair, lightened by occasional rays of optimism as individual films met with the approval of the intellectuals who ran such key institutions as *Close Up* magazine and The Film Society. Paul Rotha summed up the attitude in his massive and magisterial *The Film Till Now*, first published in 1930, reprinted in 1949 and long regarded as authoritative. He wrote of British cinema:

> The British film has never been self-sufficient, in that it has never achieved its independence ... It has no other aim than that of the imitation of the cinema of other countries. ... British studios are filled with persons of third rate intelligence who are inclined to condemn anything that is beyond their range.[7]

British intellectuals of the 1920s and 1930s tended to favour Continental European cinema, experimental and avant-garde film-making and the British documentary movement.

By contrast with the despair of the interwar period, the late 1940s positively glowed with an optimism inspired by the belief that film had been accepted as an art form and British cinema was now valued as a serious and respect-worthy national cinema. This optimism took the form of the foundation of the British Film Academy in 1946, the launching of the *Penguin Film Review* in 1946, the revitalisation of the British Film Institute and a plethora of book publishing on British cinema issues. The dominant critical ethic of the late 1940s and the viewpoint from which British cinema was judged was the one identified by John Ellis in his seminal article on late 1940s film criticism. After a careful, thorough analysis of a broad range of newspaper and journal reviews, he established this critical stance as one which placed greatest value on documentary realism, literary quality and a middle-class improvement ethic.[8] But the moment of self-confidence was brief and the optimism waned in the early 1950s.

As it did so, other critical voices began to be heard. The magazine *Sequence* (1946–1952) began to pay serious critical attention to Hollywood cinema. Lindsay Anderson, one of its editors, wrote later that:

> By the end of the War, British films were respectable and over-praised. They had made their contribution to the mood of national self-confidence. They reflected the class divisions of the country faithfully enough ... the industry remained a closed shop ... Why should we join in the chorus of praise? It was much more useful surely, to draw attention to the vision and vitality of American cinema – then much despised.[9]

It was an attitude picked up and developed by the next important development in the cinema culture, the magazine *Movie*, founded in 1962. *Movie* saw itself as a response to the failure of British film criticism, which it defined as having been epitomised by the BFI's magazine *Sight and Sound*, still wedded to reverence for declining European art cinema and characterised by 'a set of liberal and aesthetic platitudes which stood in for a deeper and more analytical response' which 'meant that the critical approach to all films was equally impoverished'.[10]

Movie's approach to films was clearly influenced by that of *Cahiers du cinéma*. It is impossible to overestimate the significance of *Cahiers*; it was *the* major influence on the development of Film Studies both in Britain and America in the 1960s. This influence led to the foregrounding of the *auteur* theory, which saw the director as the dominant artistic and creative force in film-making. The editors of *Movie* shared with *Cahiers* a passion for Hollywood cinema, a belief in directorial authorship, a reverence for Hitchcock and Hawks and a fondness for rank-ordering directors. They constructed a pantheon that appeared in the first issue of *Movie*. The American section was headed by Hitchcock and Hawks, the only directors entered in the category 'great', followed by eleven in the category 'brilliant', twenty-one in the 'very talented' category and twenty-four in the 'talented' category. By comparison there were no British directors working in Britain in the 'great' category – Hitchcock's greatness for *Movie* lay in his Hollywood films. There was only one in the 'brilliant' category (Joseph Losey, an expatriate American), one in 'very talented' (the Argentinean Hugo Fregonese who made only three British films) and only three in 'talented' (Robert Hamer, Seth Holt and Karel Reisz, all directors with a distinctively European sensibility). All the rest, including Michael Powell, Carol Reed, David Lean and so on, were rated merely competent or worse. V.F. Perkins underlined *Movie*'s stance in an essay written on behalf of the editorial board:

> The British cinema is as dead as before. Perhaps it was never alive. Our films have improved, if at all, only in their intentions. We are still unable to find evidence of artistic sensibilities in working order. There is as much genuine personality in *Room at the Top*, method in *A Kind of Loving* and style in *A Taste of Honey* as there is wit in *An Alligator Named Daisy*, intelligence in *Above Us the Waves* and ambition in *Ramsbottom Rides Again*.[11]

It is perhaps a measure of the way in which Cinema History and Film Studies have evolved in the last thirty years that it would now be perfectly possible to read a journal article or hear a conference paper entitled 'Issues of gender and genre: the cases of *An Alligator Named Daisy*, *Above Us the Waves* and *Ramsbottom Rides Again*'.

This is the product of new perspectives and a new respect for British cinema which has its roots in the 1970s and the appearance of such books as Raymond Durgnat's *A Mirror for England*, David Pirie's *A Heritage of Horror* and Charles Barr's *Ealing Studios*, which with its combination of sensitive film analysis and thorough historical contextualisation remains to my mind the best single volume written on British cinema.[12] They pointed us in new directions away from the preoccupations and priorities of *Movie*. This is in no way to denigrate the work of *Movie* in revaluing Hollywood, something which then needed doing. But it did not need to be done at the expense of British cinema. There has been a tendency in recent years to downplay the auteurism that characterised *Movie*'s approach. But auteurism still has value as a critical tool. It would be impossible to deny that such directors as Thorold Dickinson and John Baxter are *auteurs*; and auteurist criticism has in recent years helped to rehabilitate critically directors like Michael Powell, David Lean, Carol Reed and Basil Dearden, all of them dismissed by *Movie*. At the time of writing, a new series of monographs on British directors to be published by Manchester University Press will assuredly give us fresh insights into both familiar and neglected figures from British film production and we still await definitive studies of such important figures as Anthony Asquith, Maurice Elvey, Victor Saville, Cavalcanti, Marcel Varnel and Herbert Wilcox, to name but a few.

New approaches to British cinema

In their thoughtful overviews of the course of British cinema history, both Charles Barr and Andrew Higson stress the richness and diversity of British cinema by contrast with an earlier and narrower concentration on realism as the defining characteristic of authentic British cinema.[13] The focus on realism produced much excellent and enlightening work on politics, class and the documentary movement.[14] But there were vast unexplored areas awaiting appraisal. Several landmark collections of essays began to shed light on these areas of darkness. Notable among them were James Curran's and Vincent Porter's *British Cinema History*, and Charles Barr's *All Our Yesterdays*, and more recently Andrew Higson's *Dissolving Views* and Robert Murphy's *The British Cinema Book*.[15] Many of the contributors to these collections pointed us towards the new approaches and emphases that are now helping us to rethink British cinema, approaches which more often than not productively combine Film Studies and Cinema History.

Particularly fascinating is the application of the idea of genre to British cinema. Marcia Landy, Sarah Street and Robert Murphy in their various histories of British cinema have demonstrated a new way of approaching British cinema in terms of genre analysis.[16] Some genres – the horror film, for instance – have received detailed and in-depth attention.[17] Sue Harper in her superb book on the costume film, *Picturing the Past*, provided a powerful model for the application of generic ideas: establishing a taxonomy of the genre, analysing its social, sexual and class functions, and exploring the forces which produce images of history and determine their consumption. Other genres still await the same kind of systematic exploration.[18]

Next to genre, one of the most rewarding areas of exploration today is the role and significance of film stars. Stars were and remain one of the principal attractions of the cinema and it is vital to any understanding of the medium to interpret their images and their appeal, their rise and fall in popular esteem, the nature of their performances, the shaping of films to act as vehicles, their importance in providing role models of masculinity and femininity. Richard Dyer's works form the foundation for the study of stars.[19] Although there have been valuable individual essays on British film stars, we still need full-length studies of, among others, Tom Walls and Ralph Lynn, Jack Hulbert and Cicely Courtneidge, Jack Buchanan, George Arliss, Margaret Lockwood, Googie Withers, John Mills and Jack Warner, to name only a few. They were stars who regularly topped box-office popularity lists and film magazine polls and until we understand the reasons for their popularity we will not fully comprehend the power and significance of the star system.

An integral part of star studies is the study of gender. When in the early 1980s I was writing *The Age of the Dream Palace* I gave more weight to class than to gender.[20] In recent years, class has been downplayed and other factors

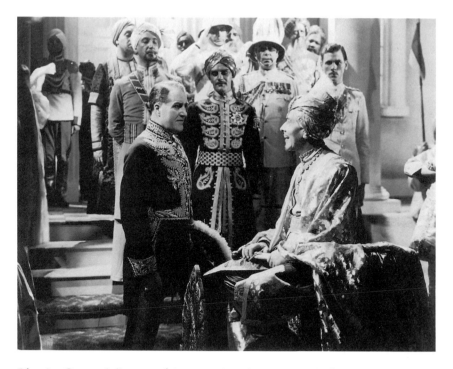

Plate 3   George Arliss, one of the many British stars in need of reappraisal, seen here in *East Meets West* (Herbert Mason, 1936) with Godfrey Tearle and Ballard Berkeley.

such as gender and ethnicity have taken greater prominence. Class is still to my mind significant. A viewing of any half-dozen films from the 1930s, 1940s or 1950s demonstrates this point. But gender studies have considerably deepened and enriched our understanding of British films. I have only one slight criticism. Gender is often taken to be synonymous with women. But gender is a gender-neutral word and applies equally to men and women. The flood of work on women and femininity in film – some of it very good – has so far been met by only a trickle of work on masculinity.[21] A full consideration of the operation of cinema on the audience requires both approaches.

The matrix of both stars and genres is the studio. Much important work has been done on the nature and function of the Hollywood studio system. Most film scholars can recognise the distinctive qualities, visual, aural and narrative, of the films of Warner Bros, Paramount, 20th Century-Fox, MGM, RKO and Universal, but much work remains to be done on what constitutes the look, style, feel, sound and ambience of the British studios. One studio – Gainsborough – has received detailed scholarly attention, in particular Sue Aspinall's and Robert Murphy's pioneering *Gainsborough Melodrama*, and Pam Cook's admirable edited collection, *Gainsborough Pictures*, which enriches the discourse by 'tracing shifts of identity across different historical moments and cultural contexts'.[22]

One of the key issues in the question of the studio look is the influence of the major influx of continental émigrés who from the 1930s on lent their considerable talents to British film-making. Kevin Gough-Yates has undertaken a major study of their contribution.[23] But did they create a Teutonic aesthetic in British films? Tim Bergfelder says they did not, Sue Harper suggests that they did.[24] Further research is needed here. But as we look at Continental influences, we should not neglect the American influence. There was a regular flow of directors, cinematographers and stars from Hollywood to Britain, some of whom – Tim Whelan for instance – did their best work in Britain. What was their impact? In a fascinating article, Tim Bergfelder suggests that what was distinctively British about British films was a merger of continental *mise-en-scène* and Hollywood narrative drive, an idea that deserves further exploration.[25] The impact of technology – sound, colour, widescreen, etc. – on the British film aesthetic also needs in-depth examination.[26]

In Britain, unlike America, film studio records are very hard to come by. But other documentation exists which enables scholars to chart some of the constraints under which the film industry operated in this country. It is impossible to understand fully the structure, nature and development of the British film industry without an appreciation of those constraints. The Board of Trade records provided the information which enabled Margaret Dickinson and Sarah Street to write their valuable study of government policy towards the film industry, *Cinema and State: The British Film Industry and the British Government 1927–1984*. James Chapman utilised Ministry of

Information records for his admirable work, *The British at War: Cinema, State and Propaganda 1939–1946*. Few periods of British cinema history are as encrusted with myth and misconception as the Second World War. The received view of the period has been heavily coloured by the opinions and reminiscences of the participants, often recalled years afterwards in memoirs which sometimes embellished the facts for the sake of a good story and sometimes sought to settle old scores. The judicious use of contemporary government records helps to dispel many of the misconceptions and set the record straight. Like the government, the censors influenced film content directly. They dictated the limits of what was permissible on the screen. An understanding of this process requires a careful and systematic analysis of the censorship records. The British Board of Film Censors' records were very effectively quarried by James C. Robertson for his indispensable studies, *The British Board of Film Censors, 1896–1956* and *The Hidden Screen*, and by Anthony Aldgate for his *Censorship and the Permissive Society*. Anthony Slide was the first scholar to investigate the records of the American Production Code Administration as they relate to the release of British films for his *'Banned in the USA': British Films in the United States and their Censorship, 1933–1960*, a work which is a major addition to our knowledge and understanding of the censorship process.[27]

Perhaps the hottest topic of current film scholarship is the question of national identity. Britain is currently undergoing a crisis of national identity, precipitated by the end of the Empire, the failure to engage with Europe, the arrival of devolution, the uncertainty over the status of Northern Ireland, unprecedented criticism of our traditional institutions (the monarchy, the law, Parliament, the Church of England) and the polarisation of the nation by eighteen years of Tory rule under Margaret Thatcher. This crisis has provoked a stream of conferences, articles, books and collections, and film scholars have turned to cinema to interrogate its role in the creation and promotion of national identity. This interest has produced my own *Films and British National Identity*, Sarah Street's *British National Cinema*, Kenton Bamford's *Distorted Images: British National Identity and Films in the 1920s* and Andrew Higson's excellent *Waving the Flag*, which thoughtfully and productively embraces both Film Studies and Cinema History and suggests an evolving identity through analyses of production strategies, genres and star images.[28]

Beyond the actual process of film-making lies the question of what audiences went to see, what stars, genres and productions they liked best, where they went to see their films and what they made of them. John Sedgwick, in a valuable series of articles, has been seeking to establish by statistical analysis which British films and which British stars were most popular in the 1930s.[29] This work is complemented by that of Allen Eyles, who has produced a meticulously researched series of studies on cinema buildings, cinema chains and the role of cinema in local communities.[30] Cinema-going was part of a wider cinema culture and that culture has been the subject of a major Economic and Social Science Research Council research project undertaken by Annette Kuhn, following the pioneering work done in the 1930s by Mass Observation and in the 1940s by J.P. Mayer.[31] Annette Kuhn is in the process of converting her findings into a series of articles.[32] She has made extensive use of oral history techniques and this is an approach which has recently received a new stimulus, from such works as Brian McFarlane's *Autobiography of British Cinema*, a series of interviews with film industry veterans, and Charles Drazin's *The Finest Years* which also draws on interviews with survivors of the 'golden age of British film-making'.[33] The cinema culture itself had specific appeal to women and children. Terry Staples' book *All Pals Together* charts the history of the Children's Cinema Club Movement and Annette Kuhn's study is likely to highlight the importance of films to the lives, imaginations and self-images of women of the 1930s, in much the same way that Jackie Stacey's *Stargazing* has done for women of the 1950s.[34]

Rethinking the 1930s

Many of these issues were in my mind when I recently returned to investigate the 1930s for an edited volume *The Unknown 1930s*, for which I recruited a band of cinema historians to explore some of these new areas.[35] For many years the 1930s was a neglected decade in the history of British cinema. It was seen as the era which produced a host of largely unmemorable British films and in which the mass audience preferred Hollywood's cinematic output.[36] When the histories of British cinema came to be written, the 1930s was characterised as the decade of Alexander Korda's epics, the regional comedies of Gracie Fields and George Formby, the polished thrillers of Alfred Hitchcock and the documentary movement led by John Grierson, claiming to present the only authentic picture of contemporary life in Britain. All of these aspects are important and worthy of study and have received, and are receiving, careful scholarly attention. But there is much more to the 1930s than that.

When I came to write my book on British cinema in the 1930s, *The Age of the Dream Palace*, I tried to rethink the conventional approach to the decade and to deepen and widen our understanding by the establishment of context. The questions I raised and sought to explore then – imperfectly and incompletely as is inevitable when you venture into new territory – were: what were the patterns of cinema-going and what was the actual experience of film-watching in the 1930s? What were the production strategies and policies of the film companies? What made up the contemporary debates within the culture about the influence of cinema? What were the aims, principles, operation and effects of censorship? What was the function of the star system and the role and appeal of particular British stars (I chose Gracie

Fields, George Formby, Jessie Matthews, Robert Donat and Leslie Howard)? Only when I had looked at these questions did I come to the films themselves, examining the debate about how Britain should be depicted on the screen, the messages about the present contained in two particular genres – the historical and the science fiction film – and an assessment of how cinema dealt with issues of class. *The Unknown 1930s* by contrast contains essays on neglected genres (the thriller, the society melodrama, the musical), on neglected stars (Conrad Veidt and Tod Slaughter), on neglected directors (Bernard Vorhaus, Berthold Viertel, Robert Stevenson), on an unresearched studio (Twickenham), on MGM's quotas films, and on audience preference in British stars and films. The essays addressed among other subjects the issues of star image, studio style, performance, generic conventions, the contribution of émigrés and audience context. But there is still more to do. I am struck by the absence of systematic studies of the role and influence of the fan magazine; of the richly productive symbiosis between the cinema and popular fiction, records, radio and stage; on the nature and preoccupations of British film critics in the 1930s. There is as yet no complete and systematic study of the films of the works of Ben Travers and Edgar Wallace, the two most filmed British authors of the decade. The whole field of 'quota quickies', hitherto despised, is suddenly attracting attention with, for instance, the rediscovery of Bernard Vorhaus. In a fascinating essay Lawrence Napper interprets 'quota quickies' both in their formal and thematic concerns as 'narratives of resistance to American values of mass consumption', an intriguing idea that deserves development at length across a wide field of filmic examples.[37] The whole vast range of quota quickies clearly provides potentially rich pickings for exponents of the many new approaches.

What we need in rethinking the 1930s is a creative and constructive concert of voices, a range of approaches, a variety of theoretical positions, seeking to explore and analyse and chart every aspect of the decade, from every possible perspective, male and female, left and right, producer and audience, director and writer, studio and star, British and foreign, until we can appreciate to the full the richness and complexity of the period. This is also the best way forward in rethinking British cinema in general. There is still so much to do that we cannot afford fruitless internecine strife. Let us therefore brace ourselves to tasks and so conduct our dialogue and our researches that people in future looking back on this era of cinema history may well say, 'This was their finest hour'.

NOTES

1 See, for instance, A. Medhurst, 'This Septic Isle', *Sight and Sound*, February 1998, vol. 8, no. 2, pp. 28–9; P. Cook, *Fashioning the Nation: Costume and Identity in British Cinema*, London, BFI, 1996, pp. 18–19.
2 David Bordwell, 'Textual analysis etc.', *Enclitic*, 1981–2, nos. 10–11, p. 135.

3 The approach is exemplified by A. Aldgate and J. Richards, *Best of British: Cinema and Society from 1930 to the Present*, London, I.B. Tauris, 1999 (revised edition), and A. Aldgate and J. Richards, *Britain Can Take It: The British Cinema in the Second World War*, Edinburgh, Edinburgh University Press, 1994.

4 A.J.P. Taylor, *English History 1914–1945*, Harmondsworth, Penguin, 1975, p. 392.

5 J. Richards, *Films and British National Identity*, Manchester, Manchester University Press, 1997. For criticism of its lack of coverage of the 1970s and 1980s, see J. Helbig, *Journal for the Study of British Cultures*, 1998, vol. 5, no. 2, pp. 233–4 and I. Christie, 'Book of the Month', BBC Radio 3, September 1997.

6 For a fuller discussion of R. Low's career and contribution, see my introduction to R. Low, *The History of the British Film*, London and New York, Routledge, 1997 (seven-volume reprint). The volumes were originally published between 1948 and 1985.

7 P. Rotha, *The Film Till Now*, London, Vision Press, 1949, pp. 313–14.

8 J. Ellis, 'Art, culture and quality', *Screen*, Autumn 1978, vol. 19, no. 3, pp. 9–49. A revised version of the article appeared as 'The quality film adventure: British critics and the cinema, 1942–1948', in A. Higson (ed.) *Dissolving Views: Key Writings on British Cinema*, London, Cassell, 1996, pp. 66–93.

9 L. Anderson, '*Sequence*: Introduction to a reprint', unpublished essay in the possession of the author, p. 7.

10 I. Cameron (ed.) *The Movie Reader*, New York, Praeger, 1972, p. 6.

11 Ibid., pp. 7–8.

12 R. Durgnat, *A Mirror for England*, London, Faber, 1970; D. Pirie, *A Heritage of Horror*, London, Gordon Fraser, 1973; C. Barr, *Ealing Studios*, London, Studio Vista, 1993 (revised edition).

13 C. Barr, 'Introduction: amnesia and schizophrenia', *All Our Yesterdays: 90 Years of British Cinema*, London, BFI, 1986, pp. 1–29; A. Higson, 'British Cinema' in J. Hill and P. Church Gibson (eds) *The Oxford Guide to Film Studies*, Oxford, Oxford University Press, 1998, pp. 501–9.

14 I. Aitken, *Film and Reform: John Grierson and the Documentary Film Movement*, London, Routledge, 1990; P. Swann, *The British Documentary Film Movement 1926–1946*, Cambridge, Cambridge University Press, 1989; S. Jones, *The British Labour Movement and Film, 1918–1939*, London, Routledge, 1987; B. Hogenkamp, *Deadly Parallels*, London, Lawrence and Wishart, 1986; P. Stead, *The Working Class and Film*, London, Routledge, 1989; J. Hill, *Sex, Class and Realism: British Cinema 1956–63*, London, BFI, 1986; S. Laing, *Representations of Working Class Life 1957–1964*, London, Macmillan, 1986; D. MacPherson (ed.) *Traditions of Independence*, London, BFI, 1980; A. Aldgate, *Cinema and History: British Newsreels and the Spanish Civil War*, London, Scolar Press, 1979.

15 J. Curran and V. Porter (eds) *British Cinema History*, London, Weidenfeld and Nicholson, 1983; Barr, *All Our Yesterdays*, op. cit.; Higson, *Dissolving Views*, op. cit.; and R. Murphy (ed.) *The British Cinema Book*, London, BFI, 1997.

16 M. Landy, *British Genres: Cinema and Society, 1930–1960*, Princeton, Princeton University Press, 1991; S. Street, *British National Cinema*, London, Routledge, 1997; R. Murphy, *Realism and Tinsel: Cinema and Society 1939–1949*, London, Routledge, 1989, and *Sixties British Cinema*, London, BFI, 1992.

17 D. Pirie, *A Heritage of Horror*, London, Gordon Fraser, 1973; P. Hutchings, *Hammer and Beyond: The British Horror Film*, Manchester, Manchester University Press, 1993; D. Meikle, *A History of Horrors: The Rise and Fall of the House of Hammer*, Lanham MD and London, Scarecrow Press, 1996.

18 S. Harper, *Picturing the Past*, London, BFI, 1994.

19 R. Dyer, *Stars*, London, BFI, 1979, and *Heavenly Bodies: Film Stars and Society*, London, Macmillan, 1987. See also C. Gledhill (ed.) *Stardom: Industry of Desire*, London, Routledge, 1991.

20 J. Richards, *The Age of the Dream Palace*, London, Routledge and Kegan Paul, 1984.

21 On femininity, see, for instance, A. Lant, *Blackout: Reinventing Women for British Wartime Cinema*, Princeton, Princeton University Press, 1991; C. Gledhill and G. Swanson (eds) *Nationalising Femininity: Culture, Sexuality and British Cinema in the Second World War*, Manchester, Manchester University Press, 1996; C. Gledhill (ed.) *Home is Where the Heart is: Studies in Melodrama and the Woman's Film*, London, BFI, 1987.

22 S. Aspinall and R. Murphy (eds) *Gainsborough Melodrama*, London, BFI, 1983, and P. Cook (ed.) *Gainsborough Pictures*, London, Cassell, 1997; see also Vincent Porter's chapter in this volume, on the films of ABPC in the 1950s.

23 K. Gough-Yates, 'The British feature film as a European concern: Britain and the émigré film-maker, 1933–45', in G. Berghaus (ed.) *Theatre and Film in Exile: German Artists in Britain 1933–1945*, Oxford, New York and Munich, Berg Publishing, 1989, pp. 135–66.

24 T. Bergfelder, 'The production designer and the *Gesamtkunstwerk*: German film technicians in the British film industry of the 1930s', in Higson (ed.) *Dissolving Views*, op. cit., pp. 120–37; Harper, op. cit.

25 Bergfelder, ibid., p. 36.

26 On the importance of technology, see B. Salt, *Film Style and Technology: History and Analysis*, London, Starword, 1983.

27 M. Dickinson and S. Street, *Cinema and State: The British Industry and the British Government 1927–1984*, London, BFI, 1985; J. Chapman, *The British at War: Cinema, State and Propaganda 1939–1946*, London, I.B. Tauris, 1998; J.C. Robertson, *The British Board of Film Censors 1896–1956*, London, Croom Helm, 1985; J.C. Robertson, *The Hidden Screen*, London, Routledge, 1989; A. Aldgate, *Censorship and the Permissive Society*, Oxford, Oxford University Press, 1996; A. Slide, *'Banned in the USA': British Films in the United States and their Censorship 1933–1960*, London, I.B. Tauris, 1998.

28 J. Richards, *Films and British National Identity*, Manchester, Manchester University Press, 1997; Street, *op cit.*; K. Bamford, *Distorted Images: British National Identity and Films in the 1920s*, London, I.B. Tauris, 1990; A. Higson, *Waving the Flag: Constructing a National Cinema in Britain*, Oxford, Clarendon Press, 1995.

29 J. Sedgwick, 'Cinemagoing preferences in Britain in the 1930s', in J. Richards (ed.) *The Unknown 1930s*, London, I.B. Tauris, 1998, pp. 1–36; 'Film "hits" and "misses" in mid-1930s Britain', *Historical Journal of Film, Radio and Television*, August 1998, vol. 18, pp. 333–51; 'The comparative popularity of stars in mid-30s Britain', *Journal of Popular British Cinema*, 1999, no. 2, pp. 121–7. The whole of issue 2 of *Journal of Popular British Cinema* deals with questions of audience and reception in Britain.

30 A. Eyles, *ABC, The First Name in Entertainment*, London and Burgess Hill, CTA/BFI, 1996; *Gaumont British Cinemas*, London and Burgess Hill, CTA/BFI, 1996; M. O'Brien and A. Eyles (eds) *Enter the Dream House*, London, BFI, 1993.

31 J. Richards and D. Sheridan (eds) *Mass Observation at the Movies*, London, Routledge, 1997; J.P. Mayer, *British Cinemas and Their Audiences*, London, Dennis Dobson, 1948.

32 The first fruits of the research can be found in A. Kuhn, 'Cinema culture and femininity in the 1930s', in Gledhill and Swanson, op. cit., pp. 177–92.

33 B. McFarlane, *An Autobiography of British Cinema*, London, Methuen, 1997, and C. Drazin, *The Finest Years*, London, Andre Deutsch, 1998.
34 T. Staples, *All Pals Together*, Edinburgh, Edinburgh University Press, 1997; J. Stacey, *Stargazing*, London, Routledge, 1993.
35 Richards, *The Unknown 1930s*, op. cit.
36 See, for instance, B. Wright, *The Long View*, London, Secker and Warburg, 1974, p. 103: 'The basic content of feature films in Britain, at least during the first eight or nine years of the talkie era, was trivial and without contemporary emphasis.'
37 L. Napper, 'A despicable tradition? Quota quickies in the 1930s', in Murphy, *The British Cinema Book*, op. cit., p. 46.

2

THE INSTABILITY OF THE
NATIONAL

Andrew Higson

To write about British cinema is to operate, however implicitly, with some understanding of what that cinema is, what its limits are, what distinguishes it from other cinemas. Innocent though they may seem, these are far from straightforward matters, which can be approached from a variety of perspectives. Each perspective will inevitably offer a different way of thinking through what it is that makes cinema 'British'. Legislation laid down by the state provides one set of definitions, but critics and historians have rarely seen legislation as a sufficient means of defining the Britishness of British cinema. Ideological criticism might explore the role that cinema has played in shaping and maintaining the idea of the British nation, imagining its inhabitants as members of a national community with a shared identity. A cultural historical perspective might explore the ways in which British films are rooted in national traditions. A reception studies approach might look at the ways in which promotional discourses, reviewing practices and audiences have worked with particular ideas of national identity and nationhood.

My own earlier work on British cinema draws on all of these approaches in various ways. Like many others using these approaches, I was perhaps at times rather too ready to find British films presenting an image of a coherent, unified, consensual nation.[1] In what follows, I want to engage more thoroughly with those approaches that resist the tendency either to seek out images of national consensus or to maintain rigid boundaries between nations, cultural formations and identities. In other words, I want to engage with those perspectives that call attention to cultural diversity.

Such approaches seem particularly suited to the examination of contemporary cinema. In recent years, new types of film-making have embraced multiculturalism, transnationalism and devolution. While such developments may be limited, they still constitute a powerful critique of traditional ideas of Britishness and consensual images of the nation. I will suggest that such films should be seen less as products of a national cinema, more as postnational films. But I will also suggest that this unravelling of traditional ideas of British nationhood is increasingly a feature of historical work on the

British cinema of the past. The films of the 1930s and 1940s are fertile ground in this respect, for if some have argued that they were dominated by images of national consensus, others are now drawing attention to the cultural diversity of British cinema in those years and the degree of engagement with transnational impulses.

The indigenous and the exotic

I want first to persevere with some problems of definition. It would seem reasonable to define a national cinema as one that draws on indigenous cultural traditions, one that invokes and explores the nation's cultural heritage. But what exactly is an indigenous cultural tradition? According to a strict dictionary definition, an indigenous action, event or idea is one whose origins can be found in the locality in which the action, event or idea is performed; the indigenous is, strictly speaking, the opposite of the exotic, that which is of foreign origin. Yet in the field of culture, how many actions, events or ideas can really be seen as indigenous in this sense, without any exotic, foreign influences? Is the national heritage ever really 'pure', or is it always to some extent a cultural collage, an amalgam of overlapping and sometimes antagonistic traditions, a mix of ingredients from diverse sources? What does it mean to talk about the indigenous in a multicultural community that is 'home' to various diasporic peoples? Whose heritage are we talking about? It is questions such as these that begin to trouble the concept of indigeneity.

The concept of tradition is equally problematic. We may speak loosely of a film being deeply rooted in national or indigenous cultural traditions. But what exactly counts as traditional? How many times, or over how long a period, does an action or event or idea have to be repeated before it becomes a tradition? It is conventional to speak of our heritage as that which we inherit from or which is transmitted to us by past generations. But what about invented, imposed or imported traditions, rather than inherited traditions? How far back must the line of inheritance stretch within the nation-state before an action, event or idea counts as deeply rooted in the national culture or as an indigenous tradition?

Howards End (James Ivory, 1992) is the sort of film that could easily be described as deeply rooted in national cultural traditions. In many respects, it seems perfect material for absorption within the idea of an indigenous British national cinema, or, perhaps better, an English national cinema. From this perspective, it would not be eccentric to read the film as invoking a mythology of England as, at its spiritual heart, ruralist and traditional, a place of antiquity, a place with a long history, in which questions of inheritance become crucial. The film clearly plays on the idea of national tradition in various ways. Thus it invokes familiar discourses and images of landscape, architecture and place; it is steeped in traditions of propriety, gentility, behaviour and manners; and it re-works Britain's literary heritage, adapting the work of a canonical author, E.M. Forster.[2]

It makes just as much sense, however, to read *Howards End* as the product of *invented* tradition rather than *inherited* tradition. If the film-makers made strenuous efforts to establish that *Howards End* inherited the sensibility and periodicity of E.M. Forster's novel, they in effect re-invented Forster as an antiquarian rather than a modernist and his story as a costume film rather than a contemporary drama. The cinematic celebration of Forster can also be seen as part of a longer tendency by which modernist writers become part of the established literary heritage. The same process of innovation and encrustation can be seen at work in the recent cycle of British heritage films to which *Howards End* belongs, from *Chariots of Fire* (Hugh Hudson, 1981) and *A Room with a View* (James Ivory, 1986) to *Sense and Sensibility* (Ang Lee, 1995) and *Elizabeth* (Shekhar Kapur, 1998). This is a cycle of recent construction, whose conventions were very rapidly established, its traditions very quickly invented. And of course those conventions are in part designed to establish the veneer of tradition and antiquity in the films.

Forster's narrative might also be said to interrogate rather than to assume the nature of Englishness, not least in the Anglo-German cultural formation of the Schlegel sisters, the central protagonists of the drama. This sense of hybridity, and of a concomitantly fluid identity, is also emphasised in the cinematic presentation of the narrative, which is prefaced in the credits sequence by a Fauvist painting by the French artist André Derain and by a title card which uses Art Nouveau lettering. This situates the film not in relation to parochial national tradition, but in the context of European modernism and international art connoisseurship. This is perhaps hardly surprising, given the multi-national nature of both the financial backing for the film and the production team that made it (the film was funded primarily by British, American and Japanese capital and made by an American director, James Ivory, and an Indian producer, Ismail Merchant, from a script by Ruth Prawer Jhabvala, a Polish Jew now resident in India).

National cinema or post-national cinema?

As an example such as this suggests, tradition and heritage, indigeneity and the national, are complex matters, not issues we can afford to take for granted. Was it always thus, or was there a time when questions of national identity were less problematic? There is certainly a fairly well established line of argument that there has been a shift in representation in the last half century of British cinema, from images of homogeneity to images of heterogeneity. This can be exemplified in the journey from the Ealing films of the 1940s and early 1950s to the new British cinema of the 1980s and 1990s. Thus the Ealing films seem to offer a consensual vision of the nation, while films like *My Beautiful Laundrette* (Stephen Frears, 1985), *Bhaji on the Beach*

(Gurinder Chadha, 1993), *Trainspotting* (Danny Boyle, 1995) and *My Name is Joe* (Ken Loach, 1998) articulate a much more ambivalent image of contemporary Britain. What is perhaps more surprising is my suggestion above that we might also find evidence of this shift in a film like *Howards End*, apparently such a solidly and conservatively English film. In general terms, the shift from homogeneity to heterogeneity seems inevitable, given the dramatic changes in the economic, political, social and cultural landscape of postwar Britain. The shift responds especially to the emergence of new sociocultural and subcultural communities organised around particular ethnic allegiances or youth styles and responding to local circumstances. These specific developments can be tied to the more general sense of cultural fragmentation and diversification that is widely assumed to have taken place following the loss of faith in the modernist project and the emergence of postmodern sensibilities. The shift from a British cinema of consensus to one of heterogeneity and dissent does then indeed seem inevitable, whether in the more covert guise of *Howards End* or the more self-conscious difference of *My Beautiful Laundrette*, *Bhaji on the Beach*, *Trainspotting* and *My Name is Joe*.

In recent debates about identity, culture and nation, concepts such as instability and transnationality have come very much to the fore, with the key metaphors now travel and mobility, liminality and the diasporic, marginality and the hybrid.[3] With reference to British cinema, we can see this tendency at work in the way in which films like *My Beautiful Laundrette* and *Bhaji on the Beach* have been taken up. Tim Corrigan's evocative discussion of *My Beautiful Laundrette*, for instance, stresses the way in which the security of home and the stability of identity are always in this film the temporary products of circumstance rather than deeply embedded in tradition; identity is in fact always fluid, the sense of belonging always contingent.[4] Similarly, Sarita Malik argues of *Bhaji on the Beach* that 'the "pull" between British and Asian identities and British and Indian cinema aesthetics generates the pleasures of hybridization in the cinematic form'.[5]

These are of course relatively recent films that take the contemporary experiences of multiculturalism and transnationality as their central themes. They thus explore the complex and occasionally aggressive negotiations and resistances that take place between different cultural identities and formations in post-colonial England. The emergence of such films, but also of the critical discourses which validate them, might quite reasonably be seen as indicative of a shift away from a national cinema which imagined the nation as a singular, consensual and organic community.

Should such films still be seen as the products of a national cinema? It might in fact be more useful to think of them as embodying a new post-national cinema that resists the tendency to nationalise questions of community, culture and identity. The concept of post-national cinema surely better describes films that embrace multiculturalism, difference and hybridity. John Hill thinks not, insisting that what I am calling a post-national cinema

Plate 4 *My Beautiful Laundrette* (Stephen Frears, 1985): a key film of the post-
national cinema, offering ambivalent images of a contemporary Britain
marked by difference and dissent.

can equally claim the mantle of national cinema: simply because films made
in Britain no longer adhere to entrenched ideas of the nation does not mean
that we should junk altogether the concept of national cinema. We should not,
he writes, 'underestimate the possibilities for a national cinema to re-imagine
the nation, or rather nations within Britain, and also to address the specificities of a national culture in a way that does not presume a homogeneous and
"pure" national identity'.[6]

Hill is not simply engaging in an academic theoretical debate but is in
part mounting an argument about policy. Given that the nation-state
remains a vital and powerful legal mechanism, and that government film
policy is formulated at the national level, it remains important to conduct

debate at that level and in those terms. Thus it still seems necessary to argue for the conditions to be established at a national level that might enable films to be made that do not invoke homogenising national myths, but are sensitive to social and cultural differences and to 'the lived complexities of British "national" life'.[7] It is still important to ensure that films like *My Beautiful Laundrette* and *Bhaji on the Beach* can be made with reasonable budgets and resources and can be carefully promoted and circulated to the widest possible audiences. The question is whether it is useful to continue to promote such films in terms of a concept of British national cinema, especially 'one which works with or addresses nationally specific materials' within 'an identifiably and specifically British context'.[8]

By using such terms as 'nationally specific' and 'identifiably British', Hill seems once more to take Britishness for granted in a way which glosses over too many other questions of community, culture, belonging and identity.[9] Some of the identities and positions explored in films like *My Beautiful Laundrette* and *Bhaji on the Beach* are surely as much either local or transnational as they are national. Given the transient and fleeting nature of many of the allegiances established in these films it seems problematic to invoke the idea of a singular, indisputable British nation, however complex and devolved – hence my preference for the idea of a post-national cinema. At the same time, both these films clearly emerged from funding contexts in which a national television channel (Channel 4) played a central role: as Hill insists, we cannot simply step around the category of the national because it is so firmly entrenched at the level of policy and legality.

The increasing prominence of transnational economic developments, not least in the media industries, of course puts tremendous pressure on the boundaries between nation-states. The massive capital investment in consumerism and the extensive delivery of cultural products across national borders, from films and television drama to soft drinks, clothing, computer software and recorded music has long had a dramatic effect on the cultural repertoire of once much more parochial communities. But there is also plenty of evidence that the same cultural product will be taken up in quite unique and dissimilar ways within different reception communities, while there is little evidence that taste and cultural preference are securely framed by national boundaries.[10] Identity is far too complex an issue to be reduced to nationality. It is in this context that it seems worth persisting with the use of the term post-national.

From homogeneity to heterogeneity

I suggested earlier that the journey from a cinema of homogeneity in the 1940s to a more recent cinema of heterogeneity is fairly well established. But there are also many ways in which the British cinema of the past might be thought of as engaging with heterogeneity and plurality. By way of illustration, I want to look at three lines of development here: first, the identification of the diverse cultural strands that have over the years fed into British cinema; second, the identification of specifically foreign influences on British film-making; and third, revisionist interpretations of the films of consensus produced during the Second World War.

The first line of development, the identification of British cinema as culturally diverse, makes it difficult to see that cinema as articulating an unproblematically homogeneous vision of the nation. While such generalisations are always problematic, we might in the 1930s, for instance, contrast several broad-based cultural formations, which draw in different ways on cultural tradition. One such formation is the provincial popular cinema of Gracie Fields and George Formby, with its roots in the relatively lowbrow cultural traditions of music hall. Another is the more middlebrow cinema that relies heavily on adaptations of best-selling literature, such as J.B. Priestley's *The Good Companions* or Winifred Holtby's *South Riding*, both of which were made into films by Victor Saville, in 1933 and 1938 respectively. The case for a highbrow strand in the 1930s is of course more difficult to make. It might include reference to the self-consciously intellectual concerns of some of the work of the documentary movement, or of an avant-garde film like *Borderline* (Kenneth MacPherson, 1930), or Friedrich Feher's almost wordless music film *The Robber Symphony* (1936), described at the time as 'a novel work of art', but one with 'little appeal to other than the aesthetes of the musical world'.[11] But such examples are few and far between, not least because the highbrows of the period either disdained the cinema altogether, or favoured what they saw as the more artistically respectable work of European directors such as Eisenstein, Vigo or Renoir.

What holds together the particular examples I have cited for each of these strands, the lowbrow, the middlebrow and the highbrow, is that they seem concerned to explore identity and to stress cultural difference, and very often the clash between different cultural identities. It is from these different strands that a richly hybrid British cinema emerges. This is especially true at those points where the strands overlap – when Priestley wrote the script for the Gracie Fields vehicle, *Sing As We Go* (Basil Dean, 1934), for instance, or when Humphrey Jennings made his deliberately artful poetic documentary, *Spare Time* (1939), about the regional diversity of Britain's popular culture and leisure pursuits.

The second line of development I want to consider is the identification of foreign influences on British film-making. A key moment in British cinema history from this point of view is the late 1920s and 1930s, when two interrelated tendencies encouraged an exotic strain in British film-making. First, from the mid-1920s to the early 1930s, various business initiatives explored the possibility of a pan-European cinema, or 'Film Europe', as it was known at the time. Some of the more enterprising British film production companies were involved in these initiatives, developing co-production arrangements with companies elsewhere, but especially in Germany and France, sharing production facilities, exchanging personnel and generally attempting to make films that might appeal to audiences in several different national markets. Some of the more prominent examples of these developments include Hitchcock's well-documented production work in German studios and the five films made in Britain by the German director E.A. Dupont, including *Moulin Rouge* (1928) and *Atlantic* (1929). The early sound period also saw an intense flirtation with the production of multiple-language films (that is, films made simultaneously by the same production team in several different language versions) as well as re-makes of foreign-language films.[12]

The other closely connected tendency of the period was the emergence of the British film industry in the 1930s as a major centre for émigré film-makers fleeing Nazi persecution in Germany. This development would undoubtedly have been much less extensive had it not been for the co-operation between British and European companies during the Film Europe years. The establishment of the British film industry as a centre for émigré film-makers had an impact both on the range of personnel working in British studios and the aesthetic and technical standards of the 'British' films they worked on.[13]

It is difficult to see such developments as anything other than transnational, in both conception and achievement. Both films and film-makers were mobile, travelling across political, economic, cultural and linguistic borders as part of the effort to establish a transnational film culture and film market. Their mobility was not of course without limits and constraints. The movement of films was dependent on the vagaries of film distribution and held in check by the quota regulations or other import restrictions imposed in various nation-states. The movement of film-makers was dependent on reputation and linguistic ability, as well as contractural agreements, though by the mid-1930s it was provoked as much by political terrorism as anything else: the movement of political émigrés could hardly be described as free. For many émigré film-makers, London was a liminal space, a threshold between the persecutions of Germany and the real Mecca, Hollywood. But while the diasporic film-making community that gathered in and around London may in some respects have been forced into a marginal position, they were able to have what was in many respects a central and long-lasting influence on British film culture and film-making. Thus witness the status and reputation of the Hungarian producer-director Alexander Korda, who became one of British cinema's most powerful figures. Or another Hungarian, Emeric Pressburger, Michael Powell's collaborator for many years. Or Alfred Junge, who started his career at Germany's UFA studios but became one of the most important art directors working in Britain in the 1930s, 1940s and 1950s.

The theme of travel, the movement through different geopolitical spaces and the mapping of a transnational landscape can be seen in films as diverse as *Atlantic*, *The Tunnel* (Maurice Elvey, 1936), *Rome Express* (Walter Forde, 1933) and *The Lady Vanishes* (Alfred Hitchcock, 1938). *Atlantic*, Dupont's multiple-language film made in English, German and French versions, depicts the fateful journey of a luxury ocean liner between Europe and North America. *The Tunnel*, a remake of a successful German film (also made in a French version), follows the efforts of a multinational team to build a trans-Atlantic tunnel. *Rome Express* and *The Lady Vanishes* are both thrillers set on trains occupied by passengers of different nationalities, travelling through various European states. Each of these four films had a multinational cast and/or crew; each dealt in different ways with the tension between the national and the transnational, between that which is rooted in national cultural traditions and that which is uprooted and in transit. The exotic influence can also be seen clearly in films closely associated with the émigré film community, such as those directed by Karl Grune: *Abdul the Damned* (1935), a political thriller set in Turkey, *Pagliacci* (1937), a vehicle for the Austrian opera singer Richard Tauber, and *The Marriage of Corbal* (1936), which inspired Graham Greene to write a notorious review:

> What is an English film? There are times when one cannot help brooding with acute distress on the cheap silly international pictures exported under that label. *The Marriage of Corbal* is a fairly harmless example. It is incredibly silly and incredibly badly written but there is a kind of wide-eyed innocence about this story of the French revolution which is almost endearing. But an English film? Is that a fair description of a picture derived from a novel by Rafael Sabatini, directed by Karl Grune and F. Brunn, photographed by Otto Kanturek, and edited by E. Stokvis [*sic*], with a cast which includes Nils Asther, Ernst Deutsch and the American, Noah Berry? The result is appalling ... England, of course, has always been the home of the exiled; but one may at least express a wish that émigrés would set up trades in which their ignorance of our language and our culture was less of a handicap: it would not grieve me to see Mr Alexander Korda seated before a cottage loom in an Eastern county, following an older and a better tradition. The Quota Act has played into foreign hands, and as far as I know, there is nothing to prevent an English film unit being completely staffed by technicians of foreign blood. We have saved the English film industry from American competition only to surrender it to a far more alien control.[14]

This extreme anxiety about 'cultural invasion' is typical of certain strands within 1930s British film culture. Asserting a very restricted understanding of English culture, it fails completely to recognise the potential benefits of such transnational influences, which clearly enrich British cinema's cultural repertoire.

A de-centred film culture

So to the third line of development illustrating the way British film historians and others are producing a new vision of a heterogeneous British cinema: the return to the films of the 1940s as signifiers of difference and insecurity as much as an imagined consensus. Charles Barr's work on Ealing films has long been central to debates about British cinema as a national cinema. In his classic *Ealing Studios*, he wrote of how Michael Balcon and his colleagues at Ealing set out to make films that projected Britain and the British people.[15] Barr argued that Ealing films imagined the nation as a community, and a relatively centred, stable and consensual community at that. His work also suggested that there was a core national identity, which these films sought to tease out. This same sensibility has been identified in other British films of the period, especially those produced during the latter half of the Second World War, such as *Millions Like Us* (Frank Launder and Sidney Gilliat, 1943) and *This Happy Breed* (David Lean, 1944).[16]

Critics are increasingly calling into question this vision of a consensual 1940s cinema imagining a stable, centred nation. Pam Cook and others have argued that to focus on what she calls the consensus films is to ignore the number of other immensely popular British films of the mid-1940s which offered very different, and often much more transgressive, visions of the nation.[17] Cook focuses in particular on the Gainsborough costume dramas of the period, films like *Madonna of the Seven Moons* (Arthur Crabtree, 1944), *The Wicked Lady* (Leslie Arliss, 1945), and *Caravan* (Arthur Crabtree, 1946) which, she argues, 'celebrate an itinerant spirit in British cinema, an urge to move beyond fixed national boundaries to a more hybrid notion of national identity'.[18]

One line of argument against the perceived homogenising tendency in 1940s British cinema has thus been to push new films into the critical light. Another line of argument involves reinterpreting the consensus films themselves in terms of the metaphors of difference rather than consensus, mobility rather than groundedness, and fragmentation rather then centredness. Some of the consensus films of the 1940s, such as *San Demetrio, London* (Charles Frend, 1943), or *Millions Like Us*, are surely comparable to later films such as *My Beautiful Laundrette* and *Bhaji on the Beach* in terms of the ways in which they depict contemporary social interaction and the contingent meetings of people from different walks of life and cultural backgrounds. Is it not possible to see the 1940s films as offering a vision of a plural, complex, heterogeneous and hybrid nation, and a sense of multiple 'British' identities, similar to that of the later films? Is the wartime community of *San Demetrio, London*, *Millions Like Us* and the rest of the consensus films not just as contingent, just as fluid, just as temporary as the allegiances established in *My Beautiful Laundrette*? To ask such questions is to employ the critical insights of post-structuralist, postmodernist and post-colonialist theories not simply to investigate the films of the present, but to return to the classic British films which, according to another interpretation, 'projected Britain', imagining the nation as a consensual space. To ask such questions is to demonstrate a fascination with the social and cultural voyages undertaken in the consensus films, the travel across boundaries, the forming of new relationships, the mixing of different identities, rather than the safe enclosure within familiar boundaries.

It is striking that, in constructing a vision of a potentially consensual community, several Ealing films explore a liminal space on the margins of the nation in order to be able to grasp its apparent centre. The construction of 'home' thus involves leaving home, moving away. In *Passport to Pimlico* (Henry Cornelius, 1949), for instance, a war-damaged space at the centre of London temporarily becomes a part of the kingdom of Burgundy and leaves the United Kingdom. In *Whisky Galore* (Alexander Mackendrick, 1949), the tight-knit, insular community inhabits a tiny island off the coast of Scotland. Later films might also be said to return to similarly liminal spaces on the metaphorical edge of the nation. Thus the youthful protagonists of the working-class Midlands communities in *Saturday Night and Sunday Morning* (Karel Reisz, 1960), *Billy Liar* (John Schlesinger, 1963) and other early 1960s 'kitchen sink films' seem thoroughly alienated from the metropolitan centre of the nation. Later still, *My Beautiful Laundrette*, set in South London like *Passport to Pimlico*, might in some ways be said to rehearse *Passport's* themes and spatial awareness, to explore the exotic within the national. In a different way, as Justine Ashby shows, the female protagonists of several woman's films of the 1980s and 1990s, from *Letter to Brezhnev* (Chris Bernard, 1985) to *Shirley Valentine* (Lewis Gilbert, 1989) to *Enchanted April* (Mike Newell, 1991), literally escape from the claustrophobic confines of Britishness by entering a liminal space elsewhere, beyond the boundaries of the nation.[19]

In the light of such arguments, British national cinema appears increasingly heterogeneous, eccentric, even unhomely. On the one hand, unfamiliar films are given a new significance. On the other, the films that were once seen as constructing a familiar consensus, imagining the nation as a solid, stable, centred space and people, now seem to express the contingency and fragility of the national, and the fractured and shifting nature of identity. The distinction between the national cinema of the past and the post-national cinema of the present no longer seems so clear-cut. Is this simply a question of critical fashion? Is what is at stake here no more than a question of interpretation, one reading of a film replaced by another?

This question of interpretation, the question of where meaning resides, or how it is created, has of course become a central issue in Cinema Studies. An increasing number of scholars now question the legitimacy of textual analysis divorced from historical context. Interpretation is increasingly grounded in the historical study of reception. We should be wary then of cultural analysis that lacks such grounding. But that should not stop us asking questions about how we arrive at the conclusions we propose, or about such familiar concepts as 'national cinema' or 'cultural tradition'. Empirical history will often take such concepts for granted, but we should remember that the boundaries between different geopolitical spaces, and the status and meanings of cultural identities, are almost always contested: the national is almost always a fragile and contingent compromise. Hence my preference for the term post-national to describe a contemporary cinema which takes such matters to heart.

Empirical history should in any case alert us to the diversity of British cinema. It should also alert us to the difficulty of distinguishing between the indigenous and the exotic. And while the historical fact of the nation-state cannot simply be ignored, perhaps it would be fruitful sometimes to focus less on the national and more on the local, or on the border-crossing elements of the transnational. Like Hill, I want to celebrate the cinema of diversity. But I'm not sure how productive it is to use the borders of the nation to contain and label this cinema.

NOTES

1 See, for example, my *Waving the Flag: Constructing a National Cinema in Britain*, Oxford, Clarendon Press, 1995.

2 I discuss *Howards End* in greater detail in my *English Heritage, English Cinema*, Oxford, Oxford University Press, forthcoming.

3 See, for example, H. Naficy (ed.) *Home, Exile, Homeland: Film, Media, and the Politics of Place*, New York and London, Routledge, 1999; M. Hjort and S. MacKenzie (eds) *Cinema and Nation*, London, Routledge, 2000 (forth-coming); P. Cook, *Fashioning the Nation: Costume and Identity in British Cinema*, London, BFI, 1996; P. Cook, 'Neither here nor there: national identity in Gainsborough costume drama', in A. Higson (ed.) *Dissolving Views: Key Writings on British Cinema*, London, Cassell, 1996, pp. 51–65; T. Bergfelder, 'Negotiating exoticism: Hollywood, Film Europe and the cultural reception of Anna May Wong', in A. Higson and R. Maltby (eds) *'Film Europe' and 'Film America': Cinema, Commerce and Cultural Exchange, 1920–1939*, Exeter, University of Exeter Press, 1999, pp. 302–24; T. Bergfelder, *The Internationalisation of the German Film Industry in the 1950s and 1960s*, unpublished Ph.D. Thesis, University of East Anglia, 1999; T. Elsaesser, 'Heavy traffic: Perspektive Hollywood: Emigranten oder Vagabunden', in J. Schöning (ed.) *London Calling: Deutsche im britischen Film der dreissiger Jahre*, Munich, Edition Text + Kritik, 1993, pp. 21–41.

4 T. Corrigan, *A Cinema Without Walls: Movies and Culture After Vietnam*, London, Routledge, 1991, pp. 218–27; see also J. Hill, *British Cinema in the 1980s*, Oxford, Oxford University Press, 1999, chs 10 and 11.

5 S. Malik, 'Beyond "the cinema of duty"? The pleasures of hybridity: Black British films of the 1980s and 1990s', in Higson, *Dissolving Views*, op. cit., p. 212.

6 J. Hill, 'British cinema as national cinema: production, audience and representa-tion', in R. Murphy (ed.) *The British Cinema Book*, London, BFI, 1997, p. 252.

7 J. Hill, 'British film policy', in A. Moran (ed.) *Film Policy: International, National and Regional Perspectives*, London, Routledge, 1996, p. 111.

8 J. Hill, 'The issue of national cinema and British film production', in D. Petrie (ed.) *New Questions of British Cinema*, London, BFI, 1992, p. 16.

9 I develop this argument at greater length in 'The limiting imagination of national cinema', in Hjort and MacKenzie, op. cit.

10 See, for example, A. Silj *et al.*, *East of Dallas*, London, BFI, 1988, and T. Liebes and E. Katz, *The Export of Meaning*, Oxford, Oxford University Press, 1991, on the transnational reception of *Dallas*, and Bergfelder, *The Internationalisation of the German Film Industry*, op. cit., on the different reception of Edgar Wallace films in Germany and Britain.

11 *Kinematograph Weekly*, 23 April 1936, p. 32.

12 For details of all these developments, see Higson and Maltby, op. cit.

13 K. Gough-Yates, 'Exiles and British cinema', in Murphy, op. cit., pp. 104–13; T. Bergfelder, 'The production designer and the *Gesamtkunstwerk*: German film technicians in the British film industry of the 1930s', in Higson, *Dissolving Views*, op. cit., pp. 20–37; Bergfelder, 'Surface and distraction: style and genre at Gainsborough in the late 1920s and 1930s', in P. Cook (ed.) *Gainsborough Pictures*, London, Cassell, 1997, pp. 31–46; A. Higson, '"A film League of Nations": Gainsborough, Gaumont-British and "Film Europe"', in Cook, ibid.; and Higson, 'Way West: Deutsche Emigranten und die britische Filmindustrie', in Schöning, op. cit., pp. 42–54.

14 G. Greene, '*The Marriage of Corbal*', *The Spectator*, 5 June 1936, reprinted in D. Parkinson (ed.) *The Graham Greene Film Reader: Mornings in the Dark*, Manchester, Carcanet, 1993, pp. 107–8.

15 C. Barr, *Ealing Studios*, London, Cameron and Tayleur/David and Charles, 1977.

16 See, for instance, chapter 5 of my *Waving the Flag*, op. cit.

17 See Cook, 'Neither here nor there', op. cit.; R. Murphy, *Realism and Tinsel: Cinema and Society, 1939–1949*, London, Routledge, 1989; J. Petley, 'The lost continent', in C. Barr, *All Our Yesterdays: 90 Years of British Cinema*, London, BFI, 1986, pp. 98–119.

18 Cook, 'Neither here nor there', op. cit., p. 64.

19 Writing as J. King, 'Crossing thresholds: the contemporary British woman's film', in Higson, *Dissolving Views*, op. cit., pp. 216–31.

Part II

THE DISTRIBUTION AND
RECEPTION OF BRITISH
FILMS ABROAD

Introduction

The ways in which audiences watch and make sense of films and the range of films made available to them are crucial to our understanding of cinema. The study of patterns of distribution, exhibition and reception has become a growth area in recent years. The three contributions to this section extend this interest. British cinema is often conceived as a national cinema addressing domestic audiences. As Sarah Street, Marcia Landy and Pierre Sorlin make clear, British cinema is also an international cinema, its films travelling extensively across national and cultural borders. The history of how British films have fared in export markets, as Sorlin points out, is an under-researched aspect of Cinema Studies. Yet as all three contributions demonstrate, there is much to be learnt from both the economics of the export business and the processes of cultural transference by which films from one national context are taken up and absorbed by audiences in another national context.

Street and Landy consider the distribution and reception of British films in the US. Sorlin undertakes a preliminary mapping of how British films fared in western European markets. Sorlin and Street draw on available box-office statistics, which Street supplements with information from the trade press and company records. They also look at patterns of promotion and critical reception. The latter is central to Landy's account, which is at the same time a fascinating personal history, an autobiography of an American with a passion for British cinema. Like Sorlin's and Street's chapters, Landy's carefully contextualised account of the transition from youthful viewing of Gainsborough melodramas to teaching British cinema at an American university yields much about the way films travel across cultures. It becomes abundantly clear from these contributions that the same films can have very

49

different impacts in different countries and exhibition contexts. The extent and relative success of British exports to the US and western Europe are also very revealing. As Street shows in her case study of the promotion and reception of *The Private Life of Henry VIII* (Alexander Korda, 1933), it is often the most distinctive films that make their mark in export markets. Cultural specificity and specialised appeal can actually be the keys rather than the obstacles to success.

3

STEPPING WESTWARD

The distribution of British feature films
in America, and the case of *The Private Life of
Henry VIII*

Sarah Street

It's costume and history of another country, but it has laughs,
spice and its presentation is of the best. The business this film
will do should convince England's flicker producers that their
contention of prejudice on this side has always been a fallacy.
(Review in *Variety* of *The Private Life of Henry VIII*)[1]

Most discussions of British cinema as a national cinema focus on how British
films have fared with British audiences. But audiences in other countries
also watch British films, while the export market has long been considered
vital to the health of the British film industry. The most important market
in this respect has been America. It has commonly been assumed, however,
that the careers of most British films in the USA were disastrous, providing
further evidence of the relative weakness of the British film industry *vis-à-vis*
Hollywood.[2] In this chapter, I will present a different view: while many
British films experienced problems finding distribution outlets and in
winning audiences, some did manage to occupy a space in a highly competitive market. They did so for a variety of reasons, often to do with timing and
purely economic factors, but also because of their ability to appeal to specific
American audiences. When British films travelled westwards they were
received into a new market context, attracting critical commentary and
audience responses which can be related to American concerns. This process
of cultural transference and absorption can be seen very clearly in Alexander
Korda's *The Private Life of Henry VIII* (1933). A detailed study of the
American distribution of this film also indicates trends that subsequently
characterised the reception of later British films in America.

The lure of the American market

From the early years of the twentieth century British film producers were keen to obtain screenings for their films abroad.[3] Further encouraged by the common language after the introduction of sound, access to the American market was held up as the highest ambition of any film company, an ambition that implied financial rewards and approval from audiences whose main preference, as in the UK, was for Hollywood films. It also implied a degree of Anglo-American cultural *rapport* and was perceived as a sign of the health of the British film industry as well as an indicator of Anglo-American co-operation. Hollywood's success at home and abroad made it the dominant model of world cinema, a capitalistic blueprint for a successful movie industry – surely, many argued, Britain should follow suit. British films did not dominate their home market, so any extra revenue was welcomed, especially when the lure of the American market implied the possibility of deals with the major companies who controlled distribution in the USA and more or less in the UK.[4] The aim to distribute British films in the USA was therefore bound up with two key themes: the profitability of the British film industry and the importance of Britain as America's prime overseas market.

British policymakers sought to exploit American vulnerabilities in this second area once they became aware that the American film industry was dependent on the British market for much of its overseas revenue. From 1938 British protective measures for the film industry were accompanied by incentives for American companies to produce in Britain, thus encouraging them to give their 'British' films, as well as those financed by British capital, fair distribution in the USA.[5] American companies, anxious to prove that they did not discriminate against British films and keen to protect their own overseas markets, made a concerted attempt to show that if British films were good enough, they would get a fair chance in the USA. Somewhat ironically, therefore, American corporate attitudes towards British films cannot be considered without reference to their interest in preserving the flow of Hollywood's films to the UK.

The favourable trend towards 'reciprocity' between British and American companies found its clearest expression in Korda's links with United Artists in the 1930s and Rank's much publicised deals with Universal which were largely responsible for the relatively high number of British films distributed in America in the 1940s and 1950s. In 1946–7, for example, America imported forty-six British films (approximately half the annual output of British feature films) and their gross income was $3,700,000.[6] According to the *Motion Picture Film and Television Almanac* in the 1950s an average of 150 British films were listed as available for distribution each year. This was at a time when the Hollywood majors' output was decreasing sharply: between 1953 and 1958 the combined annual average number of films released by the major studios was 247; in the 1930s it had been approximately 370.[7] Access to the American market was impossible without an arrangement with one of the major American companies, some of which were keen to oblige in order to gain reciprocal favours for their films in the UK. Since American films dominated the British market this was hardly a pressing concern for the largest 'majors' (Warner Bros, MGM, Paramount and 20th Century-Fox) who had little trouble persuading exhibitors to show their films. Consequently, it is no surprise that both United Artists and Universal, the two companies Korda and Rank did business with, were not the strongest of American companies: neither owned cinemas. Yet their commercial interests in British companies and their willingness to take the concept of 'reciprocity' seriously did have an impact, ensuring that a certain level of visibility was maintained for British films. While a cynical interpretation might conclude that their dealings with British films were motivated purely by self-interest, it can be argued that their history of assisting British films indicates a more positive attitude towards them and implies a degree of faith in their viability for the American market.

Purely economic incentives like the devaluation of the pound in the mid-1940s, or legislation restricting the amount of dollars American companies could remit home, also provided an incentive for the production of American-financed 'British' films in the UK. The Anglo-American Film Agreements of the late 1940s and early 1950s, for example, confined dollar earnings in the UK as 'blocked' currency, resulting in some production activity. It was assumed that, because of their financial parentage, the films would be distributed in the USA on an equal basis with those produced in California. This was not always the case, and many complaints were made in the 1950s about the lack of assertive distribution for these films in the USA: while they may have been available, they were often not actively promoted. Nevertheless, during 1950–7 American companies produced over 100 films in Britain, and American dollars financed British films to an unprecedented degree in the 1960s: 'success' stories in this tradition include *Tom Jones* (Tony Richardson, 1963), the Beatles films and the James Bond films.[8]

Changes to the structure of the American film industry also proved to be significant. In the late 1940s and 1950s the divorcement decrees freed up some of the market for foreign films, facilitating the development of the American art film market that flourished until the 1970s. British films played a prominent part in this market, which grew from a circuit of eighty-three cinemas in 1950 to one of 664 by 1966.[9] While few British films were treated as art films at home, it is interesting to trace how they were often received as such in the USA, a notable example being *The Red Shoes* (Michael Powell and Emeric Pressburger, 1948).[10] In the 1950s British films occupied an awkward place in relation to other 'foreign' imports. While these were frequently marketed as salacious challenges to the Production Code, British films did not always escape being marketed along similar lines. When *The Private Life of Henry VIII* was re-released in Chicago in 1950, for instance, it was advertised with the following text: 'Rumors, Scandals, Shame/What a King, What a Lover, What a Man'.[11]

The vagaries of distribution

Particular distribution policies could be decisive in influencing the careers of films in the USA. One example is Sidney Bernstein's 'rota' scheme, instituted during the Second World War, whereby eight American companies each agreed to distribute at least one British feature film and eight shorts annually. Also important were the 'roadshow' distribution tactics favoured by United Artists for films like *Henry V* (Laurence Olivier, 1944; released in the USA in 1946) and *The Red Shoes*.[12] Intelligent distribution was often identified as the key to the American market: as early as 1926, statistician Simon Rowson was one of the first commentators to argue for 'reciprocity' agreements and for the establishment of a special distribution company exclusively concerned with handling British films abroad.[13] More recently, Miramax's astute marketing of British films as diverse as *Four Weddings and a Funeral* (Mike Newell, 1994) and *Trainspotting* (Danny Boyle, 1995) has created something of a viable market space for British films in America. *The Full Monty* (Peter Cattaneo, 1997), for instance, distributed by Searchlight, a division of 20th Century-Fox which markets 'unusual' films with special care, earned £26,800,000 in eight weeks.[14]

Despite the above factors that gave British films a greater chance of being shown in the USA, their distributors nevertheless experienced distinct problems. The most pressing of these was the power of the majors and the associated difficulty of establishing a distribution network for British films outside of the weaker companies which handled them (United Artists and Universal). Exhibitors' attitudes and audiences' tastes also proved to be significant obstacles if the films were released indiscriminately and on an unequal basis in terms of financial remuneration to the production company. Fox's mass distribution of London Films' *An Ideal Husband* (Alexander Korda, 1947) and *Anna Karenina* (Julien Duvivier, 1947) provides interesting examples. Both films were released at the same time as Fox's own productions, in large theatres that usually supported long runs of American feature films and with no careful 'roadshow' treatment; neither was able to attract a high number of bookings.[15] An inappropriate and misleading advertising campaign by United Artists contributed to the poor box-office career of *The Life and Death of Colonel Blimp* (Michael Powell and Emeric Pressburger, 1943, American release 1945). The sensationalist posters depicted Colonel Blimp as a lascivious old man: audiences who expected to see this promise delivered in the film were disappointed.[16]

As far as the market was concerned, the sheer geographic enormity and cultural diversity of the USA militated against the extensive exhibition of British films. They did, however, gain some popularity among audiences in

New York (a success that was associated with the development of the art-film market) and in larger cities, although establishing accurate information can be difficult. In contrast to the British situation, where since 1927 renters and exhibitors had to deal with and show a quota of British films, American exhibitors had no statutory obligation to exhibit British films. Grosses reported in *Variety* and *Motion Picture Herald*, supplemented with ledgers from studio archives therefore provide the main evidence of rental and box-office earnings. These reveal that some British films, often being held over for several weeks after their first week's exhibition and holding their own against American competition, occupied a significant place in the market during particular years.

In the sound period, for instance, British films enjoyed comparative success in the American market in 1933–9, 1945–8, 1963–7, 1981–2, 1985–8 and 1992–9. Even in the 1950s, there were good openings for British films in the 'art' market. Some genres and cycles were more popular than others, among the most consistently successful being historical films, costume dramas and literary adaptations, including *Nell Gwyn* (Herbert Wilcox, 1926), *The Private Life of Henry VIII*, *Henry V*, *Caesar and Cleopatra* (Gabriel Pascal, 1946), *Tom Jones* and *A Room With a View* (James Ivory, 1985); melodramas such as *The Wicked Lady* (Leslie Arliss, 1945), *Brief Encounter* (David Lean, 1945) and *The Seventh Veil* (Compton Bennett, 1945); comedies, including those produced at Ealing, the St. Trinians films and the Monty Python films; romantic comedies such as *A Fish Called Wanda* (Charles Crichton, 1988), *Four Weddings and a Funeral* (Mike Newell, 1994) and *Notting Hill* (Roger Michell, 1999); youth/'cult' films like *A Hard Day's Night* (Richard Lester, 1964) and *Trainspotting*; and films made by directors whose names had come to mean something at the box office – the films of Hitchcock, and Powell and Pressburger, for example.[17]

Distributing *The Private Life of Henry VIII*

The Private Life of Henry VIII is something of a *cause célèbre*: it broke box-office records on its first day's showing at the Radio City Music Hall, New York, in 1933 and encouraged other British producers to aim at world markets. Many blamed the example set by Korda for promoting profligacy and overextension, contributing to the famous 'crash' of many British film companies in 1937. Encouraged by confidence in film production as an investment, banks and insurance companies had financed film companies to an unprecedented extent in 1935–7. When returns on their investments proved to be disappointing the City financiers withdrew their support and many film companies were declared bankrupt.[18] This version of events is oversimplified, however: in many respects *The Private Life of Henry VIII* became a convenient scapegoat for the film industry's domestic problems in the 1930s. There is a degree of controversy about the impact and significance of the film's American experience. Ian Jarvie has speculated that 'close analysis of the career of the film in the USA would, I believe, show that it had in fact a limited release, confined to major cities, and that it gained, by Hollywood's standards, a modest return'.[19] In fact, what 'close analysis' of the film's career (in *Variety* and *Motion Picture Herald*) shows is that it did do well outside New York, extremely well in some places, holding its own against films like *I'm No Angel* (Wesley Ruggles, 1933). Far from being an insignificant example, I would argue that this was a major step forward for British films and was certainly perceived as such by contemporaries. A report from Pittsburgh in *Variety*, for example, commented that:

> leading town comparatively by a wide margin is *Henry VIII* at Fulton, which shows signs of hitting $9,000 and indicating possibility of h.o. [hold over]. Picture has been in the air for some time now, with intelligentsia eating it up and giving house carriage trade it hasn't seen since *Cavalcade* [Frank Lloyd, 1932]. Also marks first time in history of house that Friday's business, usually a cropper due to preponderance of other openings, has topped inaugural day's trade. All the more amazing since Charles Laughton is cast's only name and he has meant just a bit more than nothing here in the past.[20]

Reports of comparative good business also came from Boston, Buffalo, Chicago, Cleveland, Denver, Detroit, Los Angeles, Providence, San Francisco, St. Louis and Washington.[21] The film occupied seventh place in United Artists' top grossing rental figures for 1933.[22]

Korda's film was the product of many advantageous circumstances that help to explain its success. United Artists, who financed the film, marketed it in an astute manner in New York and beyond, pitching it at 'highbrow' audiences but at the same time remaining aware of its box-office potential as a comedy with broader appeal. *Motion Picture Herald* reported on the campaign, introducing several key themes that highlight aspects of the American context of reception:

> Every British and Canadian club and organisation in NY [New York] was informed of the date, and bulletins were posted at all headquarters and clubrooms. High and elementary school history and English department heads were asked to inform their classes of the historical interest of the picture, and the various NY colleges also cooperated in bringing this information to the attention of students. Special screenings were held for representatives of over 600 local women's clubs, National Council of History Teachers, the Daughters of the American Revolution, and other prominent organisations, whose secretaries signed endorsements of the picture on

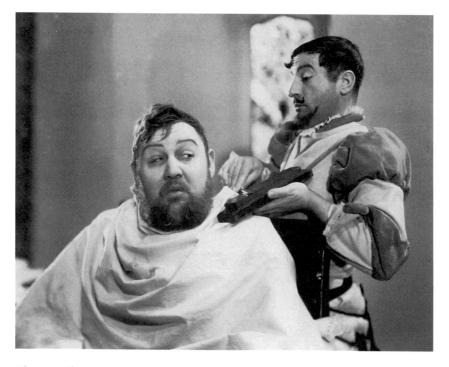

Plate 5   *The Private Life of Henry VIII* (Alexander Korda, 1933): at the mercy of the populace? A close shave for Henry VIII (Charles Laughton).

postcards sent by UA to all individual members. Other screenings were held for magazine and newspaper picture editors and critics with excellent advance publicity results. The local Liggett drug stores carried special 40 by 60 window cards done in the Ripley manner showing the highlights of Henry's matrimonial career, and book stores also plugged the Hackett edition of the king's biography. A clever and humorous angle was carried out in the newspaper ads, wherein the entertainment values of Henry's roaring romances was stressed, and managers who do not choose to sell the historical angle too strongly, should utilize this slant which is carried out in the press books ads.[23]

The film's progress was assisted by the recession in Hollywood, creating a 'space' for new or unusual films. Attendances and box-office takings were down in 1933 and America was just beginning to recover from the worst effects of the Depression, assisted by Roosevelt's 'New Deal' programme.[24] *Gold Diggers of 1933* (Mervyn Le Roy, 1933) had been released in June, a film which along with *42nd Street* (Lloyd Bacon, 1933) articulated the New Deal's philosophy of a united community and a benevolent President fighting against the Depression. This ideology is also evident in *The Private Life of Henry VIII*, with its representation of a benevolent king whose subjects understand and support him. At one point, for example, 'the people's will' is declared to constitute 'the king's law'.

As David Reynolds has shown, in the 1930s many Americans were both fascinated by and critical of British traditions and institutions, especially the class system.[25] From this perspective, *Henry VIII*'s comedic 'key-hole' approach to British history is important. So too is its potential for readings based on what Sue Harper calls 'aristocratic substitution'. She argues that *Henry VIII* demonstrates an 'aristocratic-proletarian alliance' and encourages the audience to sympathise with Henry and to put themselves in his place. This forges a cross-class bond that paradoxically confers on the lower echelons in the film a 'superior' status that is characterised by an apparent insight into the king's personal shortcomings and human frailties, particularly as far as women are concerned.[26] Such readings can be seen as exercising persuasive influence in America at a time when the historic sense of a common liberal tradition between the UK and the USA was being interrogated. *Henry VIII* is an example of a British film that uses comedy to critique British institutions and the film was considered irreverent and unpatriotic by some British reviewers.[27] In the film, Henry's royal status is a burden – he cannot live up to the onerous demands of monarchy, especially repeated pressures from advisers and the populace to prove his masculinity by re-marrying and siring heirs to the throne. Far from being represented as a 'divine being', Henry is weak and pathetic, longing for the personal freedoms enjoyed by his subjects. The demands of the state are depicted as crushing his spirit, with advisers and wives alike exploiting his physical weaknesses. The film is therefore far from an 'official' history, and is much more a comedic character study that nevertheless involved an address to contemporary concerns.

When pitched to 'class' audiences the film was promoted as history, conferring on it a 'highbrow' status which appealed to those seeking to acquire 'cultural capital'. English history had been widely taught in America until the mid-1920s, but by the 1930s had more or less disappeared as a separate high-school subject.[28] English authors still dominated literature classes, but it seems that *Henry VIII*'s own ambivalent engagement with the institution of monarchy fed into prevailing American attitudes towards the UK. It seems likely, therefore, that combined with the 'history' theme it was the film's irreverence and comedy that assured it of longer life at the box office. *Motion Picture Herald* commented: 'A preview of the picture will enable the exhibitor to catch innumerable flashes, situations which will make for powerful advertising copy. He may well place selling emphasis on the comedy, the flashing performance of Laughton.'[29] Other reviews highlighted these elements, as well as acting, settings, comedy and sex. Charles Laughton's star persona was a significant factor in ensuring the film's success in America. He was far from unknown to American audiences: by the time he appeared in *Henry VIII*, he had been in several Hollywood films, including *The Sign of the Cross* (Cecil B. DeMille, 1932) and *If I had a Million* (Ernst Lubitsch *et al.*, 1932). His performance was awarded with an Oscar and the film was voted one of the ten best films of 1933 by the *New York Times*' critics.

Henry VIII also appeared at an interesting moment in terms of stricter censorship in the USA. In 1933 the Payne Studies on the impact of films on children were published and from November onwards Joseph Breen initiated tougher rules for the industry's Production Code. By 1934 films needed approval from the Motion Pictures Producers and Distributors of America (MPPDA) before they could be distributed or exhibited. Between 1932–3, most films were influenced by debates about overt representations of sexuality on screen and many producers avoided taking risks. From this perspective, *Henry VIII*'s risqué subject matter and verbal sexual banter perhaps anticipated the dialogue-based innuendo upon which producers were forced to rely once the Code was in operation. The poster for the film, however, showed Henry in a lustful pose, behind Jane Seymour, pulling her back to kiss her neck. Such postures by no means typified the film, which perhaps reveals a tension between advertising concerns and pressures towards conforming to the Production Code. When the film was re-released in 1935 this poster was withdrawn at the insistence of the Advertising Advisory Council and some of the suggestive dialogue was removed from the film.[30]

Henry VIII acquired a celebrated status in American film culture as a case of a British film that deserved to do well: features praised in reviews were commonly used as standards of judgement for subsequent British films, suggesting continuities and contrasts.[31] Ian Jarvie has argued that *Henry VIII* was an isolated, freak example of British success in the USA, citing the comparatively poor reception of Korda's later imperial films, *Sanders of the River* (Zoltan Korda, 1935) and *The Four Feathers* (Zoltan Korda, 1939) as evidence for this assertion.[32] In fact, some of these later films did very well at the box office, particularly *The Four Feathers*, United Artists' sixth highest grossing film of 1939.[33] It is also productive to link *Henry VIII* with comedy, Gainsborough melodramas and similarly irreverent or lavish costume epics. A successor in this tradition is *Caesar and Cleopatra* which after a vigorous and astute marketing campaign earned 2 million dollars on its first run and was reported as 'doing strong business throughout the country and … going over particularly big in Loew houses outside New York'.[34] The film made more money in the USA than in the UK and it fared better with American critics. *Henry VIII* also displays similarities with Hollywood's late 1930s cycle of history/costume films, including *The Prince and the Pauper* (William Keighley, 1937), *The Adventures of Robin Hood* (William Keighley/Michael Curtiz, 1938) and *The Private Lives of Elizabeth and Essex* (Michael Curtiz, 1939).[35]

Conclusion

There are clearly many intriguing questions about the distribution and reception of British films in the USA, and this is a relatively unexplored area of British cinema history.[36] Films have different careers in different countries and exhibition contexts, factors that relate to wider questions of national and cultural specificities (what is a British, as opposed to an 'international' film?). Such issues are especially fascinating as far as the UK and USA are concerned because of the common language and ideas about the two countries' supposed 'special relationship'. The British film industry's historic links and conflicts with Hollywood also provide an extra commercial dimension which has both assisted and hindered the export of British films. The aim to distribute British films in the USA was a persistent feature of debates about the protection of the British film industry and could not be extricated from Hollywood's tenacious defence of its most important overseas market. American companies distributed British films in the USA as a gesture of goodwill, in the spirit of 'reciprocity' which pervaded Anglo-American film relations, and as a strategy for continued economic health. It would be tempting to interpret the distribution of British films in the USA by American companies as motivated purely by self-interest. The number of British films they handled, however, and the fact that it is possible to identify key years and decades and evidence of continuities between popular themes and genres, indicates that there was more to it than the defence of Hollywood's film exports.

Many British producers have argued that in order to succeed in the American market British films should become 'international' and de-emphasise their sense of national identity. In fact, it is clear that the films which did best in the USA were distinctive, particularly in their notions of 'Britishness' (which could often be critical) and their appeal to specific 'niche' markets. These films often needed to display a degree of product differentiation in order to find a space in a highly congested marketplace. *The Private Life of Henry VIII* is a prime example of this strategy, released at a time when American audiences were particularly receptive to its comic critique of British institutions and affinities with New Deal philosophy. Far from being a 'one off', the film was part of a longer trajectory of British films which struck a chord with American audiences. While 'Stepping westward' could be a hazardous undertaking, in many cases the economic and cultural rewards far outweighed the risks.

NOTES

1 *Variety*, 17 October 1933, p. 19.
2 G. Macnab, for example, argues that 'the USAA was resistant not merely to British cinema but to British culture in general', in *J. Arthur Rank and the British Film Industry*, London, Routledge, 1993, p. 56.

3 See A.H. Guzman, 'The exhibition and reception of European films in the US during the 1920s', unpublished Ph.D. thesis, University of California, Los Angeles, 1993.

4 According to Political and Economic Planning (PEP), the overseas earnings of British films in 1950 were £3–3,500,000 (including Australia, New Zealand, Canada, South Africa, Europe, Japan and Latin America; 1 million of this came from the USA), totalling almost as much as earnings from the home market. See *The British Film Industry*, London, PEP, 1952, p. 250.

5 See S. Street, 'The Hays Office and the defence of the British market in the 1930s', *Historical Journal of Film, Radio and Television*, 1985, vol. 5, no. 1, pp. 37–55.

6 Figures from *Kine Year Book*, 1949 and *Cine-Technician*, May–June 1947. In 1946 the Board of Trade registered eighty-three British feature films; in 1947 the figure was 107.

7 Figures quoted in C. Ogan, 'The audience for foreign films in the United States', *Journal of Communication*, Autumn 1990, p. 59; and by R. Maltby in *Hollywood Cinema: An Introduction*, Oxford, Blackwell, 1995, p. 71.

8 T. Balio, 'The recession of 1969 and Hollywood's retreat from European production', unpublished paper delivered at 'European Challenge' seminar, British Film Institute, 1993.

9 T. Balio, *United Artists: The Company that Changed the Film Industry*, Wisconsin, University of Wisconsin Press, 1987, p. 224.

10 A study by D. Smythe, P. Lusk and C. Lewis of audiences in Champaign-Urbana, eastern Illinois, 1951–52, 'Portrait of an art-theatre audience', showed that *The Red Shoes* was one of the most popular films to play in the previous year. See *Quarterly of Film, Radio and Television*, Fall 1953, vol. 8, no. 1, p. 41.

11 *Chicago Tribune*, 26 April 1950, pt. 3, p. 7.

12 For a discussion of the various distribution mechanisms see R. Roud, 'Britain in America', *Sight and Sound*, Winter 1956–7, vol. 26, no. 3, pp. 119–23.

13 S. Rowson in *The Times*, 23 March 1926, p. 14.

14 *Guardian*, 27 October 1997, p. 5.

15 Examples given by R. Griffiths in 'Where are the dollars?' (2), *Sight and Sound*, January 1950, vol. 18, p. 40.

16 J.E. Williams, 'They stopped at nothing', *Hollywood Quarterly*, April 1946, vol. 1, no. 3, pp. 271–3.

17 For further details of genres and themes see S. Street, *The Projection of Britain: British Feature Films in America*, London, Cassell, forthcoming.

18 F.D. Klingender and S. Legg, *Money Behind the Screen*, London, Lawrence and Wishart, 1937; and M. Dickinson and S. Street, *Cinema and State: The Film Industry and the British Government, 1927–84*, London, British Film Institute, 1985, pp. 76–88.

19 I. Jarvie, *Hollywood's Overseas Campaign: The North Atlantic Movie Trade, 1920–1950*, Cambridge, Cambridge University Press, 1992, p. 144.

20 *Variety*, 14 November 1933, p. 10.

21 See reports in *Variety*, 7 November 1933, p. 25; 14 November 1933, p. 8; 21 November 1933, p. 11; 28 November 1933, p. 8; and 5 December 1933, p. 9.

22 It grossed $469,646.01. I am grateful to Mike Walsh for providing me with this information from the U[nited] A[rtists] Archive, State Historical Society, Wisconsin.

23 *Motion Picture Herald*, 21 October 1933, p. 6.

24 See tables in M. Cormack, *Ideology and Cinematography in Hollywood, 1930–39*, London, Macmillan, 1994, p. 45.

25 D. Reynolds, *The Creation of the Anglo-American Alliance*, London, Europa, 1981, pp. 23–5.

26 S. Harper, *Picturing the Past: The Rise and Fall of the British Costume Film*, London, BFI, 1994, pp. 20–3. See also S. Street, *British National Cinema*, London, Routledge, 1997, p. 40.

27 Street, ibid., p. 23. In the House of Commons pressure was put on the Secretary of State for India (Sir Samuel Hoare) by Sir Frank Saunderson to urge the Indian Government to ban *The Private Life of Henry VIII* on the grounds that it was likely to have a 'detrimental effect on the audience'. The film, however, passed the censors. See *Kinematograph Weekly*, 30 November 1933, p. 1, and 4 January 1934, p. 12; *Parliamentary Debates (Commons), Official Report, 5th series, 1933–34*, vol. 283, 27 November 1933, cols. 484–5, HMSO, 1934.

28 See Reynolds, op. cit., p. 23.

29 *Motion Picture Herald*, 23 September 1933, p. 40.

30 Production Code Administration files, Margaret Herrick Library, Los Angeles and press books file, Billy Rose Theatre Collection, New York.

31 *Variety* reviewed fifty-nine British films in 1933. Those which received the best reviews were: *The Private Life of Henry VIII*, *Rome Express* (Walter Forde), *The Good Companions* (Victor Saville), *Sleeping Car* (Anatole Litvak), *It's a Boy* (Tim Whelan) and *Orders is Orders* (Walter Forde).

32 Jarvie, op. cit., p. 143.

33 See UA figures, UA Archive, op. cit.

34 *Variety*, 11 September 1946, p. 27.

35 For a discussion of Warners' 'Merrie England'/historical cycle see N. Roddick, *A New Deal in Entertainment: Warner Brothers in the 1930s*, London, BFI, 1983, pp. 235–48. The review by *Variety* of *The Private Life of Henry VIII* predicted this trend: 'With Hollywood on the verge of a biographical cycle *Henry VIII* will likely provide the slight shove needed to send the coast into an era of historical and costume pictures', 17 October 1933, p. 19.

36 Existing work includes R. Murphy, 'Rank's attempt on the American market', in J. Curran and V. Porter (eds) *British Cinema History*, London, Weidenfeld and Nicholson, 1983, pp. 164–78; Macnab, op. cit.; and J. Sedgwick, 'Michael Balcon's close encounter with the American market, 1934–36', *Historical Journal of Film, Radio and Television*, 1996, vol. 16, no. 3, pp. 333–48.

4

THE OTHER SIDE OF PARADISE

British cinema from an American perspective

Marcia Landy

If, as the cliché would have it, 'travel broadens the mind', there may be things to be learned about British cinema, particularly popular British cinema, from its travels across the Atlantic. In what follows, I map the journey of British films on several levels – personal, pedagogical and scholarly. My essay is not a conventional treatment of a subject that has, over the last decade, begun to engage scholars and film critics. My emphasis is largely anecdotal, singular and impressionistic. Two questions in particular underpin the expedition. First, is there a British national cinema and, if so, in what ways is it recognized abroad? And second, how might such a transatlantic journey alter conceptions about past and present British cinema?

First impressions

My experience with British cinema from this side of the Atlantic began in the 1940s with my viewing British films at my neighborhood movie theater in the mid-West city of Cleveland, Ohio – not 'sophisticated' New York City. I remember vividly *The Man in Grey* (Leslie Arliss, 1943), *Madonna of the Seven Moons* (Arthur Crabtree, 1944), *The Seventh Veil* (Compton Bennett, 1945), *The Wicked Lady* (Leslie Arliss, 1945) and *They Were Sisters* (Arthur Crabtree, 1945). Each made a profound and indelible impression on me at that time, though it's only now that I have a language (thanks primarily to the work of Sue Harper, Pam Cook and Sarah Street) to describe my encounter with these films.[1] I did not assimilate the films as 'British'. To me, the concept of 'national cinema' was alien. As far as I was concerned, there was then only one cinema – Hollywood. Yet my friends and I sensed a difference from the usual melodramatic and adventure features to which we were accustomed. The films were shown in the early evenings of weekdays, since Saturday matinees were largely devoted to adventure films: Gene Autry and Roy Rogers Westerns, science fiction films featuring Buck Rogers and the Charlie Chan detective film serials. If memory serves me correctly, the British films were shown mainly in neighborhood theaters, of which there were many at the time, as distinct from the downtown theaters that offered Hollywood first-run features.

At that time, I was an avid reader of movie magazines. For adolescent moviegoers in the 1940s like myself, removed from the New York cultural center, our responses to cinema were influenced in part by our reading of movie magazines and their stories about particular stars and the cultural and cinematic roles into which they were cast. Such magazines as *Silver Screen* and *Photoplay* featured stories with photographs about the life styles of British stars – David Niven, Laurence Olivier, Merle Oberon, Charles Laughton, to name but a few – who made their homes and careers in Hollywood. These stories were not only conducive to heightening awareness about these stars in their off-screen and on-screen roles but to a blurring of lines between American and British culture. The émigré community, identified as the Hollywood Raj, was not a mere anecdotal fabrication manufactured by later writers such as Michael Korda.[2] An active publicity machine contributed to a fascination and engagement with Hollywood versions of British culture on the part of viewers and fans like myself. The stories were a vital source of

Plate 6   The Gainsborough films invited young American women of the 1940s into a titillating world of romance, sexuality and violence, inhabited by exotic figures: here, Margaret Lockwood and James Mason in *The Wicked Lady* (Leslie Arliss, 1945).

cultural folklore and the popularity of certain British films was enhanced by a mythology of Britishness.

Gainsborough and melodrama

Gainsborough films offered young women of the mid-1940s like me a timeless and titillating world of romance, sexuality and violence at a time when sex was appealing but threatening. When the earliest of these films was released in the USA, the war was waging, but the short films and newsreels with their patriotic messages accompanying the feature films struck me as an intrusive and annoying distraction barely to be tolerated until the feature began. By contrast with newsreels and feature films devoted to war, service and sacrifice, the Gainsborough films, inhabited by exotic figures played by Margaret Lockwood, Stewart Granger and James Mason, opened the door to what Sue Harper has described as a 'world of fantasy where freedom and pleasure were coterminous'.[3]

The most engaging aspect of these films was not their reproduction of official and mythic representations of British wartime and postwar culture. Their appeal, for better or worse, was their location within the parameters of Hollywood popular cinema and their resistance to documentary realism. Their melodramatic modes opened up vistas in relation to gender and sexuality that can hardly be dismissed as mere escapism. They seemed to offer no political prescriptions, no polemic and no direct challenge to the *status quo*. Through images of the feminine body, the unspecified landscape of romance and the attractive images of 'evil', the films raised suspicions about prevailing and inhibiting values concerning sexuality, the family and morality. To a young, motherless and naïve young girl, these films validated unspoken erotic desires and, even more, fantasies of rebellion.

One might be surprised to learn that Gainsborough films appealed to American audiences beyond cosmopolitan New York, introducing them to new forms of narrative, new faces, a different iconography of Britishness and novel treatments of history. In my case, my decision to teach and to write about British cinema later in life arose from this very personal – not academic – interest in films that were part of my initiation into the subversive potential of popular cinema, particularly subversive in relation to my then inarticulate conceptions of gender and sexuality. That I chose to write about British genre films, not documentary or experimental films, I blame on the Gainsborough melodramas. I wonder how many other lives, especially of American women, were touched by these films in ways that inflected their discontent with the prevailing strictures on sexual behavior and social conformity. Yet while important work has been done on the character and reception of these films by British and American critics, little, to the best of my knowledge, has been done in the USA to track the films' impact on segments of the American cinema-going public.[4]

Responses of American audiences to British films can be gleaned, in part, from an examination of reviews in newspapers and magazines of the time, limited though they might be as a reliable means for fully gauging the circulation and reception of the films. These reviews give a modest indication through the language adopted to advertise them of how the films were received and of the criteria employed to describe their style and content. In general, these film reviews reveal uncritical but excited responses to the films, focusing mainly on their treatment of sexuality. For example, *Variety*, commenting on *Fanny by Gaslight* (Anthony Asquith, 1944; US title, *Man of Evil*), wrote that: 'For all of its being toned down from Michael Sadler's [*sic*] frank treatment in the novel, the way the curvaceous femmes do their stuff in the underground joint hardly makes for the best family trade.'[5] A review of *Madonna of the Seven Moons* criticized the film for having an implausible narrative but conceded that 'there are moments in the picture which are strikingly dramatic and fraught with a passionate frankness that must have caused the Production Code moral guardians to pause'.[6]

The acting of the Gainsborough films was consistently praised even if reviewers hesitated about the pace of the films as well as their sexual innuendo. The *Variety* reviewer for *Caravan* (Arthur Crabtree, 1946) compared this 'sockeroo' to *The Wicked Lady*, commenting how 'one melodramatic situation [was] piled on another', and on the 'strong direction, ... brilliant individual performances' and high production values, adding that 'this production augurs well for the J. Arthur Rank organizers'.[7] While reviews emphasized the British origins of the films (predictably commenting on 'whether the ultra-English accents will be palatable to US patrons'), the reviewers were more interested in discussing the films for their sexually transgressive and violent content. *Variety*'s review of *The Upturned Glass* (Lawrence Huntington, 1947) provides a typical example: 'Many will squirm at two operations performed on children, sparing the audience nothing and not a few will shudder at the three principals strewing the stage as corpses.'[8]

One of the pleasures of these films was the way in which they used their historical settings to explore contemporary themes. Serious historians were of course less impressed with this viewpoint. On the dubious historicity of melodrama, a review of *The Wicked Lady* in *Variety* pointed out that

> In a way, *The Wicked Lady* serves a useful purpose. For years London critics have lambasted Hollywood for picturizing England as forever fog-bound, or staging fox-hunting in mid-summer, or for showing the Grand National against a background of waving palm trees. Now a British film outfit has produced a film which distorts 17th century England no less grotesquely.[9]

So much for the reviewer's general sympathy for 'historical pleasures'. The comparison with Hollywood's liberal treatments of history and of landscape is, nevertheless, a backhanded compliment and operates as a positive recognition of the British industry's contribution to (and competition with) the Hollywood cinema of the era, in particular its fascination with spectacle, the gothic and the grotesque.

By contrast with the reception of the Gainsborough films, David Lean's adaptation of Noël Coward's play, *This Happy Breed* (1944), a Two Cities/Cineguild film, received more restrained, though respectful, reviews. Bosley Crowther in the *New York Times* described the film as 'mild and episodic' and 'no world-beater as a dramatic exercise'. The film provoked Crowther to acknowledge that he was 'not sufficiently familiar with the English to say for sure how accurately Mr. Coward reports them'.[10] These reactions were echoed by *Variety*'s reviewer, who found the film a 'bit choppy and episodic at the start', although he contended that the film had 'special interest' for contemporary society 'as families everywhere try to hold anchor in an uncertain time'.[11] As a viewer of the time, I did not share these concerns. Living in a children's home, I was not at all conscious of or troubled about the tenuousness of the family in 'an uncertain time'. *Brief Encounter* (David Lean, 1945) got a more enthusiastic review for the acting and direction. In particular, *Variety* praised the acting of Trevor Howard as Alec, 'whose performance is calculated to win the sympathy of femmes of all ages' and added the film to 'the growing list of British-made pictures qualified to appeal to world audiences'.[12] Though I found the film absorbing, I was deeply disappointed at Laura (Celia Johnson) and Alec's failure to consummate their romance and escape their constraining milieu and found the film a bit tedious.

After the war, British films continued to be screened and reviewed beyond the New York landscape and several films from the war years enjoyed a revival in the early 1950s. I saw the films as an undergraduate at Ohio University where the notion of studying cinema was still remote. They played in the movie theaters of the small university town of Athens, Ohio and in neighboring Columbus, where I traveled when opportunity permitted. My hometown paper featured interviews with Margaret Lockwood and tracked the vicissitudes of various films. W. Ward Marsh, film reviewer for *The Cleveland Plain Dealer*, commented on James Mason's role in *The Seventh Veil* as 'making quite a sensation here'. In a later review, he was enthusiastic about the 'return' of British films to the Cleveland cinema: 'It will make many a film fan happy to learn that such British films as *Brief Encounter*, *Black Narcissus*, *Great Expectations*, *Seventh Veil* and many others are again available for showings in this territory.'[13] His list included some Ealing films and more Gainsborough films. Although Marsh identified 'a new celluloid bond between Britain and America',[14] he did not favor all British films. *The Wicked Lady*, for instance, was 'mechanical' and 'clichéd', although Lockwood's low-cut gowns and, more generally, the 'gorgeously attired human puppets' were noteworthy.[15]

The Gainsborough films vied with Hollywood in offering validation for the possibility of undermining the sacred truths of history and, even more, the values attached to nation and family. In short, these films were and are a window on to the ways in which popular cinema loosens the attachment to both civil society and the state, creating a 'politics of style' divested of socially sanctioned meanings. If the reviewers reiterated the need to chastise the commercial cinema as un-historical, they reaffirmed that the uses of history in films are an important point of contention, if not analysis, an issue that is only now garnering critical attention.

Ealing comedy and Hammer horror

Other popular films from Britain that wreaked havoc with heritage conceptions of British culture were the Ealing comedies of the late 1940s and early 1950s and the horror films produced by Hammer in the late 1950s and early to mid-1960s. The largest audience for these films was located in metropolitan centers such as New York, Boston and Chicago, but these films also made their way to college campuses and to a dwindling but still viable cinema-going public. Despite the penchant toward Anglophilia among members of this audience, these films were able to communicate vulnerable aspects of British national culture, presenting an image of crisis rather than legitimation in relation to social class, gender and community. The Ealing films received enthusiastic responses from reviewers in the USA, particularly such films as *Passport to Pimlico* (Henry Cornelius, 1949), *Whisky Galore* (Alexander Mackendrick, 1949), *Kind Hearts and Coronets* (Robert Hamer, 1949), *The Lavender Hill Mob* (Charles Crichton, 1951) and *The Man in the White Suit* (Alexander Mackendrick, 1951). Charles Barr has described these films as a 'national institution' belonging 'to both the landscape and the mood of postwar Britain', but the Ealing comedies were also very much part of the international postwar world.[16]

Thanks to the Ealing comedies, the American movie-going public, familiar with Alec Guinness from David Lean's *Oliver Twist* (1948), was soon to celebrate Guinness' screen image. What accounts for the popularity of this so ostensibly British actor? Is it worldliness as suggested by a *Time* review: 'Though remaining British to the core, he [Guinness] somehow achieves an element of Latin intensity in the role of a little man in happy revolt against society'?[17] Crowther in the *New York Times* stressed *The Lavender Hill Mob*'s 'indulgence in a serene and casual tolerance for the undisguised lawlessness in man', and found Guinness' character 'wickedly droll ... [and] one big chuckle from beginning to end'.[18] *Film Daily* advertised the film as 'the best of the modern British comedies, Guinness hilarious, delightful all the way'.[19]

If the Ealing films lacked the sexually transgressive aspects of Gainsborough films, they appealed and accommodated to the cynical taste of members of the Cold War and Keynsian generation while competing successfully with neo-realism. It is also significant that reviewers likened the films to the heyday of Hollywood comedy, thus indicating that favorable comparison of British films with Hollywood products was a potential key to their success in the USA. John McCarten in the *New Yorker* wrote that '*The Lavender Hill Mob* has plunged into the broadest cops-and-robbers slapstick that you've encountered in the movies since Mack Sennett retired the Keystone boys'.[20] This positive comparison also implied that the films were not exclusively or claustrophobically British. For good or ill, they were admitted into and registered as part of international film culture. However, while these Ealing comedies were largely praised for their acting, their audacious wit and their satire, there were some complaints about their 'whimsy growing thin' and the scripts being 'too full of Anglicisms … for the parochial American ear'. These were not complaints made earlier about Gainsborough films or later about Hammer films.[21] My recollection is one of little difficulty with the films' comprehensibility or of the problem of 'whimsy'. Instead, for me, the films' satire was a bracing relief from the moral platitudes of the 1950s and, even more, the repressive aspects of the anti-communism of the Cold War.

In my recollection, my response and those of my classmates to these comedies was not predominantly critical. We were not immersed in the travails of the postwar British state and empire or the condition of British culture. What we recognized, if perhaps inchoately, was that the films were an antidote to the rhetoric and actions of Cold War America. We identified the films with a certain form of hipness. They seemed to express emerging but still unconsolidated disaffection with authority in all aspects of the social life of the time, toward the government, familial and filial relations and prescriptions about the need for normality and conformity. These films seemed to travel across cultures in ways far different from the films of Second World War society. In particular, Britishness was not easily separable from Americanness and cinema was no longer Hollywood. International cinema had arrived.

If the Ealing films crossed over from popular to art-house audiences, the Hammer films appealed mainly to fans of the popular horror genre. In their anti-realism, their focus on sexuality, violence and power, these films maintained a form of film-making characteristic of Gainsborough films. Singles and married couples, my friends and I, while not critically astute about cinema, were impressed with the sophisticated acting of Christopher Lee and Peter Cushing, though we did not associate them with stardom. We were also impressed by the narratives, their connections to the Frankenstein and Dracula literature with which we were familiar, and with the films' exotic settings. These horror films constituted yet another instance of British popular cinema as opposed to high art cinema that received a favorable (and profitable) response in the United States. This response has been well documented over the years by British critics and to a lesser degree by American critics, particularly in the case of the horror genre. Like so many of the science fiction and horror films of the postwar era, *Dracula* (Terence Fisher, 1958; US title, *The Horror of Dracula*) (and those films that followed it from the Hammer studio) capitalized on the anxieties of the time. Such films worked over issues of authority gone awry and of beleaguered masculinity and femininity in an anti-realist cinematic language that invoked the sexual images and scenarios earlier identified with Gainsborough melodramas.

At the time of the films' appearance, the reviewers echoed earlier responses to the transgressive aspects of the Gainsborough films. The publicity campaign for the films and their actors heightened the sense of the films' lurid aspects. For example, *The Quatermass Experiment* (Val Guest, 1955; US title, *The Creeping Unknown*) was described by a reviewer as 'crammed with incident and suspense'.[22] Terence Fisher's *Dracula* was advertised with the intriguing question, 'Who will be his bride tonight?' The film was described in the *New York Times* as 'One of the best horror films ever made ... [a] lavishly mounted, impressive production ... Excitement and intrigue permeate the film'.[23] In addition to commenting on its 'vivid color' and the disturbing 'impeccable Oxonian accents', the reviewer, A.H. Weiler, commented on the 'damsels who look delectable enough in diaphanous shifts to turn the head of a red-blooded observer'.[24] Once again, the appeal of British cinema in the USA seemed to reside less in visual and narrative encomiums to the British Empire, its monarchy and its heritage than in its adherence to British styles of acting and settings and its violation of canons of taste, especially those involving sexuality.

From the Cold War to Swinging London

In the late 1950s, I had moved to Rochester, New York, with my husband and child and I began graduate study in literature at the University of Rochester. The city was the location of film archives at the George Eastman House where I saw a number of rare silent films and began to appreciate the potential for studying film. Meanwhile, local theaters were featuring such British films as *Room at the Top* (Jack Clayton, 1959), *Saturday Night and Sunday Morning* (Karel Reisz, 1960) and *The Loneliness of the Long Distance Runner* (Tony Richardson, 1962), films which challenged us with different images of British culture and different forms of cinematic expression. Britain's Cold War filmic versions of neo-realism crossed national boundaries with a vengeance. They elicited largely favorable responses in the USA without concern about their undermining the 'family trade'. Reviewers commented on their 'distinctiveness', especially their differences from Hollywood. These differences were largely attributed to the milieu of the films, their cynical edge and the style of acting, physical appearance and personalities of the performers, especially the defiant stance of the male actors. *Newsweek* described *Saturday Night and Sunday Morning* as 'Arthur's Cold War' and Albert Finney was singled out for his potential star appeal:

'Arthur [the character played by Finney] emerges as one of the few really distinctive characters of recent movies – a scoundrelly young haymaker whose cynicism is balanced by a thoroughly contagious addiction to the wine of life.'[25]

Edith Oliver, in the *New Yorker* in 1961, asserted that the film spoke to a certain *Angst* and crisis of masculinity of the time. Of Arthur's character, she wrote: 'what we have been seeing all along is a rowdy Peter Pan, and just as Peter was partly right in his view of stuffy Edwardian society, so our hero is partly right to fear for his future.'[26] A favorable contrast with Hollywood acting was made in *The Nation*, which described Finney and the two women who play opposite him, Shirley Ann Field and Rachel Roberts, as 'authentic in a way that our celebrated Hollywood fidelity seldom achieves'.[27] Reviewers again emphasized the film's flouting of social and sexual morality, praising the film for being 'a loud, hilarious, indignant, malodorous belch of prosperous protest from the British working class'.[28] While I might not have used such language to describe the films, I recollect being drawn to them by their different class configuration and by their assault on cultural and social values. I did not question the film's positioning of women, however (though I recall vividly that I lamented Alice's suicide in *Room at the Top*). In general, I found myself aligned with the male protagonists in their ill-fated struggles to escape the prison house of social class.

The Loneliness of the Long Distance Runner elicited a different response from *Time* magazine, which took issue with the politics of the film, suggesting that the film's social and cultural perspective had not been lost on the reviewer. *Time* found the film 'a piece of skillful but specious pleading for the British proletariat, [which] ominously suggests that the battles of World War III may be lost on the playing fields of Her Majesty's reform schools. ... [T]he hero is too palpably holier-than-thou, his case is too obviously rigged. Fortunately, actor Courtenay is excellent.'[29] Hollis Alpert, in *The Saturday Review* avoided the issue of politics and focused on the actors and their importance to changes in the star system and on the appearance of a new type of director:

> England's angry young director Tony Richardson is clearly a menace to the star system. He first discovered Rita Tushingham who in *A Taste of Honey* bore not the least resemblance to the usual pretty young movie ingenue ... and now in *The Loneliness of the Long Distance Runner*, he has discovered Tom Courtenay who is the least likely looking movie star since Ernest Borgnine. ... As an actor ... he is devastating; he achieves expressiveness with no palpable effort, and sends you home both heartbroken and uplifted.[30]

The Nation commented favorably on Courtenay's 'slouching posture' and on his 'projection of personality'.[31] Once again, British cinema was perceived by reviewers and movie-goers like myself as instituting new cultural images through the physical appearance and performance of the actors and also of introducing new subject matter different from Hollywood's. This appreciation of difference soon extended to British music, fashions, films and film stars identified with 'Swinging London' as part of the growing internationalization and commodification of popular culture. From the 1960s onward – a time of heightening global awareness – the American movie-going and television audience became enamored of British popular culture. *The Girl with Green Eyes* (Desmond Davis, 1963), *The Knack* (Richard Lester, 1965), *Darling* (John Schlesinger, 1966), *Alfie* (Lewis Gilbert, 1966), *Georgy Girl* (Silvio Narizzano, 1966) and *Smashing Time* (Desmond Davis, 1967) introduced American audiences to different styles of narrative and acting, new stars such as Julie Christie and Rita Tushingham and a different sense of the physical and cultural landscape of Britain. Critical reviews stressed the youthfulness and vitality of the films, their union of realism and poetry. Commentary was devoted to their 'far out romps' and their use of landscape, music and popular culture, aspects of the films not lost on popular audiences.

Reviewers expressed some reservations. While responses to *The Girl with Green Eyes* were complimentary, a few were critical about the film's potential for popular appeal. *Film Daily* described it as a film aimed at the 'discriminating viewer', at 'patrons of superior taste', thus suggesting that it was an 'art' film with a limited audience and meager financial prospects. Despite the concerns expressed about box-office receipts, Rita Tushingham was singled out for her 'big eyes, big mouth, and pointed nose ... her odd and wistful looks'.[32] I recall that, for certain men of my generation among my acquaintances, Rita Tushingham was as popular and appealing as the more glamorous Julie Christie. Aside from the predictable preoccupation with the acting and appearance of British stars, a less obvious selling point was the Britishness of the film. British cinema history was not lost on Bosley Crowther, for example, who described the film as a '"brief encounter," a "love story," between a youthful protagonist and an older man'.[33]

Comparisons and predictions are the stock in trade of the reviewer, and Michael Caine as Alfie was described in the *Hollywood Reporter* as 'a contemporary Tom Jones'. The same review commented on the sexual exploits of the male protagonist: 'His object is sex: cheery and irresponsible. He is caught up and changed when he finds responsibility inescapable.' With this role, it was suggested, 'Caine moves into the select cast of top international stars'.[34] *Georgy Girl* was commended for providing 'the warmest and funniest import of recent years for "arties"'[35] and the reviewer predicted stardom for Lynn Redgrave. In these films of Swinging London, traditional images of British culture collided with unsettling views of an unfamiliar urban landscape. The focus on youth, the introduction of people of color, if only as part of the background, the appearance of regional inequities and the focus on disaffection between classes were British but could be appreciated by a discerning American audience.

British cinema and Thatcherism

With the demise of the Swinging London films (brought on not least by the withdrawal of American funding for British film production), British cinema all but disappeared and would not again find a niche in the American market until the 1980s. I do not recollect seeing many British films in commercial theaters until then, although films like *Sunday, Bloody Sunday* (John Schlesinger, 1971) had successful runs at metropolitan centers along with other 'foreign' imports. British films could also occasionally be seen in university theaters and in museums.

These years also witnessed changes in the exhibition practices of the film industry and in the movie-going habits of the American public. Multiplexes had replaced neighborhood theaters; films of different nations shared the marquee with Hollywood films. VCRs had become popular and a whole new outlet in home videos flourished. Moreover, cinema audiences now included the young, the bored and middlebrow art types with cash to spend. More experimental films were seen at museums and film festivals. The cinema-going experience in the USA had become eclectic and de-centered. The experience of films paralleled politics, inflected by a confusion about the nature and meaning of national identity. On the one hand, many films came packaged in terms of their country of origin – its history, mythology, languages and landscapes, and so on. On the other hand, the issue of national identity was more mystified than ever, tied closely to the increased internationalization of the media and to the commodification of identity politics. In the USA, perhaps more than in Europe, the national had blurred into the international. That is, one might recognize a 'British film' as the critics do, but this designation is more a matter of classification rather than a sign of a critical engagement with the specifics of national identity. Some films crossed the Atlantic; others did not. Anglo-American co-productions and British genre films, despite problems of language and milieu, might cross national borders more successfully than intellectual films that experimented with form. Intensive publicity campaigns may be responsible for the success of some films, such as *Trainspotting* (Danny Boyle, 1996), but the reputation of the stars, the director or the literary source might also mitigate the difficulties of travel.

The years of Thatcherism (1979–1990) in Britain paradoxically offered a plethora of films that challenged long-held and insular values concerning British national identity – Terry Gilliam's *Brazil* (1985), Chris Bernard's *Letter to Brezhnev* (1985), Stephen Frears' and Hanif Kureishi's *My Beautiful Laundrette* (1985) and *Sammy and Rosie Get Laid* (1988), Peter Greenaway's

The Cook, the Thief, His Wife and Her Lover (1989) and Mike Leigh's *High Hopes* (1989) among others. These films resembled films of the late 1960s in their experimentation with media and in their focus on under-represented social groups and political fragmentation. They stand in contrast to many of the heritage films that specularize British cultural and architectural landmarks.[36] Continuing into the 1990s, the 'hybrid',[37] if not quite oppositional, cinema produced in Britain and supported by British, American and European capital explored history and memory, race, gender, ethnicity, sexuality and regionalism. In so doing, this cinema offered American audiences a portrait of British life that highlighted difference and disaffection with both tradition and modernity.

The responses to these films were mixed. At issue were questions of politics and national identity. Stanley Kauffmann, in a review of *Sammy and Rosie Get Laid*, was respectful of the film and of other Channel Four productions. He compared *Sammy and Rosie* to the British social-realist film of the 1960s 'as daring new furniture is to a sturdy old table'.[38] By contrast, Terrence Rafferty suggested that 'in this brave, incendiary failure … [Kureishi has] burned away too large a part of himself in trying single-handedly to put the torch to Thatcherism'.[39] Some of these films, like the Ealing comedies before them, were described as 'little' films and John Simon complained 'about the inability of Americans to make good small films such as *My Beautiful Laundrette* and *Letter to Brezhnev* … small films of undeniable quality'.[40] Likewise, Peter Greenaway's films received mixed acclaim from reviewers. There was a pious recognition of their 'erudition, and their visual imagination'. At the same time, Richard Alleva found that 'the whimsy in Greenaway's work … repels me, not the ferocity … it's the whimsy that makes the ferocity sickening'. He disavowed the political allegory, finding the work 'postmodernist par excellence'.[41] His responses, similar to other reviewers and dissimilar to academic critics such as Marcia Pally, revealed annoyance with the political and intellectual dimensions of Greenaway's films.[42]

Neither politics, erudition, local situations nor language stopped *The Crying Game* (Neil Jordan, 1992), *Four Weddings and a Funeral* (Mike Newell, 1994) or *Trainspotting* from successfully crossing the Atlantic. These films enthralled American intellectuals, members of diverse ethnic groups, the young, feminists and anti-feminists, gay and anti-gay groups. There was, however, moral – not linguistic – caviling in the case of *Trainspotting*. Richard Grenier wrote in *American Enterprise*:

> The dithyrambic praise for the film from our quality press ('brilliant,' 'dazzling,' 'hilarious,' 'fresh,' 'jubilant,' 'exultant,' 'stylish,' 'irresistible') doesn't connect easily with, for instance, the delightful scene when one of the characters dives into a very dirty toilet bowl for a heroin suppository that slipped out. … Unlike the Cheech and

Chong movies of some years back, in which the leading characters had comic adventures while under the influence of marijuana, the heroin addicts of *Trainspotting* are deprived of any redeeming virtues.[43]

Reviewers avoided the politics of these films. David Sprague in *Billboard* devoted most of his review of *Trainspotting* to the music in the film.[44] Others singled out the film's 'nihilism', its 'depiction of violence, destructiveness and intimidation'.[45] Did *Trainspotting*, like its predecessors of the 1960s, cross national boundaries with the help of characters and situations that challenged prevailing values? Or are these films indicative of a situation perennial to the reception of British cinema, namely, the need to comment on sexual practices as both interdiction and incitement of interest? The reviews of *The Crying Game*, for example, focused on the sexual attractions of Jaye Davidson and the sensationalism of the revelation that she was 'after all a man'.[46] The Irish political dimensions of the film in the hands of many of the reviewers paled beside 'the over-the-top metamorphosis',[47] the fact that it was 'a love story with a difference'.[48] The reactions of reviewers to British cinema largely revealed an absence of concern for the specific social and historical context of the films, although they continued to exhibit a fascination with films that violate dominant social norms, particularly sexual norms. In

Plate 7　　*The Crying Game* (Neil Jordan, 1992) was one of several British films to find favor in the US in the 1990s, though perhaps more for its sexual intrigue than for its 'Britishness'.

75

general, their reviews exposed a bias toward genre films and a lack of under-standing or sympathy for films that departed too widely from these con-ventions.

British cinema goes to university

The altered perceptions of British cinema in the USA are due in some measure to the creation of film and media studies programs in the late 1970s and early 1980s. National cinema has been one of the growth areas of American university film culture. The one-semester British Film course that I developed in the early 1980s was one of the first courses on British cinema offered on my side of the Atlantic. Of course, there had been literature courses in the English curriculum that included versions of Shakespeare on film, but the idea of focusing on popular British culture was another matter entirely. It violated the canonical and sacrosanct role that British literary classics played in the curriculum. My decision to offer a course on British cinema was based on my assumption that film constituted another means for understanding and representing British culture and society despite the assimilationist tendencies of the American film industry and monolithic readings of Hollywood films. In more personal terms, my decision was animated by my early attachment to British cinema, my curiosity about the identity of these films and the desire to understand their fate, which I now linked to that of 'popular culture'.

In offering my course on British cinema, I had to confront a number of objections from colleagues. Not the least of these was their belief (which they no longer mention) that there was no cinema culture in Britain, that British films, such as they are, were not visually and culturally innovative or interesting. I persevered and to my surprise not only did students exhibit interest in the course, but they also began to appreciate that there was indeed something to be learned about British popular cinema from the films I showed and from the readings that I assigned for the course. The films seemed challenging, familiar and yet different from the customary Hollywood fare. No longer did I have to tolerate the querulous comment, 'Is there a British cinema?'

In my first years of teaching the course, critical and historical readings were sparse. There were a few histories that could be used as assigned texts, popular biographies of stars, reminiscences on the Hollywood Raj, some material on censorship and some writing on melodrama, produced by British scholars.[49] Since the late 1980s, the number of courses on British cinema in American universities has grown. So has the number of students who focus on British films with some enthusiasm for what lies in store for them. At the same time, so has the available writing on British cinema grown, offering a larger repertoire of critical readings for the course.[50] These books, including my own *British Genres*,[51] focused more intensively on the critical analysis of various decades, documentary film production, genre study, star studies, director studies and questions of nation formation in relation to the role of cinema. Critical studies of British cinema have also attended to questions of history, the uses of history in British cinema and issues of race, ethnicity, class, sex and gender. As a consequence of this scholarship and the growing interest in national cinemas, some American film scholars have begun to undertake work on British cinema,[52] even graduating students with Ph.D. dissertations based on British film-makers.[53]

One of the initial problems I confronted in a course designed to cover various genres, themes and styles of film-making was the limited amount of films available, but over time, videos became obtainable, enabling a more diverse representation of film production. As for students' responses to the films, they were also revealing in their contrasts and similarities to reactions of audiences to earlier British cinema. Students tolerated politely such films as *Oh, Mr. Porter!* (Marcel Varnel, 1937) and *This Happy Breed*. They were mildly appreciative of such films as *Pimpernel Smith* (Leslie Howard, 1941) and *2000 Women* (Frank Launder, 1944). Gainsborough melodramas received a mixed response. Film majors were intrigued by the films' excessive style, star images, uses of costume and gender representations. Others, especially non-film majors, suffered these screenings and discussions. Ealing comedies got a more positive response from the latter group, particularly *Kind Hearts and Coronets*, a film that seemed more witty and cynical than *Passport to Pimlico*. The *Carry On* films were received with interest and enthusiasm as were Monty Python films and, more recently, *The Full Monty* (Peter Cattaneo, 1997). Students appeared respectful of the heritage dimensions of British cinema, though occasionally, as in the case of more recent films such as *Carrington* (Christopher Hampton, 1995), students were attracted to the film's sexual politics and to uses of landscape rather than to historical issues. In general, the course received positive evaluations for the film selections and for the recommended scholarly readings. In particular, the students were, like their movie-going predecessors, fascinated with films that treated aspects of British character and social life irreverently and excessively.

Epilogue

How do I now answer the question, 'Is there a British cinema?' I agree with Pierre Sorlin's position on national cinema that 'there is no clear-cut answer',[54] but there are clues in the reception of British national cinema from this side of the Atlantic – from reflections on personal history and from reviews of and scholarship on British cinema. I have learned that beyond the familiar narrative of Hollywood's colonization of British cinema are other and more diverse narratives. Along with positive responses to films that reinforce official and Anglophilic versions of Britishness, I find that there is greater enthusiasm for films that violate and undermine these myths and present transgressive sexual, gendered and historical portraits of culture. In particular, I find generally that responses to the texts are less preoccupied with British national identity (it is either taken for granted or ignored) than with those films that create a sense of commonality between American and British popular culture. That is how British cinema looks from the 'Other Side of Paradise'.

NOTES

1 S. Harper, *Picturing the Past: The Rise and Fall of the British Costume Film*, London, BFI, 1994; P. Cook, 'Melodrama and the woman's picture', in S. Harper and R. Murphy (eds) *Gainsborough Melodrama*, London, British Film Institute, 1983, pp. 14–28; and S. Street, *British National Cinema*, London, Routledge, 1997.
2 M. Korda, *A Charmed Life: A Family Romance*, New York, Avon Books, 1979.
3 Harper, op. cit., p. 131.
4 But see Chapter 3 by Sarah Street in this volume.
5 *Variety*, 7 June 1944, p. 8.
6 *New York Times*, 23 May 1946, p. 18.
7 *Variety*, 17 April 1946, p. 32.
8 *Variety*, 25 June 1947, p. 8.
9 *Variety*, 5 December 1945, p. 10.
10 *New York Times*, 14 April 1947, p. 24.
11 *Variety*, 16 April 1967, p. 8.
12 *Variety*, 5 December 1945, p. 10.
13 *Cleveland Plain Dealer*, 8 June 1951, p. 18.
14 *Cleveland Plain Dealer*, 17 January 1948, p. 14.
15 *Cleveland Plain Dealer*, 23 February 1947, p. 8.
16 C. Barr, *Ealing Studios*, Woodstock, New York, Overlook Press, 1980, p. 5.
17 *Time*, 15 October 1951, p. 118.
18 *New York Times*, 16 October 1951, p. 35.
19 *Film Daily*, 15 October 1951, p. 6.
20 *New Yorker*, 20 October 1951, p. 78.
21 *New Yorker*, 5 November 1949, p. 110.
22 *Variety*, 7 September 1955, p. 6.
23 *New York Times*, 29 May 1958, p. 24.
24 Ibid.
25 *Newsweek*, 10 April 1961, p. 103.
26 *New Yorker*, 15 April 1961, p.154.
27 *The Nation*, 29 April 1961, p. 380.
28 *Time*, 31 March 1961, p. 64.
29 *Time*, 26 October 1962, p. 60.
30 *The Saturday Review*, 22 September 1962, p. 42.
31 *The Nation*, 10 November 1962, p. 316.
32 *Film Daily*, 29 July 1964, p. 5.
33 *New York Times*, 11 August 1964, p. 37.
34 *Hollywood Reporter*, 23 August 1966, p. 3.
35 *Hollywood Reporter*, 10 October 1966, p. 3.
36 A. Higson, *Waving the Flag: Constructing a National Cinema in Britain*, Oxford, Clarendon Press, 1995.

37 J. Hill, 'British cinema as national cinema', in R. Murphy (ed.) *The British Cinema Book*, London, BFI, 1997, p. 251.
38 *The New Republic*, 30 November 1987, p. 24.
39 *The Nation*, 21 November 1987, p. 608.
40 *National Review*, 4 July 1986, vol. 38, p. 44.
41 *Commonweal*, 1 June 1990, vol. 117, no. 11, p. 351.
42 M. Pally, 'Order vs. chaos', *Cineaste*, Summer 1991, vol. 18, issue 3, pp. 3–6.
43 *American Enterprise*, November/December 1996, p. 12.
44 *Billboard*, 29 June 1996, p. 68.
45 B. Cardullo, 'Fiction into film, or bringing Welsh to a Boyle', *Literature/Film Quarterly*, 1997, vol. 25, issue 3, p. 158.
46 *Time*, 1 March 1993, p. 57.
47 *Esquire*, December, 1992, vol. 118, issue 6, p. 42.
48 *Films in Review*, May/June, 1993, vol. 44, issue 53, p. 188.
49 R. Armes, *A Critical History of British Cinema*, New York, Oxford University Press, 1978; J. Curran and V. Porter (eds) *British Cinema History*, London, Weidenfeld and Nicholson, 1983; Barr, op. cit.; J.C. Robertson, *The British Board of Film Censors: Film Censorship in Britain*, London, Croom Helm, 1985; Cook, op. cit.
50 J. Hill, *Sex, Class and Realism: British Cinema, 1956–63*, London, BFI, 1986; J. Richards and A. Aldgate, *British Cinema and Society 1930–1970*, London, Croom Helm, 1986; R. Dyer, *Stars*, London, BFI, 1986; T. Ryall, *Alfred Hitchcock and the British Cinema*, Urbana, University of Illinois Press, 1986; Murphy, op. cit.; Higson, op. cit.; Street, op. cit.; J. Richards, *Films and British National Identity: From Dickens to Dad's Army*, Manchester, Manchester University Press, 1997; J. Richards, *The Unknown 1930s: An Alternative History of British Cinema 1929–39*, London, I.B. Tauris, 1998.
51 M. Landy, *British Genres: Cinema and Society 1930–1960*, Princeton, Princeton University Press, 1991.
52 L. Friedman (ed.) *Fires Were Started: British Cinema and Thatcherism*, Minneapolis, University of Minnesota Press, 1993; W.W. Dixon (ed.) *Reviewing British Cinema: Essays and Interviews*, Albany, SUNY Press, 1994; A. Lawrence, *The Films of Peter Greenaway*, Cambridge, Cambridge University Press, 1997; R. Rosenstone (ed.) *Revisioning History: Film and the Construction of a New Past*, Princeton, Princeton University Press, 1995.
53 A. Ciecko, *Gender, Genre and the Politics of Contemporary Representation: Contemporary British Films by Women*, unpublished Ph.D. Dissertation, Pittsburgh, University of Pittsburgh, 1997.
54 P. Sorlin, *Italian National Cinema, 1896–1996*, London, Routledge, 1996, p. 4.

5

FROM *THE THIRD MAN* TO *SHAKESPEARE IN LOVE*

Fifty years of British success on Continental screens

Pierre Sorlin

The discussion of national cinemas is very often parochial and insular – and the discussion of British cinema is no exception. British cinema is more than the sum of the films produced in Britain. Audiences at home, for instance, have for several decades watched American films as much as, if not more than British films. But British films have also had a life abroad. The circulation of films in export markets is a neglected aspect of Cinema Studies that has only recently begun to attract the attention of scholars. My purpose in this chapter is to begin a preliminary mapping of the role of British films in Continental Europe in the postwar years. My interest is in ascertaining which films did well at European box offices, whether the same films performed equally well in different countries, and how we might account for the various successes and failures. A full analysis along these lines would require detailed attention to matters of taste and audience preferences, matters that are very difficult to research. For the purposes of this chapter, I have relied upon the available statistics for cinema audiences, as well as press reviews and commentary. The latter, of course, can tell us something about taste, but it should be remembered that published reviews do not necessarily reflect spectators' opinions.

Postwar success: to what extent?

With few exceptions British cinema had been of little interest to the rest of Europe in the 1920s and 1930s. After 1918 movie theatres on the Continent became easily accessible to American imports so that in the mid-1920s two-fifths of all pictures screened in Germany or France and 90 per cent of those shown in Austria came from Hollywood.[1] Most countries reacted to this influence by introducing protective legislation for native film industries; there were also some attempts at making 'Continental' pictures that might compete more equitably with American films. The German company UFA was particularly effective in this respect, managing to secure second place, after Hollywood, in the Austrian, Dutch and Danish markets as well as exporting to France, Spain and Italy. There was little room left for the United Kingdom; the outburst of nationalism that marked the 1930s, especially in Italy and Germany, only worsened the situation. France was the only European country that continued to screen British movies up to 1940. While critics praised British documentaries, Hitchcock's thrillers and some Korda productions, notably *The Private Life of Henry VIII* (Alexander Korda, 1933) and *The Four Feathers* (Zoltan Korda, 1939), their interest in these British pictures was overshadowed by images of American films which seemed to them superior.

After the Second World War, the role of British films in Europe changed dramatically. Not only did movies like *The Man in the White Suit* (Alexander Mackendrick, 1951) have a sensational impact upon west European audiences, but journalists became accustomed to taking British cinema seriously instead of measuring it against Hollywood standards.[2] It is rare to observe such a swift transformation, especially one that has been so long lasting; and it is the continuing success of British films on Continental screens that I want to explore here. Success is an elastic notion and several points must be borne in mind when expanding upon the fame of such an ill-defined object as 'British cinema'. The first point is that Continental movie theatres have long been the scene of fierce competition between Hollywood and local producers, so that only a limited portion of the market has been, and is still, open to other European producers. If a few British movies are commercially rewarding, they still only account for 5 per cent of the screenings in the best years and in some years as little as 2 per cent.[3] Success does not come at random but has to be prepared for. Another important point is that, alongside the intrinsic quality of the pictures, we must take into account the astute export policy developed by British distributors, a policy that has had no equivalent in Europe. Having captured a secure audience thanks to their sales in the American market, British distributors have been able to build up audiences on the Continent. Unlike the strategy of the American studios, their marketing technique has consisted not in selling as many pictures as possible but in promoting a limited cluster of original, offbeat movies. I do not want to expand on this side of movie distribution but it is worth remembering that in 1993, the worst year of the decade from a financial point of view, Britain's film exports to the Continent amounted to £95 million whereas imports from the Continent ran to only £69 million.[4]

The last point to consider is that a film may be popular because many spectators enjoy it, but also because it is much talked about, even by people who have not seen it. Take the biggest British hits of the late 1940s and 1950s, *The Third Man* (Carol Reed, 1949) and *The Bridge on the River Kwai* (David Lean, 1957). The latter was a must-see film in the late 1950s, topping box-office charts in France and ranking second in Italy and Germany; in the latter country it was seen by more than six million people, which made it one of the top foreign moneymakers in the history of German cinema. After an initial outburst of enthusiasm, however, it was almost forgotten and rarely screened again. Attendance for *The Third Man* was about four times less than for Lean's movie,[5] but the film was endlessly commented on and discussed throughout Europe, even after the end of its run in movie theatres. I shall try to account for the enduring fame of Carol Reed's movie in due course; what I want to stress here is that it is often difficult to explain why a particular film is so highly appreciated. The European reputation of the British films in the second half of the century is partly explicable but it must also remain partly inexplicable.

When attendance was booming

We may be tempted to conclude from these statistics that during the latter half of the twentieth century Continental spectators valued British films very highly. But this is an imprecise, almost meaningless claim since 'Continental spectators' do not exist as such. Cinema-goers behave differently according to their country, their cultural background and, above all, according to the evolution of the market. For the purposes of the present chapter, however, it will be necessary to resort to such generalisations in order to allow a preliminary mapping of a complex topic. Trying to define periods in an evolution is equally risky and the divisions I will suggest must be regarded as propositional rather than as an elaborated scheme. However, it does not seem arbitrary to consider three successive moments, the first stretching from the end of the Second World War to 1960, the second including the 1960s and 1970s, and the third bringing the story up to the present.

The first period was one of intense movie-going on the Continent. This may sound strange since both Britain and the USA witnessed a dramatic decline in cinema attendance in the 1950s: between 1951 and 1960, British audiences diminished by 60 per cent. During the same period, Continental audiences increased by 16 per cent.[6] In 1957 more than 3,000,000,000 tickets were sold, which means that, statistically speaking, every Continental, including the new-born, went to the movies sixteen times that year. From 1947 to 1962, movie-going was a major leisure activity on the Continent. The fascination with cinema resulted in the opening of new theatres and the creation of film societies or film clubs.[7] In order to fill their programmes, exhibitors had recourse to old movies and to American imports, but that was not enough. British studios, which were then by far the most active in Europe,[8] seized the opportunity and succeeded in selling many pictures. Let us consider two difficult markets, Germany and Spain: a defeated Germany was reluctant to watch movies made by an occupying country, while the Spanish government, outlawed by democratic countries, was doing its best to boycott products from abroad. Nevertheless, Gallup polls suggest that the European films that most appealed to German audiences were British while, in Spain, British movies came third at the box office in the 1950s, behind Hollywood and locally produced pictures.[9]

But statistics provide too abstract a picture, since they can tell us neither who saw what film, nor what motivated people's choices. While an 'elite' of film buffs, who had learnt a foreign language at school, was keen to see films with their original soundtrack, the vast majority of spectators preferred dubbed versions. This is an aspect of cinema attendance that has not yet been explored in any detail but it does explain why some pictures that had been very successful in Britain were never screened on the Continent. The choice, for distributors, was simple: if they could lure the urban middle-class public into attending first-run screenings they would make money rapidly with subtitled prints; otherwise, they would dub more 'popular' movies and turn a profit over longish periods. The case of Laurence Olivier's screen adaptations of Shakespeare is typical in this respect: these pictures were considered masterpieces, particularly for their use of colour, by a small minority of city dwellers; they were thus distributed in subtitled prints but were soon taken out of distribution.[10]

Dubbed films took most of their earnings from second-run screenings but the clientele of small cinemas had a choice between national, American and other foreign pictures. Distributors were therefore obliged to be extremely selective, and when they decided to promote a British production they had to advertise it very carefully. This is precisely what happened with *The Third Man*: the musical score was extensively broadcast on radio (something exceptional at the time), a great splash of publicity was made with the casting, the fame of Graham Greene, and the Best Picture award it won at Cannes so that, when the film was released on the Continent, the public was anxious to see it. The film did well in first- and second-run screenings. Cinema-goers' reactions were unpredictable, however. Powell and Pressburger's movies, which were also intelligently promoted, met with a weak response in France and Italy, while in Germany, *The Red Shoes* (1948) and *The Battle of the River Plate* (1956) ranked among the top ten in 1950 and 1957 respectively, matching the success of local productions.[11] *The Red Shoes* was well received by critics who stressed the pleasant blend of melodrama, fairy tale and psychological drama, the recurring intervention of the red colour, its connection with love, dance and death, the emphasis placed on ballet shoes, the play on obscurity and shadows – but nothing allows us to say that this is what enthralled the public. That critics did not share the same tastes is demonstrated by *The Battle of the River Plate*, which was not highly praised by journalists, but was nevertheless very successful at the box office.

Urban cinemas routinely accrued large receipts but the takings from local picture houses and even fairground cinemas were far from negligible. There, exhibitors who had little money bought at bargain prices prints which could no longer run in the cities; for the viewers, the only choice was between attending or not attending a unique programme. Local monographs show that British (and other foreign) films seldom reached the provinces, apart from the Ealing productions.[12] It was thought initially that *Whisky Galore* (Alexander Mackendrick, 1949) and *Passport to Pimlico* (Henry Cornelius, 1949) would merely complete second-run programmes. The films were consequently poorly advertised, and the Italian distributors went so far as to refuse them because they were 'based on cultural traditions and habits which could not be easily exported'.[13] In the event, the films actually did very well in first-run cinemas. Urban screens were then under the sway of two cinematic models, the Hollywood genre movie with its superb photography and the European art film which was strongly influenced by Italian neo-realism. Continental spectators were delighted by the freshness of Ealing comedies; the film buffs enjoyed a funny, critical but unpatronising self-portrait of British life, while the 'popular' public liked the absence of sophistication and the humorous dialogue. Even the Italians overcame their prejudice: *The Man in the White Suit* was a success in the peninsula, while the French preferred *Kind Hearts and Coronets* (Robert Hamer, 1949). National preferences as revealed by the box office often resulted from clever distribution strategies. They also tell us something about European spectators and the way they looked at Britain at the time. Italy was on the verge of what has been called 'the economic miracle' and Italians, interested in teasing out analogies between their country and more industrialised societies, enjoyed the spectacle of inefficient factories, corrupt industrialists and lazy unionists in the UK. As for France, the Revolution having democratised the old aristocracy and vulgarised it in the process, the French were sensitive to any image of degenerate, resentful nobles!

While a few British films met with an excellent response on the Continent during the 1950s, they were isolated cases. The Ealing films, without ever being among the box-office top ten, were always moneymakers. As a series, they demonstrated the capacity of English studios to make funny, gripping films on a regular basis. They were also the only pictures to appeal to all sectors of the film audience and their role in creating a favourable image of British cinema must be fully appreciated. Another important factor was the blossoming of film societies which, aiming to develop an interest in 'realist' cinema among film buffs, often screened British documentaries of the 1930s as well as more recent movies dealing with social problems.[14] The members of these clubs were mostly students or young people, many of whom would later become directors, producers or film critics. It is always difficult to gauge the influence of the press but it is quite possible that the journalists who had frequented the film societies played a part, ten or fifteen years later, in persuading spectators that British films were worth a visit.

The time of the New Waves

During the 1950s, Continental spectators showed a taste for pictures they had not known before and which would not last long afterwards. Obviously, there were quite diverse film-viewing behaviours at the time, but the fact that cinema was the dominant form of entertainment, while distribution was dominated by American companies selling more or less the same films in different countries, tended to homogenise film consumption. The following decade was characterised by an increasing differentiation between countries and between generations.[15] The dominant trend in this second period, which began in the early 1960s and lasted until the 1980s, was the decline of cinema attendance: in 1965, admissions across Europe had fallen to 2,000,000,000, a good 30 per cent less than ten years before. However, while the Germans, Austrians and Belgians deserted the cinema on a massive scale, the decrease was slow in France and the Netherlands and began much later in Italy, Spain and Portugal. In Germany, where more than 3,000 picture houses closed in two decades, cinema became a purely urban form of entertainment.[16] But even in southern countries, a shift occurred in the way people conceived of cinema. Previously, going to the pictures was both a weekly routine, almost detached from the nature of the programmes on offer, and a family rite. In the 1960s youngsters began visiting cinemas in groups and audiences began to care about what they saw. Spectators no longer put up with indigenous quickies and preferred foreign movies when they were of better quality. Of course Hollywood had the best share, but Britain also did very well, as can be observed in Germany. There, until the early 1960s, all the top ten films were national productions; in 1963 *Lawrence of Arabia* (David Lean, 1962) was only thirtieth at the box office; the following year *Tom Jones* (Tony Richardson, 1963) was thirteenth. I have discounted the fantastic success of the James Bond films, which were among the top ten in every country, because the series was Anglo-American rather than British. But even if we leave these aside several British films were among the top ten in Germany during the 1960s and 1970s.[17]

Film specialists have long noted important changes in the 1960s, with the advent of various 'new waves' or 'new cinemas'. How did Britain's New Wave fare in European markets? While the movies of the 'angry young men' were unanimously lauded by critics, only *Saturday Night and Sunday Morning* (Karel Reisz, 1960) met with a favourable response from the Continental public – with the interesting exception of Spain. In France, Italy and slightly later in Germany, young film-makers were trying to get rid of old patterns; spectators interested in these developments found Britain's 'angry young men' too embedded in social problems and questions of class status. But in Spain, where escapism had long been the dominant trend in film production, 'el cine de la disidencia' was introducing in its films a critical view of the country akin to the picture of provincial, industrial Britain offered by the British New Wave.[18] Some of the films directed by Juan Antonio Bardem, especially *A las cinco de la tarde* (1960), which showed that bullfighters were often poor, exploited people, dealt with similar problems to those examined in *The Loneliness of the Long Distance Runner* (Tony Richardson, 1962) and *This Sporting Life* (Lindsay Anderson, 1963). In effect, the films of Bardem and others like him introduced Spanish viewers to the atmosphere of the British movies.

I do not have the space here to explore all the films that appealed to Continental audiences: I will therefore focus instead on two examples, *Darling* (John Schlesinger, 1965) and *The Go-Between* (Joseph Losey, 1970), chosen because they are very different from one another. *Darling* was favourably received in Germany. There was nothing particularly original in the story, which could have been shot in many other countries. The Germans, for instance, had tackled similar issues with films like *Die Sünderin* (Willie Forst, 1951) and *Das Mädchen Rosemarie* (Rolf Thiele, 1958). But, at least according to the critics, *Darling* did not indulge in moralising, unlike its German predecessors. Its main character was both admired for her independence and denigrated for her inability to establish a stable relationship with her partners. The film explored the new consumerist age while emphasising the disparity between what commodities promised by way of seduction and what they were actually about. It was this amalgam of criticism and enthusiasm which distinguished the film and which accounts for its success. In France and Italy, *The Go-Between* was one of the most widely discussed films of the period.[19] It is of course the presence of the beautiful, energetic and seemingly invulnerable Julie Christie in both *Darling* and *The Go-Between* that allows one to draw parallels between the two films. But journalists reacted in quite different ways in different countries. The Germans pragmatically emphasised the confrontation of *Darling*'s main character with the four temptations typical of the time – television, money, politics and advertising. The French and the Italians, on the other hand, expanded much more on the sumptuous and playful take on the end-of-the-century period in *The Go-Between* and applauded the uncertainty resulting from the shift from one epoch to another. The films are, of course, very different, but it is worth noticing that some critics admired the simplicity of *Darling*, others the complexity of *The Go-Between*.

The television era

Criticism in the end matters less than the box office. During the third period of my study, the 1980s and 1990s, Europe proved an excellent outlet for selected British films. In the 1990s, for instance, British films attracted as many Italian spectators as all other European films put together. The most successful films were not necessarily those that had proved popular in the UK, such as *Chariots of Fire* (Hugh Hudson, 1981) or *A Room with a View*

(James Ivory, 1986).[20] Nor were they necessarily the most critically acclaimed films. To take a simple case: in France the biggest British hit of the 1980s was *Octopussy* (John Glen, 1983), which received hostile reviews but was seen by one million spectators; *My Beautiful Laundrette* (Stephen Frears, 1985), on the other hand, interested only 1,000 viewers while *The Draughtsman's Contract* (Peter Greenaway, 1982) hardly did better.

The response of the public must be interpreted in the context of an audio-visual market dominated by television.[21] Television networks have played a major part in familiarising Europeans with the history of British cinema. In the 1980s the Italian public network, RAI, for instance, broadcast a whole cycle of Ealing productions, which was a revelation for most viewers. During the 1990s, the German networks put on more than 600 British films, with special series dedicated to the great actors and main directors. Television was also a very influential advertiser. *Shakespeare in Love* (John Madden, 1999), for example, was extensively discussed on the small screen because of its Oscars and the award it won at the Berlin Film Festival, and the distributors took the opportunity to release it while spectators were still hearing of the movie. More important, television channels bought films. *The Remains of the Day* (James Ivory, 1993), which was not a moneymaker in cinemas, was seen by some twenty million people on the small screen. Broadcast films were usually dubbed; although there were more and more Continentals who had been taught English at school, there was still a clear divide between those who were willing to read subtitles and those who were not. Dubbed films and subtitled films necessarily attracted different publics, both on television and at the cinema. In the case of the latter, dubbed films showed in the big film centres frequented by suburban families, whereas subtitled films were on offer in the limited circle of art cinemas.

There were, once again, two kinds of publics but, in so far as we can interpret their views, a wide spectrum of spectators enjoyed the difference of British movies from the dominant trends of Continental films. Italian and French comedies were often extremely sophisticated, their implicit concept a 'what if ...?': what if the world were different, what if virtual characters could meet real ones? Pictures like *Four Weddings and a Funeral* (Mike Newell, 1994), one of the biggest hits of the 1990s, seemed simply funny, however; with their intentionally comic moments, and interweaving multiple narrative strands with dazzling assurance, they were not pretending to picture things simply for the sake of art. As for so-called 'modern' Continental films, they made nothing happen, they were not places where events or adventures might take place: the viewer was meant to care less about the thing pictured and more about the way of picturing it. Such films avoided the major concern of the period, unemployment. Critics were thus prone to contrast them with British films like *The Full Monty* (Peter Cattaneo, 1997), which seemed to tackle such issues head on, displaying the endless repetitive days and empty weeks redundant people had to go through as well as the pleasure

Plate 8   The Full Monty's (Peter Cattaneo, 1997) humorous take on life in post-industrial Britain ensured it was a major success in Europe.

of comradeship. We cannot know for sure why audiences were so taken with such films, but the reaction of the press was unequivocal: journalists praised the depiction of current anxieties within society. These films showed that poverty had robbed people of options. They offered a persuasive look at life in post-industrial areas rarely visited by film-makers and an acute study of contrasted types of rebels. If there was much that was grim in these stories, film journalists (and audiences?) applauded the fact that the films, while acknowledging these problems, never indulged in sorrow or misery.

Britishness?

The successive movements in British cinema of which Ealing comedies, the sophisticated pictures of the 1960s and the half-fantasy, half-serious movies of the 1990s were a key part, helped modify the way Europeans looked at Britain. What did Continentals retain from British films? Roughly speaking a clearer, if relatively biased view of British society, and a notion of what constitutes 'Britishness'.

Reading the commentaries written on the Continent after the war, it is surprising to learn that film critics felt they were discovering a little-known world: British society. There was much argument about the class structure of the United Kingdom.[22] The class system was a dominant feature of many European films in the middle of the twentieth century. It was much criticised in French or German movies which blamed the selfishness and arrogance of the establishment, while the Italians laughed at the aristocracy. British films impressed many spectators because, instead of condemning, they seemed accurately to depict a sharply class-divided society in which the gentry retained complete dominance of the public sphere, while ordinary Britons seemed more interested in improving their welfare than in changing the features of the country. This was rather confusing for Continental audiences fussy about equality and reluctant to acknowledge that class remained the chief determinant of individuals' life-chances and experiences. Bewilderment did not vanish during the second period, the 1960s and 1970s. If many British movies seemed to turn upside down the traditions of deference and politeness on which social relations were based, social mobility was still restricted as a result of education: penniless people had to stay where they were born, or to use guile to progress socially. Enjoyable stories often turned out to be extremely cynical, the comedy coming from the contortions the plot had to perform in order to keep the class stratification intact despite apparent attacks against established customs.

The 1950s were an epoch of violent political conflicts in most Continental countries, with liberal parties, especially the Christian democrats, taking control from the communists and the left. Many cinema-goers were thus impressed by the description of firmly settled British communities and often missed the hints of much subtler divisions, such as the opposition between the English and the Scots in *Whisky Galore*.[23] The films of the 'angry young men' in the 1960s might have dispelled these illusions but they were not popular. The pictures of the 1980s and 1990s were consequently a shock because they depicted a divided, scattered population and revealed new communities of immigrant origin. Few Continental films have tackled the risky problem of immigrants' inclusion in European societies and most have preferred simply to denounce the apartheid newcomers have to endure. British films such as *My Beautiful Laundrette* or *Sammy and Rosie Get Laid* (Stephen Frears, 1988) look at Britain from the view-point of well-adjusted young Pakistanis. Despite considerable prejudice, they have embraced western culture and western lovers in a way that sets them apart from their immigrant parents without integrating them into the life of British society. Other movies like *My Son the Fanatic* (Udayan Prasad, 1997) go further when they present Pakistanis who, having painfully adapted to British life and given their children a good education, have to face the rebellion of their sons who reject the west and its immoral ways. What disconcerted many Continental spectators in the 1950s and still impresses many today is the explicit picture of social partitions offered by British films as well as their absence of moral judgement. What has long been repressed in Continental cinemas, namely the awkward compromise between national consensus and class and racial conflicts, actually figures quite centrally in British pictures and is treated in a transparent, accessible manner so that nobody can ignore it.

British films were also important in helping develop the idea of Britishness. I would argue that this concept, which has no precise meaning, was part of a fashion that flourished during the second half of the century and consisted in attributing to each nation so-called distinctive characteristics. Britishness was merely what foreigners labelled 'typically British'. Alec Guinness was initially seen as the perfect embodiment of Britishness because of his seemingly restrained, over-controlled way of acting. But things soon changed, and an unstable notion of Britishness evolved with the James Bond series. There was nothing strikingly original in the plots of these films, their all-action references and allusions stretching back to the spy movies of the previous decades. The most recent James Bond films have abundant special effects of always more ambitious proportions but there were no brilliant tricks in the first items of the cycle. What most viewers seemed to like, and what may have made them remodel their idea of Britishness, was Bond himself. Here was the personification of a new kind of hero, whose mark was less his ability to take a beating or seduce enemy women than his aptitude to commit acts of violence while always looking well-dressed in the finest evening attire with a clean shirt and polished shoes. It was impossible to take these stories too seriously and the perfect amorality of a character who mixed murder and sex was all the more pleasurable because it seemed totally fictitious. Bond's cool, unemotional behaviour, his dispassionate way of mastering sophisticated gadgets and killing people, his impeccable wanderings through corpses and car chases, were miles away from the professional competence of Continental detectives. Against Alec Guinness' command of understatement, Bond was seen as the symbol of a United Kingdom that made fun of everything, especially of the sacred values of patriotism and defence of liberty.

How was it possible to reconcile this vision of a swinging, careless Britain with the other conception of a class divided society? That scheme was, of course, totally impracticable. But movie-goers do not look for coherent, logical impressions. What they want are strong images, however conflicting these images may be. The most successful British films did not provide Continentals with a better knowledge of the United Kingdom – but they made them realise that the British cinema existed and was worthy of consideration.

NOTES

1   K. Thompson, *Exporting Entertainment: America in the World Market, 1907–1934*, London, British Film Institute, 1985, pp. 104, 125, 131.
2   Eastern European countries will not be considered in this chapter because statistics for the Soviet Union and East Germany are incomplete and unreliable.
3   ANICA, *Cinema d'oggi*, August 1997, nos. 14/15, p. 21.
4   *Overseas Transactions of the Film and Television Industry, 1995*, London, ONS, 1996, p. 83.

5 See K. Sigl, W. Schneider and I. Tornow, *Jede Menge Kohle? Kunst und Kommerz auf dem deutschen Filmmarkt der Nachkriegszeit*, Munich, Heyne, 1986, p. 124.

6 Statistics drawn from M. Gyory and G. Glas, *Statistics of the Film Industry in Europe*, Brussels, European Centre for Research on Cinema and Television, 1992, and A. Finney, *The State of European Cinema*, London, Cassell, 1996. All subsequent statistical information is from these sources unless otherwise indicated.

7 In 1955 there were 6,000 cinemas in Italy, 5,800 in France and 6,500 in Germany, against 4,500 in Great Britain.

8 Producing 1,365 films between 1951 and 1960, against 1,029 in Germany.

9 Ludwig Thome, 'Der Film und sein Publikum: Der deutsche Filmbesucher', *Internationale Film Revue*, 1951/52, vol. 1, no. 4, p. 280; Román Gubern (ed.) *Historia del cine español*, Madrid, Catedra, 1995, p. 263.

10 In Germany, despite good reviews, both *Henry V* (1945), released in 1950, and *Richard III* (1955) were commercial flops; see Sigl, Schneider and Tornow, op. cit., pp. 124 and 129.

11 Sigl, Schneider and Tornow, ibid., pp. 124 and 131.

12 L. Pinna, M. MacLean and M. Guidacci, *Due anni col pubblico cinematografico*, Rome, Bianco e Nero, 1958; C. Fleer, 'Vom Kaiser-Panorama zum Heimatfilm', in W. Mueller and B. Wiesener (eds) *Schlachten und Stätten der Liebe. Zur Geschichte von Kino und Film in Ostwestfalen und Lippe*, Detmold, Streifenweise, Film Archive Lippe, 1996.

13 See 'Film critica', *La Stampa*, 15 October 1951, p. 4.

14 V. Spinazzola, 'Circoli del cinema e organizzazione cella cultura', *Cinema nuovo*, October 1954, vol. III, no. 44, pp. 13–28; A. Paech, 'Schule der Zuschauer: Zur Geschichte der deutschen Film-Club Bewegung', in H. Hoffman and W. Schobert (eds) *Zwischeb Gestern und Morgen: Westdeutscher Nachkriegsfilm, 1946–1962*, Frankfurt, Deutsches Filmmuseum, 1989, pp. 108–23.

15 On the evolution of the film audience, see V. Spinazzola, *Cinema e pubblico: lo spettacolo filmico in Italia, 1945–1965*, Milan, Bompiani, 1974; L. Thome, op. cit., p. 280 ff.; S. Pozo, *La industria del cine en España, 1896–1970*, Barcelona, Universitat de Barcelona, 1984.

16 In 1970 there were less than 100 million tickets sold in Germany.

17 Notable box-office successes include *Those Magnificent Men in their Flying Machines* (Ken Annakin) in 1966, *Blow-Up* (Michelangelo Antonioni) in 1967, *A Clockwork Orange* (Stanley Kubrick) in 1973, and *Barry Lyndon* (Stanley Kubrick) in 1976.

18 For an evaluation of this critical stance, see Filmoteca Nacional de España (eds) *El cine realista británico*, Madrid, Filmoteca, 1978.

19 Few films were so extensively reviewed. There were more than twenty substantial articles in French and Italian magazines and there was even a long-lasting debate in the Italian magazine *filmcritica* (see the issues of January and February 1972).

20 On the reception of British films of the 1980s and 1990s, see P. Pilard, *Le nouveau cinéma britannique*, Paris, Hatier, 1989; *Cinema d'oggi*, August 1997, nos. 14/15; *Internazionale Filmfestspiele*, Berlin, Filmfestspiele, 1999.

21 On the screening of films on television, see H. Riedel, *Fernsehen. Von der Vision zum Programm. 50 Jahre Programmdienst in Deutschland*, Berlin, Deutsches Rundfunk-Museum, 1985; and J. Hill and M. McLoone (eds) *Big Picture, Small Screen: The Relation Between Film and Television*, Luton, John Libbey Media, 1996.

22 Reviews of *The Go-Between*, for instance, frequently emphasised this question.

23 Something that Italian distributors overlooked in 1950.

Part III

CINEMA, POPULAR CULTURE AND THE MIDDLEBROW

Introduction

The three chapters in this section each deal with tensions between different cultural traditions in Britain. For John Ellis, the tension is between the more middle-class tradition of the classical narrative film and the more populist cinema organised around performative rather than narrative traditions. For Lawrence Napper, the tension is between lowbrow, middlebrow and highbrow cinema as understood by cultural commentators of the late 1920s and 1930s. For Jane Stokes, it is between the working-class popular entertainment of Arthur Askey and the more elitist traditions he satirised. Each elucidates these cultural traditions by focusing on a key film or films: Ellis compares the structure and appeal of *Radio Parade of 1935* (Arthur Woods, 1934) and *Brief Encounter* (David Lean, 1945); Napper examines *The Good Companions* (Victor Saville, 1933) as archetypal 1930s middlebrow fare; Stokes looks at two Askey vehicles, *Band Waggon* (Marcel Varnel, 1940) and *Make Mine a Million* (Lance Comfort, 1959).

Relations between cinema and broadcasting between the late 1920s and the late 1950s also figure strongly, as all three contributors explore the ways in which both the BBC and British cinema struggled to achieve a consensual national audience. Each chapter is thus much more than a simple history of films and looks variously at the contexts of production and reception. Stokes draws links between Askey's work inside and outside the cinema and especially the interdependence of his broadcasting and film careers. Napper is as interested in the cultural debates of the period as in the films themselves, especially the debates about how broadcasting, literature and cinema in Britain should respond to the perceived threat of an emergent superficial, Americanised culture. Ellis too is interested in how films are absorbed into the prevailing culture. His central concern is with the modes and conditions of film performance: the cinema buildings themselves, what was on offer inside them, and how audiences were prepared for the experience of the main event, the projection of a feature film. While most of what he has to say is about the classical period, and the tension between narrative and performative experiences, he also makes some telling contrasts with today's cinema exhibition experience. This common concern with cultural history, with non-canonical films (especially of the 1930s) and with the different layers of British (film) culture allows some very rich associations to emerge across these three chapters.

6

BRITISH CINEMA AS PERFORMANCE ART

Brief Encounter, Radio Parade of 1935 and the circumstances of film exhibition

John Ellis

For some time I have been concerned that it is not enough to write about historic films from seeing them on video, or even in the context of screenings under contemporary cinema conditions. They were made for a different kind of cinema, whose practices are only just being rescued from historical oblivion by today's oral historians.[1] This chapter sets out the case for cinema as a performance art rather than a textual art: for an integration between the examination of film texts and the mode and conditions of their performance. The classic narrative film requires a relatively quiescent audience, paying attention to the screen rather than participating in the activity of the performance space. My interest is in how cinema as an institution persuades this audience to sit down quietly, without interacting with their neighbours, when this is not perhaps the first thing most people would do in a crowd out for fun.

In looking at the classic period of mass sound cinema in Britain (the 1930s and 1940s), I argue that, throughout the period, an extensive work of preparing the audience for feature films took place within the performance space of the cinema itself. This contrasts with the modern cinema, where this work of 'getting the audience in the mood' takes place elsewhere than in cinema. I then examine *Radio Parade of 1935* (Arthur Woods, 1934) as an example of a film that was able to use this performative relationship with the audience as the basis for its own textual construction. Seen in this context, the film becomes an invaluable record of popular entertainment and of popular views of radio and television. In this respect, it contrasts sharply with a more classical film such as *Brief Encounter* (David Lean, 1945), whose very different textual construction and reception I briefly consider.

Cinema management as risk management

Films have a spurious solidity. Cans of celluloid or videotapes seem to give them an existence as objects, but they exist as texts only through their projection for audiences. They are realised through performance, but the nature of their performance is a fleeting moment, a transient set of moods and emotions that exist within a temporary collectivity of individuals. Unlike film scholars, cinema managers have long known how volatile this audience can be. The cinema owners' history of cinema dwells upon orange peel and juvenile delinquency, sexual activity, mechanical breakdowns and local advertising. Now scholars are beginning to re-evaluate these mundane considerations. Recent studies, both of audience statistics and oral history, have opened a way to understanding the importance of the performance of films in the cinema. Cinema is a performance art in the vital sense that films have always anticipated how they will be performed.

Cinema performance is always a risk. A group of individuals assemble; they are attracted by advertising, by habit, by desire for a particular kind of aesthetic experience, by simple lassitude, by the need to escape from home or to be together in the dark. They are individuals from diverse backgrounds, with different expectations of the movies and different levels of connoisseurship. Their histories are different and so are their moods. In her trailblazing study of early American cinema performance, Miriam Hansen paints a picture of a constant struggle to weld together these diverse individuals into an audience in the polyglot cities of America at the beginning of the twentieth century.[2] British exhibitors had similar problems. Audrey Field records an interview with Charles Brown, the manager of the Mile End Empire in 1918:

> The Mile End Empire was a roughish sort of place ... Some of the toughs in the audience there gave trouble to my usherettes, one of whom came to me in tears. 'Out,' I said to the young fellow, and helped him to go. The only trouble was, some of his friends encouraged him to bring a case against me, which he won. It seems you must not use more force than is necessary, and you must not go on using force in the street.[3]

Brown used an undue level of violence to expel unruly audience members. Most of the time, in Britain as in America, cinemas used more subtle strategies to create a common mood within the audience. Exhibitors used both architecture and ambience. Denis Norden describes his time as a cinema manager just before the Second World War:

> Cinemas themselves were special. Nobody had central heating, so it was warm. ... And it was opulent in the way nothing else in your life was. They were called 'picture palaces' for a very good reason. At the Empire Leicester Square, the toilets were truly lavish: 'I dreamt I dwelt in marble halls' had real meaning. Before the cinema opened

men were given cigars to puff, so that when you came into the foyer it had the smell of luxury.[4]

Audiences in large cinemas were segregated by price into sub-groups, with the balcony costing more than the stalls. Subdued by the monumental architecture, relaxed by the comforts and secure in the sense of being in the company of 'your own type', the members of the audience were then treated to live entertainment shows. At Upton Park, a 2,100-seat supercinema that was one of the first British cinemas to convert to sound, the audience had

> the very best of the new talking films, [...] Tommy Trinder, Naughton and Gold, an eight-piano show and an early variant of *In Town Tonight* which gave them glimpses of such famous personalities as Cloria, the famous model, and Alcock and Brown [the aviators]. For this, they paid between sixpence and two shillings.[5]

Other kinds of hall offered competitions: in Rawenstall, Lancashire 'the men were nearly all out of work. But somehow, the families still managed to come to the cinema. One reason was the prizes for lucky tickets – tea, sugar, packets of bacon and all kinds of groceries.'[6] Other cinemas staged local talent shows and even bingo.

All this live entertainment activity did not just sell tickets; it also created an audience out of the disparate individuals. It was a warm-up for the main event of film projection. But, like the warm-up of a studio audience before the recording of a television show, it was highly necessary to create a community of response within the audience, and to eliminate interpersonal friction. The film alone could not be trusted to do this: hence the continuing pattern of live entertainment in both large and community cinemas well into the sound period. Live performers could interact with the audience, dealing with hecklers, allowing audience members to settle down and get things out of their system. Cinema in its classic, mass audience phase was a social activity, filling a wide range of needs and desires which are now dealt with by a wide range of social and entertainment institutions. Sometimes even live entertainers were challenged by what they encountered in the cinemas of the 1930s and 1940s:

> At the Troxy, in Commercial Road, Stepney, they'd have American stars coming over. One big American came out to do his act and I saw him blanch, and then visibly pull himself together before proceeding. I went round afterwards and asked him what was the problem. He said 'I've never seen anything like this'. It was an early show. He had to come on and be funny at 1.30 in the afternoon. And the whole front row was full of women who were breastfeeding their babies.[7]

Nicholas Hiley has analysed data relating to the 1930s in which this multi-purpose cinema developed.[8] By combining statistics relating to the changing size and nature of cinemas with audience attendance figures, he proposes a shift in the very nature of cinema-going through the period as an explanation for the drop in cinema attendance through the 1920s. This levels off at the beginning of the Depression in 1929 (so eliminating a simple economic explanation) and picks up again only in 1939. Hiley proposes that 'we might be looking at the successive rise and decline of two separate forms of cinema, whose appeal was quite distinct, but whose audiences overlapped during the interwar period'.[9] His first model of cinema is that of the small communal halls offering a cinema of attractions, which includes an element of live performance and the opportunity to be unruly in a controlled space. His second is that of the large supercinema constructed during the 1920s and then confirmed in their dominance by the advent of sound with a new form of cinematic performance. According to Hiley,

> the controllable frame replaced the uncontrollable auditorium as the true location of cinema, and the decline of the auditorium as the site for production of meaning was completed by the emphasis on dialogue in the new sound films. This not only imposed a discipline of prompt attendance and silent attention, but also reduced the need for the audience to flesh out the screened image with its own emotions.[10]

Hiley's argument is persuasive, but overstated. In particular, he draws two alarming bell-curves over the attendance figures to demonstrate this possibility and thereby shows the flaw in his argument. For although it is an overdue contribution to argue that long-term shifts were occurring in the nature of cinema performance, it is an overstatement to posit two distinct forms of exhibition, one in full decline and the other struggling to ascendancy.[11]

Rather, as the cinema managers quoted above seem to indicate, the two forms of exhibition continued to exist side by side, sometimes in tension with each other, but more often providing mutual support. Even the 'better class of patron', as cinema managers were fond of calling them, were given forms of live entertainment as well as a reassuring sense of luxury in their halls. The successful performance of sound films just as much as that of silent films depended upon the ability of the cinema as an institution to create an audience out of the bunch of disparate individuals who happened to buy a ticket. Both the circumstances of the cinema and, as we shall see, the films themselves, played their part in doing this.

It is important to understand the nature of cinema as performance because the circumstances of performance have changed and evolved to an even greater extent than even Hiley proposes, if we take a longer time perspective. By the 1990s, cinema performance had changed to such an extent that many films made for cinema performance in the 1930s and 1940s had become difficult if not impossible to understand. The cinema of the separately ticketed shows, of the lack of any supporting programme, of the multiplex and marketing of individual titles is far removed from Denis Norden's supercinema of the 1940s where 'people came anticipating a double feature. They'd ring me up and say "what's the also?". You had two films, the first feature and then the "also"'.[12] Norden's was still to a crucial extent a cinema of event, of attractions. Audiences went to the cinema rather than to see a particular film. Even a major film would be surrounded and led up to by a second feature and a panoply of shorts, advertisements and even live acts. These were crucial performative preparations for any classic narrative film text: they 'got the audience into the mood', as managers would put it.

Today, by contrast, the experience of going to the cinema is organised much more around the textuality of the film, where the film is the whole and entire purpose of the screening. Gone is the multi-part screening event of the 1930s and 1940s, where a series of entertainments welded an audience together for the main feature. In contrast to the cinema of the 1930s and 1940s the surrounding apparatus of cinema performance is perfunctory: a few advertisements and trailers, the sale of popcorn and so on. Of course, the surrounding non-cinematic material, the hype preparing for the cinema performance of the film can be considerable, if not all-pervasive in the case of the modern blockbuster film. Crucially, however, this promotional activity takes place outside the cinema itself.

In the modern cinema, tickets tend to be bought by individuals wanting to see a specific film, attracted by publicity of various kinds, from previews and listings to the front-of-house publicity material displayed in multiplexes. For the blockbuster, this process becomes one of both anticipating and extending the experience of the film. A whole raft of merchandising and pre-publicity ensures that the film's narrative images are spread as widely as possible.[13] This extends as far as the idea of people paying simply to see the trailer for the *Star Wars: The Phantom Menace* (George Lucas) prequel of 1999 and not bothering to stay for the film it preceded, which is perhaps a new urban myth of film performance. At the other end of the process, so to speak, there is the phenomenon of the TV spin-off series, repeating and permutating the blockbuster's narrative elements.

In this context, it is important to understand the differences between these two forms of cinema performance. In the 1930s and 1940s, the cinema performance itself had to prepare and condition its audiences. There was relatively little popular cultural activity to support its work, despite the existence of fan magazines and the pervasive habit of cinema attendance. Now, with cinema attendance less of a habitual practice, there are many more networks of publicity and anticipation for cinema performance to rely upon, the crucial one being television with its constant re-screening of films and references to cinema culture. Much of the work of getting the audience in the mood now takes place beyond the confines of the cinema performance itself. At the risk of overstatement, it is possible to say that in the classic mass cinema, audiences were formed by the cinema as performance event, with all its rituals of anticipation, placing and audience formation. In the modern cinema, audiences are formed beyond the cinema institution for the precise and pre-known form of the performance of a text.

Modern cinema can be seen as a rite of passage for a narrative text, the means by which an audio-visual fiction gains the right to be called 'a film'. This gives it a claim to self-sufficiency and a cultural standing that is not available to the 'made-for-TV' fiction or the 'straight-to-video' film. Both these forms have a circumscribed circulation and a subordinate cultural role that confirms their disposability. The fiction that has gained a cinema release and has had some success in that market comes with an entirely different valuation. Garnished with extracts from the critics and an image that has circulated through advertising and editorial copy, picked out in TV listings, it claims its rightful place as a fiction to be watched with the attention that a cinema film requires. It promises to reward that attention with a degree of coherence and intensity that the made-for-TV or straight-to-video film provides only occasionally. A cinema release endows fictions with this cultural valuation in subsequent markets, even if, as often, the cinema release itself is not financially rewarding for the investors. Modern cinema performance is geared towards generating this validation for its products. There is the minimum of surrounding performance, and the maximum of veneration of the unique text in and for itself. This performance style has now become so ubiquitous that critics and students have to beware of reading it back onto films produced for the very different circumstances of the mass cinema that prevailed until the 1950s. Anyone who tries to understand the films of the 1930s and 1940s through the optics of the modern cinema will misunderstand much of what made it vital as well as much of what made its texts what they are.

Film performance and film text in mass cinema

The contrast is not a simple duality, however. The modern type of cinema performance can be seen as the culmination of a tendency that is present from the beginnings of the feature film itself: the event of the 'special presentation' which established the possibility of a film being constructed as a self-contained text rather than an unfolding performance event negotiating with its audience.[14] Indeed, it can be said that many films, especially in the era of mass cinema, participate to a greater or lesser degree in both models, which is why Hiley's distinction between them is over-emphatic. In contemporary discussions, David Lean's *Brief Encounter*, became a kind of limit-case for the cinema performance culture of the day as the word spread that the preview audiences had 'laughed it off the screen' in Rochester, Kent, then a tough naval dockyard town.[15] Today, the film can be seen as a perfect example of postwar British narrative film construction, a classic text that strives towards completeness, much as Lean sought to achieve technical perfection in the film.[16] The film is constructed as an almost hysterical attempt to control its meanings, from the heavy use of Rachmaninov's *Piano Concerto No. 1*, through the burlesque of the main theme provided by the working-class flirtation on the station, to Laura's narration of the flashback structure, which enables a double closure of the narrative. The restricted range of characters further simplifies and intensifies the structure.

In an analysis of the film's uneven commercial career, Lean identified a new sensibility in British cinema audiences as a result of the war:

> British films have got themselves into their present position on what audiences call their 'reality'. [...] You will be wondering why, in the light of all this, *Brief Encounter* did not 'go' with this great new and enlightened British audience. I think the answer is that in this particular case we went too far; too far, that is, from a box-office point of view. We defied all the rules of box-office success. There were no big-star names. There was an unhappy ending to the main love-story. The film was played in unglamorous surroundings. And the three leading characters were approaching middle-age. A few years ago this would have been box-office disaster, but this wasn't the case with *Brief Encounter*. The film did very well in this country in what are known as 'the better-class halls'.[17]

This assertion links to Lean's earlier characterisation of the behaviour of the average cinema-goers, Bill and Mary 'sitting in the back row of the stalls. Main titles and first sequence – general settling down and lighting of cigarettes. Introduction of female star – Mary makes a comment on her general appearance and her clothes in particular ... '.[18] The account continues in this vein, using a crude model of identification: 'The screen Bill is speaking for the real Bill and putting things rather better than the real Bill, *and* to the accompaniment of a vast orchestra. They kiss. Fade out. So do Bill and Mary ... '.[19] Lean then draws the conclusion towards which his stereotype has been moving:

> Long after Bill has married Mary, they *might* be interested in seeing the story of 'a respectable British matron'. But then they don't go to the cinema so often. They have their own home, and don't have to escape from Mum and Dad; and besides, there's that other film up the road with Betty Grable, Tyrone Power, four bands and Technicolor. And life is very drab. I see their point.[20]

Tangled up in the rhetoric of class and the easy category of escapism is an important statement from Lean. *Brief Encounter* did not suit the performance conditions predominant in British cinemas of the 1940s. It is a self-contained text whose very perfection of construction, even its classicism, puts it at the extreme edge of what was possible within those performance conditions.

If *Brief Encounter* is a limit-text for the cinema performance habits of the period, what then constitutes the predominant style? Here we encounter all the hesitations and the sense of inadequacy that have bedevilled both British film-making and, until recently, the study of it as well. For those films that reach out the most to their audiences, which anticipate the conditions of their performance the most, are those deemed to have the least cultural value. However, British cinema cannot be understood without constant reference to its status as performance. The most extreme example of the cinema of performance in this sense is the style exemplified by the *Carry On* series. Uneven, loose or non-existent at the level of narrative, these films depended on the *mise-en-scène* of particular, isolated sequences which are paced specifically to create and deliver a sense of audience communality. They depend upon stars, and on a 'common knowledge' circulating between audience and film-makers. The *Carry On* series had other characteristics, too, not least a miserly attitude to budget. Whether the budget was large or small, such films are accorded lesser status as cultural objects simply because they depend much more explicitly on their performance within a particular cinematic institution. Such films form a large part of the films listed in Denis Gifford's catalogue, films whose ephemeral existence has condemned them to oblivion: critical oblivion in almost all cases, and physical oblivion for a substantial number. Seen without a sense of their performative context, whether judged by the standards of the 'classic narrative film' or those of modern cinema, they appear poor things indeed, narratively unsophisticated, even incomplete and incoherent. By contrast, the textual classicism of a film like *Brief Encounter* retains both its critical and its market value in the differing performance conditions of modern cinema. Mainstream cinema today tends more towards the classicism of *Brief Encounter* and away from the performative mode of films like the *Carry On* series. Such films continue in the fringes of cinema, seeing occasional successes (particularly when lampooning cinema conventions as with the work of the Brothers Zucker and Farrelly), but their characteristics can be found much more readily in the popular genres of television. The coming of television did not simply reduce the scale of cinema-going, it seems; it altered the relationship between cinema audiences and film performance in ways that we are only just beginning to understand.

Radio Parade of 1935: a compendium of the performative

There were many ways that the British film of the 1930s and 1940s could emphasise and exploit its performative aspects. Andrew Higson has examined some of them in his enlightening comparison between *Sing As We Go* (Basil Dean, 1934) and *Evergreen* (Victor Saville, 1934).[21] A third film released in 1934, *Radio Parade of 1935*, offers a compendium of the available techniques, because it is explicitly contemporary in its address. It concerns the problems of a radio broadcasting organisation, the National Broadcasting Group or NBG, in the grips of an overly bureaucratic management lead by the indolent tyrant William Garlon (Will Hay). Its output consists of arcane lectures, aetiolated classical music and dull middle-of-the-road dance music. The ambitious complaints manager, Jimmy Clare (Clifford Mollison), manages to persuade Garland into an experiment involving the public televising of variety acts, and almost falls foul of a boycott by the sinister head of the Theatre Trust, Carl Graham (the egregious Alfred Drayton). Clare manages to fill his broadcast with the unrecognised talent found in the NBG's art deco headquarters which uncannily resemble the BBC's new Broadcasting House, and television is well and truly launched by transmitting to crowds in London's public spaces. The spectacular entertainments begin with Alberta Hunt's soulful *Black Shadows*, then burst into colour with an elaborate music and dance piece, *There's No Excusin' Susan*.

Radio Parade of 1935 is an extraordinary satire of the BBC, which strongly suggests that the BBC was not a popular institution at the time.[22] The film assumes that its audience will respond favourably to the image of a top-heavy bureaucracy staffed by such assistants to the Director General as 'Sir Egbert Featherstone Haugh-Haugh' and 'Lt.-Commander Vere de Vere de Vere' with bellies and whiskers to match; a commissionaire who spends most of the film keeping the anonymous inventor of television from entering the building; a complaints department that files everything and acknowledges nothing; and a Director General who never listens to the station but spends his time admiring pictures of himself. This was the year in which audiences for commercial broadcasting from the Europe-based English language Radio Normandie and Radio Luxembourg began to outstrip those for BBC Radio.[23]

Satire was a dangerous weapon in the attempt to weld together an audience, yet *Radio Parade of 1935* manages to carry it off. In some ways, the film is even more ambitious in its contemporary references. It is a film *à clef*, with names echoing those of real life characters: Reith ('wreath') becomes Garlon ('garland'), for instance. The transposition from 'BBC' to 'NBG' plays on the popular use of 'NBG' to mean 'No Bloody Good'. The name Carl Graham of the Theatre Trust bears a linguistic resemblance to that of Charles Gulliver of the Entertainment Protection Association, which had in

Plate 9   Radio Parade of 1935 (Arthur Woods, 1934): the assistants to the Director
General take the salute at the start of the day at the NBG.

March 1927 banned their artistes from appearing on the BBC. They 'launched
a furious campaign against the BBC. [...] Abandoning their unqualified
opposition to broadcasting as such, they demanded large block sums for the
"use" of their artists and threatened that they might seek to open a broadcasting station of their own.'[24] Edward Black was the first to break ranks in
October 1928 with fortnightly broadcasts from the London Palladium, a
move 'bitterly criticised by the Variety Artists' Federation' who accused the
BBC in writing of ' "giving their talents away" '.[25] The boycott was a formative event in the history of BBC radio entertainment, just a few years before
Radio Parade of 1935.[26]

Radio Parade of 1935 may be a topical satire of the BBC, but it still
depends upon the BBC for its very existence. As Rachael Low records, 'in
the spring of 1933, reflecting the news that there were 5.5 million radio
licences in the country, BIP began an annual series of *Radio Parade* films
featuring many acts known through radio'.[27] The opening credits list many
of its artists under the generic heading of *In Town Tonight* which as virtually
every audience member would have known was the title of the BBC's most
topical entertainment-based show. First broadcast on 18 November 1933, it
'established itself as a popular favourite, bringing to the microphone at the
same time each week a great medley of characters who either lived in or were

visiting London. A sense of spontaneity was achieved'.[28] It was the invention of the then Head of Variety, Eric Maschwitz, who is also credited by Asa Briggs with the discovery of some of the acts appearing in *Radio Parade of 1935*, including the suggestive gibberish of Clapham and Dwyer; the aggressive and surreal Ronald Frankau, a forerunner of Spike Milligan; the impressionist Beryl Orde; and the obtuse 'piano tuner' Claude Dampier.

Many of the other artists appearing in the film had also broadcast with the BBC, and as the commercial broadcasters were only just consolidating their position in the market, the BBC was the most likely route for the audience to have heard them. As most would recognise them by sound alone, a significant part of the novelty and appeal of the film is that it enabled its audiences to put faces to the voices. Although the predominant style of cross-talk comedy has fallen from favour nowadays, there is little doubt that this crucial process of recognition would have taken place. The acts are introduced cursorily, as though to confirm an audience's guess at their identity rather than to provide it for them. All are listed in the opening titles, however, and this would have produced a pleasant sense of anticipation among a radio-oriented audience. The acts themselves show different levels of adaptation to the visual. Beryl Orde stands and delivers her vocal impressions with no attempt at the physical impersonation we expect of a performer like Rory Bremner. Ronald Frankau, however, is a visual revelation, handing his cigarette to an astonished Director General, shaking the assembled assistants by the hand with the mocking establishment phrase, 'I was at Oxford you know', before launching into a surreal song every bit as wild as his looks. Other acts could never have appeared on radio, even in the 1930s when radio in the USA had the ventriloquist Edgar Bergen as its number one star. Havers and Lee, the effects men, for instance, provide a heavily visual slapstick show.

The film connects in another way with its audience through its anticipation of television, which eventually began regular transmissions in 1936. Indeed, it could almost be construed as a lobby for television of a particular kind, one that could use cinemas themselves as television venues (the film was produced by British International Pictures which was part of the group that owned the ABC chain of cinemas). Publicity surrounding the coming of television – radio with pictures – had been a part of public imagination and visions of the future since Baird had displayed his early experiments in Selfridges' Oxford Street store in London in 1925. The BBC's first experimental broadcast, *The Man with the Flower in His Mouth*, coincided with the initial sale of Baird Televisors in 1930, though there were few takers. And in April 1934 the Prime Minister attended a demonstration of the Baird system at Film House in Wardour Street.[29] The Selsdon Committee of Enquiry into television broadcasting was set up on 16 May 1934 and at one of the preparatory meetings between the Post Office and the BBC on 5 April, many matters were discussed including 'the possible use of film television to serve a chain of cinemas'.[30] This potential of the technology, only fitfully exploited in subsequent years, is the form energetically proposed by *Radio Parade of 1935*, which imagines television as an essentially communal viewing activity somewhere between the cinema and the public concert.

The television broadcast is the spectacle that completes the film. The final number is an experiment in Dufaycolour, a British process that accentuated greens, oranges and yellows at the expense of red saturation. *There's No Excusin' Susan* tops the opening dance spectacular *Good Morning* in its use of the massed geometric ranks approach of Busby Berkeley. These two spectacles probably helped the film on its American release (entitled *Big Broadcast of 1935*), but even they display a peculiarly British reticence. In the midst of the opening number, showing the disciplined staff of the NBG arriving for work, two lugubrious weather forecasters intrude with a verbal routine based on familiar complaints about the British weather. Even at its most international, the film remains defiantly local.

Radio Parade of 1935 connects with its audience in a wide range of ways. It uses spectacular musical numbers and adds a sense of wonder at its comparative sophistication. It uses familiar acts but gives a fresh perspective to them, allowing them to be seen for the first time outside the music halls. Their direct address performative style is central to the film's appeal to its audiences. The film also refers back to the specific and well-known historical event of the variety entertainers' boycott of the BBC, and forward to the anticipated future of television. It actualises the audiences' imaginings and desires around television, showing what it will be like. It offers a bitter satire of the BBC, based on a widespread feeling that the organisation was bureaucratic and out of touch with its audience.

Some of these are matters of address, but most trade on and increase the stock of common knowledge, 'the widely shared pool of information and perspectives from which people shape their conceptions of self, world and citizenship'.[31] Common knowledge is common because it is repeatedly offered up for inspection and renewal, as it is in this film, rather than simply 'repeated'. The diffuse sense of 'something called television' is dramatised and made concrete. Common knowledge is sustained in a dynamic process, working with the curiosity and sense of adventure of the population rather than just the dreariness associated with the idea of 'the everyday'. Common knowledge also, crucially for this argument, involves a feeling of connectedness and togetherness. It rests upon a feeling of 'yes we are together; yes we are who we are', which spreads through the audience, creating a sense of communality. But it also addresses difficulties, like the theme of class conflict, which underlies the battle of tastes that is the NBG and surfaces in Ronald Frankau's routine among others.

The 'classic text' and the performative

To examine *Radio Parade of 1935* in the light of notions of performance and common knowledge develops the argument advanced by Higson in relation to *Sing As We Go*. Higson claims that the film 'belongs to a performative genre rather than a strictly narrative genre' and so 'gains its strength from the tension between the linear forces of narrative (the forces that contain), and the non-linear pleasures of the gag, the song, the spectacle, the attraction (the forces which disrupt)'.[32] This places the film alongside such Hollywood features as *Flying Down to Rio* (Thornton Freeland, 1933), according to Higson, among those 'generically licensed spaces for the intrusion of non-classical devices'.[33] Higson draws on Peter Krämer's argument that 'Classical Hollywood cinema always operated according to a double standard. Alongside the tight economic narrative feature films, the studios were also producing cartoons, comedy shorts, serials and so on – and, of course, very weakly narrativized and thereby classically aberrant, feature films.'[34]

By pleading for an increased attention to the performative aspect of cinema, I am arguing that it is misleading to propose an opposition between, on the one hand, those cartoons, shorts and so-called 'classically aberrant features', and on the other the classical text itself. 'Aberrant features', like those of *Radio Parade of 1935*, should perhaps be seen as the dominant features of cinema performance during the period of mass cinema-going. In any case, the relationship between the classical and the 'aberrant', or the performative, is a symbiotic one. The success of the classical narrative – the category that *Brief Encounter* very assertively claims for itself – depends upon the success of those more performative genres in generating an audience out of a group of people who have paid for tickets. If every film performance is a risk, then the performance of a film in the mould of the classic text is a riskier performance than most. So many so-called classic texts try to integrate performative elements of one kind or another.[35] But in the end they relied for their enduring success on the formidable work of the cinema institution itself in securing an audience for them. The architecture, the staff, the *mise-en-scène* of the cinema hall, the supporting programme of live performances and shorts, and the constant work of performance-based films like *Radio Parade of 1935* all developed the common knowledge of the audience, one element of which was how to behave at the pictures.

NOTES

1   In particular, see the ESRC-funded project, 'Cinema Culture in 1930s Britain', directed by Annette Kuhn, samples of which appear in the *Journal of Popular British Cinema*, 1999, no. 2. This issue of the *Journal* contains much else that is relevant here.

2   M. Hansen, *Babel and Babylon: Spectatorship in American Silent Film*, Massachusetts, Harvard University Press, 1991.

3 A. Field, *Picture Palace: A Social History of the Cinema*, London, Gentry Books, 1974, p. 98.
4 Denis Norden, 'Six penn'orth of dark', in I. Breakwell and P. Hammond (eds) *Seeing in the Dark*, London, Serpents Tail, 1990, p. 49.
5 Field, op. cit. (from the account of Charles Brown), p. 101.
6 Charles Brown, quoted in Field, ibid., p. 102.
7 Ibid., p. 53.
8 ' "Let's go to the Pictures": the British cinema audience in the 1920s and 1930s', *Journal of Popular British Cinema*, 1999, no. 2, pp. 39–53.
9 Ibid., p. 42.
10 Ibid., p. 45.
11 Hiley's emphasis on the position of the regular cinema-goer and their importance to the industry is, however, a vital one which has often been overlooked. It shows the unevenness of connoisseurship that existed (and exists) in the cinema audience, something that films – and film historians – ignore at their peril.
12 Norden, op. cit., p. 52. The use of the telephone shows that Norden's patrons were definitely of 'the better class'. This contrasts strongly with the Mass Observation material about the same cinema quoted in S. Harper and V. Porter, 'Cinema audience tastes in 1950s Britain', in *Journal of Popular British Cinema*, 1999, no. 2, p. 68.
13 For a discussion of the idea of narrative image, see John Ellis, *Visible Fictions: Cienema: Television: Video*, London, Routlege, 1982, pp. 29–37.
14 The model for this would be the roadshowing in the USA of *The Birth of a Nation* (Griffith, 1915), or, even earlier, the treatment given to the eight-reel Italian production *Quo Vadis* (Enrico Guazzoni, 1912) by its American importers in 1913, roadshowing in legitimate theatres at $1 a ticket. See R. Stanley, *The Celluloid Empire: A History of the American Motion Picture Industry*, New York, Hastings House, 1978, p. 19.
15 See K. Brownlow, *David Lean: A Biography*, London, Richard Cohen Books, 1996, p. 203.
16 See ibid., pp. 189–205.
17 '*Brief Encounter*' in *Penguin Film Review*, 1947, no. 4, p. 31.
18 Ibid., p. 28.
19 Ibid.
20 Ibid.
21 A. Higson, *Waving the Flag: Constructing a National Cinema in Britain*, Oxford, Clarendon Press, 1995, pp. 98–175.
22 Cf. P. Scannell and D. Cardiff, *A Social History of British Broadcasting. Volume 1. 1922–1933. Serving the Nation*, London, Blackwell, 1991.
23 In an unpublished paper, Sean Street reveals how the BBC's own audience research discovered this distressing fact, especially on Sundays.
24 A. Briggs, *The History of Broadcasting in the United Kingdom, vol. II: The Golden Age of Wireless*, Oxford, Oxford University Press, 1965, p. 78.
25 Ibid., p. 82.
26 Clapham and Dwyer, who appear in *Radio Parade of 1935*, are reported as being reluctant to broadcast when invited in 1926. They recalled: 'we only had one act at that time and we really didn't want to give it away to thousands listening in.' Cited by Briggs, op. cit., p. 84, drawing on a radio programme of 1951.
27 R. Low, *Film Making in 1930s Britain*, London, George Allen and Unwin, 1985, p. 123. *Radio Parade of 1935* was the second in the series.
28 Briggs, op. cit., p. 107. The cinema manager Charles Brown, cited earlier, uses the show to define the nature of his live stage performances in Upton Park.

29 Ibid., p. 579.

30 Ibid., p. 581.

31 J. Gripsrud, 'An Introduction', in J. Gripsrud (ed.) *Television and Common Knowledge*, London, Routledge, 1999, p. 2.

32 Higson, op. cit., p. 162.

33 Ibid.

34 Krämer, 'The double standard of classical Hollywood cinema', paper presented at the Society for Cinema Studies, Bozeman, Montana, USA, 29 June–3 July 1988, quoted ibid.

35 Any number of examples exist even in today's movies: films made for holiday release that refer to that holiday; the diegetic use of contemporary or retro music; the means by which the star is introduced by reference to their then currently circulating persona; topical gags; even the massive, physically felt, rumble of bass sounds that seems to inaugurate most contemporary Hollywood films, ordering the audience to sit down and shut up.

7

BRITISH CINEMA AND THE MIDDLEBROW

Lawrence Napper

> The worst of Mr Rotha, as of all highbrow writers about the
> cinema, is that he will not recognise what I should like to call
> the half-way film ... I am persuaded that what the average
> intelligent cinema-goer likes is something half-way between
> the Caligari stuff, in which people look like parallelograms
> and furniture in rhomboid, and the nit-wit film in which
> stenographers renounce diamonds and protection for the
> horny-handed wistfulness of some virginal cow-puncher. Most
> cinema-goers I am persuaded, just want a reasonably good
> story reasonably well told.
>
> (James Agate, 1930)[1]

In this chapter I shall argue that James Agate's desire for a cinema of the
middle-ground – a cinema in between Europe and Hollywood, art and
escapism, highbrow and lowbrow – was largely realised by the British film
industry of the 1930s. Operating under the curious conditions laid down by
the 1927 Cinematograph Act, that cinema was successfully able to address
its audiences through what we might, extending Agate's spatial metaphor,
describe as a 'middlebrow' aesthetic. As an institution working within that
aesthetic, British cinema has suffered a certain amount of condescension.
Until recently, British cinema has been denigrated by critics for its perceived
middlebrow qualities. Its adherents were accused of mistaking the coy
banalities of genteel film-making for a quality art form, while remaining
blind to both the intellectual rigours of international art cinema and the
vigorous and potent entertainment provided by Hollywood. Its reliance on
literary sources, its restraint, its formal conservatism, its provincialism, its
concern with middle-class characters and the naïve optimism of its vision of
community and state have, according to these critics, marked it out as bland
and essentially uncinematic.[2] Even the welcome reappraisal of British
cinema in recent years has, to a certain extent, reproduced this anxiety,
emphasising the diversity of British cinematic output, only to fetishise the
concept of the 'edges'. As Robin Buss argues,

critics trawl through the film archive for whatever lies outside the mainstream, whatever helps to relieve their feelings of embarrassment at the 'parochial', 'middle-class' world of *The Titfield Thunderbolt* [Charles Crichton, 1952], or *Doctor in the House* [Ralph Thomas, 1954] and presents itself to them as in some way 'transgressive'.[3]

The time is ripe for a reaffirmation of the centre of British film production. In pursuit of this project, I want to return to the interwar years, and to revivify the notion of the 'middlebrow'. Such a move need not necessarily imply the pejorative judgements of British cinema bequeathed by many critics. It is clear, both from the debates of the period and from many of the films produced in Britain during the time, that the term 'middlebrow' could be, and often was, invoked in an unproblematically positive way. One such film is *The Good Companions* (Victor Saville, 1933), which I shall examine later in this chapter. This film, I shall argue, refers to audiences, articulates values and evokes pleasures that we might describe as middlebrow. Crucially, it is self-conscious about its involvement in this aesthetic, and about the purpose of that involvement, for *The Good Companions* is a film which seeks quite openly to express the idea of Britain as a nation.

When highbrow meets lowbrow: the creation of the 'middlebrow'

The term 'middlebrow' is specific to the 1920s and 1930s and the expansion of the mass communications media that characterised those years. It has a peculiarly close relationship to what Buss calls the 'mainstream' of British culture. 'Middlebrow', with its companions, 'highbrow' and 'lowbrow,' form a cultural geography which dominated the critical debates of the interwar period, demarcating the landscape of taste in forums as disparate as *Scrutiny* and popular song lyrics. The terms have largely fallen out of use now, partly because the struggle over cultural value to which they refer has largely been emulsified by the postmodern condition. Today, pop videos and heavyweight literature are reviewed in the same breath by the distinguished celebrity guests of BBC2's art review show, *Late Review*, and the distinction between avant-garde art, advertising and popular cinema is blurred to annulment by constant intertextual reference across genre and medium. In this context, it is easy to forget how great the anxieties over cultural distinction attendant on the explosion of the mass communication media in the interwar years must have been. The conceptual hierarchy contained within the language of 'brows' can be regarded as an attempt to articulate that anxiety and to police the boundaries of culture from both above and below.[4]

The terms 'highbrow' and 'lowbrow' originated in America before the First World War.[5] Initially, advertisers used them to delineate the consumer market, but they soon came to be understood as marking points in the confrontation between 'high' culture and other forms popularised by mass communication technology. The 'middlebrow', however, was a term – and a market – exclusive to Britain, identified by *Punch* in 1925. 'The BBC,' it quipped, 'claim to have discovered a new type, the "middlebrow". It consists of people who are hoping that some day they will get used to the stuff they ought to like.'[6] The 'middlebrow', then, even at the very moment of its birth, is associated with a British cultural institution that owes its existence to a desire to protect the nation from the excesses of American market forces.

The BBC secured an exclusive licence to broadcast in 1922. Its monopoly was the result of a recognition within both the government and the press of the potential power of radio as a mass medium. This was coupled with an anxiety over the consequences of conceding that power to the kind of uncontrolled market exemplified by both the internationalist expansion of Hollywood, and the development of American broadcasting. In the USA, numerous small, commercial broadcasters, whose output was financed by advertising and sponsorship deals, served a rapidly expanding market. The British government balked at the lack of control such a free market implied. The popular press, too, opposed the idea of commercial radio, seeing it as a potential drain on their own advertising revenue.

Thus, even before John Reith's appointment as General Manager, two guiding principles were enshrined within the BBC's structure. First, it was to be free from the kinds of commercial interests that dictated the populist broadcasting of America. Second, as a monopoly funded by licence fees, it was expected to address the whole nation, remaining in consequence ultimately, if subtly, answerable to the state. On his appointment, Reith imbued these principles with a remarkable energy and zeal, making explicit the public service ethos that they already implied. The BBC's broadcasts were, through the 'brute force of monopoly', to become a force for the moral and cultural improvement of the nation.[7] By maintaining a careful balance between genuinely popular programming and items of a more specialist cultural appeal, the BBC sought to develop the public's cultural taste, rather than pander to it. As Reith himself maintained, 'The BBC must lead, not follow its listeners, but it must not lead at so great a distance as to shake off pursuit.'[8] In maintaining this balancing act, the BBC refused to demarcate its audience or its broadcasts. Thus in 1928 it explicitly rejected the distinction between 'highbrow' and 'lowbrow' broadcasting, preferring instead to conceive of a 'great audience' whose tastes might be as catholic as they were upwardly mobile.[9]

If the BBC refused to recognise 'brows', its audience and critics did not. *Punch*'s derision of the BBC's public service position, its plain incredulity at the possibility that a 'great audience' might exist, can be regarded as an early example of a tradition of criticism that survives to this day. As D.L. LeMahieu has shown, the BBC came under increasing pressure throughout the 1930s, both from the radio critics of the popular press, and from the more concrete threat of Continental commercial rivals such as Radio Luxembourg, to acknowledge more fully its popular audience. The BBC was accused by such figures as Collie Knox, the radio critic of the *Daily Mail*, of catering only for 'pseudo highbrows'. 'Why in the name of Beecham does the BBC expect listeners to sit through more than two hours of symphonic music?' he asked.[10]

Jane Stokes and John Ellis argue elsewhere in this volume that films such as *Radio Parade of 1935* (Arthur Woods, 1934) and *Band Waggon* (Marcel Varnel, 1939) brought criticisms of the BBC to an even wider audience. My own view is that as the 1930s wore on, the BBC was able substantially to revise its output to include the popular broadcasts of such figures as Arthur Askey, star of *The Band Waggon*, without appearing to relinquish its public service commitment. Such figures, and the programmes and films in which they appeared, enabled the BBC to contain criticism, articulating it within its own entertainment output in a move which at once conceded to populism while at the same time reinscribing the BBC as the central binding force for a national audience.

Criticism of the BBC came not only from populists, however. For Constant Lambert writing in *Music Ho!* in 1932, it was not the content of BBC programmes which was objectionable, but rather their availability: 'One's complaint is not with the programmes themselves, which through an independence of advertising interests are of an admirably eclectic nature, but with their intolerably wholesale diffusion through portable sets and loud speakers.'[11] Such wholesale diffusion, he complained, was leading to a homogenisation of taste that robbed both low and high culture of their vitality:

> Here is yet another example of the gradual fusion of highbrow and lowbrow ... Instead of the admirable old distinction between classical and popular which used to hold good ... classical music is vulgarised and diffused through every highway and byway, and both highbrow and lowbrow are the losers.[12]

It was out of this 'gradual fusion of highbrow and lowbrow' that the 'middlebrow' was formed. Lambert was not the only person to be alarmed at the tendency of new technology to democratise culture in Britain. As John Baxendale and Christopher Pawling suggest, the derogatory use of the term 'middlebrow' became a useful defensive strategy for those who felt under threat, marking 'a new boundary of cultural discrimination, which divided the general educated audience from the high intelligentsia'.[13]

If the concept of the middlebrow was co-opted by the high intelligentsia to protect them from the vulgarities of the general educated audience, the aesthetic itself arose out of a concern within the general educated audience and within government. Their concern was to protect British culture from the vulgarities of the unfettered commodity and leisure capitalism originating from America. Such writers as Virginia Woolf and F.R. Leavis and Q.D. Leavis fetishised 'lowbrow' culture as the traditional vital production of organic working-class communities. Others characterised it as a foreign culture of consumption originating from America and threatening to swamp British cultural integrity by operating the standard of the lowest common denominator. If the BBC represented one attempt to protect British cultural life from such a fate, in 1927 the government set itself the task of achieving the same objective with regard to cinema, in the form of the Cinematograph Act.

The projection of England: a middlebrow cinema

The deleterious state of the British film industry had been a cause for concern for some time before 1927. The exhibition sector had been subject to large-scale expansion both during and immediately after the war. Hollywood had supplied the majority of the films and had thus achieved a stranglehold over the British exhibition market that threatened to squeeze British producers out of business altogether. The ensuing industrial crisis was of concern to the Board of Trade, who felt that British films could potentially operate as an advertising medium for British goods, thus indirectly benefiting the whole economy as the Americans freely admitted Hollywood did. Nevertheless, much of the rhetoric which surrounded the Cinematograph Act remained cultural. Not only British audiences, it was suggested, but also the subjects of the Empire were exposed to films from America that were familiarising them with 'ways of thinking and acting and speaking which were not British ways'.[14]

The Cinematograph Act was certainly effective in boosting the volume of British film production. By legally obliging distributors and exhibitors to handle an annually increasing proportion of British films, the Act created a protected home market within which British producers had the opportunity to develop and expand. As with the creation of the BBC, the government had acted to temper the pressure of the market, in the interest of maintaining a culture of 'national ideas and national atmosphere'.[15]

Critics in both the national press and the trade papers were unanimous in their support of this project, described by Stephen Tallents in 1932 as 'the projection of England'.[16] L'Estrange Fawcett reminded the industry that,

> Sooner or later we must justify the Government's action in promoting the industry's welfare so munificently. The film producer has a responsibility outside purely business considerations. He cannot avoid the incidence of the film as an instrument of culture, and he knows perfectly well that ... the intelligent film is the only one to bring credit and glory to the industry.[17]

How to achieve this goal was a subject of considerable controversy, however, and each critic held his or her own view about what constituted an appropriate version of the nation, and how best to portray it. For John Gammie in 1934, the answer was to 'to make at least one or two films, historical or modern, reflecting the character of Britain as a nation'.[18] C.A. Lejeune felt that the answer lay in putting the industrial life of the nation on the screen: 'there is still unemployment, there is still shipbuilding, and there is still farming. We have an industrial north that is bigger than Gracie Fields running round a Blackpool funfair.'[19] Alfred Hitchcock, on the other hand, argued that British producers should portray 'that vital central stratum of British humanity – the middle-class ... In them lies the spirit of England that, for some unknown reason is almost entirely ignored by the screen.'[20]

The production industry that arose from the Cinematograph Act was thus forced, like the BBC, into a balancing act between the cultural demands of government and critics and the need to address and entertain a popular audience. Given these pressures, it seems hardly surprising that British producers chose to make films imbued with a 'middlebrow' aesthetic. Such films were largely flattering to the Baldwin government's conception of the nation as an essentially stable society, but addressed an audience whose very existence was the result of the social and economic dynamics of the interwar period.

This period is often characterised as split between the declining heavy industries associated with the north and the new light industries and spreading suburbs of the south. I would suggest that it was to the tastes of the new suburban middle classes that British cinema primarily addressed itself. Their numbers increased dramatically during the period, attendant on the growth of the Civil Service, banking and insurance companies, the expansion of the new science-based industries and the increase of the service sector. It was this new class, anxious to consolidate a hard-won, but precarious improvement in social position and living standards, which had the greatest investment in the stability which the Baldwin government's version of national culture appeared to offer.[21] For such audiences, consumption of British texts was one of the crucial activities that distinguished them from the industrial working classes who tended towards Hollywood. Accordingly, British film producers offered films which would surely have satisfied Agate's desire for a cinema which was neither pretentious, nor overly sentimental, but consisted rather of 'good stories ... well told'.

Unlike the modernist texts emerging from the political and social upheavals of Continental Europe in this period, these films tended to emphasise the stability and continuity of British cultural life, both formally and thematically. Agate's conception of a 'good story, well told' is best understood as involving a believable setting, with rounded characters participating in a well-constructed narrative. The emphasis is on the traditional, the transparent realism of nineteenth-century literary forms, rather than the formal stylistic experimentation of European art cinema, or the predictable generic narratives of Hollywood. Unlike the critics, then and now, the producers and their audiences were less interested in cinema as a pure new art form than as a new medium for the dissemination of established cultural property.

Many of the productions of the 1930s were careful adaptations of known literary or theatrical successes such as R.C. Sheriff's *Journey's End* (James Whale, 1930), J.B. Priestley's *Laburnum Grove* (Carol Reed, 1936) and G.B. Shaw's *Pygmalion* (Leslie Howard and Anthony Asquith, 1938). Solid realist narratives of family and community life by such authors as H.G. Wells, Margaret Kennedy, Winifred Holtby and of course Priestley also attracted producers and included such titles as *Things to Come* (William Cameron Menzies, 1936), *The Citadel* (King Vidor, 1938), *South Riding* (Victor Saville, 1938) and *The Good Companions* (Victor Saville, 1933). Other staple successes included such historical dramas as *The Private Life of Henry VIII* (Alexander Korda, 1933), *Fire Over England* (William K. Howard, 1937), *Victoria the Great* (Herbert Wilcox, 1937) and *Sixty Glorious Years* (Herbert Wilcox, 1938).

While some of these films were literary or theatrical adaptations, others were original stories steeped in the landscape and the heritage of the nation. Either way, they were suitable fare for the educated audiences of the new suburban middle classes who were keen to emphasise the cultural barrier between their own taste and the surface sophistication and mechanised narrative thrills of Hollywood. We should not perhaps lose sight of quite how far the very Englishness of these productions was responsible for the reactions they provoked. For this general educated audience it was their Englishness that guaranteed their quality. The crisp English accents reassured provincial middle-class audiences as often as they infuriated others.[22] Not surprisingly, such an attitude was anathema to those 'highbrow' critics for whom the formal cinematic achievements of international art cinema was the benchmark of quality. Graham Greene could hardly contain his irritation on finding English cinema being championed against Hollywood by a provincial, female acquaintance in 1937. It was a middlebrow cinema, he suggested, that appealed to her underdeveloped intellect, 'an intelligence which has grown up as little as her face, so that the books and art which once seemed ... so lively and cerebral still excite her'.[23] Ironically, the expression of taste for British films which Greene's hapless female friend takes as a mark of cultural distinction is precisely what betrays her to him as intellectually inferior. In the ensuing discussion, Greene affects to demonstrate the falseness of British cinema through a series of comparisons with the vitality of American film and the sincerity of the documentary movement. British entertainment cinema emerges in his view as bland, false and stagy. His judgements, however, start from that cultural prejudice, rather than arriving at it. Like his friend, Greene is using cinematic taste primarily to mark out cultural territory. For him, good cinema is defined by qualities found elsewhere than in the British entertainment film, thus it must *de facto* be inferior.

Greene was certainly not alone in his contempt for middlebrow tastes. Indeed sniping over the parapet of the brow became so endemic in the writings of the period that it might almost be regarded as a national sport. Its prevalence is perhaps a marker of the extent of the social and economic changes occurring in Britain at the time, and the effect they were thought to have on the very notion of Culture. Even the BBC joined in. In October 1932 it ran a series of its eponymous 'talks', with J.B. Priestley and Harold Nicolson putting the case for the lowbrows and highbrows respectively. It was this exchange that prompted Virginia Woolf to write her withering attack on 'The Middlebrow', intended as a letter to the *New Statesman* but never sent.[24] Like Greene, Woolf identifies the middlebrow with provincial taste, and with British provincial taste in particular. She describes the middlebrow as being 'betwixt and between' and dubs the BBC the 'Betwixt and Between Company'. Also like Greene, she displays in her contempt an interesting slippage between the aesthetics of middlebrow taste, and that section of the population who are deemed to possess it. Affecting to propose a natural affinity between the vitality of the pure 'art' of the highbrow and the pure 'life' of the lowbrow, she identifies the middlebrow population as the enemies of both because they are involved in a compromise which, according to Woolf, resulted in a fake culture. In their aspiration to unite the nation, their anxiety to express stability through 'Queen Anne furniture ... [and] houses in what is called "the Georgian style",' Woolf warned against a middlebrow that would end up 'obscuring, dulling, tarnishing and coarsening even the silver edge of Heaven's own scythe'. Indeed, she goes so far as to wonder 'what will become of us, men and women, if Middlebrow has his way with us, and there is only a middle sex but no husbands or wives?'[25] Thomas Sharpe echoed Woolf's fear in 1932 when he argued that 'there is no avoiding the figures, town and country is male and female, suburbia is hermaphrodite'.[26]

Q.D. Leavis too identified the threat of the middlebrow as one of impotency through cultural miscegenation. She claimed that middlebrow novels such as Priestley's *The Good Companions*, while aspiring to the status of artistic endeavour, were little more than faked sensibility, providing their readers with 'the agreeable sensation of having improved oneself without incurring fatigue'.[27] As William Hunter suggested in *Scrutiny of Cinema*, the public and even some critics had become so inured through exposure to these texts, that they had lost the ability to distinguish between the true and the false:

> If a critic is capable of properly responding to *Storm over Asia* [V.I. Pudovkin, 1928], or *The End of St Petersburg* [V.I Pudovkin, 1927], he should equally be capable of detecting the blatant falseness of *The Forsyte Saga*, *The Good Companions*, Gershwin's *Rhapsody in Blue*, or Academy Art. But unfortunately he is not. Almost every critic

who has written on the films ... has sooner or later shown himself to be quite incapable of detecting ... what constitutes goodness or badness in any work of art.[28]

This conception of culture – the rigid and static distinction between what is 'true' and what is 'false' – effectively denied the optimism for consensus that was at the heart of the middlebrow project for a national culture. The arrangements between state and industry that resulted in the BBC and the Cinematograph Act had been predicated on an idea of *taste* both fluid and dynamic, rather than the rigid structures of value espoused by such critics.

Not surprisingly, middlebrow writers responded energetically to their accusers, characterising the 'highbrow' in turn as pretentious, irrelevant and infected with snobbery. 'For myself,' wrote Agate airily, 'I have carefully avoided telling readers of the *Tatler* that the neo-vorticism of Olga Preobrashenkaia is not to be confounded with the centrifugal Platonism of Dziga-Vertov.'[29] E.G. Cousins, writing in 1932, found the rigid cultural position of highbrow critics 'totally artificial and misleading', precisely because it threatened the unifying project of British cinema:

> It postulates ... a kind of declaration of taste, a fixity of outlook, a definite classification. The Highbrow likes highbrow films, the Lowbrow likes lowbrow films, and that's that! – and that matter being satisfactorily settled, the great and worthy Middlebrow public (of which everyone considers himself a member) can forget about them both and go to the pictures. ... The fact is that we are nearly all catholic in our tastes. There are times when we like what old Kipps called 'a simple chune,' and there are times when we are attuned to the Melody of the Spheres.[30]

For Cousins, it is the 'great and worthy Middlebrow public' which is identified with sincerity, honesty and truth, rather than the bogus highbrow with 'his assumption of superiority to the common herd of filmgoers, his scornful ignorance of the ordinary filmgoer's requirements, his lofty contempt for the commercial side of film-making ... and the abstruse jargon with which he endeavours to conceal his paucity of ideas'.[31]

Priestley, too, identified the highbrow with fake pretension, and *The Good Companions* was written explicitly as an antidote to what he considered a dangerous tendency of modern literature. Writing to his publisher before the book came out in 1928 he declared, 'I am of course deliberately breaking with everything that is characteristic of highbrow fiction of the moment, the vague crowds of clever idlers, the dreary futility and all the rest of it. Let's have some real people says I.'[32] Towards the end of her essay on the middlebrow, Virginia Woolf had fantasised about a place from which the middlebrow had been banished, where 'priests are not, nor priestesses, and, to be quite frank, the adjective "priestly" is neither often heard, nor held in high esteem'.[33] For Q.D. Leavis too, Priestley's *The Good Companions* is the definitive example of the middlebrow aesthetic whose popularity she found so unsettling, 'with its complacent hearty knowingness ... coarse in texture'.[34]

The Good Companions

Given its centrality in this debate, we should hardly be surprised when we turn to *The Good Companions* to find it energetically involved in the middlebrow project of expressing the nation through consensus.[35] 'This is a story of the roads and the wandering players of modern England', declares the narrator (Henry Ainley) at the very beginning of the Gaumont-British adaptation. Indeed the film, like the best-selling book from which it is so carefully adapted, structures its narrative as a journey through the different versions of England fought over in the films debate. Ainley's prologue continues over a map of England marked with the strategic locations of the characters he introduces: Jes Oakroyd (Edmund Gwen) in C.A. Lejeune's industrial north; Indigo Jollifant (John Gielgud), a teacher in the fen country; Miss Trant (Mary Glynne) in the rural idyll of the West Country so favoured by Baldwin and the Shell guide posters, and the Dinky Doos concert party in the Midlands.

As we move into the narratives of each character, the film follows Priestley's descriptive technique in the novel very closely. In the book, each character's narrative is introduced by a long descriptive passage, purporting to look down onto a section of the landscape of the nation itself and celebrating those aspects of English heritage and culture which it represents. Thus Oakroyd represents the honest respectability of the British working man, Jollifant the public school tradition and Miss Trant the responsibility of the rural gentry. In the film, these different Englands are presented again in sequences of symbolic montage reminiscent of documentary film-making. However, while the symbolic sequences are largely celebratory of English culture, the narratives they introduce are more ambivalent. Each character, we discover, feels trapped in the particular version of the nation that they occupy and the expectations of those around them. Independently, they each decide to leave in search of new horizons. Each travels through England, observing and partaking in 'the jostling pageantry of insignificant faces', until they join forces with the Dinky Doos concert party, renaming it The Good Companions.

It is not difficult to see why *The Good Companions* might have appealed to the middlebrow audiences of interwar suburban England. One might describe it as a narrative of economic and social migration, where a series of characters leave various old, static, regional versions of England behind, in order to create a new, dynamic, centralised one. Ostensibly this new England offers greater freedom to its inhabitants – it is less bound by considerations of tradition, gender and class; it is transient, based not on authenticity, but

Plate 10   A consensual middlebrow vision of Britain: from all corners of the nation, the members of the concert party in *The Good Companions* (Victor Saville, 1933) gather to toast their collective achievement.

on acting and performance. Its symbolic centre is Susie Dean (Jessie Matthews), the young soubrette star, who is defined by her ability (and her desire) to sham. She is continually play-acting, dressing up, parodying and imitating. In a key scene she dresses up in Jollifant's cap and gown, making fun of his intellectual pretensions; in another scene she refuses his proposal of marriage in a parody of the cut-glass accents of the West End theatre – a remarkable feat for the over-elocuted Jessie Matthews.

Despite her play-acting, however, Susie's ambition for modern stardom is no sham. It is based on a recognition of the authenticity of her own heritage, a desire both to celebrate and to escape from the dreary, thankless lives her parents endured touring the Halls. For Susie Dean, the democratisation of culture is an opportunity for her to reap the benefits that her parents were denied. For the others as well, the limited freedom of the 'new' nation that they have created is crucially predicated on a recognition of the authenticity of traditional values. The difference is that, because of their widening horizons, those values are defined centrally, rather than in terms of region or class. Cultural values, in effect, become national.

Contemporary reviewers championed the middlebrow aesthetic of *The Good Companions*, identifying it unequivocally with an authentic British film-making tradition. Hailing it as a 'very British picture', the *Daily Telegraph* singled out its 'sound characterisation ... quiet charm ... commonplace dialogue and incident ... and quite funereal tempo'. It added that 'as many people find the rapid action and quick-fire wit of American pictures rather bewildering, its slowness may not greatly detract from *The Good Companions*' popularity in this country, whatever its chances abroad'.[36] C.A. Lejeune, in the *Observer*, was less equivocal. Directly reversing Graham Greene's notion of good cinema as discussed above, she declared:

> We have waited over twenty years for *The Good Companions*. We have watched the British producers trying to copy the film manner of Hollywood ... [and] of Berlin. We had almost given up hope of seeing them strike out for themselves a national manner in film-making – an English manner, with the characteristic slow, packed development of the best English art – a picaresque manner, which has always been, in writing, painting, drama, and music, the English heritage.[37]

Central to many of the reviews is the notion that *The Good Companions*, having been adapted from a best-selling book, is already a known text and thus a common point of contact for its audience. The *Telegraph* warns that its readers mustn't 'expect to come on every old friend and familiar incident'.[38] Critics debating the issue of the 'projection of England', then and now, tend either to focus on whether British cinema successfully reflected the lifestyles of its audience (as implied in the title of Raymond Durgnat's book, *A Mirror For England*), or to engage in a search for an authentic version of the nation to which everyone might subscribe.[39] More important for a middlebrow aesthetic, I would suggest, is the creation of a common culture – a series of cultural texts with which everyone is familiar, and which act as a common point of contact, whether or not they refer to the lived reality of the audience. The architects of the Cinematograph Act, as is clear from their oversight with regard to a quality clause, were likewise less interested in the content of British films than they were in the fact that there should be a British cinema at all, a common point of contact for domestic audiences.

The Good Companions is involved in the creation of that common culture through its metaphor of the concert party of individuals. All are involved in a common project, despite their individually disparate regional and class origins. They literally tour through the nation, linking the towns they visit through the common experience of their show. In the same way, the novel and the film reach out to their disparate regional audiences, making *The Good Companions* itself the link, the common point of contact that creates the nation.

This optimism with regard to the creation of a common national culture through mass media forms is central to the middlebrow aesthetic. Its promise motivated the curious negotiation between state, industry and audience that characterised both the creation of the BBC and the regeneration of the British film industry in the late 1920s. Those media developed in the way that they did mainly because of that formative negotiation. As Robin Buss points out, critics even now express embarrassment at the centrality of the common culture posited by the middlebrow aesthetic that was adopted. While British film production was diverse enough to allow space for marginal and oppositional voices, its main gravitational force, like that of the BBC, was nevertheless towards an optimistic version of the nation as a site of utopian consensus. One might argue, given its history, that this expression of national centrality is the function of the British cinema which evolved from the 1927 Cinematograph Act, just as the expression of marginality is the function of avant-garde cinema. To criticise it for its 'middlebrow' qualities seems somewhat tautological. Such criticism would seem to be based on the misapprehension that the 'middlebrow' vision is complacent and reactionary. That need not be the case. Embracing new technologies of communication, assuming both social and cultural dynamism in audiences, one might suggest that middlebrow texts attempted to articulate a unified nation which was genuinely modern in form, even while they acknowledged the tensions underlying that unity. British cinema was central to this process during the 1930s, no less so than it was during its 'Golden Age' in the war years, when the middlebrow project of articulating the nation took on a more immediate significance, one where complacency had no place. It is high time we stopped feeling ashamed of being 'middlebrow'.

NOTES

1 J. Agate, 'The Film Till Now' (1930), in Around Cinemas, London, Home and Van Thal, 1946, p. 80.
2 See C. Barr, 'Amnesia and schizophrenia', in Barr (ed.) All Our Yesterdays: 90 Years of British Cinema, London, BFI Publishing, 1986, for a thorough examination of this tradition of British film criticism.
3 R. Buss, 'The bitter Truffaut', Independent on Sunday, 14 September 1997, p. 33.
4 See J. Baxendale and C. Pawling, Narrating the Thirties, London, Macmillan, 1996, pp. 48–56.
5 R. Graves and A. Hodge, The Long Weekend, London, Hutchinson, 1985 (first published 1940), p. 50.
6 'Charivaria', Punch, 23 December 1925, p. 673.
7 A. Briggs, The History of Broadcasting in the United Kingdom. Vol. II, Oxford, Oxford University Press, 1965, p. 56.
8 Ibid.
9 See ibid., p. 28. The more familiar division of the service into Home, Light and Third Programmes was a development of the 1940s.
10 D.L. LeMahieu, A Culture For Democracy, Oxford, Oxford University Press, 1988, p. 275. For further discussion of the early BBC, see R. Blythe, The Age of Illusion, Harmondsworth, Penguin, 1964, pp. 55–76.

11 C. Lambert, *Music Ho!*, Harmondsworth, Pelican, 1948 (first published 1934), p. 171.
12 Ibid., p. 169.
13 Baxendale and Pawling, op. cit., p. 49.
14 M. Dickinson and S. Street, *Cinema and State*, London, BFI Publishing, 1985, p. 16.
15 P. Cunliffe-Lister, in the debate on the Cinematograph Bill, *Hansard*, 16 March 1927, p. 2039.
16 S. Tallents, *The Projection of England*, London, Faber and Faber, 1932.
17 L'Estrange Fawcett, 'Story values this year', *Kinematograph Weekly*, 9 March 1933.
18 J. Gammie, 'If I were a British producer', *Film Weekly*, 4 May 1934, p. 34.
19 C.A. Lejeune reviewing *Jew Süss* in the *Observer*, 1934, quoted in J. Richards, *The Age of the Dream Palace*, London, Routledge, 1984, p. 246.
20 A. Hitchcock, 'The real spirit of England', *World Film News*, February 1937, p. 15.
21 See N. Branson and M. Heinemann, *Britain in the Nineteen Thirties*, St Albans, Panther, 1973, pp. 165–79.
22 Such attitudes extended beyond the suburbs, even to industrial Bolton; see, for example, responses in J. Richards and D. Sheridan, *Mass Observation at the Movies*, London, Routledge and Kegan Paul, 1987, pp. 51–131.
23 G. Greene, 'The middlebrow film', *The Fortnightly Review*, March 1936. Reprinted in D. Parkinson (ed.) *Mornings in the Dark: The Graham Greene Film Reader*, Manchester, Carcanet, 1993, pp. 397–403.
24 See L. Marcus, 'Virginia Woolf and the Hogarth Press', in I. Willison, W. Gould and W. Chernaik (eds) *Modernist Writers and the Marketplace*, New York, St Martins Press, 1996, p. 150.
25 Ibid., p. 118.
26 T. Sharpe, *Town and Countryside*, Oxford, Oxford University Press, 1932, p. 43.
27 Q.D. Leavis, *Fiction and the Reading Public*, London, Bellew Publishing Company, 1990 (first published in 1932), p. 37.
28 W. Hunter, *Scrutiny of Cinema*, London, Wishart and Co, 1932, p. 13.
29 Agate, op. cit., p. 79.
30 E.G. Cousins, *Filmland in Ferment*, London, Denis Archer, 1932, p. 282.
31 Ibid., p. 283.
32 Quoted in J. St John, *William Heinemann – a Century of Publishing 1890–1990*, London, Heinemann, 1990, p. 207.
33 V. Woolf, 'The middlebrow', in Woolf, V., *The Death of the Moth, and Other Essays*, London, Hogarth, 1942, p. 119.
34 Leavis, op. cit., p. 77.
35 I am indebted to Charles Barr for drawing my attention to *The Good Companions*. See his reading of the film in C. Barr, 'Desperate yearnings: Victor Saville and Gainsborough', in P Cook (ed.) *Gainsborough Pictures*, London, Cassell, 1997, pp. 47–59.
36 *Daily Telegraph*, 27 February 1933. Reproduced without page numbers on *The Good Companions* microfiche at the BFI Library, London.
37 *Observer,* 26 February 1933, reprinted in A. Lejeune (ed.) *The C.A. Lejeune Film Reader*, Manchester, Carcanet, 1991, pp. 87–9.
38 *Daily Telegraph,* op. cit.
39 R. Durgnat, *A Mirror for England: British Movies from Austerity to Affluence*, London, Faber and Faber, 1970.

8

ARTHUR ASKEY AND THE CONSTRUCTION OF POPULAR ENTERTAINMENT IN *BAND WAGGON* AND *MAKE MINE A MILLION*

Jane Stokes

Cinema has never been a pure medium and has benefited immensely from its links with other cultural practices. This is particularly the case with popular British film comedy, whose stars have often enjoyed parallel careers in music hall, radio and television. This chapter makes a case for Arthur Askey (1900–1982) to be recognised as a definitive British popular entertainer and argues that Askey made a distinctive contribution to our understanding of both 'British' and 'popular' culture in the twentieth century. This is not to detract from the importance of other performers such as George Formby or Gracie Fields, who are more frequently acknowledged within British Cinema Studies. These and other entertainers have been the subject of much scholarship, focusing typically on their role as archetypal working-class entertainers.[1] Askey's significance for British cinema, however, remains much less well documented, yet he made several successful films, besides his work on the stage and in radio and television.

Irrespective of the medium, Askey's act involved him in direct engagement with the idea of the popular. Always critical of arbitrary authority, the 'Little Man', as Askey was known, used the tools of his trade – satire and silliness – to lambaste autocratic prigs. With his keen sense of what was popular, Askey readily ridiculed the Reithian ethos of using culture for social ends and reserved special opprobrium for the BBC mandarins who seemed to dictate public taste. The definition of 'popular taste' is a key element in Askey's work and is especially evident in the two films I will explore in some detail here. Both *Band Waggon* (Marcel Varnel, 1940) and *Make Mine a Million* (Lance Comfort, 1959) interrogate popular access to the medium of television at key points in British cultural history. Made almost twenty years apart, they reflect something of the revolution in British popular entertainment in the 1930s and 1950s.

In a long career that spanned half of the twentieth century, Askey saw many changes in popular entertainment first hand as he worked in almost every branch of show business. As Andy Medhurst has observed, Askey was part of a generation that saw British comedy shift from the music hall to mass mediated entertainment.[2] Indeed, he was more successful than many in making the transition from stage to radio and subsequently to film and television. He began his career in a concert party in the 1920s, the heyday of the British music hall.[3] In the 1930s he was a pioneer in the state sanctioned public radio but also in the less frequently acknowledged, although in many respects more popular, commercial broadcasts of the period.[4] In the late 1930s he became a national celebrity following the enormous success of the BBC radio variety programme *Band Waggon*.[5] Gracie Fields introduced Askey to television in 1932, and his act was among the first to be broadcast using John Logie Baird's experimental system.[6] In the postwar period Askey became one of Britain's leading television entertainers with such shows as *Before Your Very Eyes* and *Living it Up*. In 1961 he had his own situation comedy, *The Arthur Askey Show*, and in the 1970s was a regular on numerous television variety and panel shows.

Throughout his career, Askey remained loyal to his stage origins and kept up a busy schedule of live appearances in music hall and pantomime. His film career, on the other hand, was intermittent. During the Second World War, he starred in eight features for Gainsborough Pictures, including *Charley's (Big Hearted) Aunt* (Walter Forde, 1940), *I Thank You* (Marcel Varnel, 1941) and *King Arthur was a Gentleman* (Marcel Varnel, 1942). More than ten years elapsed between the release of his last film for the studio, *Bees in Paradise* (Val Guest, 1944), and his next feature, *The Love Match* (David Paltenghi, 1955), which was based on his stage show. The 1970s saw him in a few more films, mostly in minor roles exploiting his television success, including *The Alf Garnett Saga* (Bob Kellett, 1972) and *Rosie Dixon – Night Nurse* (Justin Cartwright, 1978).

Askey's films have received relatively little attention from historians of British cinema, William K. Everson's evaluation constituting a fine exception.[7] Perhaps this is because he is more closely identified with his roles in television and as a pantomime dame. But perhaps the films have received scant attention because they have not stood the test of time very well: quite shamelessly made for popular consumption, many of the films are interesting now as ephemera only. It is precisely because his work was so diverse, however, and his films so much of the moment, that Askey is such an archetypal British popular entertainer who warrants further study.

As a comedian who 'achieved a national fame which transcended class barriers',[8] Askey's film roles are typically characters called Arthur who frequently refer to the performer's extra-diegetic fame. When Arthur is irritated that his landlady anticipates the punchline of a joke in *Make Mine a Million*, he grumbles to her: 'Oh, you know all my jokes.' 'Who doesn't!' she quips back, alluding to his corny humour and his high exposure. *Band Waggon* and *Make Mine a Million* play on Askey's well-established public persona as a popular performer prepared to speak his mind and challenge authority. The films see Arthur and his chums taking on the broadcasting establishment in the interests of the taste of ordinary folk. They constitute manifestos for popular entertainment – a phenomenon that the films define against the BBC, which is seen as the promulgator of elitist and divisive notions of culture.

Getting on the *Band Waggon*

Askey's appeal to working-class audiences was something that the BBC could well benefit from in the early days of radio. The BBC was frequently criticised for its lack of entertainment-oriented programmes in the 1920s and 1930s and faced serious challenges from commercial radio broadcasts of the time, especially those of overseas concerns such as Radio Luxembourg.[9] Established theatrical and music hall artists frequently appeared on the English-language transmissions from Europe, which were of marginal legality.[10] Commercial broadcasters acquired a greater credibility with working-class audiences as a consequence, especially as the leading theatrical agent of the day, George Black, forbade his artists from appearing on the BBC in a long-running feud over remuneration. The BBC at first treated commercial radio with disdain. Even Asa Briggs, the historian of British broadcasting, refers to non-BBC broadcasts as 'the lightest and most ephemeral of all light and ephemeral fare'.[11] The success of commercial radio made a mockery of the BBC's claim to be a national institution, however, and Britain's monopoly broadcaster began to look to commercial radio from Europe and the US as models for enhancing the popularity of its programming.

Band Waggon was a radio programme launched by the BBC in 1938 specifically to boost its appeal to working-class audiences.[12] Based on an American concept, the variety show featured comedians Arthur Askey and his sidekick Richard Murdoch, and top musical acts Jack Hylton and his orchestra and singer Patricia Kirkwood. After a lacklustre start, the programme soon 'became a cult'[13] and proved 'pre-war radio's biggest comedy success',[14] enabling the BBC to compete more successfully with their commercial rivals. *Band Waggon* also launched Askey as a national household name: as a result of his star billing on the show he featured in several films, a touring show and various publishing deals.[15]

Askey had an ambiguous relationship with the BBC, however, claiming that it was he who first gave it the nickname 'Aunty'.[16] The BBC may have ensured his status as a national star by launching *Band Waggon* and he may have boasted of being known as the Corporation's 'resident comedian',[17] yet as Everson points out, 'Askey had enough clout to make the BBC itself the butt of many of his jokes'.[18] He habitually ridiculed his erstwhile employers in his act, lampooning the bureaucracy and satirising the mandarins for being out of touch with the tastes of ordinary people. This was one of the central features of his first film, *Band Waggon*.

Band Waggon, a spin-off from the radio show, was made with the permission of the BBC by Gainsborough Pictures. It featured a number of the regulars and some of the plot-lines from the radio series.[19] Several other BBC radio personalities were also given cameos, including Michael Standing, C.H. Middleton and Jasmine Bligh. The film went into production in 1939, only to be interrupted during the first week of shooting by the declaration of war. This resulted in a rapid story change to incorporate a wartime theme of Nazi spies using a secret television station to relay home images of British planes. The film reprises Arthur's and Dickie's roles from the radio series as squatters on the roof of Broadcasting House from where they can launch satirical missiles at the venerable old lady, the BBC. As Scannell and Cardiff note, the humour of the radio show relied on the saturnalian possibilities offered by this running gag: 'Arthur and Dickie's tenancy of the flat at the top of Broadcasting House symbolised the occupation of that "damned awful erection", that monument of Reithian sobriety, by the forces of innocent mayhem and fun.'[20] The film plays on these same forces of 'mayhem and fun', undermining the authority of the BBC and proposing Arthur and his entourage as the true advocates of popular entertainment. Their attitude towards the Corporation is summed up in the scene in which Arthur and Dickie are evicted from their rooftop squat. They bump into Michael Standing in the lobby of Broadcasting House and invite him to join them in their new venture. Standing demurs, saying that he is 'under contract here', to which Arthur quips: 'Oh, bad luck. Why don't you try and get with a decent firm?'

The character of the BBC executive John Pilkington is established early on in *Band Waggon* as a synecdoche for the BBC. We learn from the Broadcasting House porters that Pilkington 'hates music' and is unlikely to listen to the jitterbug band recently arrived for an audition. In his chauffeur-driven car, Pilkington is a caricature of the British toff: he wears morning dress, speaks in an upper-class accent and is dismissive of the popular entertainers like Jack Hylton who write to him requesting auditions. Pilkington's negative attitude towards popular music is further established when Hylton and his band ensnare Pilkington into hearing them play. Despite putting on one of the film's most lavish acts, the band's efforts are ignored and Pilkington reads his newspaper, oblivious to the big band, its soloists and the dance troupe.

When Arthur and his chums gain access to an illegal television transmitter, they tune into the BBC television broadcasts and intercept them with their own messages. Arthur seizes this opportunity to challenge the authority of the BBC directly. At first, the mockery is for the amusement of

Plate 11   *Band Waggon* (Marcel Varnel, 1940): staid BBC officials attempt to contain Arthur Askey's and Richard Murdoch's fun-making on the roof of Broadcasting House.

his chums in the studio, but when the gang superimpose the image of Arthur onto the BBC broadcast, Arthur is able to share a frame with the pompous Pilkington. When Pilkington addresses the BBC audience on the Corporation's plans for the future of television, Arthur cannot resist the opportunity of answering back: 'Put me through,' Askey demands, 'I'll tell him a few things.' Pilkington addresses the audience: 'As you know, I'm always looking for fresh talent.' Askey retorts: 'Don't you believe it. You can't get near the old – gentleman.' The exchange continues when Pilkington affirms: 'In fact, all of us here are anxious to find new faces.' 'And blimey, could you do with it,' chips in Arthur, asking the television audience: 'Did you ever see such a clock in your life?' Arthur's cheeky jibes undermine the authority of the autocratic, self-serving Pilkington. The BBC executives withdraw their broadcast, leaving Arthur free to make a declaration of independence for popular entertainers:

> Well, playmates, I've done you one good turn: I've got rid of him. And now I can tell you what really does happen. He says he spends his time searching around for fresh talent. Shall I tell you what

happens when he finds it? He keeps it hanging about for three months and then gives it the sack ... Him and his experts! Why I could do better than him with my hands tied behind my back and what's more I will! You tune in on this wavelength at 8 o'clock tonight and I'll show you – I'll show you some of the talent that he's missed: Jack Hylton and his band, Pat Kirkwood, Arthur Askey, Richard Murdoch!

Pilkington is enraged at the scam. 'I'll have this man in jail!' he declares. 'Get the police!' The forces of law and order side with the BBC, eventually arresting Arthur and Jack for 'obstruction to public service and trespass on the BBC charter'. In the end, however, the BBC succumbs to the power of popular taste and grants the gang their own show. The revolutionaries are happy to be co-opted by the establishment broadcaster and the show is declared a hit.

The making of *Make Mine a Million*

Band Waggon was the first of the eight films Askey made at Gainsborough, and the first of three under the direction of Marcel Varnel. During the war, Askey's film work proved reliable at the box office and he was especially successful with such films as *Charley's (Big Hearted) Aunt* and *I Thank You*.[21] After the war, Askey returned to the stage, working with his friend Jack Hylton, the bandleader turned independent producer.[22] Hylton produced several stage shows and films as vehicles for Askey who continued to enjoy national recognition. *Ramsbottom Rides Again* (John Baxter, 1956) was a hugely successful Hylton production, based on Askey's stage show, which the pair followed up with *Make Mine a Million*. This satire on the 1950s television industry was released in 1959, almost two decades after *Band Waggon*, by which time the landscape of British entertainment had been revolutionised. The recognition of working-class tastes following the end of the Second World War resulted in an upheaval in all areas of culture and the arts, nowhere more clearly than in the realm of television. After the introduction of commercial television (ITV) in 1955, access to television was extended to those with expertise in popular entertainment such as the music hall and the cinema. Film producers who had been excluded from television in the BBC monopoly era now owned television stations; cinema studios that had been idle were now given over to television production. Jack Hylton was one of many impresarios who found lucrative outlets for their work in the expanding broadcasting medium. The new commercial stations served working-class audiences more fully than the BBC had done, and British television became a popular medium in every sense for the first time.[23]

In the mid- to late 1950s, Askey's career, and that of many other entertainers, was altered dramatically by the changes heralded by ITV. Postwar entertainers were better able to negotiate for improved terms and conditions of service when there was an 'other side' to which they could go for work. Askey was typical in that he worked for Jack Hylton in commercial television from 1957 to 1961 before switching allegiance back to the BBC.[24] While working for Hylton, Askey starred in and co-financed *Make Mine a Million* which addresses the revolution in the television industry by satirising the rivalry between public- and commercially-funded television.

Askey's ridiculing of the BBC as a bastion of legitimate, anti-popular taste in *Band Waggon* returns as a theme of *Make Mine a Million*. Despite the dramatic changes in the landscape of British television between the 1930s and 1950s, it is remarkable how the image of 'Aunty' remains unchanged in these two films. According to Askey, *Make Mine a Million* was 'based on my own idea of a make-up man at the BBC being bribed to put out commercials during the BBC programmes'.[25] Askey plays Arthur Ashton whose old variety act has been made obsolete by television, compelling him to work backstage at the National Television Service (NTV), a thinly disguised BBC. *Make Mine a Million* has Arthur team up with Sid Gibson (Sid James), the archetypal spiv, who pressurises Arthur into doing the unimaginable – advertising on the National.

Make Mine a Million plays on the popular stereotypes of the BBC and ITV in the early years of commercial television in Britain. For the first time there was a regional, popular and advertising supported television service to challenge the dominance of the national, elitist and publicly-funded BBC. In Britain in the 1950s, television was the subject of much debate and the film industry reflected this public interest.[26] A high public profile was given to the rivalry between the two systems in *Make Mine a Million*, which puts forward the perspective of the British working class for whom advertising was seen as a symbol of the end of postwar austerity. The BBC is trenchantly associated with the ascetic and anti-popular cultural elite, an image engendered in the Reith period, but lingering well into the 1950s.

The Director General (Clive Morton) and his cronies are harshly satirised in the film, with the entire Board of Directors lampooned for its haughty and self-satisfied stance. At the beginning of the film the Board congratulate one another on the good taste of their fare as they watch an NTV programme in their private viewing room. Removed from the ordinary context of viewing, they are oblivious to the preferences of ordinary folk such as Arthur's landlady, who prefers to watch 'a good play' on the other side; even the loyal Arthur admits that the NTV programming is 'lousy'. The Board of Directors, on the other hand, revels in the fact that their programmes, unlike those on the commercial channel, are 'unmarred by unsavoury interruptions'. Their smug self-congratulation turns to outrage when the pirate broadcasters insert a placard for 'Bonko! The Wonder Detergent' at the end of an NTV programme. The Director General declares: 'Heads shall roll for this!'

When culpability for the wheeze is traced to Arthur, he is summoned to the Director General's office. The soundtrack establishes a mood of doom as Arthur is marched to the Board Room, with the Little Man dwarfed by the gigantic door and its ornate decoration. The Director General stands before him like a hanging judge and leans down to pass judgement on Arthur. Asked whether he realises what he has done 'to the pattern of National Television', Arthur replies with a cheeky grin, 'dropped a stitch, I suppose'. The Director General glowers at him: 'And it'll take at least three poetry readings and a visit to Glyndebourne to fix it up again.' The contrast between Arthur's homely cultural references and the highbrow ones of the Director General could not be clearer. Nor could the implication that the BBC believes it has a duty to defend cultural pursuits like poetry and opera against the onslaught of popular, commercial influences. Even so, as in *Band Waggon*, *Make Mine a Million* concludes with the official broadcasters employing the rebels: Sid is rewarded with a job at TAA, the commercial television station, while Arthur is given his own show on NTV.

Although the BBC receives the brunt of the satire, commercial television is not given a particularly easy ride either in *Band Waggon* and *Make Mine a Million*. When Arthur and his chums decide to take over the television station in *Band Waggon* they have to oust the spies who are posing as commercial broadcasters purveying baked beans. Arthur argues that the gang has the right to commandeer the station for popular entertainers on the basis that they have 'more than baked beans to show the world'. Rank commercialism is not defended here. In *Make Mine a Million*, TAA is caricatured as sexist, Americanised and decadent, especially in contrast to the National. The films don't permit any direct equation of 'commercial' with 'popular' television. Askey's anti-establishmentarianism is as readily extended to the purveyors of 'baked beans' as to the cultural arbiters at the BBC.

'Hello, playmates!' – the group and the popular

In *Band Waggon* the BBC's dismissive approach to popular entertainers is criticised; in *Make Mine a Million*, the focus of satire is more on the official broadcaster's attitude toward advertising. In both films, the challenge is launched by a group of buddies working together as a team, with Askey playing a pivotal figure. The core of the gang in *Band Waggon* comprises the unlikely double act of the diminutive working-class music hall entertainer Arthur and his tall, good-looking and witty 'playmate', Cambridge graduate Richard 'Stinker' Murdoch. The two do not disregard their readily apparent differences in social class and even incorporate them into their act. For example, when the pair arrive at the Jack in the Box restaurant, Dickie teases Arthur: 'Seems a bit posh. I hope they don't throw you out.' In the restaurant, the gang is formed when Arthur and Dickie meet up with Jack Hylton, an old buddy of Arthur's from his music hall days, who introduces them to musician Freddy Schweitzer and singer Patricia Kirkwood.

Group solidarity is immediately established when they all learn of their common experience of being rejected by Pilkington and the BBC. The exclusion from legitimate broadcasting of these heroic outsiders compels the comrades to take matters into their own hands. They find an opportunity to display their team spirit when they first discover the abandoned illegal television station. Dickie is the one who realises the significance of the find. 'This is the biggest break we've ever had,' he tells the gang. 'We don't need the BBC now!' 'That's right,' says Jack Hylton, 'We can broadcast without them!' 'What a swell idea!' chimes in Pat, 'We can get the band and the girls and put on a terrific show!' With technical expertise provided by Freddy, whose facility with broadcast technology is explained by the fact that he once worked in a radio shop, and with Arthur's performing skills, the working team is formed.

Their roles are established as equals with different skills and the show they produce is seen to be a collaborative effort. The grand finale of *Band Waggon*, a number called *Booms-a-Daisy*, is an ensemble piece featuring the cast of the show in nineteenth-century evening dress dancing in formation and bumping bottoms with every 'booms-a-daisy'. The group successfully challenges the authority of the BBC to define taste by affirming the value of the working-class, communal culture of slightly lewd group dancing. There is an irony in the closure when Pilkington, obliged to recognise their victory, grants the performers their own show. For the film's heroes have fought for something that, in the extra-diegetic world, their actors have already been granted. The film's close suggests that the BBC will allow the chums on air as a result of their revolutionary demonstration of the popularity of their acts, whereas, in reality, the BBC produced the radio show that established the national reputation of the performers. The idea that the BBC will have to change its attitude as a result of the insurgency of the entertainment revolutionaries does a disservice to the actual role the BBC played in promoting popular performance at this time. This paradox is emblematic of Askey's ambiguous relationship with the BBC.

Like *Band Waggon*, *Make Mine a Million* also focuses on the cohesive, inclusive gang, working for the common goal of undermining the hegemony of the official broadcaster. Sid and the Professor have developed the formula for Bonko, the Wonder Detergent, but have trouble selling it because 'it hasn't been advertised on the telly'. Arthur is at first reluctant to help advertise Bonko on non-commercial television, but Sid is a cocky cockney who proves too persuasive to resist. He finally convinces Arthur and Jack (the cameraman) that they should come and work with him after they are sacked from their jobs at NTV. 'We could set up our own little television station,' he tells them. He flatters the ex-NTV men: 'I'll leave all the technical details to you two – after all, you're the experts.' He tells Arthur: 'With your organising genius and Jack's technical ability, I don't see why we shouldn't pinch a couple of minutes on National Television sometimes. After all, there

have been pirate radio stations. Why not television, too?' From being sceptical, even hostile, at the beginning of the scene, Arthur is finally persuaded:
'I say, what a lark,' he says to Jack.

The working team is formed and in the next scene we see them all
mucking in to help churn out the extra boxes of Bonko needed to meet the
increased demand created by television advertising. Sid exhorts the gang:
'We've got to start operating like a wartime underground movement!' The
group is able to reject the bureaucracy and hierarchy of the official broadcaster by dint of collective effort. The cohesive gang of people of different
social classes, working together to achieve the common goal of undermining
legitimate broadcasting and affirming popular entertainment values is thus
a feature of both films.

Askey: the popular hero of the entertainment front

In both *Band Waggon* and *Make Mine a Million*, a popular television service is
shown as something that people have to fight for and which television
bureaucrats, with their limited, class-bound tastes, prefer to stifle. The resolution to both films involves those formerly excluded from television finally
gaining access. Askey organises around himself a popular front of diverse
workers who successfully challenge established cultural values. In the
process, these films offer a definition of popular entertainment that is inclusive of all British people. Askey achieves this by attacking the claims of the
BBC to represent national cultural taste.

In both films, however, Askey and the gang are incorporated into the
television industry and given employment, which rather neuters the radical
edge of their rebellion. The BBC is shown as capable of adapting and
responding to the subversives by co-opting them if necessary. Askey is thus
the BBC's conscience and its carnival fool: he draws attention to the ludicrous nature of the Corporation's power, but in the long run this is so that it
may evolve and prove a more efficient ruler over the cultural domain. None
the less, Askey is a hero who champions the right of access to popular entertainment by working-class entertainers. He deserves a place in the pantheon
of British performers who stand up for ordinary people by challenging
cultural autocracy. His persona expresses popular values of resistance to
authoritarianism through the exercise of collective action; he is a definitive
British popular entertainer.

NOTES

1 See, for example, J. Richards, *Films and British National Identity. From Dickens to
   'Dad's Army'*, Manchester, Manchester University Press, 1997.
2 A. Medhurst, 'Music hall and the British cinema', in C. Barr (ed.) *All Our
   Yesterdays: 90 Years of British Cinema*, London, BFI Publishing, 1986, pp.
   168–88.

3 R. Wilmot, *Kindly Leave the Stage*, London, Macmillan, 1985; A. Askey, *Before Your Very Eyes: An Autobiography*, London, Woburn Press, 1975.

4 A. Briggs, *The Golden Age of Wireless. The History of Broadcasting in the United Kingdom. Volume 2*, London, Oxford University Press, 1965.

5 R. Hirst, *Three Men and a Gimmick*, Kingswood, Surrey, The World's Work (1913) Ltd., 1957; B. Took, *Laughter in the Air. An Informal History of British Radio Comedy*, London, BBC/Robson Books, 1976.

6 V. Hanna, 'Television was ludicrous, but it was fascinating that it was possible at all', *Radio Times,* 30 October 1976, vol. 213, no. 2764, pp. 74, 75 and 81.

7 W.K. Everson, 'Arthur Askey', *Films in Review*, March 1986, vol. 37, no. 3, pp. 169–75.

8 R. Dacre, 'Traditions of British Comedy', in R. Murphy, *The British Cinema Book*, London, BFI Publishing, 1997, p. 200.

9 P. Scannell and D. Cardiff, *A Social History of British Broadcasting. Volume 1. 1922–1933. Serving the Nation*, London, Blackwell, 1991; Briggs, op. cit.

10 Briggs, op. cit.

11 Ibid., p. 364.

12 S. Neale and F. Krutnik, *Film and Television Comedy*, London, Routledge, 1990, pp. 221–2.

13 Scannell and Cardiff, op. cit., p. 272.

14 Took, op. cit., p. 21.

15 Scannell and Cardiff, op. cit.; Askey, op. cit.

16 D. McGill, 'Hello, playmates', *TV Times*, 7 December 1972, p. 75.

17 Askey, op. cit., p. 93.

18 Everson, op. cit., p. 169.

19 Although Askey's name appears on the credits for a 1937 revue picture, *Calling All Stars* (Herbert Smith), Askey explains in his autobiography that the small scene he shot for this film was dropped before the film was finally released; see Askey, op. cit., pp. 85–6.

20 Scannell and Cardiff, op. cit., p. 272.

21 A. Aldgate and J. Richards, *Britain Can Take It. The British Cinema in the Second World War*, Edinburgh, Edinburgh University Press, 2nd edn, 1994, p. 91.

22 P.W. Logan, *Jack Hylton Presents,* London, BFI Publishing, 1995.

23 J. Corner (ed.) *Popular Television in Britain,* London, BFI Publishing, 1991.

24 McGill, op. cit.

25 Askey, op. cit., p. 167.

26 C. Barr, 'Broadcasting and cinema 2: Screens within screens', in Barr, *All Our Yesterdays*, op. cit., pp. 206–24.

Part IV

AUTHORSHIP AND AGENCY

Introduction

Debates about authorship have long been central to the study of cinema. The numerous publications on the work of individual directors and the various attempts since the 1970s to challenge the critical supremacy of the director or *auteur* have meant that questions of authorship and agency remain a significant frame of reference for Film Studies and Cinema History. Generally though, this trend has been rather less prevalent in accounts of mainstream British cinema than it has in critical discourses about Hollywood or European cinema. Aside from the attention certain canonical directors and avant-garde film-makers have attracted, there have been few attempts to consider how authorship functions in the context of mainstream British cinema.

The four contributors to this section go some way to redressing this absence. In their different ways, Sue Harper, Vincent Porter, Justine Ashby and Peter Hutchings all consider the practicalities and possibilities of tracing the exercise of agency in the institutional and cultural practices of commercial British cinema. None of the writers takes the tenets of authorship for granted, however; nor do their analyses depend upon an orthodox concept of the author. Thus Harper maps out a series of star types to which most actresses working in British cinema in the 1930s conformed, and considers how far these actresses were permitted performative agency. In a very different vein, Porter looks at the institutional ideology and practices of the Associated British Picture Corporation, a British film company responsible for some of the most famous British films of the 1950s, and highlights the ways in which individual directors were all too often straitjacketed by intrusive budgeting policies and working practices that subscribed as much agency to scriptwriters and musical directors as it did to its film directors. Ashby also discusses the limitations and pressures studios often imposed on the individual film-maker in the 1950s in her study of Britain's most successful female producer, Betty Box.

Of the four contributors to this section, Hutchings engages most explicitly with debates about authorship and considers the ways in which these debates need to be modified to be wholly salient to an analysis of British cinema history. In a case study of Roy Ward Baker, Hutchings shows how studio style was often more distinctive and more influential in Baker's films than the director's agency. Above all else, what these four contributors seek to establish is that orthodox concepts of the author need to be extended: they need to be rooted in culturally and historically specific moments; and they need to be revised to include agents and influences beyond the romanticised figure of the *auteur*.

9

FROM WHOLESOME GIRLS TO DIFFICULT DOWAGERS

Actresses in 1930s British cinema

Sue Harper

The way actresses are deployed in the cinema is the result of industrial and cultural constraints. Although there have been a few exceptions, actresses' autonomy has usually been limited. They may choose their roles, but the way they nuance them by body language, gaze pattern and voice timbre is often subject to others' control. Both male and female roles in film are determined by the prevailing agency within the industry. In the 1930s and 1940s, the producer operated as the ultimate determinant of the way actors and actresses functioned in film texts. In the 1950s, it was the distribution company; in the 1960s, the director. In the 1970s, 1980s and 1990s, it was an unpredictable *mélange* of different types of agency.

Of course, film roles are intimately connected to the shifting demands of historical convention and fashion. Every period contains recognisable social stereotypes (the flapper, the bluestocking, the sex kitten) which are the consequence of historically specific constraints, and which are determined by shifting definitions of class identity and sexual respectability. Cultural forms do not automatically reflect these social stereotypes; rather, they engage with them – sometimes critically, sometimes tangentially. Just as there is an ebb and flow of social stereotypes, so codes and patterns of cultural representation shift too. In British as in other national cinemas, there are discrete 'clusters' of actors or actresses, which develop and dissolve over quite short periods of time, and vary according to their topicality and intensity. Some have longer cultural roots than others. Jeffrey Richards and Andrew Spicer have valuably demonstrated that, in the case of male film roles, the short-rooted clusters constitute radical innovations, whereas some have deeper historical roots that make them function as a kind of cultural *ancien régime*.[1] Female groupings in British cinema tend to be more varied and unstable than their male counterparts, possibly because of the anxieties unconsciously evinced by the 'masters' of the texts. All clusters, whether of long or short duration, feed important social hungers, and address specific parts of the audience. It might be argued that to sketch out such clusters is unduly speculative; but I think it is important for the film historian to progress from a basis of detailed empirical discovery to more tentative work, and to make suggestions about the social function of cultural forms.

If we consider 1930s British cinema, what is remarkable is the range and quantity of female clusters. On one level, this can be attributed to the volatility of the industry, which was characterised by flexibility, informality and financial crisis. Studios were acutely prone to market fluctuation, and they depended upon the instincts of their producers. Their cultural entrepreneurialism meant that risk-taking strategies had to be buttressed by a canny sense of contemporary mores.

Working conditions for film actresses were often parlous. Competition was fierce, and actresses would sometimes go to outrageous lengths to secure a part.[2] The financial rewards were mixed. Potential starlets were given small retainers (sometimes £5 a week) and then paid on a daily basis if they were chosen to appear.[3] Bigger companies would pay £20 a week on a five-year contract. Sometimes actresses were only paid per foot of completed film, and in order to survive, they doubled up by filming during the day and appearing on stage at night.[4] However, once they achieved star status, significant sums were earned. Evelyn Laye, for example, earned £5,000 per picture.[5] Jessie Matthews earned much more, and Gracie Fields earned £40,000 per film in a four-picture deal struck in 1933.[6]

Young actresses were the cheapest unit of exchange. When Alexander Korda had money problems during *The Private Life of Henry VIII* (1933), Binnie Barnes recalled that:

> he lent me out to BIP which was right next door. It was for a film called *An Old Spanish Custom*, so I played a Spanish woman in the morning and Catherine Howard for Alex in the evening. I got sprayed with a bucket of water at BIP and then I had to run across the street and be glamorous.[7]

The symbolic function actresses could fulfil varied according to their nationality. Non-British stars were cast in exotic roles, but this often made them marginal to the social themes of the films. British stars were more thoroughly assimilated into the main body of the texts.

Exotics

There was considerable transnational traffic in film personnel in 1930s Britain, and this extended to actresses as well as to actors, directors and designers. European women such as Elizabeth Bergner were invited to bring a sense of sophistication to the bill of fare. The French actress Renee Saint-Cyr, for example, completely transformed Gainsborough's workaday *Strange*

Boarders (Herbert Mason, 1938). Saint-Cyr's performance is remarkable for its sophistication. When she discovers her husband masquerading in a boarding-house as a Mr Bullock, she signs herself in as Miss Heifer, and her manner is a double entendre in itself.

European actresses could be given lines expressing a cynicism that would probably have been polluting if spoken by British females. The French comedienne Yvonne Arnaud appeared in a range of films in which her plump persona administered correctives to bourgeois respectability. Arnaud was aware of the difficulties which her urbanity and age posed for producers:

> I am not what you would call a sweet young ingenue – no? That is what they really wanted ... I think I would like to be something like a younger Marie Dressler. You see, I am an awkward age. I am not so young, but I am not old.[8]

Arnaud thought only Tom Walls was capable of making good use of her talents. His *Cuckoo In the Nest* (1933) is an example of her best work. Arnaud played an MP's wife who is wrongly accused of adultery with an old flame. Her performance is marvellously knowing. With a po-faced expression, she displays her supposed lover to her husband with a shrug: 'Go on! Look at him!' The husband replies, 'You're right. It's impossible.' Her manner suggests that she has avoided adultery not because it is wrong, but because the co-respondent is too silly.

Many 'exotics' were marketed in studio press books as the leaven that would raise the dough of ordinary films. Producers intended exotic actresses to allude to the mystery of the unknown, which could not be invoked by more forthright British actresses. Nina Mae McKinney, for example, was brought over from America to star in *Sanders of the River* (Zoltan Korda, 1935). In *Sanders*, her role is so thoroughly integrated into the debate about responsible Empire leadership that there is no space for any acting manoeuvres. Instead, McKinney's function is to be decorative and to endorse western definitions of the family: 'one paper, one wife', as Sanders instructs her and Bosambo after their marriage. The exotic heroine is only important for the events she can set in train.

The same can be said of the Chinese-American actress Anna May Wong, who made four films in Britain: *Piccadilly* (E.A. Dupont, 1929), *Tiger Bay* (J. Elder Wills, 1933), *Java Head* (Basil Dean, 1934) and *Chu Chin Chow* (Walter Forde, 1934). In the first three, her racial 'otherness' is signalled as a source of visual pleasure and moral danger.[9] In the musical *Chu Chin Chow*, Erno Metzner's florid sets display Wong as their chief piece of dressing. She symbolises a love object that is profane because it is heavily inflected. Sacred love objects, by implication, are single-faceted and familiar.

Tamara Desni was used for different purposes. Her fractured accent and ethereal appearance was always used as an index of vulnerability. In *Fire Over*

England (William K. Howard, 1937), Desni plays Spanish Elena, who falls in love with the English hero. It is necessary for the patriotic resolution of the narrative that he reject her. In *The Squeaker* (Howard, 1937), she plays a nightclub singer fatally in love with an arch-burglar. Her performance throughout is like someone walking under water. Desni's voice has a thrilling vibrato, and she intones the keynote song ('He was my only one/He's gone') while walking backwards and wearing a transparent dress. The signs of excess weigh too heavily in the scales against the signs of reason, and accordingly Desni's power is overcome by the cool righteousness of the character played by Ann Todd. This pattern is replicated in Desni's other films: her Tamara in *By-Pass to Happiness* (Anthony Kimmins, 1934), Conchita in *Jack Ahoy!* (Walter Forde, 1934) and Tanya in *Love in Exile* (Alfred Werker, 1936).

Other companies were ambitious for the status which Continental stars could confer. The German star Camilla Horn was brought over for *Matinee Idol* (George King, 1933), *The Love Nest* (Thomas Bentley, 1933) and *The Luck Of a Sailor* (Robert Milton, 1934). As these were low-budget items, Horn felt insulted, and thought that British producers tarred all foreign actresses with the same exotic brush.[10] The English/German actress Lilian Harvey was signed for a three-picture deal with BIP, but only completed *Invitation to the Waltz* (Paul Merzbach, 1935) because she felt her roles were predictable soubrettes with no emotional breadth.[11]

When American-owned companies imported exotic women into their British films, they over-egged the pudding. Fox's *Wings of the Morning* (Harold Schuster, 1937) was structured around the French actress Annabella.[12] First she is a gypsy, then she is disguised as a boy, and lastly she is the aristocratic heir to a great estate. The film almost collapses under the overload of motifs, and the range of symbolic functions borne by the heroine makes her role preposterous.

Marlene Dietrich was the biggest international actress to be imported. Alexander Korda brought her over to star with Robert Donat in *Knight Without Armour* (Jacques Feyder, 1937). Dietrich's reputation was based on films in which her sublime ambiguity intrigued the viewer. *Knight Without Armour*, however, which dealt with the rescue of a Countess from the marauding hordes of the Russian revolution, required Dietrich to function in a more one-dimensional way. Artistically the film is a wonderful achievement, but the designs by Lazare Meerson concentrate on the light rather than the dark aspects of Dietrich's persona. She is there in order to be saved, but she cannot be understood.

The case of Merle Oberon provides us with interesting problems. She was of Indian/Eurasian descent, but took great pains to conceal this. Korda discovered her in 1932 and married her in 1939. She starred in a range of his productions in the 1930s, such as *The Private Life of Don Juan* (Alexander Korda, 1934), *The Scarlet Pimpernel* (Harold Young, 1935) and *The Divorce of*

Lady X (Tim Whelan, 1938). Her performances in these films suggest that she was split between the desire to exploit her exotic charisma and the need to conceal her racial origins by assuming an extreme refinement and impassivity.[13] She also had to operate as the central female symbol for Korda's philosophical system. These conflicting demands account for the acute inconsistency of Oberon's persona and performative styles.

One home-grown British actress, Chili Bouchier, was used as an 'exotic', but the typecasting inhibited her career. When producer/director Herbert Wilcox discovered her 'Latin looks', he set about constructing her as a star with non-English allure. Bouchier recalled that:

> He confessed to a fantasy in which he discovered an actress who could be a true Trilby to his Svengali – a girl whom he could control completely both professionally and privately.[14]

According to Bouchier, her spirited rejection of Wilcox's amorous advances caused him to take revenge by loaning her out for lacklustre films. When Anna Neagle replaced Bouchier in his affections, the débâcle was complete. With Wilcox's final words ringing in her ears ('you are going to find it very difficult'), Bouchier noted that hers was 'a cautionary little tale which demonstrated what happens to little actresses when they refuse to reward their mentors'.[15] The 'foreign' persona Bouchier had acquired in Wilcox's films proved hard to shed, and all she could get were Romany roles. In *Gypsy* (Roy Neill, 1936), she was presented in the words of a contemporary reviewer as 'a wild half-naked creature with fuzzy-wuzzy hair who fought like a wild-cat'.[16] Bouchier's career declined steadily, and an actress of great versatility was lost to the cinema.

Thus, an 'exotic' persona was a disadvantage in the British film industry, but only if you were female. Male stars with such qualities were presented in a different way. Sabu always appeared as fresh, eager and inventive. Conrad Veidt's saturnine qualities were used to positive effect by British producers.[17] Female exotics were used by British producers to throw advantageous light on indigenous and more restrained actresses, and they were directed so as to emphasise their profane allure.

Ladylike ladies

If we now turn to the home-grown clusters of female film types, it seems likely that their main function was to operate as an exhortation to unexceptionable behaviour. This differentiated them from the Awful Warnings symbolised by the foreign 'exotics'. One such cluster was the 'ladylike' actresses whose entry into films was often via C.B. Cochran's revues.[18] Evelyn Laye was one, who appeared in such Ruritanian musical comedies as *Princess Charming* (Maurice Elvey, 1934), and whose function was to raise the tone of events. Sarah Churchill was another Cochran graduate.[19] So was Florence Desmond, who allowed film and revue to cross-pollinate in her work. She 'quoted' the furniture-touching scene from *Queen Christina* (Rouben Mamoulian, 1933) in her revue *Why Not Tonight?*, and implicitly referred to her Cochran act in many of her films.[20] Like the other 'ladylike' types, Desmond used her revue connections to give status to her film persona. So did Gertrude Lawrence. Her role in *Rembrandt* (Alexander Korda, 1936) is of particular interest. She uses the housekeeper role to suggest a combination of sexual hunger with a desire for social revenge. Her performance as Desdemona/the wife in *Men Are Not Gods* (Walter Reisch, 1936) saturates the film's central issues (jealousy, duplicity and control) with upper-middle-class resonance. Interestingly, Lawrence was marketed as a star with particular appeal to women.[21]

Other 'ladylike' actresses functioned in a similar manner: for example, Kathleen Nesbitt in *The Passing of the Third Floor Back* (Berthold Viertel, 1934). Binnie Barnes invested her role in *The Private Life of Henry VIII* with such a degree of controlled calculation that she undermined some of the intentions of the script.[22] Benita Hume did the same in *Jew Süss* (Lothar Mendes, 1934).[23] The 'ladylike' characters always raised the tone of events. Their textual function was to operate as a brake on the narrative, and to encourage the viewer to recall a period when definitions of class and culture were comfortably stable.

Wholesome sensible girls

An emergent cluster of actresses counterbalanced the socially residual effect of the 'ladies'. They included Nova Pilbeam, Wendy Barrie, Renee Ray, Googie Withers, and Ann Todd, who all projected an air of modernity. They were all cool in their delivery, and gave the impression of competence and energy; they had the forthright manner of a socially emergent group, and could imbue realist tales with an aura of contemporaneity. 'Wholesome sensible girls' always had middle-class aspirations. Their verbal delivery was brisk (no slurring or drawling) and their gaze was direct. Their textual effect is bracing, and they are clearly intended to evoke confidence in a new social order.

Consider the contribution made by Edna Best to *South Riding* (Victor Saville, 1938). She plays the young headmistress, Sarah Burton, who has a social conscience and a degree of feminism. Best plays her entirely without nuance. Her gaze has a minimum of searching movements so that she appears incisive; her body language lacks redundancy, making her seem straightforward. Best's performance throws into sharp relief that of her rival, the mad wife, who is made to seem far more asymmetrical and dangerous by comparison. Best therefore carries a great deal of the moral weight of the picture.

Another 'wholesome sensible girl' was Madeleine Carroll, who had been a schoolteacher before becoming an actress. Carroll's stock-in-trade was her ability to appear unfazed; like Best, she could express stillness amidst confusion. This was what characterised her performance in *I Was a Spy* (Victor Saville, 1933). Carroll plays a Belgian nurse who becomes a spy during the First World War, and the film is structured and edited to favour a feminist interpretation of her role. For example, in an early scene she is reminded that she is a Belgian. With remarkable firmness she replies: 'I am a woman first. And a Belgian afterwards.' In between the two sentences there is a cut; she is shown glancing at a nun, as if to affirm their common gender which supersedes nationality. The shooting style too favours an heroic view of Carroll's function. The final sequence frames her centrally throughout; when she pushes open the door of her prison and walks out into the sunlight, her courage is emphasised by the composition and lighting style.

We cannot impute the construction of Carroll's persona merely to director- or producer-led procedures. If we consider her performance in *The 39 Steps* (Alfred Hitchcock, 1935), we can see continuities with her earlier films. Carroll is minimalist, with the ability to express emotion intelligently. Hitchcock himself presented Carroll as the first of the blondes he pushed to the edge: 'Nothing gives me more pleasure than to knock the lady-likeness out ... That is why I deliberately deprived Madeleine Carroll of her dignity and glamour in *The 39 Steps*.'[24] There is no evidence of such strain in Carroll's performance. Indeed Hitchcock's British films feature many 'sensible girls' who take matters into their own hands. Either the female sexual/social stereotypes in British cinema were too intractable for Hitchcock, or his control of the scripting process was not as complete as in his later films. The issues of authorial control, acting style and female narrative function are highlighted in his British films in an acute manner.

Margaret Lockwood is an interesting case. Of course, she became the eponymous Wicked Lady in the 1940s, and played roles in which she outraged every decorous convention. But in her 1930s films, we can safely categorise her as a 'wholesome sensible girl'. In *The Lady Vanishes* (Hitchcock, 1938), Lockwood's persona is resourceful; she is able to decode the meaning of words on a windowpane, and to recognise the old lady as the 'mummy' swathed in bandages. Lockwood was also forthright in *Lorna Doone* (Basil Dean, 1935) and *Owd Bob* (Robert Stephenson, 1938). It looks as though the 'wholesome girls' cluster was sufficiently powerful in the 1930s to disrupt casting more sympathetic to the actresses' own proclivities. In any case, the dense population and the intensity of the 'wholesome girls' group is probably indicative of a desire on the part of some producers to give the audience confidence in modernity – to let them see that women could be both brisk and pure. 'Wholesome girls' had the double function of comforting and challenging the viewers, who were being gradually acclimatised to newer, more combative female types.

Mannish women

1930s British cinema contained a small cluster of 'mannish women' – females who are not conventionally beautiful and who engage in quasi-masculine activities. These women can feasibly struggle for power and status, since they waste little textual time in the pursuit of romance. The film scripts present these mannish women as wistful. They are made to regret their position as men by proxy, and the narrative structures ultimately consign them to the position of female eunuchs. There are tensions between the powerful energy of the actresses' performative styles, and the painful social exclusion imposed on them by the scripts.

Flora Robson possessed an extraordinary spiritual beauty and technical virtuosity. During the 1930s, she made films in which she played powerful women who suffer because they are extraordinary, such as her role as the Empress in *Catherine the Great* (Paul Czinner, 1934). The screenplay by Marjorie Deans required her to express some feminist sentiments. Robson turned in a performance of great subtlety, in which her demeanour bears witness to the loneliness of power and promiscuity. She played Elizabeth I in *Fire Over England* (W.K. Howard, 1937). The screenplay by the female playwright Clemence Dane presents the monarch as someone torn apart by internal conflict. Elizabeth wishes to symbolise victory over the flesh, but also to enjoy being that flesh. Robson's most intense scenes are those where she is driven by desire to be young like her ladies-in-waiting, and to be old in wisdom like the monarchy itself. This conflict makes her unreasonable and interesting. Elizabeth's original speech at Tilbury saturates political power with gender:

> My people, I am come to live or die among you all. I know I have the body of a weak and feeble woman, but I have the heart and valour of a king, aye, and of a king of England too.

Robson's intonation and emphasis suggest that it is feasible to be both a monarch and a citizen, to be both alive and dead and to be both male and female. Robson knew she had turned in an unusual performance:

> Elizabeth was essentially a woman of action, and that is just the kind of woman I like best to portray. Whether they are characters of actual history, or just folklore, or of pure fiction, such women – women whose lives and works were far more important than their loves – are much more in tune with our modern idea and tempo of life than many of the sexy sirens who have figured as heroines of sexy and sentimental films in the past.[25]

Another 'mannish woman' was Cecily Courtneidge, who specialised as a male impersonator in revue.[26] She and her husband Jack Hulbert were friends of Michael Balcon, and they both appeared in a range of Gaumont-British comedies. Courtneidge's style was robust, and her body language foursquare. In *Soldiers of the King* (Maurice Elvey, 1932) she doffs and assumes the appearance of manliness with aplomb, and makes it seem an artificial disguise. Her transgressive brio is even more evident in *Me and Marlborough* (Victor Saville, 1935). The scenario by Marjorie Gaffney required Courtneidge to masquerade as a soldier. Even in female dress Courtneidge is a better man than most; legs akimbo, she halloos loud, and bewails her unconsummated marriage. She persuades Marlborough to dress as a woman and tells her husband that 'I've enough intelligence for both of us'.[27] Yet the editing makes her operate as the mouthpiece of authority. In a prolonged dissolve, she appears superimposed over images of the army and weaponry at the end of the film.

Courtneidge was very popular, coming second as favourite British film star to Gracie Fields in 1933. But her popularity was short-lived, and by 1937 she had slipped to thirty-first place.[28] Fields had a much longer pedigree in the popularity charts. We might tentatively assign Fields to the 'mannish' group, not because she aspired to power in any literal way in her films, but because her persona in them was so resolutely desexualised. Jeffrey Richards has rightly suggested that 'during the 1930s Gracie was able to embody simultaneously Rochdale, Lancashire, Britain, the Empire, women and the people at large'.[29] But one might add that she could only embody women with workaday looks, who show their mettle through their talent rather than their dress sense. Fields could only attain broad symbolic status because she lacked glamour. Instead, she had vigour and persistence. Glamour would have located her in an internationalist and de-classed context.

Madcap girls

A more combative cluster was the 'madcap girls'. This was an ensemble of small, feisty females who were social parvenus. Their role is to bring about a minor perturbation, and then to encourage the audience to turn from the textual maelstrom to still waters. Evelyn Dall, for example, was an American vaudeville star who appeared in a range of musicals. Her persona was abrasive, and her diminutive height was used to good effect.[30] Mary Morris was a 'madcap' too. Openly lesbian in her private life and in her acting style, Morris played a reform school inmate in *Prison Without Bars* (Brian Desmond Hurst, 1938) and the Nazi chauffeuse in *The Spy in Black* (Michael Powell, 1939). In these and later roles, Morris gave the impression of a tiny whirlwind, liable to change or destroy at will.[31]

The most important 'madcap' was Jessie Matthews, whose musicals were a vital part of Michael Balcon's production policy at Gaumont-British.

Matthews had been successful in Cochran's stage revues, but became a much bigger star with her film roles. She had humble origins, which she disguised with elocutionary zeal. Matthews' accent was both a social asset and a coping mechanism: 'At high-class dinner parties ... I was petrified of making mistakes. I used to sit and listen, making mental notes, learning all the time, learning how to produce words, how to use the English language properly.'[32] This insecurity underpins all Matthews' performances and fuels their energies and ambiguities.

Physically, Matthews was extraordinarily talented: lissom, sinuous and uncannily alert, she could shift from high kicks to a sashaying, shimmering glide. Matthews owed much to the lessons and choreography of the great black dancer, Buddy Bradley. But her physical prowess (and her management of it) was her own. Matthews exhibited a wilful persona, acutely at issue with duty. In *The Good Companions* (Victor Saville, 1933), her vigorous performance rescues what would otherwise be a sexually conservative film, with her character Susie Dean suggesting that the will for happiness motivates women as well as men.

Matthews' persona works by alluding to important anxieties and then resolving them. The optimism of her performance encourages audiences to

Plate 12   'Madcap girl' as box-office hit: Jessie Matthews demonstrates her high-kicking potential in *Evergreen* (Victor Saville, 1934).

feel that the social and sexual system is flexible enough for any eventuality. In *Evergreen* (Victor Saville, 1934), for example, Matthews has to masquerade as her mother, and pretends that her boyfriend is her son; her manner deals superbly with embarrassment. *First a Girl* (Victor Saville, 1935) also concerns masquerade, this time between the sexes rather than generations. Matthews has to assume the part of a drag artist, and is a woman playing a man playing a woman. However, her body language evokes a passionate femininity. In one scene, her beloved still thinks she is a man. Lying supine on the sand in a clinging swimsuit, Matthews' expression changes utterly. It glows with erotic power, and there can no longer be any doubt as to which gender she is. But Matthews specialised in social masquerades as well. In *It's Love Again* (Victor Saville, 1936), she impersonates the ideal woman who can be East and West, virginal and loose, huntress and hunted. Matthews' persona was classless, and this holds good for all the 'madcaps', who have a destabilising effect on the narratives of their films. By contrast, larger, older and more combative women had quite a different textual function.

Difficult dowagers

There was a group of older actresses, such as Grace Edwin, Marie Lohr, Mary Brough and Norma Varden, whose wryness could transform the most unpromising material. The 'difficult dowagers' are unruly women who have transgressed the boundaries of modesty and respectability. They are freed from the time-consuming pursuit of sexual desire. Significantly, their textual spread is not confined to one class, but it is confined to the genre of comedy. These ladies of misrule usher in a short saturnalia, in which anarchy and bad behaviour are the just rewards for a long life of conformity.

Varden was the most inventive of the dowagers. She was trained as a Shakespearean actress, but found her comic form when she appeared in the Ben Travers farces at the Aldwych Theatre. Varden turned in superlative performances in two Travers films, *Turkey Time* (Tom Walls, 1933) and *Foreign Affaires* (Tom Walls, 1935). She also starred in two Will Hay films, *Boys Will Be Boys* (William Beaudine, 1935) and *Windbag the Sailor* (William Beaudine, 1936).[33] In all these roles Varden deployed her majestic size to full effect. Tall, deep-breasted and moving like an ocean liner, she delivered withering admonishments to hapless males. Varden's phrasing and pattern of gaze were very precisely orchestrated. No one understood the art of deprecation better than she; with a downward glance and a small *moue*, she could administer a universe of pain. Varden's roles were all middle class, but there were other 'difficult dowagers' who played working-class characters. Mary Brough, for example, played comic landladies full of rage, righteousness and self-determination. Like Yvonne Arnaud, she aspired to be a Marie Dressler type, and practised looking like 'a paper bag, blown up and ready to burst'.[34]

Plate 13   Norma Varden, the most inventive of the 'difficult dowagers', with Tom
Walls and Ralph Lynn in *Turkey Time* (Tom Walls, 1933): 'No-one
understood the art of deprecation better than she'.

We cannot discuss older, unruly females without dealing with the Old
Mother Riley films. The first of the cycle was *Old Mother Riley* (Oswald
Mitchell, 1937), and the series continued until the early 1950s. In all the
films, the heroine is uninhibited in her pursuit of self-expression. But
Mother is played by a man, Arthur Lucan, and 'her' daughter Kitty is played
by Lucan's wife, Kitty MacShane. (In one sense, of course, the whole act can
be construed as a loud bellow of marital pain.) The Old Mother Riley films
had their roots deep in vaudeville, where the tradition of drag was well
assimilated. Cross-dressing encourages the audience to play a kind of sexual
hide-and-seek. But what you think might be there is not; what *is* there is
not what you expect. Old Mother Riley plays this game with vigour. The
most interesting example is a filmed extract from Lucan's act in a revue,
Stars on Parade (Oswald Mitchell, 1936). Mother waits up as usual for the
erring daughter; she disrobes for bed, and in a grotesque parody of the dance
of the seven veils, seven petticoats are removed, four vests, and a corset.
Finally the awful truth is revealed: the flat chest, the scrawny arms, the
desexualising effects of age. What gives Mother her insane energy is that
time has made her like a man. The fact that 'she' *is* a man deliberately
muddies the issue.

The 'difficult dowagers' were the most transgressive of all the clusters of female film types. Their assumption of masculine behaviour is not threatening, because the comic mode defuses it. The terrors elicited by their large or ageing bodies are safely neutralised by comedy. In general, though, the other female film clusters in the 1930s tended not to be confined to one genre. Certainly each of the groups comes from a range of production companies. It looks as though actresses' creative freedoms varied according to the degree of hands-on control exacted on the studio floor, and the shooting speed or economy of the film. The smaller and cheaper the outfit, the more there was room for performative manoeuvre. If the director was fairly liberal (as in the case of Victor Saville) or the producer was very busy (as with Michael Balcon), then the controls were not so intractable and some of the social complexities of the film 'cluster' could emerge.

There remains the case of Anna Neagle, the one 1930s star who fits into no category at all. Or all of them. She poses acute interpretative problems, which have to do with conflicting agendas of artistic control. We cannot ascribe the variety of Neagle's roles to her acting ability, since on the technical level they are all the same. The same mannerisms inhabit them all: the infrequent blink rate, the measured uninflected tones. Neagle's movements are curiously uncoordinated; they are like building blocks wedged together without cement. Her manner is consistent, but the social meaning inscribed into it is inconsequential.

Neagle's career was utterly dependent on Herbert Wilcox, who was both uxorious and domineering. As her director, producer and husband, he had massive control over her performances. There was little space left for her in which to make her own mark. It is tempting therefore to interpret Neagle as Wilcox's cipher. For actresses to have social or cultural meaning, a degree of autonomy is necessary; or if not autonomy, then some small gaps or interstices through which they can slip to evade the controls of script or studio. Such were the dispositions of power in the Neagle/Wilcox films that there were no gaps at all. He is her author, and the representations of womanliness in the films are solely his.

Such a firm degree of individual control over the filming process permits the emergence of a Wilcoxian female type that is presented as outside historical and social forces. On the other hand, the 'madcaps', 'wholesome sensible girls' and the other clusters emerge as cultural phenomena because of the conflicts and contradictions within the production process. The fluidity and flexibility of the clusters is a testament to the richness of the film culture of the period.

NOTES

1   J. Richards, 'From Christianity to paganism: The new middle ages and the values of "medieval masculinity"', *Cultural Values*, April 1999, vol. 3, no. 2. A. Spicer, *Typical Men: Masculinity in British Cinema*, London, I.B. Tauris,

forthcoming. See also R. Samuel, 'Introduction: The figures of national myth', in R. Samuel (ed.) *National Fictions*, London, Routledge 1989.

2 Roye, *Nude Ego*, London, Hutchinson, 1955, pp. 65–6.

3 C. Bouchier, *Shooting Star: The Last of the Silent Film Stars*, London, Atlantis, 1996, p. 67.

4 See C. Nesbitt, *A Little Love and Good Company*, London, Faber, 1975. Gertrude Lawrence worked on stage while filming *Rembrandt*: see her *A Star Danced*, London, W.H. Allen, 1954, p. 197. Binnie Barnes was moonlighting as well: see interview in *Films in Review*, May 1990, p. 281.

5 E. Laye, *Boo, To My Friends*, London, Hurst and Blackett, 1958, p. 93.

6 G. Fields, *Sing As We Go*, London, Frederick Muller, 1960, p. 90.

7 Barnes interview, op. cit., pp. 281–2.

8 Interview with Arnaud in *Film Weekly*, 8 March 1933, p. 11. See also *Picturegoer*, 20 April 1945, p. 10.

9 See T. Bergfelder, 'Negotiating exoticism: Hollywood, film Europe and the reception of Anna May Wong', in A. Higson and R. Maltby (eds) *Film Europe and Film America: Cinema, Commerce and Cultural Exchange, 1920–1939*, Exeter, University of Exeter Press, 1999, pp. 302–24.

10 C. Horn, *Verliebt in die Liebe*, Berlin, Herbig, 1985, pp. 169, 177.

11 C. Habichon, *Lilian Harvey*, Berlin, Hande und Spoener, 1990, p. 49.

12 For material on Annabella, see *Classic Images*, November 1996, p. 56. For a 1936 interview with Annabella, see *Picturegoer*, 25 July 1936, p. 10: for a 1983 interview, see *Films and Filming*, October 1983, pp. 25–8.

13 She went to great pains to remove Indian traces from her accent; see C. Higham and R. Moseley, *Merle: A Biography of Merle Oberon*, Sevenoaks, New English Library, 1983, p. 27.

14 Bouchier, op. cit., p. 73.

15 Ibid., p. 84.

16 *Evening Standard*, 7 October 1936.

17 See S. Harper, 'Thinking forward and up: the British films of Conrad Veidt', in J. Richards (ed.) *The Unknown 1930s: An Alternative History of British Cinema 1929–39*, London, I.B. Tauris, 1998, pp. 121–38.

18 C.B. Cochran, *Cock-A-Doodle-Do*, London, Dent, 1941, pp. 124–36.

19 S. Churchill, *Keep On Dancing*, London, Weidenfeld, 1981.

20 F. Desmond, *Florence Desmond By Herself*, London, Harrap, 1953, pp. 72–3.

21 G. Lawrence, *A Star Danced*, London, W.H. Allen, 1954, pp. 194–5.

22 For interviews with Barnes, see *Picturegoer*, 3 June 1933, p. 11; and 2 December 1933, p. 11.

23 See *Film Weekly*, 23 March 1934, p. 7.

24 Quoted in D. Spoto, *The Dark Side of Genius: The Life of Alfred Hitchcock*, London, Plexus, 1994, p. 153.

25 *Film Weekly*, 2 January 1937, p. 8.

26 C. Courtneidge, *Cicely*, London, Hutchinson, 1953, p. 77.

27 See interview with Courtneidge in *Film Weekly*, 11 January 1935, p. 11.

28 Bernstein Polls of 1933 and 1937.

29 J. Richards, *Films and British National Identity: From Dickens to Dad's Army*, Manchester, Manchester University Press, 1997, p. 265.

30 L. Levy, *Music For the Movies*, London, Sampson, Low and Marston, 1948, pp. 158–9.

31 S. Bourne, *Brief Encounters: Gays and Lesbians in British Cinema*, London, Cassell, 1996, pp. 48–51.

32 J. Matthews and M. Burgess, *Over My Shoulder: An Autobiography*, London, W.H. Allen, 1974, p. 5.
33 See *Film Fan Monthly*, March 1975.
34 See interview with Brough in *Film Pictorial*, 14 October 1933, p. 6.

10

OUTSIDERS IN ENGLAND

The films of the Associated British Picture Corporation, 1949–1958

Vincent Porter

The vertically integrated Associated British Picture Corporation (ABPC) was one of the two most powerful organisations in the British film industry from the beginning of the sound period until the 1970s. When its founder John Maxwell died in 1940, Warner Bros became a major shareholder, buying first 25 per cent and later a further 12.5 per cent of the company's shares. Two of the company's directors were appointed by Warners and two by the Maxwell estate, one of whom was Robert Clark. From 1947, Clark took charge of the company's new Elstree studios, and between 1949 and 1958 he was in charge of production at Elstree. Over a period of ten years, Clark produced or co-financed some eight films a year which were designed to fulfil the quota of British films for the company's chain of ABC cinemas. The relative stability of the production system during these years makes for a valuable, self-contained case study of that process.

The aim of the ABPC board of directors was to make money for shareholders, and to this end it insisted that production budgets were kept as low as possible. A project as expensive as *The Dam Busters* (Michael Anderson, 1955) was only approved because of Clark's personal commitment, although it then went on to become one of the company's most successful films.[1] Generally, though, Clark and his accounts staff imposed a tight financial regime on the business of turning British stories into British films. Everything was costed down to the last penny, and printed at the bottom of all the studio's memoranda sheets were the admonitory words, *'No Verbal Orders to be Given or Accepted'*. Furthermore, the heavily bureaucratic managerial regime and the clear division of creative labour meant that the contributions of different production departments often failed to sustain each other. 'It was a dreadful place,' Richard Attenborough recalled, 'It created nothing in terms of a feeling of commitment.'[2] Given their production context, it is perhaps unsurprising that few of the company's films commanded either critical approval or box-office success.

Faced with the evidence of this production system, it is difficult to accept the conventional wisdom that it is the director who has creative control over a film. Authorship in such a tightly controlled environment might more usefully be attributed to the studio as a whole, or to those who carefully managed it. This can be demonstrated by a particular leitmotif that recurs across a great many of ABPC's films made in the 1950s, regardless of who was directing them. As I shall show, the motif of the outsider or the visiting stranger to England seems to owe more to the influence of Clark's scenario editor, the German émigré Frederick Gotfurt, than to the inclinations of individual directors or even scriptwriters.

Managing production

Clark was comparatively inexperienced when he took charge at Elstree. 'He's smart but doesn't know much about making pictures,' Jack Warner told Vincent Sherman when he sent him to Elstree to direct *The Hasty Heart* (1949).[3] Clark appointed four key people to help him manage his production programme. His scenario editor and head of the script department was Frederick Gotfurt, a theatre critic, playwright and occasional scriptwriter. Walter Mycroft, previously Maxwell's head of production, was his chief scenario advisor. Culturally and politically, Gotfurt and Mycroft were poles apart. Gotfurt was a German-Jewish émigré, ideologically committed to the realist mode, whereas Mycroft was a Putney Conservative who had held extreme right-wing views before the war.

In the position of casting director, Clark appointed Robert Lennard, who built a new roster of studio contract artistes. Wherever the story allowed, Lennard tried to pair the contract artistes with American stars in order to build their profile in the US market.[4] Finally, Clark hired Louis Levy as his musical director. All four appointments played key roles in shaping the films that ABPC produced or co-financed.

Clark's previous production experience had mainly been in buying stories as cheaply as possible for John Maxwell, a policy he continued during the 1950s. For him, a story only had what he termed 'a public value' if it had successfully been produced as a play or published as a book. Furthermore, the author would not fully realise that value until the story had been produced as a film.[5] He was singularly suspicious of stories that were specially written for the screen. Indeed, only two of the twenty-one films produced by the studio during the 1950s came from original stories.[6] Clark also had to be able to marry a star to the story and to be sure that its plot had no recognisable resemblance to any developments in world affairs that might jeopardise its commercial success. Finally, of course, the film had to satisfy public taste. Search and sift was his motto.[7]

Relations with the National Film Finance Corporation

Clark originally intended to finance and produce all ABPC pictures in-house and in 1949 he announced a £2 million production investment.[8] However, the following year he adeptly modified his approach in order to exploit the arrival of the National Film Finance Corporation (NFFC) and the British Film Production Fund (the Eady Fund).

During the 1950s, ABPC financed, or co-financed, three types of production, over which Clark exercised varying degrees of creative control. He had total control over ABPC productions, but his powers were more limited on projects that were co-financed by the NFFC. Although financially less risky, and although Clark could insist that the film was shot at Elstree, an NFFC loan commitment gave the producer a degree of creative autonomy over the choice of the story, the screenwriter and the director.[9] The third type of investment was for Clark simply to sign a distribution deal for an independent British project. For a comparatively small financial outlay, he could bring a picture to Elstree studios and pick up the UK distribution revenues.

Table 1 Films distributed by Associated British Pathé, 1950–1959

Year	Total	First features			Second features			Shorts
		ABPC Production	NFFC Loan	Other	ABPC Production	NFFC Loan	Other	
1950	10	6	2	1	–	–	1	
1951	5	3	2	–	–	–	–	
1952	11	1	7	1	–	2	–	
1953	6	4	–	–	1	1	–	
1954	10	–	3	3	–	2	2	
1955	4	1	2	–	–	1	–	
1956	8	–	3	4	–	–	1	
1957	12	2	3	–	1	1	2	3
1958	9	3	3	2	1	–	–	
1959	6	1	3	1	1	–	–	
Total	81	21	28	12	4	7	6	3

Source: Denis Gifford, *British National Film Catalogue* and *NFFC Annual Reports*.

As can be seen from Table 1, ABPC only produced about a third of the first and second features that it distributed during the 1950s. It co-financed nearly half with the NFFC, while the remainder were merely finance and distribution deals with independent producers. Although nearly all the films were shot at Elstree, each category exhibits marked differences in the manner in which it tells British stories and deploys British backgrounds. In general, the 'Britishness' of the films made with independent producers varied widely, while the stories of those co-financed with the NFFC are generally marked by the personality of their producer, be it Marcel Hellman, Maxwell Setton, Herbert Wilcox or Mario Zampi.

There are strong similarities, however, between the films produced by Victor Skutetsky and those produced in-house. For Victor Skutetsky was independent in name only. Originally an ABPC staff producer, he made three films for ABPC through his company, Marble Arch: *Father's Doing Fine* (Henry Cass, 1952), *The Yellow Balloon* (J. Lee Thompson, 1952) and *It's Great to Be Young* (Cyril Frankel, 1956). He was also closely associated with Frederick Gotfurt. They were fellow émigrés from Berlin and Skutetsky had previously employed Gotfurt as his scriptwriter on two ABPC films: *It Happened One Sunday* (Karel Lamac, 1943) and *Temptation Harbour* (Lance Comfort, 1947). Furthermore, as Skutetsky normally used ABPC staff writers and directors on his Marble Arch films, they share similar characteristics to ABPC's own productions.

Gotfurt the dramaturg

As chief scenario editor, Frederick Gotfurt became the dramaturgical gate-keeper to ABPC's in-house productions, advising Clark on which stories to buy. Gotfurt knew how to restructure a scenario in order to modify an audience's perception of the tale being told. In 1942, for instance, he co-scripted a satirical revue *Mr. Gulliver Goes To School*, for the *Freier Deutscher Kulturbund*, an anti-fascist centre for German refugees living in London. The story opens conventionally enough in 1704, but Swift's Gulliver becomes a time-traveller who has just returned from 1942 Germany to report on the internal opposition to Hitler.[10] At ABPC, Gotfurt and Skutetsky restructured Simenon's novella *Affairs of Destiny*, calling the film *Temptation Harbour* and switching its locale from Dieppe to Newhaven, thus setting it literally on the edge of Britain.

Once in place at ABPC, Gotfurt set about building the scenario department into a vast bureaucratic machine for reading and evaluating literary properties. By 1955, his reader, Kathleen Leaver, was responsible for monitoring and making reports on a wide range of material. She had to read and summarise six or seven books a week and identify which should be acquired.[11] By the end of the 1950s, Gotfurt was casting his net so widely that he had to employ others to assess new plays.[12]

The stories that ABPC bought were then turned into scenarios that were stored and filed, although only one in every four or five made it to the studio floor.[13] Indeed, Gotfurt seemed to have great difficulty in choosing appropriate subjects for studio projects. Not one of the various scripts and storylines that he offered Richard Todd when he returned from the Oscar ceremonies in 1950 appealed to Todd, even though he spent a month or two discussing them.[14] It was the same for Audrey Hepburn. Although Clark wanted her to fulfil her contractual obligations to star in an ABPC production, the only projects that Gotfurt could come up with were totally unsuitable: a life story of Gracie Fields, a Graham Greene comedy and a romantic drama.[15] In 1955, four of the five scripts that Gotfurt sent Cyril Frankel to read were so bad that he threw them aside. The only one that caught his imagination was a scenario by Ted Willis, which ultimately became *It's Great to Be Young*.[16]

Gotfurt's weakness lay in his poor ear for English dialogue. Richard Todd thought his fractured English so weak that he seriously doubted Gotfurt's ability to assess the qualities of the dialogue in any script.[17] Gotfurt therefore relied heavily either on the dialogue in the original novel or play, or on that contributed by ABPC staff writers. In *Temptation Harbour*, for instance, he and Skutetsky relied on Rodney Ackland's dialogue, although the fact that they gave the lines that Ackland had written for Mabel (Kathleen Harrison) to Camelia (Simone Simon) in the final scene demonstrated a disregard for character and vernacular.[18] On *The Dam Busters* and *Ice Cold in Alex* (J. Lee Thompson, 1958; US title, *Desert Attack*), Walter Mycroft did important work.[19]

Outsiders and insiders

Although Gotfurt's dramaturgical skill in restructuring a cheap story probably led Clark to appoint him as his scenario editor, there were other things that he and Gotfurt had in common. Both saw the film industry as a business, and each in his own way was an outsider to English life and English institutions. Indeed, Gotfurt had been an outsider in psychological terms, long before he came to Britain. In 1921, he defended Dostoevsky because his mental landscape was similar to his own: that of a visitor walking through the wet streets of a foreign city.[20] He rejected the expressionism of Weimar Germany as the sickness of the age and turned instead to the realism of Ibsen and Strindberg.[21] But he recuperated Hoffmann, as a realist in a higher sense, arguing that he recognised unreality as part of the way in which the individual experiences the real world.[22]

The theme of the visiting stranger or the outsider to society recurs as a leitmotif in several ABPC films of the early 1950s for which Gotfurt was scenario editor. This serves to indicate the degree of editorial control he was able to exert over the authorship of the company's films. In *Last Holiday*

(Henry Cass, 1950) for instance, George Bird (Alec Guinness) is mistakenly informed by his doctor that he has only a few weeks to live. Deciding to enjoy his last few weeks on earth, he checks into an expensive hotel, where he observes the foibles of the English middle class, persuading them to fend for themselves when the hotel staff go on strike.

The Franchise Affair (Lawrence Huntington, 1951) is set in the middle England town of Melford. Robert Blair (Michael Denison) a solicitor, agrees to act for two newcomers to the town, Marjorie Sharpe (Dulcie Gray) and her mother (Marjorie Fielding), when a Scotland Yard detective intends to arrest them for allegedly kidnapping a local girl, Beth Kane (Ann Stephens). The two outsiders live in a house that is symbolically called 'The Franchise'. Needless to say, once Blair re-interviews Kane's relatives and friends, the apparently innocent kidnapped girl turns out to be a liar. Despite Blair's evidence, the citizens of Melford are not prepared to accept the outsiders' version of events until Blair provides incontrovertible proof that Marjorie Sharpe and her mother have been telling the truth all along.

Clare (Margaret Johnston), the heroine of *Portrait of Clare* (Lance Comfort, 1950), is an emotional outsider to the social order of Edwardian England, who looks back on a life of emotional aridity. Having lost her first husband, she compliantly marries the family solicitor, who insists on sending her son to boarding school, leaving Clare emotionally starved and thoroughly alienated from English social life. Although attracted by a barrister, social convention demands that she has to remain emotionally unfulfilled for the remainder of her days.

Although the origins of these films were markedly different – an original script by J.B. Priestley and novels by Josephine Tey and Francis Brett Young – the centre of the drama always concerns the troubled relationship between an outsider (two in *The Franchise Affair*) and English society. The production history of *The Dam Busters* is also revealing in this respect.

Although Gotfurt originally acquired the screen rights to Paul Brickhill's book as a vehicle for Richard Todd,[23] he lost control of the film during production. Initially, Barnes Wallis (Michael Redgrave) was more of an outsider to RAF High Command than he appears in the final film. When ABPC circulated its final screenplay to those members of the RAF or their relatives who were still alive, Air Marshall Sir Arthur Harris objected to being portrayed as 'an irascible unapproachable moron' who 'had time to discuss cricket and private affairs but no time for "inventors" of Wallis' calibre'.[24] Producer William Whittaker therefore asked Walter Mycroft to rewrite a key scene.[25] In the final film, Mycroft's rewrite conveys the impression that Harris and the RAF High Command immediately welcomed Wallis' plan for a bouncing bomb, and did not consider him an eccentric outsider.

The leitmotif of the outsider in English society extended into the films produced by Victor Skutetsky, for which Gotfurt was also scenario editor.

They regularly used a stranger to take a tough and often critical look at the impact of English institutions on the ordinary individual. The perceptions of these institutions expressed by these particular individuals were often at odds with received views of contemporary English life. In *The Yellow Balloon*, the young Frankie (Andrew Ray) (misguidedly) mistrusts the police. In *The Weak and the Wicked* (J. Lee Thompson, 1954), middle-class gambler Jean Raymond (Glynis Johns) has to experience the emotional degradation of a year in gaol. In *It's Great to Be Young*, the equable and popular music master Mr Dingle (John Mills) cannot tolerate the authoritarian regime of head-master Mr Frome (Cecil Parker). In *No Time for Tears* (Cyril Frankel, 1957), trainee nurse Margaret (Sylvia Syms), who is a new entrant to the hospital, has to learn from the experienced and emotionally disciplined Sister Birch (Flora Robson) that there is no place for spontaneous affection in a profes-sional children's nurse.

The opposition between the individual and society reaches its apogee in *Yield to the Night* (J. Lee Thompson, 1956; US title, *Blonde Sinner*), which starred Diana Dors as convicted murderess Mary Hilton. Indeed, the emotional sufferings of Hilton in her condemned cell were so harrowing that the censor originally wanted to ban the whole film, although he was later persuaded to give it an X certificate.[26] Although adapted from an original story by Joan Henry, the film fitted in with Gotfurt's general belief in the troubled relationship between the individual and society, a view that shaped so many ABPC dramas before they reached the studio floor.

The role of the director

The freedom of the film director at ABPC was therefore often tightly circumscribed, as management normally took the key creative decisions on scripting and casting. Sometimes the director was merely required to transfer other people's characters and dialogue onto film. In order to circum-vent this division of labour, an astute director, such as J. Lee Thompson, would also involve himself in writing the scenario.

Gotfurt was sometimes accused of exercising 'a sort of kid glove dictator-ship'.[27] As scenario editor, he always had numerous working sessions with the creative triumvirate of writer, director and producer. This enabled him 'to ensure that nothing reached the studio floor unless he was satisfied that it was the best possible job they could all achieve'. For him, the director, 'like an army commander in the field, had plenary powers once he was on the studio floor', but 'the best directors never extended this power to imposing important changes of story line, or even dialogue'.[28] As far as Gotfurt was concerned, 'it is the screenplay that tells the story, and it is the director who interprets it to the actors and through them to the public'.[29]

Gotfurt's exploitation of the division of creative labour at Elstree and his use of a military metaphor to describe the director's creative role are revealing. They pay no regard to the contributions that lighting, camera movement, point of view or narrative pace can contribute to the interpretation of the screenplay. More important, they ignore the aesthetic challenges faced by a director in telling a tale that articulates the ambiguities of the dialectical relationships between the outsider and the community, or the different ways in which an individual and the socially dominant group may perceive the same world.

ABPC's regular directors were a mixed bunch. Henry Cass demonstrated little directorial flair in his films. *No Place for Jennifer* (1949) suffered from 'stilted dialogue, uninspired direction and an overdose of uninspired psychotherapy', while in *The Last Holiday* 'the shortcomings of the script [were] emphasised and its values minimised' by Cass's slow and unimaginative direction.[30]

Gilbert Gunn initially expressed an interest in folksy realism. 'The movies haven't said nearly enough about the British people ... I want to make good entertaining movies that spotlight the ordinary simple folk of this country.'[31] After the failure of *The Good Beginning* (1953), he turned to comedy. *My Wife's Family* (1956), *Girls at Sea* (1958) and *Operation Bullshine* (1959) all sought to make audiences laugh at situations of sexual misunderstanding. But the critics were not impressed. *Girls at Sea* laboriously hammered home comic clichés and was shot 'as if to emphasise its stage origins against a studio background of stationary clouds'.[32] *Operation Bullshine* was a stumbling production that 'never successfully resolves the problem of whether it is a comedy of errors or a barrack-room farce'.[33]

Cyril Frankel, who came to ABPC from Group 3, directed four ABPC films: *It's Great to Be Young* (1956), *No Time for Tears* (1957), *She Didn't Say No!* (1958) and *Alive and Kicking* (1959). Although he tried to turn Ted Willis' script for *It's Great to Be Young* into 'a joyous exuberant film',[34] his direction was so weak that Raymond Durgnat suggested Willis was the film's true *auteur*.[35] Casting director Robert Lennard's choice of Anna Neagle as the star of *No Time for Tears* was as safe and reliable as his casting of John Mills in Frankel's previous film. If Frankel's *mise-en-scène* in *No Time for Tears* was more convincing, it was probably because he worked closely with camera operator Norman Warwick, whom he found 'very helpful'.[36]

Like Gunn, Frankel turned to comedy. His next two films had an Irish theme and each became progressively more whimsical. The direction of *She Didn't Say No!*, in which the illegitimate children of Irishwoman Bridget Monahan (Eileen Herlie) are all sired by different fathers, was 'heavily unsubtle and the playing coyly emphatic'.[37] As for *Alive and Kicking*, which had a preposterous plot in which three idiosyncratic old women escape from an old people's home, get picked up by a Russian trawler and deposited on a remote Irish island, Frankel chose to 'exploit the implicit archness of the idea at the expense of its genuine comic possibilities'.[38] The picture sank without trace, as did Frankel's career at ABPC.

Michael Anderson directed five ABPC films, four of them photographed by Erwin Hillier. *Will Any Gentleman?* (1953), a comedy starring George Cole, was quickly followed by another second feature, *The House of The Arrow* (1954) which Edward Dryhurst had adapted from ABPC's 1940 version at Clark's behest.[39] Anderson's first concern was whether the script had a good story. 'It's nine-tenths of making a picture … spectacle is subsidiary to story. Storyline is a hobby horse that can ride a director – but it's a reliable steed really.'[40] The nearer the story was to everyday life, the better Anderson liked it. When Clark offered him *The Dam Busters*, Anderson paid meticulous attention to authentic historical detail. He was particularly attracted by the sense of realism he was able to achieve from being close to a stirring historical event, taking great care to get the people in each plane to look as similar as possible to those who took part in the actual raid.[41]

Anderson was especially proud of the silent scenes of the men's faces as they prepare to take off for the raid on the Möhne and Eder dams. He filmed them in one continuous take in order to set the mood of the people about to embark on a dangerous mission.[42] He particularly strove for authenticity from a *British* perspective; and he was proud that *The Dam Busters* was the first war picture which took its audiences with the pilots on their bombing

Plate 14   Turning British stories into British films: *The Dam Busters* (Michael Anderson, 1955) was one of the few big budget films in ABPC's otherwise tight financial regime.

missions, showing them no more than the bombers and the pilots saw. The explosions on the Möhne and Eder dams were filmed in high-angle long shot and barely showed the impact of the raids on the Germans.[43] Cinematographer Erwin Hillier produced some powerful chiaroscuro day-for-night images of 617 squadron and shot some spectacular footage from the gun turret of a Wellington bomber. According to Hillier, Anderson was superb at handling actors and saved the studio 30 per cent of its costs by not wasting footage.[44]

The most prolific ABPC director during the 1950s was J. Lee Thompson. A teenage playwright, he returned after war service to script *For Them That Trespass* (Alberto Cavalcanti, 1949) and *No Place For Jennifer* (Henry Cass, 1949). He subsequently directed and co-scripted nine films for ABPC. His first, *Murder Without Crime* (1950), a second feature that he adapted from his own stage play, is an old-fashioned melodrama of apparently accidental murder and the fortuitous death of the villain, which he filmed with pretentious camera angles, a cynical American commentator and a crashing musical score by Philip Green.

For *The Yellow Balloon*, Thompson gathered around him the technicians who would become his regular collaborators: cameraman Gilbert Taylor, art director Robert Jones and editor Richard Best. Thompson's direction reinforces the tensions in Anne Burnaby's script between the safe and respectable working-class home of the innocent and gullible Frankie Palmer (Andrew Ray) and his disturbed view of the dangerous world outside. Frankie falls for the wiles of a blackmailer who seeks to use him in a robbery, by persuading Frankie that the police think he is responsible for murdering his friend, whom he had witnessed being accidentally killed. Thompson's *mise-en-scène* for the sequence in which Frankie is pursued by the blackmailer through the deserted passages of a disused underground station was so powerful that the censor gave the film an X certificate, as he was concerned to prevent it from disturbing children.[45]

In *The Weak and the Wicked* (1954), adapted from Joan Henry's autobiographical novel, *Who Die in Gaol*, Jean Raymond (Glynis Johns) is convicted for a gambling debt and has to spend a year in prison. Co-starring John Gregson and featuring Jane Hylton and Diana Dors, the film convincingly conveys the shock of the claustrophobic prison system to Raymond's middle-class sensibility. The film did well at the box office, although most critics found it overly melodramatic.

By his own admission, Thompson sometimes accepted scripts simply because he loved the feel of the cables under his feet and the buzz of working with actors on the set.[46] *For Better, For Worse* (1954; US title, *Cocktails in the Kitchen*) and two comedies he shot at Pinewood, *As Long As They're Happy* (1955) and *An Alligator Named Daisy* (1955), followed in quick succession. The screenplay of his next ABPC film, *Yield to the Night*, won an award at the Cannes Film Festival. It is arguably Thompson's most powerful piece of film-making. His subtle camera movements in Mary Hinton's cell and the mundane routine of everyday prison life, intercut with flashbacks to her earlier life outside, heighten the claustrophobic impact of this anti-capital punishment film. Once again, Thompson uses his moving camera to get to the emotional root of his scenes, often changing the point of view of the audience from the objective to the subjective or vice-versa. Although the censor's insistence on an X certificate limited the film's commercial success, its two showings at the House of Commons probably made a substantial contribution to the campaign to abolish the death penalty in Britain.

Thompson next agreed to make *The Good Companions* (1956), out of loyalty to Robert Clark.[47] But his stimulating *mise-en-scène* and rhetorical tracking shots could not save an out-of-date story from being a box-office flop. He then set up his own production company with producer Frank Godwin and writer Ted Willis. They made two films for ABPC: *Woman in a Dressing Gown* (1957) and *No Trees in the Street* (1959). The combination of Willis' domestic realism and Thompson's edgy, claustrophobic *mise-en-scène* for *Woman in a Dressing Gown*, won the film four awards at the Berlin Film Festival, including the Golden Globe as the Best Foreign Language Film.

In between, Thompson also directed *Ice Cold in Alex* (1958). Once again, he carefully planned his camera movements in advance.[48] Significantly, he was mainly interested in the relationship between the South African, Captain Van Der Poel (Anthony Quayle), and the British personnel in the ambulance. He considered it an anti-war film, mainly because of the humanity and camaraderie between the group, even though Van Der Poel turned out to be a Nazi spy.[49]

Beyond the studio floor

Few ABPC directors saw the film after it left the studio floor. The picture still had to be edited and a music score added. Here Louis Levy, Elstree's musical director, took charge. For Levy, music could contribute as much to a film as its story; a film script was a silent canvas to be decorated with sound. But it could also overwhelm the visual and the verbal aspects of the film. Although he recognised that too long a melodic line might distract the attention of the audience, Levy often underlined climaxes with the full power of a symphony orchestra.[50] His use of music often completely undermined the narrative and visual strategies of ABPC films. For one critic writing in the *Monthly Film Bulletin*, 'the sugary American-style songs' in *It's Great to Be Young* struck 'an alien note in such emphatically British surroundings'.[51] Levy also refused to allow Thompson to use contemporary music on *Woman in a Dressing Gown*, insisting on a conventional melodramatic score for this relatively realist film.[52]

The different use of music in *The Dam Busters* and *Ice Cold in Alex* is also instructive. In the former, it was not Levy's work that made the film, but Eric Coates' 'Dam Busters March', which Leighton Lucas rearranged for the rest of the picture, that gave the emotional lift-off to Anderson's scrupulous historical reconstructions.[53] By the time *Ice Cold in Alex* was ready for music, Levy had died, so producer William Whittaker and editor Richard Best were able to adopt a different strategy, using music only where it was absolutely necessary.[54]

The end of an era

Clark's reign as head of production ended in January 1958, although he continued to be a director of ABPC. Managing Director C.J. Latta, a Warner Bros appointee, and Clark's assistant James Wallis took charge of production. Walter Mycroft retired and both Michael Anderson and Thompson left for Hollywood. The company filled Elstree with television productions and restricted its film investments to comedies featuring television stars and the UK distribution rights to independent productions. The following year, ABPC's profits soared and Warner Bros and the other shareholders purred with delight.

The results of Clark's project to make British films from British stories were mixed. In part, this must be put down to the reluctance of the company to spend a penny more than was necessary. But it must also be put down to the manner in which Clark divided the screen-writing and music departments from directing, so that only writer-directors like Thompson were able to develop the subtle *mise-en-scène* necessary to articulate the dialectical relations between the individual and the social order that underpinned Gotfurt's and Skutetsky's scenarios. Even then, Levy's overpowering use of music could smother all the care that a director had put into shooting the visuals. What becomes very clear is that authorship at ABPC in the 1950s was the product of a tightly managed business, dominated by the accountants, the scenario and music departments, in which the films' directors had little opportunity to make their own creative input. If they couldn't collaborate with the permanent managers, they usually turned in indifferent films.

Finally, although ABPC's films were often about England, they were not of it. Most of those that dealt with contemporary reality were slightly dated and were frequently unpopular with younger audiences. The two most popular, *The Dam Busters* and *Ice Cold in Alex* looked back to the Second World War and attracted the occasional cinema-goer back to the cinema.[55] It is perhaps significant that the role of the outsider was heavily repressed in both of them.

NOTES

I would like to thank the BECTU Oral History Project for permission to use their interviews with Richard Best, Edward Dryhurst and Cyril Frankel; Richard Best, Stuart Black, Alan Goatman, Robert Lennard and J. Lee Thompson for talking to me about Robert Clark's regime at ABPC; and Tim Bergfelder and Sue Harper for respectively telling me about and translating Fritz Gottfurcht's pre-war theatre criticism.

1　A. Goatman, interviewed by the author, 5 October 1998.
2　Richard Attenborough, in B. McFarlane (ed.) *An Autobiography of British Cinema*, London, Methuen, 1997, p. 36.
3　V. Sherman, *Studio Affairs: My Life as a Film Director*, Lexington, KY, University Press of Kentucky, 1996, p. 177.
4　Robert Lennard, interviewed by the author, 26 October 1998.
5　N. Lee, *Money For Film Stories*, London, Sir Isaac Pitman and Sons, 1937, p. 191.
6　*The Good Beginning* (Gilbert Gunn, 1953), scripted by Janet Green; and *No Time for Tears* (Cyril Frankel, 1957), scripted by Anne Burnaby.
7　R. Clark, 'Making a picture 1: finding the story', *ABC Film Review*, February 1951, p. 13.
8　N. Hunter, 'A good news story', *Picturegoer*, 10 September 1949, pp. 8–9.
9　J. Lee Thompson, interviewed by the author, 25 January 1999.
10　H. Rorrison, 'German theatre and cabaret in London', in G. Berghaus (ed.) *Theatre and Film in Exile: German Artists in Britain, 1933–1945*, London, Oswald Wolff/Berg, 1989, pp. 47–77.
11　P. Scofield, 'Backroom boys at Elstree Studios: reading for a living, Kathleen Leaver', *ABC Film Review*, July 1955, p. 15.
12　Stuart Black (ex-ABPC scenario department), interviewed by the author, 3 November 1998. Other ABPC readers included Richard Bates and Raymond Durgnat.
13　F. Gotfurt, 'Where credit is due', *Films and Filming*, May 1959, p. 8.
14　R. Todd, *Caught in the Act*, London, Hutchinson, 1986, p. 269.
15　A. Walker, *Audrey: Her Real Story*, London, Weidenfeld and Nicolson, 1994, pp. 88, 100.
16　Cyril Frankel, BECTU Oral History Project, no. 264, side 2; copy held in British Film Institute Library.
17　R. Todd, *In Camera: An Autobiography Continued*, London, Hutchinson, 1989, p. 11.
18　R. Ackland and E. Grant, *The Celluloid Mistress or the Custard Pie of Dr. Caligari*, London, Allan Wingate, 1954, pp. 159–60.
19　C. Sweeting, 'Walter Mycroft 1891–1959', *Journal of the Society of Film and Television Arts*, no. 1, Winter, 1959–60, p. 13.
20　F. Gottfurcht, 'Dostojewski', *Der Feuer = Reiter. Blätter für Dichtung Kritik/ Graphik* (hereafter *DFR*), I Jahrg (1921), p. 26.
21　F. Gottfurcht, 'Die Bühne/Berliner Theater: Von Fulda bis Baudisch Oder Woher Sie Kommen', *DFR*, I Jahrg (1921), p. 85.
22　F. Gottfurcht, 'Hoffmann Der Realist', *DFR*, I Jahrg (1921), p. 225.
23　R. Todd, *In Camera*, *op. cit.* p. 11.
24　RAF Museum, Hendon: Sir Arthur Harris Papers, Arthur T. Harris to W.A. Whittaker, 30 January 1954.
25　Memorandum from Walter Mycroft to Alistair Bell, 26 May 1954 (held in British Film Institute Special Collections). 'Please see me about the Harris scene (bouncing bomb) in above script.', filed in R.C. Sherriff's final revised screenplay for *The Dam Busters* (S. 384).
26　Thompson, loc. cit.
27　Gotfurt, op. cit.
28　Ibid.
29　Ibid.

30 *Monthly Film Bulletin* (hereafter *MFB*), January 1950, vol. 17, no. 193, p. 4; and June 1950, vol. 17, no. 197, pp. 80–1.

31 R. Stephens, 'The good beginning of Gilbert Gunn', *ABC*, July 1953, pp. 12–13.

32 *MFB*, November 1958, vol. 25, no. 298, p. 143.

33 *MFB*, August 1959, vol. 26, no. 307, p. 110.

34 Frankel, loc. cit.

35 R. Durgnat, *A Mirror For England: British Movies from Austerity to Affluence*, London, Faber and Faber, 1970, p. 57.

36 Frankel, loc. cit.

37 *MFB*, July 1958, vol. 25, no. 294, p. 91.

38 *MFB*, February 1959, vol. 26, no. 301, p. 17.

39 Edward Dryhurst, BECTU Oral History Project, no. 36, tape 6, side 11; British Film Institute Library.

40 F. Oughton, 'Bantam-heavyweight director', *Films and Filming*, April 1955, p. 13.

41 R. Jones, 'At Elstree realism was the order of the day for *The Dam Busters*', *ABC Film Review*, August 1954, pp. 28–9.

42 Michael Anderson, interview with Terence Heelas (*The Movies*, job no. 5627/0077, British Film Institute Library), 21 January 1967, pp. 1, 3 and 10.

43 Anderson, loc. cit.

44 Anon, 'He gets the best out of stars', *Picturegoer*, 29 March 1958, p. 14.

45 J. Trevelyan, *What the Censor Saw*, London, Michael Joseph, 1973, p. 82.

46 Thompson, loc. cit.

47 Ibid.

48 Richard Best, BECTU Oral History Project, no. 8, tape 2, side 4; British Film Institute Library.

49 Thompson, loc. cit.

50 O. Langley, 'Backroom boys 2: Musical Director Louis Levy', *ABC Film Review*, June 1955, p. 15.

51 *MFB*, July 1956, vol. 23, no. 27, p. 91.

52 Thompson, loc. cit.

53 Richard Best, interviewed by the author, 6 October 1998.

54 Ibid.

55 For the box-office significance of the occasional cinema-goer, see S. Harper and V. Porter, 'Cinema audience tastes in 1950s Britain', *Journal of Popular British Cinema*, 1999, no. 2, p. 69.

11

BETTY BOX, 'THE LADY IN CHARGE'

Negotiating space for a female producer in postwar cinema

Justine Ashby

If, in the precarious fortunes of the British film industry, success may be measured in terms of staying power, then Betty Box must surely be counted among British cinema's highest achievers. In 1946 Box was appointed head of production at Gainsborough's Islington studios at the remarkable age of twenty-six, thus overcoming the dual obstacles of gender and youth. She produced ten films in two years for Gainsborough (a staggering output given the cramped and dilapidated conditions of the Islington unit),[1] and went on to become one of Rank's most prolific and consistently profitable producers throughout the 1950s and 1960s. Collaborating with director Ralph Thomas on over thirty films, Box produced some of the most popular (if often critically reviled) British films of the postwar era (the *Huggett* series for Gainsborough and the *Doctor* films for Rank, for example). Yet, curiously, Box's substantial contribution to the industry seems to have made little impression on existing historical and critical accounts of British cinema.

What follows is a first step towards a long overdue critical evaluation of Box's work, a project that seems all the more timely and poignant since she died in 1999 while I was researching this chapter. I do not have the space here to do full justice to her rich and complex career.[2] Instead, I will offer two different but interrelated narratives of her work and professional status. First, I will sketch in a history of Box's career at Verity, Gainsborough and Rank and consider the specific conditions that facilitated her unprecedented success as a woman producer in mainstream British film production. Second, I will analyse the diverse and often contradictory ways the popular press and film magazines mediated Box's professional image, since these texts offer some important and historically immediate insights into a postwar Britain coming to terms with new professional roles for women such as Box. While these two narratives draw on different historical and textual sources, they are ultimately coterminous and informed by the same overarching questions.

166

What were the specific historical, cultural and personal conditions that enabled Box, against the odds, to achieve and maintain a position of substantial power in a profession generally barred to women? And, since Box has so seldom received critical attention, how should she be written into British cinema history?

The woman behind the scenes

In *Sixty Voices*, Brian McFarlane astutely introduces his interview with Betty Box by quoting James Mason: 'she sailed with her tide and became the most sensible and hard-working producer in the British industry, where she remained one of its few survivors'.[3] I too can think of no more appropriate way to open a discussion of Box's career since Mason's tribute sums up neatly Box's attitude to her work and the climate in which she operated. As on so many other occasions, Box is characterised as a pragmatist who succeeded by exercising shrewd business sense and diligence rather than artistic ambition. Put bluntly, Box is perhaps best remembered as a conformist who fully understood the industrial, commercial and cultural constraints of the conditions in which she worked, and indeed generally seemed happy to accept them.

Betty Box began her long career in films in 1942, aged 22, when she went to work for her brother, Sydney Box, at Verity Films, the company he had founded in 1940 primarily to make propaganda and information shorts for the war effort. Having begun as the 'general dogsbody',[4] she rapidly progressed to more responsible tasks and became particularly efficient at balancing the company accounts and negotiating contracts. The work was arduous and the hours long; as Box puts it, 'in the years between 1942 and 1945, I did about ten years hard work'.[5] But by the end of her time at Verity, she had virtually taken sole responsibility for the company (Sydney Box had departed to concentrate on feature films), and had maintained a prolific level of production. Above all else, she had earned the respect of a male-dominated industry and forged a reputation, which was to stand her in good stead for the rest of her career, as a safe pair of hands able to adhere to tight budgets and rigid shooting schedules.

At the end of the war, Box transferred her attention from documentary to feature film production. Sydney and his wife Muriel Box (a scriptwriter and producer who became a director in the 1950s) had taken the financially risky step of renting space at Riverside Studios to produce independent feature films. The gamble paid off: the success of *29 Acacia Avenue* (Henry Cass, 1945) and, more emphatically, *The Seventh Veil* (Compton Bennett, 1945), confirmed their status in the industry as film-makers with a golden touch for producing moderately budgeted box-office hits. Betty Box also worked on these productions in a capacity that can loosely be described as 'assistant producer', and though she received screen credits for neither film, the experience must have eased her transition from documentary to feature film production.

When Sydney Box accepted J. Arthur Rank's offer to run Gainsborough Studios in 1946, he appointed Betty as head of production at Islington (Gainsborough's operation was split between Islington and a larger site at Shepherd's Bush). At that point, she had officially produced only one mainstream feature film, *The Upturned Glass* (Lawrence Huntington, 1946), which she co-produced at Riverside with the film's leading man, James Mason. Despite her inexperience, Sydney's decision to appoint her to a key position at Gainsborough seems to have met with surprisingly little resistance. According to Betty, the only note of open dissent came from Michael Balcon, who thought her appointment nepotistic (though she was later to hint that his objection was just as likely to have been motivated by her gender as her family connection).[6]

Whatever euphoria Betty Box felt after landing such a prominent job at Gainsborough must have evaporated rapidly when she realised the enormity of the task that confronted her. Sydney Box had been contracted to make twelve films a year for Gainsborough, a level of production that would have been difficult enough to meet with lavishly resourced facilities. But in the small, shabby and inadequately equipped surroundings of Islington – 'the poor man's studio', as Betty dubbed it – the contract must have presented an almost impossible challenge.[7] Nor was there any hope of renegotiating a more realistic deal. In September 1947, the Labour Government imposed an import duty on films and the Hollywood studios retaliated by boycotting the British market. The Rank Organisation (who owned Gainsborough) decided to accelerate its production to plug the gap in domestic exhibition created by the boycott, obliging studios such as Islington to work to a punishing schedule.

Against the odds, Betty Box did manage to crank up production at Islington, meeting her production target, and making some genuinely popular British films into the bargain. The films she produced were generically and thematically varied, and included such detective thrillers as *Dear Murderer* (Arthur Crabtree, 1947), melodramas like *When the Bough Breaks* (Lawrence Huntington, 1947), and three of the *Huggett* series charting the comic tribulations of an 'average' English family who had originally featured in *Holiday Camp* (Ken Annakin, 1947). While it is fair to concede that the quality of some of these films was compromised by the necessary haste and thrift with which they were produced, many of them were none the less successful on their own terms (as moderately budgeted films conceived primarily with mainstream British audiences in mind). Perhaps most important, the difficult conditions in which Box speedily produced these films afforded her ample opportunity to prove, once and for all, that she was capable of working to a relentless shooting schedule and budget while making films that generally met with popular approval.

Box often said that of all the films she made at Gainsborough, *Miranda* (Ken Annakin, 1948) was her personal favourite. Her affection for the film seems to have been shared by reviewers and audiences alike, since *Miranda* was one of the most critically and commercially successful films of Box's career. It is also in many ways exemplary of her work as a whole. With its thoroughly outlandish plot and lewd innuendo, it surely counts as one of the quirkiest films of its period. Yet not only is it typical of the form of light-hearted, non-realist comedy on which Box built her reputation as a popular film-maker, but on closer scrutiny its irreverent spin on contemporary gender relations is also symptomatic of shifting attitudes to femininity in postwar Britain.

Having quarrelled with his wife, Paul Marten (Griffith Jones), a Harley Street doctor, decides to take a 'bachelor' fishing holiday in Cornwall. While on his boat, he is kidnapped by Miranda (Glynis Johns), a spirited young

Plate 15   Negotiating new sexual identities for women in postwar Britain: Miranda (Glynis Johns) is happy to be left holding the baby in *Miranda* (Ken Annakin, 1948), produced by Betty Box for Gainsborough.

mermaid who drags him back to her underwater home. Paul is soon in Miranda's thrall and agrees to take her back to London where he will pass her off as an invalid patient (mermaids being unable to walk). Once in London, Miranda embarks on a sexual spree, charming and seducing both the Martens' chauffeur, Charles (David Tomlinson) and their close family friend, Nigel (John McCullum), a faux bohemian artist. Like Paul, both men have obligations to other women, but both enthusiastically respond to Miranda's advances. At the end of the film, Clare Marten (Googie Withers) discovers she has been harbouring a mermaid in her smart London home. Miranda flees back to the sea, but the final emblematic shot of Miranda sitting in some sunnier clime embracing a small child reveals that her various amorous encounters have not been without purpose.

Miranda's plot is undeniably eccentric and implausible, even by the standards set by its most outlandish Gainsborough forerunners. Yet, to a British audience learning to cope with the more relaxed sexual mores and the significant increase in illegitimate births that were two of the social legacies of the war, Miranda's exploits were probably not so far-fetched. After all, if one ignores the fact that Miranda is a mermaid, the basic story is that of a young, single girl who freely expresses and satisfies her sexual appetite and, quite of her own volition, winds up becoming a mother out of wedlock. Of course, the fact that Miranda *is* a mermaid shifts the film into the realms of the fantastic and thus permits the representation of a sexually predatory woman that might otherwise have been considered too racy. In addition, the final scene appears to suggest that Miranda's sexual antics have really been motivated by the more socially respectable desire to conceive a child. Ultimately though, whatever ideological compromises the film makes, it cannot – or will not – recoup the playful irreverence with which it explores the fragility of traditional heterosexual relationships, nor the way it tentatively acknowledges that postwar Britain must come to terms with more liberated attitudes to female sexuality.

And so to Pinewood

When Hollywood lifted its boycott in 1948, a backlog of Hollywood films flooded the British market, making it difficult for a raft of hastily made British films to find adequate exhibition. Declaring a loss of over £16 million in 1949, the Rank Organisation was forced to scale down its operations considerably, selling off the studios at Shepherd's Bush and Islington and fully subsuming Gainsborough into the organisation. Betty Box transferred to Rank's Pinewood studios where she was based for the remainder of her career, although she was involved in various independent production companies during the 1950s and 1960s.

Box's first years at Pinewood were among the toughest of her career. The financial recession – 'the seven year hitch' as Box described it[8] – continued to bite and Rank mothballed many of its planned productions. While other producers seemed to have idly despaired, [9] Box took positive action, mortgaging her own house to provide bridging finance for *The Clouded Yellow* (Ralph Thomas, 1950). Her perseverance in getting the film into production and ensuring its completion did not go unnoticed by the British press of the day who were generally all too eager to pick over the bones of the British film industry's latest crisis. As one journalist commented in 1950, 'with feminine determination, she refuses to give up the ghost of British films as some of her male colleagues among independent producers seem to have done'.[10] *The Clouded Yellow* was the first of thirty-two collaborations with director Ralph Thomas; not only did it cement an enduring partnership, but as a largely self-financed venture, it was also her first truly independent film.

With *The Clouded Yellow*, Box may have demonstrated that she possessed the necessary initiative to endure the hard times at Rank, but it was the *Doctor* films that were to make her virtually indispensable to the organisation. The series began in 1954 with *Doctor in the House*, directed by Thomas again, which proved to be one of the biggest British box-office hits of that year. As Rank realised they had a repeatable success on their hands, plans for a follow-up were soon put into action, resulting in *Doctor at Sea* (Ralph Thomas, 1955). In the years that followed, Box made five further *Doctor* films, until the formula inevitably ran out of steam in the 1970s and transferred to television as a sit-com.

It is for the *Doctor* films that Betty Box is most likely to be remembered. Like *Miranda*, they mined a vein of comedy based on innuendo and sexual stereotypes prevalent in popular British cinema. Their dependence on formulaic narrative plots, and the longevity of the series spanning the 1950s to the 1970s, also invite comparisons with the *Carry On* films (which were produced by Box's husband Peter Rogers and directed by Ralph Thomas' brother Gerald). But where the *Carry On* films tended to focus on the power dynamics of an anarchic group of stock characters, the *Doctor* films revolved around the individual rite of passage of a young man, and were particularly concerned with lampooning middle-class, professional men. Like so many films of the 1950s, they were primarily comedy vehicles for British male film stars. Thus they rarely afforded more than peripheral roles to female characters (as a convenient love interest, an amorous patient, or an interfering landlady, for example). But they were by no means celebrations of masculinity; their staple was to send up the inept, pompous, feckless or randy male characters that invariably reappeared in different guises throughout the series.

The perennial popularity of the *Doctor* films played no small part in keeping Rank (just about) financially afloat, and thus made Rank reliant on Box's willingness to continue the flow of films. But although the *Doctor* films rendered Box's professional position far less vulnerable, she eventually found them tiresome. It seems that Rank would have been content to retain

Box's services solely to make as many *Doctor* films as her schedule would allow. As Box was later to recall, pitching a new idea to Rank became a predictable exercise: 'every time we took a new script to Rank, they said, "oh make another *Doctor*". It got very boring.'[11] Wising up to the situation, Box began to use Rank's dependence on the successful *Doctor* formula as a bargaining chip to push other, less commercially viable films into production: 'I always made a little bargain. [I said] I'd make them a *Doctor* after I'd made the film I wanted to make. And very often that's how it went: another film, a *Doctor* film, another film, a *Doctor* film.'[12]

It was as part of this bargaining strategy that she secured the finances to make two films in which she had a personal or political investment, with another *Doctor* film sandwiched between them (all three were directed by Ralph Thomas). The first was *Conspiracy of Hearts* (1960), the tale of a group of Italian nuns who operate an escape route for Jewish children rescued from a nearby concentration camp. With its blend of politics and melodrama, religion and female heroism, Rank was sceptical about its potential. However, Box's enthusiasm for the project was vindicated when it topped the box office alongside the other film she released that year, *Doctor in Love*.[13]

The second film for which Box traded the *Doctor* film was *No Love for Johnnie* (1961). Rank considered its theme of the adulterous behaviour of a Labour politician controversial and poor box-office material. In this instance, Rank's reservations seem to have been well-founded since, unlike *Conspiracy of Hearts*, *No Love for Johnnie* was neither critically nor commercially successful. However, Box always maintained that it was a film for which she felt a special pride and conviction and as her only real foray into the social problem genre, *No Love for Johnnie* certainly stands apart in an *œuvre* dominated by more light-hearted populist films.

Whatever frustration Betty Box may have felt from time to time about the range of work available to her, ultimately she seems to have been content to accept her role as a popular film-maker. I described Box earlier as a conformist, which seems to me the most fitting way to convey her ability to gauge the mood of the time and place in which she worked, and her willingness to cater to popular audiences. Box was no thwarted maverick straight-jacketed by an oppressive, unimaginative industry. She genuinely believed that making commercially successful and much-loved movies was an achievement in itself, and knew the measure of her contribution to British cinema in this field: 'I honestly do think I had an instinct for subjects, a woman's instinct for what other people wanted to see, and even if they weren't great epics, even if they weren't artistic dreams, they were very popular films.'[14]

'Betty Box-Office' and the press

The title of this chapter, 'The lady in charge' is taken from an article in a 1946 issue of *Picturegoer* heralding Box's appointment at Islington. The article provides some valuable insights into the historical and cultural moment in which it at last became possible for a woman to gain access to a prominent and powerful position within mainstream British film production. Box is presented as a trailblazing young woman making a significant inroad into a male province. The article opens with an almost sensationalist announcement: 'From now on, all pictures made at Gainsborough Studios, Islington, will be produced by a woman.'[15] While it is not entirely clear whether readers are invited to feel shocked or gratified by this news, it is certainly the novelty value of Box's gender rather than her professional credentials that is the primary point of interest. The feature goes on to give an uncompromising assertion of the power Box would wield in her new post at Islington:

> She is the first woman ever to hold so responsible a job. It is her ultimate responsibility to see that nearly half a million pounds are wisely spent ... She controls the film and the people who make it. One way and another hers is quite a considerable job.[16]

Box's position at Islington is perceived to be one of real power: governing finances and administration; overseeing day-to-day production; and perhaps most significantly, controlling decisions about the kinds of films to be made at the Islington unit. According to *Picturegoer*, Box would enjoy almost ubiquitous power over her small empire at Islington. The relish with which Box's extensive responsibilities and power at Islington are described by *Picturegoer* must have had a familiar ring to a generation of women well rehearsed in the 'You Can Do It' morale-boosting wartime slogans and representations, which had so recently urged them to step into traditionally male jobs. Bolstered by such rhetoric, Box's appointment in 1946 is represented as further proof that new opportunities for women were still there for the taking in postwar Britain.

Later in Box's career, her unprecedented professional position in mainstream British film production was not always so positively presented by the popular press who often struggled to assimilate her into a traditionally masculine business. For example, in 1955, a correspondent for the *Daily Mirror* wrote: 'Men who make movies in Britain today had better look out. The women are after them, hot and strong. One British girl is already the most successful film producer in the world. Her name is Betty Box.'[17] While the writer acknowledges Box's ability to chalk up some significant successes during some difficult years for British film production, her professionalism and ability to exercise power effectively in a tough, male-dominated industry is undermined and trivialised by the ludicrously eroticised characterisation of her as a 'hot and strong ... girl'.

The challenge that Box's status in the industry posed to conventional ideals of femininity was also sometimes allayed by drawing analogies between her professional role and skills traditionally designated as 'feminine'. The *Picturegoer* article of 1946 foregrounds Gainsborough's new 'lady' producer's 'rather rigorous financial training' and her reputation for remaining in budget and on schedule. In those years of austerity and rationing when good housekeeping skills were at a premium, it is highly likely that such expertise would have had a special resonance for *Picturegoer's* female readers. Box's work is presented less as glamorous and highly technical, more as housekeeping on a grand scale. Ironically enough, since one of Box's most time-consuming responsibilities at Verity and Gainsborough was to manage the ration books needed to acquire props and costumes, some of Box's responsibilities may not have been so very different to those performed by many of Britain's housewives. Indeed, Box herself seemed happy to draw comparisons between her professional role and that of the housewife's, claiming that 'she didn't overstep the budget' and therefore considered herself 'a very good housekeeper in that way'.[18]

In the hope of attracting women who had worked in the public sphere during wartime back into their traditionally prescribed roles as homemakers in peacetime, the 1940s and 1950s saw various attempts to dress up the housekeeping role in the garb of professional rhetoric. Thus domestic labour often came to be described as 'domestic science', and the minutiae of household chores were detailed and professionalised in numerous 'how to' magazines and books for women. The same rhetoric was used to describe women's roles in the workplace and the home; their roles in both spheres were thus presented as complementary rather than in conflict with one another. In light of this, it would be easy to argue that women's new professional status and achievements in postwar Britain were trivialised and rendered less transgressive by virtue of their apparent resemblance to traditionally undervalued feminine domestic skills. However, I would argue that such rhetoric was part of the complex ideological balancing act required to negotiate and assimilate women's changing economic and professional aspirations and status. Discursive analogies with women's traditional domestic roles provided a frame of reference with which to discuss and come to terms with new professional opportunities for women such as Box.

Inevitably enough, Box was continually asked what she could contribute to film-making as a woman. Recalling her years at Verity, she insisted that her gender had been of little significance to her work and that her male colleagues did not discriminate against her: 'the people I worked with didn't think of me as a woman, they just thought of me like everybody else.'[19] In 1946, she appeared to be only slightly less dismissive of the question, telling *Picturegoer* that, while she would like to see improvements in musical scores and costumes, she thought 'that there is little difference between the woman's angle and the man's today'.[20] By 1955 though, Box seems to have been far more willing to emphasise her 'feminine' skills:

I judge [prospective film scripts] from a woman's angle and with the cast in mind. ... For I believe in an emotional business like ours a woman's instinct helps a lot both in story construction and the selection of people to play the parts. I think that a woman can also help with dress. Frankly some women know how to dress, others, I'm afraid, do not always make the best of themselves.[21]

At face value, Box seems to succumb to a range of clichés about sexual difference. In place of the business acumen, artistic vision and strength of leadership that are the more vaunted attributes of successful producers, Box chooses to highlight those 'feminine' qualities and interests that characterise women as instinctual and emotional, preoccupied with 'trivial' concerns such as sartorial elegance. True, the very nature of the question ('what does she contribute as a woman?') steers Box into a defence of her professional status she may not have otherwise mounted. None the less, it is striking just how far her response to the question has shifted in a decade, suggesting either that the role itself had changed or that Box had decided that it had become more expedient to emphasise rather than play down her 'special' status.

There may be more to Box's increasing willingness to draw attention to her 'feminine' skills than simply an attempt to render her success more palatable to an industry (and culture) struggling to assimilate a powerful female professional. We could, for example, read her comments as a positive argument for the inclusion of feminine skills within her professional field, implying that, as a woman, she is actually better equipped to perform the producer's role. After all, when Box claims that 'ours' is an 'emotional business' (a virtual oxymoron in itself) in which the producer would do well to trust to 'instinct', she is effectively feminising an industry dominated by men. Rendered conspicuous by virtue of her gender, then, perhaps the most pragmatic and effective counter-strategy was to transform a potential handicap into an advantage. Indeed, against the grain of expectation, Box was later to make much the same claim when she rather wryly commented: 'Maybe it was an unfair advantage I took, but I always found it a bonus rather than a disability being a woman producer!'[22]

The thoroughly positive attitude towards her gendered professional position Box espoused throughout much of her career demands careful consideration. On one level, it strikes a false note in light of the clumsy sexism that often colours popular discourses about her. It is also difficult to believe that attitudes towards powerful professional women were any more progressive in the film industry than in other areas of British society. For example, Muriel Box, Betty's sister-in-law, described at length the chauvinism and hostility she continually faced in the industry in the 1940s and 1950s.[23] In contrast, Betty remained tight-lipped about any problems she encountered as a woman producer and sometimes seemed to collude with some rather patronising assumptions about her status in the industry.

Unlike Muriel, Betty appears to have had little interest in feminist politics, conceding only once in an interview with Lizzie Francke in 1991 that she might describe herself as a 'near feminist'.[24]

Whatever the problems such a stance might initially pose for a feminist assessment of her career, it is crucial that it is understood as symptomatic of the context in which she worked. Although Box worked in an industry that could ill-afford to alienate professionals of her calibre, it was none the less an industry that was probably never entirely comfortable with her presence. To measure Box's professional stance with the yardstick of contemporary cultural feminist politics would be counter-productive, anachronistic and inappropriate. What emerges from most of the journalistic accounts of her career is an impression of Box oscillating between dual and conflicting endeavours. Either she assimilates herself inconspicuously within the ranks of her male colleagues or she marks herself off as different or 'special' when that strategy seems more likely to be effective. Ultimately, her non-confrontational, apolitical attitude, her willingness to exploit her femininity if necessary, may be vindicated by the fact that she flourished in a profession where few women survived.

Conclusions

If Betty Box's professional position was indeed so culturally precarious, it seems all the more extraordinary to me that her career spanned three of the most erratic and challenging decades of British cinema. Her success, in short, flies in the face of probability. By way of conclusion, I want to offer some possible explanations for her improbable achievements, and consider what her impact on British cinema histories might be. Although Box was, quite clearly, a gifted and industrious producer, it would be rather too convenient simply to point to her individual talents and tenacity as the only factors in her success. To do so would be to ignore the historical and cultural conditions – changing attitudes to professional women, an industry destabilised by war and later by economic crisis – that enabled Betty Box to find a route into her profession and survive. (It is worth noting that these conditions also enabled two other women, Wendy Toye and Muriel Box, to become the first mainstream British women directors in the 1950s.) As a mainstream female producer in the postwar British film industry, Betty Box was a one-off. This does not mean however that we should assimilate her as the 'exceptional great woman' of British cinema history who proves the rule that film production was a domain in which women could not compete on equal terms with men. Nor should it mean that we mark her place in history as aberrant. A primary reason why her work deserves further exploration is precisely because it typifies the convoluted twists and turns, the negotiations and compromises British film production was forced to perform to remain afloat in the difficult postwar years.

I suspect, however, that Box's marginalisation in existing historical and critical discourses may have as much to do with her unapologetic populism as it does with the fact that she was a woman. In a national cinema where critical acclaim and scholarly interest have historically been more forth-coming to those who have been culturally accredited, film-makers such as Box do not always fit comfortably into established critical and historical paradigms. Although a range of revisionist histories on British cinema have begun to challenge this implicit snobbery,[25] long-established and latent stigmas are difficult to shrug off quickly. Box's marginalisation thus needs to be understood alongside the lack of attention paid to other proponents of popular British cinema. These include many of her male professional coun-terparts at Gainsborough and Rank, such as Maurice Ostrer, Edward Black and her brother, Sydney Box, whose impact on popular British film culture is only just beginning to be registered fully by film scholarship.

It is also possible to argue that many of the popular personalities and genres who are beginning to attract renewed interest have often been redeemed because of their perceived 'camp' or ironic sensibilities (the *Carry On* cast or Hammer productions, for example). This suggests that lowbrow entertainment films can be celebrated so long as they do not take themselves seriously. In some cases, this may be the best way to entice audiences and readers to revisit certain texts and personalities previously considered beyond the bounds of political correctness or 'good taste', but this is not a strategy that works for Box. Even if it were possible to claim 'camp' creden-tials for Box's most populist films (*Miranda*, or the *Doctor* series, for example), these are not the terms that best describe her career. While Box did not consider herself a 'serious' film-maker, there was little irony about the way in which she set out to make a stream of box-office hits. After all, it was on the strength of this ability to make popular British films that Box sustained her extraordinary career, and it should be on those terms that she secures a place in histories of British cinema.

NOTES

My thanks to Robert Murphy, John Ellis and BECTU for providing interview material.

1 She produced two other films during this period: *The Upturned Glass* (Lawrence Huntington, 1946), which she made at Riverside, and *So Long at the Fair* (Terence Fisher, Anthony Darnborough, 1950), which she made at Pinewood.

2 A fuller analysis can be found in my *Odd Women Out: Betty and Muriel Box,* Manchester, Manchester University Press.

3 Originally from S. Morley, *Odd Man Out: James Mason*, London, Weidenfeld and Nicolson, 1989. Quoted in B. McFarlane (ed.) *Sixty Voices: Celebrities Recall the Golden Age of British Cinema*, London, BFI, 1992, p. 36.

4 From the full transcript of Robert Murphy's interview with Betty Box, an abridged version of which is reproduced in S. Aspinall and R. Murphy (eds) *BFI Dossier 18: Gainsborough Melodrama*, London, BFI, 1983.

5 Ibid.
6 Ibid.
7 McFarlane, op. cit., p. 37.
8 Murphy, op. cit.
9 In her interview with Murphy, Box claims that while she was making *The Clouded Yellow* in 1950, Rank had no other films in production.
10 *Sunday Times*, 9 November 1950 (from British Film Institute microfiche; no page numbers given).
11 From an interview with Betty Box for *The Man Who Ruined the British Film Industry*, Large Door Ltd, 1995. My thanks to John Ellis for supplying a copy of this programme.
12 From an interview with Betty Box for *Fifties Features*, Flashback productions for Channel Four, 1986.
13 McFarlane, op. cit., p. 37.
14 *Fifties Features*, op. cit.
15 Hubert Cole, 'The lady in charge: round the British studios', *Picturegoer*, 7 December 1946, p. 8.
16 Ibid., p. 8.
17 *Daily Mirror*, 6 October 1955 (from British Film Institute microfiche; no page numbers given).
18 McFarlane, op. cit., p. 37.
19 Murphy, op. cit.
20 Cole, op. cit., p. 8.
21 *Daily Mirror*, 6 October 1955 (from British Film Institute microfiche; no page numbers given).
22 McFarlane, op. cit., p. 37.
23 See, for example, M. Box, *Odd Woman Out*, London, Leslie Frewin, 1974; Sydney Cole's interview with Muriel Box for the BECTU Oral History Project recorded in 1991.
24 L. Francke, 'The lid off the Box', *Independent*, 11 February, 1991, p.18.
25 See, for example, P. Cook (ed.) *Gainsborough Pictures*, London, Cassell, 1997; P. Hutchings, *Hammer and Beyond: The British Horror Film*, Manchester, Manchester University Press, 1993; and L. Hunt, *British Low Culture: From Safari Suits to Sexploitations*, London, Routledge, 1998.

12

AUTHORSHIP AND BRITISH CINEMA

The case of Roy Ward Baker

Peter Hutchings

On its initial release in 1955, *Passage Home*, a nautical drama starring Peter Finch and Diane Cilento, was described by one critic as 'a film made with considerable if impersonal accomplishment'.[1] The same phrase could well be used to sum up the career of *Passage Home*'s director, Roy Ward Baker. By the time of *Passage Home*, Baker was already an experienced film-maker with nine features to his credit, an eclectic mix of thrillers (*The October Man*, 1947; *Paper Orchid*, 1949; *Highly Dangerous*, 1950), a domestic comedy (*The Weaker Sex*, 1948), a romantic fantasy (*The House in the Square*, 1951) and a submarine drama (*Morning Departure*, 1950). Three of Baker's films had been made in America for 20th Century-Fox, giving him the opportunity to work with Marilyn Monroe (in *Don't Bother to Knock*, 1952) and to become one of the few British film-makers to direct a 3D film (the thriller *Inferno*, 1953). After *Passage Home* – ironically Baker's first film after his return to Britain – the director would go on to make the prestigious Titanic film *A Night to Remember* (1958) along with another thriller (*Tiger in the Smoke*, 1956), a comedy (*Jacqueline*, 1956), a war film (*The One That Got Away*, 1957), one difficult to classify generically (*The Singer Not the Song*, 1960), and a social problem film (*Flame in the Streets*, 1961). In the early 1960s, he switched to television work and then from the late 1960s onwards directed a series of low-budget horror films – including *The Vampire Lovers* (1970), *Scars of Dracula* (1970) and *Asylum* (1972) – for the two main British horror companies of the time, Hammer and Amicus.

It is certainly the case that Baker has not received the critical attention afforded other directors of the wartime and postwar period such as Michael Powell, David Lean or even Basil Dearden. In comparison with other directors associated with the horror genre – Terence Fisher or Michael Reeves, for example – he does not appear to have much of a cult status either. It might be argued that this lack of critical interest derives from the impersonality of the work itself, which is not distinctive enough to merit close scrutiny. In other words, Baker is not considered an *auteur*; his films do not express a personal vision either thematically or stylistically. Instead, to retain the French terminology that underpins auteurist writing, he is a *metteur-en-scène*, a talented journeyman skipping ably from one genre to another without significantly transforming the material with which he is working.

One of the aims of this chapter is to contest this view of Baker. This immediately suggests an approach that is in some way going to align itself with a notion of the author or *auteur* and that will seek to identify a distinctive directorial voice within a cohesive body of work. The other aim of this chapter is precisely to question the assumption that necessarily connects the study of directors with a particular kind of authorship. Bagging another *auteur* for Britain is not necessarily the best way of developing our understanding of British cinema. Conversely, ignoring or dodging round the issue of the director's role and contribution can lead to the neglect of an important level of creative agency within the British film industry.

An account of British film based on authorship sits uneasily with recent developments in the study of British cinema. I refer here in particular to an increasing interest in audiences and in studios. The stress in this work on the collective and the collaborative can make the individualistic tenor of much authorial analysis seem rather quaint and old-fashioned (just as authorship in Film Studies generally is often presented as an intellectual adventure effectively concluded in the late 1960s and long since superseded by more exciting and relevant approaches to film). I want to argue that this does not have to be the case, that an account of a director's work can not only offer inherently worthwhile and interesting insights into British cinema but can also productively develop the approaches currently being deployed in the study of British film culture. Accordingly, the comments on Roy Ward Baker that follow are intended to sketch in a way of thinking about a British film director where ideas of authorship are significant but do not wholly define or limit the sorts of questions we can ask of the material and where different ideas of authorship can emerge.

An odd career

Roy Baker was born in London in 1916 and entered the film industry in 1934. He worked for Gainsborough as both a location manager and an assistant director until 1940, when he joined the army. His first film as director, *The October Man*, was released in 1947; it was followed by a further twenty-eight films. From the early 1960s onwards, he worked extensively in television on such series as *The Saint, The Human Jungle, The Avengers, The Champions, Jason King* and *The Persuaders*. In 1967, after discovering that there was a sound editor also called Roy Baker, he changed his professional name to Roy Ward Baker.

The first question to address here is why focus on this particular director. The obvious answer if one were following an auteurist agenda would be that

Baker is a director who has been unfairly neglected and merits our attention now. To an extent I am sympathetic to this approach and would certainly argue that Baker has directed a number of films that are remarkable. At the same time, the fact that these films were not generally perceived as remarkable on their release and that Baker himself never received the sustained critical attention afforded to some of his fellow directors should not so easily be brushed aside as a past critical inadequacy shortly to be rectified. The disparity between contemporary and past perspectives on certain British directors in the postwar period might well derive from our tendency now to look for the directorial 'signature' in moments of excess and transgression within certain films. Critics in the original period of release, on the other hand, often seem to have found the director in those parts of the films which embody a more conventional approach – hence the designations 'solid', 'workmanlike' and 'professional' applied to so many film-makers of the 1950s, not least among them Roy Baker. The division apparent here between an adherence to norms and a display of excess is, I would argue, important within many British films of the postwar period and is especially significant to an understanding of Baker's work which, paradoxically, seems capable of sustaining both normative and transgressive readings.

My reason for singling out Baker as a film-maker worthy of attention is that there is something rather odd about his career, in terms both of individual films and of the overall career trajectory. Obvious examples of the former would include one-off oddities such as *The Singer Not the Song*, a baroque Mexican-set melodrama with some sado-masochistic trappings, *The Anniversary* (1968), a grotesque Bette Davis vehicle for Hammer, and *The Legend of the Seven Golden Vampires* (1974), to date Britain's only kung fu horror film. One can add to this list films which at first glance appear more conventional in terms of subject matter and generic identity, but which on closer inspection reveal themselves as decidedly idiosyncratic. *Passage Home*, for instance, must rate as one of British cinema's most relentless portrayals of sexual repression, while *The One That Got Away* is, to my knowledge, the only 1950s British war film to have a German as its hero.

A kind of oddness is also apparent in the way that Baker proceeds through different sectors of British film (and television) production between the 1940s and the 1970s. Aside from the brief excursion to Hollywood (itself an unusual departure for a British film director in the 1950s), Baker spent much of the period between 1947 and 1963 working either for companies owned by or associated with the Rank Organisation (for example, *The October Man* and *The Weaker Sex* were both produced by the Rank-owned Two Cities) or directly for Rank itself (notably *A Night to Remember*). It is not uncommon to find directors with a similar background to Baker in mid- or sometimes high-budget movie-making of the 1950s who go on to work in British television during the 1960s (Charles Crichton, Leslie Norman and Basil Dearden, all of them associated with Ealing, spring to mind). In particular, they worked on the spy and action series produced by Lew Grade's company ITC, series such as *The Saint* and *The Persuaders* that were shot on film with an eye on the international market.[2] It is very rare, however, to find a director with such a background who then works in a sustained way in the British horror genre. (Some directors best known for their contribution to British horror were also involved in the ITC series – Freddie Francis, John Gilling and Don Sharp, to name but three – but none of them had any significant directorial experience with the Rank mainstream prior to their involvement with horror.)[3] Combining work on mainstream genre films and dramas in the 1947–63 period with television in the 1960s and low-budget horror films, Baker's career is certainly out of the ordinary. This unusual combination of areas of activity represents something of a problem if one wishes to think of Baker as an author: in order to establish the existence of a cohesive authorial voice the divisions between these different areas need to be erased. Either that or one or two sections of his career have to be written off as journeyman work done to support the film-maker until fresh artistic opportunities present themselves. Failure to establish this kind of coherence means that, ultimately, the director is no author, that he or she is dominated by the material rather than dominating it.

I want to suggest that these divisions – between the Rank mainstream and the slightly more disreputable Hammer and Amicus, and between film and television – are in themselves of some interest. Furthermore, an account of Baker's work that is sensitive to such divisions or breaks – rather than seeking to efface them – can ultimately lead us to a different idea of what British film authorship might be. Given that British cinema is full of directorial careers that are truncated, interrupted or subject to sometimes bewildering transformations, it seems appropriate to think of Baker in this respect as someone whose career, for all its 'oddness', has a certain typicality about it.

Baker as author?

If we consider the 1947–63 phase of Baker's career, there is certainly enough material with which one could mount a case for his authorship in quite a traditional, auteurist manner, especially if one wished to pursue the line that a distinct morbid sensibility links his films together. Take as an example Baker's directorial debut *The October Man*. An industrial chemist (played by John Mills, who would subsequently become a regular Baker collaborator), who is suffering from mental trauma as a result of an accident in which a child was killed, lodges at a seedy boarding house. It turns out that one of his fellow guests is a murderer who functions as a kind of double for the mild-mannered chemist, expressing the violence that – the film implies – lurks within him. It is striking how this doubling, and an associated sense of Mills' mental disequilibrium, is accomplished via *mise-en-scène* and an expressive use of sound effects rather than through dialogue. At one point the murderer is shown as a shadow projected, Nosferatu-like, onto a wall, the 'dark side' made literal. Throughout the film, the chemist's capacity for violence is dramatised via the way he obsessively plays with his handkerchief, fashioning it at one moment into a child's toy, the next into a strangulation weapon (which is all the more disturbing since the film begins with a child's death). The environment is also used symbolically at the film's conclusion. Having successfully resisted the suicidal urge to throw himself under a train, the chemist's emergence from a dissipating cloud of smoke into clear air dramatises his return to mental stability.

The October Man is not unique in the way that it combines realistically presented settings with expressive moments where a character's mental disturbance is projected out into these settings. Other examples of this from British cinema in the immediate postwar period include *Dead of Night* (Alberto Cavalcanti, Charles Crichton, Basil Dearden, Robert Hamer, 1945), *Brief Encounter* (David Lean, 1945) and *A Matter of Life and Death* (Michael Powell and Emeric Pressburger, 1946). In particular, the use of the train whistle in *The October Man* to signify the chemist's suicidal despair is not dissimilar to a moment in *Brief Encounter* when Laura (Celia Johnson) contemplates suicide as a train whistle screams in the background. For all its connections with other films, *The October Man*'s *mise-en-scène* does have a distinctive and polished elegance, however, and the film's morbidity is especially insidious and seems to linger in Baker's work much longer than it does in the work of his contemporaries.

This is more than apparent in two films made by Baker in the early 1950s, *Highly Dangerous* and *Morning Departure*. The former is ostensibly a romantic thriller in which an entomologist (played, rather improbably, by Margaret Lockwood) is sent into an East European police state in order to find out about biological experiments involving insects. As it turns out, the film contains more disturbing elements than the romantic-thriller scenario suggests. One thinks here of the starkly photographed scene in which Lockwood is captured, drugged and interrogated by the state police or a moment near the end of the film where a fleeing couple are ruthlessly machine-gunned to death. The film's conclusion is interesting in this respect. Lockwood has managed to steal some of the insects that were being used by the enemy. On arrival at a British airport, she finds herself surrounded by unhelpful British officials, while the one official who could help her has failed to show up on time. To make matters worse, the insects have become hungry and are starting to eat each other. Lockwood urgently needs to provide them with sugar otherwise her mission will be a failure. As sugar is rationed, however, no one will give her any. As the unsympathetic waitress at the airport cafeteria points out, 'If they're entitled to sugar then the Ministry will issue the necessary coupons.' The mixture here of the grotesque (the cannibalistic insects) with the unappealing inflexibility and incompetence of British officialdom and the morbidly suspicious stance adopted by everyone at the airport hardly makes for an uplifting, amusing conclusion to what, initially, offered itself as being something of a romp.

A similar confounding of generic expectations can also be found in *Morning Departure*. A group of men are trapped in a submarine with too few survival suits to go round, knowing that four of them are consequently doomed to die. Ostensibly an exercise in stoicism (like Baker's other nautical disaster story, *A Night to Remember*), in actuality the film becomes a prolonged – and morbid – meditation on the futility of action. The men can do nothing but wait, and the film deals with the process of time passing. The element of chance is repeatedly stressed. Chance determines who is on the submarine and who survives the initial accident (and the accident itself is simply bad luck), and in deciding who receives the survival suits the submariners surrender themselves to chance by drawing cards. The film's key image in this respect is the captain and first officer nervously playing with a pair of dice. It's an unexpected image of helplessness and passivity to put alongside the chemist in *The October Man* turning his handkerchief into both a child's toy and a murder weapon and Margaret Lockwood's cannibalistic insects in *Highly Dangerous*. All of them hint at the peculiar character of Baker's work in this period with its penchant for upsetting our expectations of the material in various idiosyncratic ways.

But only in the period from the late 1940s to the early 1960s is this the case. After the box-office flop of *Two Left Feet* in 1963, Baker's work is different. Of the television work of his that I have seen, I can find no meaningful connections with the earlier films. As far as his horror films are concerned, a certain kind of morbidity is inevitably apparent within them, although even here there is little sense that Baker inflects the films to make them his own. Stylistically, Baker's direction for both Hammer and Amicus is arguably influenced both by his experience of television and the films' modest budgets. Thus there are more pans and zooms than tracking shots and there is less staging in depth. In addition, shots tend to be shorter and more functional than is the case in his 1950s work. Still in evidence are occasional moments of expressive excess. One thinks here of the opening of *Asylum* in which the idea of madness lurking beneath normality is first introduced when a visitor to an asylum glimpses his own reflection in the glass that covers some prints of exaggerated, stereotypical images of madness. Also worthy of mention is the splendidly atmospheric, erotically charged opening sequence of *The Vampire Lovers*. Such moments and sequences are few and far between, however, and what one generally finds instead is an efficient staging of particular narrative situations.

As already indicated, the transition apparent here from an expressive mode to an impersonally professional one is a problem if one wants to think of Baker as a distinctive author. At the same time, it's worth pointing out that a certain professional solidity is apparent in all of Baker's work, under-

Plate 16 A characteristically excessive moment from Baker's *The Singer Not the Song* (1960).

pinning the more outré elements one finds in the films from the 1950s and early 1960s – hence the 'impersonal accomplishment' assigned to *Passage Home*. This is even the case in what is probably Baker's strangest film, *The Singer Not the Song*. The *Monthly Film Bulletin* review for this suggests that the film is 'as startling as a muffled scream from the subconscious', but at the same time describes Baker's direction as 'cool, correct but unadventurous'.[4] From this perspective, there is a kind of continuity in Baker's career, although this has more to do with the exercise of a particular set of industry-specific professional competencies than it has with the expression of a distinctive authorial vision. In fact a further consideration of Baker's shifting position within the British film industry not only provides an arguably more compelling explanation of why he gives every impression of being an '*auteur*' in the 1950s and a more anonymous figure thereafter. It also potentially sheds some new light on the notion of authorship in British cinema.

Baker in context

John Ellis has noted that there seemed to be some confusion among British film critics of the 1940s about who the true artist was in cinema – the director or the screenwriter.[5] It's interesting in this respect that Baker's first film, *The October Man*, had as its main credit title '*The October Man* by Eric Ambler'. (Ambler not only wrote the screenplay but was also the film's producer.)[6] By the early 1960s, however, Baker was not only director but also producer and in one instance (*Two Left Feet*) co-writer as well. The transformation from director to producer-director was one to which a number of film directors aspired in the wartime and postwar period. In the 1940s in particular this seemed to be related to attempts to raise the status of the directing profession and, in the face of the critical doubt noted by Ellis, to establish the director as the key creative figure in cinema. Perhaps the most notable expression of such directorial ambition was the Independent Producers initiative inaugurated at Rank in 1942. Here, groups of film-makers – among them David Lean and Ronald Neame, Frank Launder and Sidney Gilliat, and Michael Powell and Emeric Pressburger – were given what was then unprecedented control over the production process. While Independent Producers did not just involve directors, the figure of the director did tend to be privileged as film-makers negotiated a relatively new industrial space for themselves. The process had as much to do with changed relationships with management, unions and other professions at it had with any artistic imperatives.[7] By the time Independent Producers came to an end in the late 1940s, it had set an important precedent for film-makers – and directors in particular – seeking to establish both creative and managerial control over their films. In an article published in 1950, British director Thorold Dickinson suggested that directors should now be thought of as 'filmwrights' in recognition of their importance.[8] (Dickinson's article provoked a furious response from Hollywood screenwriter Howard Koch who made it abundantly clear that so far as he was concerned the director had too much power as it was and that it was the screenwriter who deserved greater recognition. One suspects that most British screenwriters of the time would have agreed.) [9]

Roy Baker was one of a number of directors who began their careers in the late 1940s and early 1950s and who seemed to have been influenced by the new, ambitious ideas about direction that were circulating within the industry. Baker and some of his fellow young directors often made films which contained more obviously expressive elements than they might otherwise have done. Useful connections could be made here between Baker and, for example, John Guillermin (whose directorial debut was in 1949) and J. Lee Thompson (whose directorial debut was in 1950), both of whose careers have some parallels with Baker's. A case could probably be made for both Guillermin and Thompson as distinctive film-makers in the pre-1960 part of their careers. Like Baker, their films can be seen to contain some 'authored' elements housed within an otherwise skilful, unobtrusive servicing of particular narratives (note, for instance, the weird, expressive style of parts of

Guillermin's 1952 comedy *Miss Robin Hood*). Yet afterwards, again much like Baker, both directors move into what is apparently a more impersonal mode with international co-productions or American-financed films – Thompson with *The Guns of Navarone* (1961), Guillermin with *The Blue Max* (1966), *The Bridge at Remagen* (1968), *Shaft in Africa* (1973) and *The Towering Inferno* (1974).

Of course, one could assign this loss of a distinctive 'authorial voice' simply to the adequacy (or lack thereof) of individual directors. There is, however, something to be said for the idea that these changes in career direction relate, in part at least, to structures and working practices within the film industry itself. The medium-budget genre production with which Baker, Guillermin and Thompson were generally associated throughout much of the 1950s certainly seemed to provide a more fertile ground for the authored qualities I have discussed in relation to Baker than did other sectors of the industry (for instance, the low-budget support-feature sector which remained more firmly the province of the producer). It is revealing in this respect that Baker, Guillermin and Thompson (along with such comparable directors as Ken Annakin and Guy Hamilton) move away from this type of film-making in the early to mid-1960s, precisely the time when it is becoming a less significant feature of British film production. Indeed, in the face of the social realism of the British New Wave and the low-budget exploitation fare provided by, among others, Hammer horror and the *Carry On* series in the late 1950s and early 1960s, the 'well-made' 1950s films of Baker and others begin to look rather old-fashioned.

Admittedly a good deal more evidence needs to be amassed about the changing role and status of the director within the industry to establish this point fully and in detail. However, I do think there is a strong prima facie case for suggesting that Baker's 'authorship' in the 1947–63 period is, on a certain level, an expression of shifts in industrial definitions of the director's role. In other words, Baker directs his films in the way he does, in a particular 'authored' fashion, because this is what it means to be a director in the section of the industry where he is working at the time he is working there. This culminates in his becoming a producer-director in the early 1960s with the interesting pairing of *The Singer Not the Song* and the social problem film *Flame in the Streets*. Both are filmed in Cinemascope, a format that arguably functions in each film as an indicator of the magnitude of the ambition attached to the producer-director project in its aspirations towards a particular managerial control and authority. It follows from this that the changes in Baker's work in television and for Hammer and Amicus from 1963 onwards derive from his movement into what might be termed a different regime of directorship, one in which the director tended to be less involved in script development, casting or production design. (Indeed Baker himself once took over a Hammer film – *The Anniversary* – after shooting had commenced with another director.) In other words, the decisive break in

Baker's films that occurred in the early 1960s – a break which makes it hard to think of him as an *auteur* with a cohesive body of work – had a material basis in the industry itself. In effect, Baker moved from one director-function in the 1947–63 period to another director-function in television and horror.[10] Notions of authorship and authorial control become in this respect not merely critical tools for understanding and evaluating films but also have some significance in the way that the industry organises itself.

Looking at Baker's career in this manner draws our attention to the fact that film direction, contrary to the assumptions of some auteurist critics, is not a unitary activity. At each stage of Baker's career, there are alternative models available of what it means to be a director. Take Terence Fisher, for example. Like Baker, he started his career in medium-budget films, although at Gainsborough, which in the 1940s was a much more regimented part of the Rank empire and not a studio associated with *auteur*-directors. In the 1950s, he moved into low-budget support features and subsequently Hammer horror. While Fisher did acquire two co-writing credits in the 1950s, generally he seemed content to work self-effacingly in situations in which producers had the power and where the director had little input off the studio floor. By way of a contrast, one can cite Michael Reeves who, although twenty-eight years younger than Baker, entered British horror at more or less the same time. Reeves sought to use exploitation cinema as a means for constructing both an authorial voice and a social critique in a way that anticipated the use made of horror by a number of young American film-makers in the 1970s. Both Fisher and Reeves have in the past been described as authors. So long as this designation of authorship fails to recognise that each spoke from a different position within the industry and adhered to different definitions of directorship, however, our understanding of the role of specific directors and direction in general will be limited.[11]

The past excesses of auteurist criticism have turned some away from the study of directors. I hope this short overview of Baker's career has demonstrated that looking at film directors can aid our understanding of the film industry, and that thinking about film in terms of authorship does have some relevance within such a context. At the same time, I am aware that while British Cinema Studies offers numerous accounts of particular directors, there is still very little work on the history of film direction as a profession. Until we have a more detailed picture of the roles of direction within the collaborative and hierarchical interactions that constitute film production, the figure of the director, for all the critical value assigned to it, will remain something of an enigma.

NOTES

1   *Monthly Film Bulletin*, June 1955, vol. 22, no. 257, p. 84.

2 On ITC series, see J. Cook, '"Men behaving badly?": Basil Dearden and *The Persuaders!*' in A. Burton, T. O'Sullivan and P. Wells (eds) *Liberal Directions: Basil Dearden and Post-war Film Culture*, Trowbridge, Flicks, 1997, pp. 231–40.

3 Of the Ealing directors, Leslie Norman did receive one directorial credit for Hammer, the 1956 film X – *The Unknown*, when he replaced Joseph Losey. Seth Holt, an editor turned director, made one film for Ealing (*Nowhere to Go*, 1958) and two films for Hammer (*Taste of Fear*, 1961; *Blood from the Mummy's Tomb*, 1971) and also worked for television, although this can hardly be seen as a substantial output.

4 *Monthly Film Bulletin*, February 1961, vol. 28, no. 325, p. 21.

5 J. Ellis, 'The quality film adventure: British critics and the cinema 1942–1948', in A. Higson (ed.) *Dissolving Views: Key Writings on British Cinema*, London, Cassell, 1996, p. 86.

6 Ambler also wrote the screenplays for Baker's *Highly Dangerous* and *A Night to Remember*. Of all his screenplays for Baker, only *The October Man* seems to bear any thematic relation to Ambler's novels. In the case of *Highly Dangerous* this is a little surprising as the film, while not credited as such, appears to be a loose reworking of Ambler's own novel, *The Dark Frontier*.

7 On Independent Producers, see G. Macnab, *J. Arthur Rank and the British Film Industry*, London, Routledge, 1993, pp. 90–9.

8 Thorold Dickinson, 'The filmwright and the audience', *Sight and Sound*, March 1950, vol. 19, no. 1, pp. 20–5.

9 Howard Koch, 'A playwright looks at the "filmwright"', *Sight and Sound*, July 1950, vol. 19, no. 5, pp. 210–14. For brief discussions of some of the activities of the British Screenwriters Association and its attempts to raise the status of the screenwriter, see G. Brown, *Launder and Gilliat*, London, BFI, 1977, pp. 3–8 and S. Harper, *Picturing the Past*, London, BFI, 1994, pp. 124–5.

10 For an interesting account of working conditions at Hammer, see D. Meikle, *A History of Horrors: The Rise and Fall of the House of Hammer*, Lanham MD and London, Scarecrow Press, 1996.

11 For discussions of Fisher and Reeves, see D. Pirie, *A Heritage of Horror*, Gordon Fraser, London, 1973 and P. Hutchings, *Hammer and Beyond: The British Horror Film*, Manchester, Manchester University Press, 1993.

Part V

GENRES, MOVEMENTS AND CYCLES

Introduction

Identifying certain film genres, movements and cycles remains one of the central means by which we order and make sense of film history. While some groups of films, such as the documentary movement of the 1930s or Free Cinema of the 1950s, were very much a product of manifestos and the self-conscious endeavours of their proponents, the coherence of other cycles has been generated more by the critical discourses imposed in hindsight. None the less they remain a useful way of organising and analysing British cinema history.

The four contributors to this section discuss genres, movements and cycles that are by now familiar features of the study of British cinema. But each writer offers a revisionist account, a new perspective on a familiar landscape that demands that we rethink some established 'truths' about British cinema history. James Chapman revisits the much discussed propaganda films of the Second World War, but challenges the received wisdom that realism and documentary necessarily provided the most effective way to inspire confidence and instil a sense of national consensus in Britain's wartime audiences. Leo Enticknap looks afresh at the vicissitudes of British cinema's traditional valorisation of documentary realism, charting the fortunes of the Rank Organisation's rarely discussed cinemagazine, *This Modern Age*, and lucidly exposing the extent to which the series was motivated as much by Rank's commercial aspirations as it was from any lofty endeavour to promote a purist version of documentary realism indigenous to Britain.

Focusing on the 1960s, both Adam Lowenstein and Moya Luckett rethink another much discussed and celebrated movement in British cinema history, the New Wave. Lowenstein compares the ways in which Jack Clayton's seminal New Wave film, *Room at the Top* (1959) and Michael

Powell's once critically reviled but now reclaimed *Peeping Tom* (1960) addresses the bourgeois audience. He argues that a principal reason why *Peeping Tom* so unnerved many critics of its period was that, unlike *Room at the Top*, it insinuated its middle-class audience into a vision of an amorphous, mass consumer culture. In her discussion of the films of the New Wave and Swinging London, Luckett addresses some similar themes. She contrasts the stasis of the working-class protagonists in such films as *The Loneliness of the Long Distance Runner* (Tony Richardson, 1962) and *Billy Liar* (John Schlesinger, 1963) with the mobility of many of the heroines of 'Swinging London' epitomised by Julie Christie's role in *Darling* (John Schlesinger, 1965).

13

CINEMA, PROPAGANDA AND NATIONAL IDENTITY

British film and the Second World War

James Chapman

By common consent among film critics and historians, the Second World War is regarded as a 'golden age' for British cinema. Not only was it the period when the cinema as a social institution was at its most popular, but it was also a time when British films found greater success with both critics and audiences than ever before. 'Everyone recognises now that there has been an extraordinary renaissance in British feature-film production since about 1940,' Roger Manvell remarked immediately after the war.[1] Although the number of British feature films produced annually dropped in comparison to the 1930s, due to the closure of studios and the recruitment of industry personnel into the services, commentators such as Manvell perceived an increase in the quality of films produced. Just as the nation's health improved due to food rationing, so too did the health of British cinema. The profligate expenditure of producers like Alexander Korda in the 1930s became undesirable under the austerity regime of the war years; in its place, British cinema was deemed to have discovered a new aesthetic of sober, responsible realism, derived in large measure from the documentary movement. It was a time when a genuinely British national cinema was seen to have emerged, one that dealt with the current realities of British life, and particularly with the various processes of social change brought about by the impact of war.

This chapter sets out to examine the ways in which British cinema responded to the challenge of war, focusing in particular on the role of the government in promoting the representation of the nation through film propaganda. In order to contextualise this discussion within the contours of British film historiography, however, it will be useful first to identify the various ways in which the history of wartime cinema has been written. A survey of critical and historical paradigms will help to explain why certain films have been privileged at the expense of others, as well as illuminating the issues of text and context that inform the history of British cinema during the Second World War.[2]

Critical and historical paradigms

Most critical and historical writing about British wartime cinema falls into one of three broad traditions or schools, which, for the sake of convenience rather than the intellectual clarity of the distinction, may be termed the old film historians, the empiricists and the theorists. The old film historians include Roger Manvell, Paul Rotha and Basil Wright, all of whom were involved in film propaganda during the war, Rotha and Wright as documentary film-makers, Manvell as a critic and a Regional Films Officer for the Ministry of Information (MOI). The histories of the cinema they subsequently wrote, despite containing an element of personal narrative, are valuable for what they reveal about the critical preferences (and prejudices) of their generation.[3] They belong to the same tradition as the leading film critics of the war years (such as C.A. Lejeune, Dilys Powell and Richard Winnington) and are imbued with the same aesthetic principles that privilege realism and notions of 'quality'.[4]

By the time the war was over, a pantheon of the key British wartime films was already well on the way to being established, including *In Which We Serve* (Noël Coward and David Lean, 1942), *The Foreman Went to France* (Charles Frend, 1942), *Nine Men* (Harry Watt, 1943), *Fires Were Started* (Humphrey Jennings, 1943), *Millions Like Us* (Frank Launder and Sidney Gilliat, 1943), *San Demetrio, London* (Charles Frend, 1943), *The Way Ahead* (Carol Reed, 1944) and *The Way to the Stars* (Anthony Asquith, 1945). These films were championed for their realistic qualities, which, in the terms of the dominant critical discourse of the time, meant sober, unsensational narratives with believable characterisations and a prevailing sense of stoicism and emotional restraint. For Manvell, films such as these 'showed us people in whom we could believe and whose experience was as genuine as our own. The war film discovered the common denominator of the British people.'[5]

These films all exhibit what has been described as the 'wartime wedding' between, on the one hand, the studio-made feature film, and, on the other hand, the techniques of the documentary movement.[6] This wedding took place on several levels. On one level it involved the crossover of personnel from one branch of the film industry to another. Alberto Cavalcanti and Harry Watt, for example, both left the GPO/Crown Film Unit to join Ealing Studios. Roy and John Boulting went the other way, recruited from the commercial sector to the film units of the armed services where they worked on such documentaries as *Desert Victory* (1943) and *Journey Together* (1945) respectively. On another level, the wartime wedding involved the incorporation of narrative-documentary techniques into commercial feature film production, exemplified by the focus on groups of people in authentic

194

situations rather than the class types and caricatures familiar from British films of the 1930s. 'By the nature of their work the documentarists were expert in matters of propaganda, and it was not unnatural for the feature film-makers to turn in their direction,' Basil Wright remarked.[7]

Yet the wartime wedding did not come about immediately. Early war feature films, for example Ealing's *Convoy* (Pen Tennyson, 1940) and *Ships With Wings* (Sergei Nolbandov, 1941), were derided for their melodramatic plots and narrative focus on upper-class officer types. The latter film, a glorified drama of derring-do in the Fleet Air Arm, was criticised by the journal *Documentary News Letter* on the grounds that 'the propaganda line of the film would be more appropriate to a Ruritanian campaign than the Second World War'.[8] Most of the canonical films of the war were made during its middle years. For Manvell,

> 1942 was to be one of the richest periods for the war film in Britain. It was the year in which human considerations began to overcome the jingoistic nationalism with which most countries blinkered themselves at the beginning of the war. Similarly, the 'war story' with a patriotic slant began to give place to the 'war documentary', which derived the action and to a greater extent the characterization from real events and real people.[9]

So dominant was this view that it became the accepted orthodoxy for a whole generation of writers, and is still to be found in much film historiography even today.[10]

The first challenge to the assumptions of the old film historians came from a group of revisionist scholars who may be described collectively as the empiricist school. Grouped loosely around the *Historical Journal of Film, Radio and Television*, which was founded in 1981 and represents probably the most important development in the emergence of a new film historiography in the 1980s, this school comprises such scholars as Nicholas Pronay, Kenneth Short, Jeffrey Richards, Anthony Aldgate, Vincent Porter, Sue Harper and Philip Taylor.[11] The methodology employed by these historians is strictly empiricist, their research based on primary sources including government records, trade and critical journals, and contemporary research into film carried out by the social survey organisation Mass Observation.[12] The origins of this school date back to the 1970s and the release of official documentation relating to the cinema, especially the records of the MOI Films Division, under the Thirty Year Rule. Drawing on such sources, the empiricists reconstruct the production history of wartime films, placing them in the context of official propaganda policy and discussing the nature of their critical and popular reception. Their rigorous scholarship has done much to revise the critical prejudices and assumptions of the earlier generation of writers about how successful certain films were. For example, Richards has shown that, although *Ships With Wings* did not meet the criteria of realism and emotional restraint laid down by the old film historians, it was in fact very well received by the trade and popular press. It also proved successful with British audiences in 1941 who, far from being put off by its phoney heroics, welcomed it as a patriotic epic.[13]

A very different kind of revisionism was forthcoming in the 1980s from a third school of writers who are first and foremost film theorists rather than historians. This school is represented by the various contributions to *National Fictions*, a publication that arose out of the 1984 British Film Institute Summer School. The purpose of this publication was 'to demonstrate the extent to which the meanings accruing to a specific "event" or "period" (World War II) are *constructed*, hence subject to contestation, struggle, transformation and change'.[14] Some of the authors analyse particular films in respect of their representation of gender (Christine Gledhill, Gillian Swanson) or nationhood (Andrew Higson). Others are concerned with constructing an ideological basis for British wartime cinema (Geoff Hurd, Steve Neale). Whatever their concerns, all the essays in *National Fictions* are characterised by a highly theorised approach to the subject, determined by the application of the Gramscian theory of hegemony to explain the relationship between film and society, as the above quotation testifies. This theory assumes that culture (including films) is a site for contestation and struggle between different ideologies. In this sense, wartime cinema is seen in terms of the differing ideologies that circulated in Britain at the time (including those of official propaganda agencies, film-makers and critics). For the *National Fictions* school, the war presents an ideological paradox – the advance of the left on a popular level at a time when the country was led by one of its most totemic right-wing figures, Winston Churchill. It is how this paradox is negotiated in wartime films which interests them. It is surely no accident that this school of criticism emerged in the 1980s, the decade of Thatcherism, but the constant parallels which the writers draw between Churchill and Thatcher does raise some doubts about their understanding of the political and social conditions of the war. Nevertheless, the value of the theorists' work is to remind us that the meaning of wartime films cannot be interpreted merely from the overdetermined perspective of production discourses and propaganda policy, but is also arrived at through the reading of films by the spectator. Such readings might result in different, even contradictory, meanings being associated with the films besides those intended by producers and policy makers. Indeed, as Charles Barr has observed, the meanings that can be read into wartime films depend as much upon the political perspective of the audience as on the content of the films themselves:

> For the Right ... the war signifies pride in national defence under a belligerent Conservative leader. Emblematic film image: *In Which*

We Serve, Noël Coward on the bridge of HMS Great Britain. For the Left, it means a glimpse of socialism in action, of the achievements possible when class hierarchies and the tyranny of the marketplace are relaxed. Emblematic film image: the fire-fighting team coming together in *Fires Were Started*.[15]

These different interpretations of the ideologies of wartime films notwithstanding, however, the fact that such 'right' and 'left' films could be produced within the same national cinema gives some indication of the plurality of approaches permissible within official propaganda policy.

How do these critical and historical paradigms influence or determine accounts of British wartime cinema? Several important points emerge. First, the aesthetic assumptions of the old film historians have given rise to the perception, still quite widespread, that the 'best' (meaning the most effective) propaganda films are those made in a documentary-realist style. Thus the canon of key wartime films still exerts a strong influence, for example in television programming and retrospectives. Second, the perspectives brought to bear by both the empiricists and the theorists are essential to a full understanding of the nature of British film propaganda. Through the Gramscian perspective adopted by the theorists, it is clear that British wartime cinema, as Geoff Hurd observes, 'was not simply a vehicle for the downward transmission of ideologies which uniformly supported official needs'. Rather, it was 'a site of negotiation and transaction: between on the one hand official needs and on the other hand the aspirations of all those groups and classes whose support for the war effort had to be won'.[16] What the theorists never really get to grips with, however, is precisely what and where these points of negotiation and transaction were. This is where the empiricists come into their own, for only through the analysis of primary sources can the tensions and occasional conflicts within film propaganda be identified. The highest profile example of such conflict was Churchill's now notorious attempt to suppress *The Life and Death of Colonel Blimp* (Michael Powell and Emeric Pressburger, 1943), which has received much attention from historians.[17] However, the controversy surrounding *Colonel Blimp* has rather obscured the fact that it was an exceptional case, and that for the most part the operation of film propaganda was a smooth and consensual process. In particular, the role of official agencies such as the MOI in facilitating the smooth operation of government policy has only recently come to be acknowledged.

Official film propaganda policy

It has become one of the established myths of British cinema history that the government showed little or no interest in the role of film as a medium of propaganda and that British film-makers were left more or less to their own devices when it came to the screen representation of the nation at war. This perception owes in large measure to the initially negative impression made by the MOI, which, in the early months of the war, suffered such a catalogue of errors and mishaps that it was dubbed the 'Ministry of Dis-Information' and the 'Ministry of Muddle' by its critics. The MOI Films Division was the target of much hostility from those who felt themselves excluded from the national propaganda effort. In July 1940, *Documentary News Letter*, which had set itself up as an unofficial watchdog of the Films Division's activities, declared:

> In ten months this Division has achieved a mere fraction of what it should have achieved. Its lack of imagination, no less than its abysmal failure to be even competent at its job, have been the despair of all persons in the film trade who sincerely want to place their expert abilities at the disposal of the national effort.[18]

This wholly negative verdict is, however, significantly at odds with the opinion expressed by Michael Powell in his memoirs: 'The Ministry of Information was a great success, and its Films Division was one of its triumphs.'[19]

This discrepancy of views clearly requires some explanation. The attitude of *Documentary News Letter* was coloured by the fact that those whose opinions it represented had initially felt themselves marginalised by the MOI. 'The documentary people, all of us, were left in the wilderness,' Edgar Anstey recalled. 'We weren't used because the Chamberlain government was very much opposed to everything that we stood for, and they had their own film people, who moved into the Ministry of Information and were powerful in other quarters.'[20] But Anstey's comment tells only half the truth. While there was some hostility in official quarters to the left-wing sympathies of the documentarists, the MOI nevertheless realised from an early stage that they would be essential to the cause of national propaganda. 'We can, in addition, finance or help to finance some of the best British documentary film producers for the production of short documentary films approved by us,' said Sir Joseph Ball, the first Director of the Films Division. 'Provided such films are of first-class quality, I have already obtained an undertaking from the three big British circuits and the Cinematograph Exhibitors' Association that they will be shown throughout the cinemas of the United Kingdom.'[21]

Official film propaganda policy, in fact, was based on the understanding that there was a specific role for the different modes of film practice. This policy was laid out in the Programme for Film Propaganda, drawn up by Ball's successor, Sir Kenneth Clark. Clark accepted the MOI's three basic themes of propaganda – 'What Britain is fighting for', 'How Britain fights' and 'The need for sacrifices if the fight is to be won' – and suggested how best to adapt these 'abstract ideas to the concrete, dramatic and popular medium of the films'.[22] He considered that feature films were the best medium for the presentation of 'What Britain is fighting for':

> *British ideas and institutions.* Ideals such as freedom, and institutions such as parliamentary government can be made the main subject of a drama or treated historically. It might be possible to do a great film on the history of British Liberty and its repercussions in the world.[23]

Thus Clark outlined a theme of propaganda based on a Whiggish notion of national identity that was to be explored in historical feature films like *The Prime Minister* (Thorold Dickinson, 1941) and *The Young Mr Pitt* (Carol Reed, 1942). Although Clark thought that documentary had a less important role to play in this theme of propaganda, he saw it as central to the presentation of 'How Britain fights':

> *Documentaries.* A long series should be undertaken to show this country, France and the neutrals the extent of our war effort. There should be, in the first place, full and carefully worked out films of each of the fighting services; then shorter films of all the immediately subsidiary services, i.e. merchant navy, munitions, shipbuilding, coastal command, fishermen, etc. Most of these subjects are susceptible of detailed treatment from different angles, e.g. one-reel films on the Bren gun, the training of an anti-aircraft gunner, etc.[24]

Again, Clark anticipated the wide range of documentaries made about all aspects of the British war effort. The Crown Film Unit, for example, came to specialise in feature-length narrative-documentaries about different branches of the services, including *Target for Tonight* (Harry Watt, 1941), *Coastal Command* (J.B. Holmes, 1942), *Close Quarters* (Jack Lee, 1943) and *Western Approaches* (Pat Jackson, 1944).

The policy of incorporating both feature film producers and documentary film-makers into the propaganda effort was consolidated by Clark's successor, Jack Beddington, who actively encouraged the cross-fertilisation between the two sectors. 'The Ministry of Information Films Division, under Mr Jack Beddington, must be given credit for intermixing the documentary and studio film techniques, as well as interchanging their respective exponents,' wrote Paul Rotha.[25] The wartime wedding, therefore, was to a considerable degree the result of official policy. In particular, Beddington used his influence to persuade commercial producers to steer away from the melodramatic type of war film that typified the early years of the war and to concentrate instead on less sensational subject matter. In March 1943 he issued a policy statement to the trade through the British Film Producers' Association (BFPA), stating that what the MOI wanted were 'first class war subjects realistically treated, realistic films of everyday life, high quality entertainment films'. What it did not want were 'war subjects exploited for mere cheap sensationalism, the morbid and the maudlin, entertainment stories which are stereotyped or hackneyed and unlikely because of their theme or general character to reflect well upon this country at home and abroad'.[26]

In this respect, official policy reflected a trend that was becoming apparent across British cinema as a whole. This is exemplified by the policy of Ealing Studios, whose head of production, Michael Balcon, provides evidence that the wartime wedding identified by critics was the result of a deliberate production ideology:

> The balance between the strictly documentary and the story elements in this new type of film is still the most difficult thing to achieve. In our studios the first effort in that direction was Tennyson's last film, *Convoy*. The subject, as the title implies, was a documentary one. Cameramen were sent out with convoys and much authentic material was obtained ... I was very happy about *Convoy*, as indeed I had every reason to be. It had a great success, both as regards prestige and returns, and was even referred to in the House of Commons as fine propaganda for the Navy. Looking back at it in the light of further experience in this new type of film I should say that the balance went a little too much in favour of the story at the expense of realism. I was very much happier with the result obtained in more recent of our films, such as *The Foreman Went to France*, *Next of Kin* [Thorold Dickinson, 1942] and *Nine Men*. It is not difficult to see why, in two of these films, *The Foreman Went to France* and *Nine Men*, we struck a more satisfactory balance. By this time two of the leading makers of documentary films, Cavalcanti and Watt, had joined us at Ealing Studios, and both these films make an admirable illustration of the alliance between the two schools.[27]

The film which, in Balcon's view, best exemplified the new maturity of Ealing's output was *San Demetrio, London*, based on the true story of a petrol tanker shelled by a German pocket battleship in the middle of the Atlantic but successfully brought home by her crew. *San Demetrio, London* is now widely regarded as the quintessential Ealing war film – Charles Barr describes it as 'the culmination of Ealing's war programme, the ideal fulfilment of Balcon's policy'.[28] But although it was well received by critics, it was less successful at the box office than the earlier, more flamboyantly heroic naval dramas had been. When it was released at the end of 1943, the public's appetite for films directly about the war was already on the wane.

Heritage, spectacle and propaganda

From 1943 until after the end of the war there was a marked change in the nature of popular film culture in Britain as the war narratives that had proved popular with audiences since 1940 were overtaken at the box office by the success of the Gainsborough costume melodramas such as *The Man in Grey* (Leslie Arliss, 1943), *Fanny by Gaslight* (Anthony Asquith, 1944) and *The Wicked Lady* (Leslie Arliss, 1945). The success of the Gainsborough films is generally attributed to popular taste becoming weary of realism and craving fantasy after several long years of bombing and rationing. As early as 1942, a leading trade figure such as C.M. Woolf, President of the BFPA, observed that cinema-goers were 'already getting tired of this type of picture [war films] and were asking for films which took their minds off the tragedy now taking place'.[29] Jack Beddington was responsive to these views, telling the BFPA 'that the Ministry was prepared to support all types of pictures – both war and non-war – provided they were of the highest quality'.[30]

Laurence Olivier's celebrated production of *Henry V* (1944), which he starred in and directed, was precisely the sort of quality picture that Beddington was ready to support. Like the Gainsborough melodramas it symbolises the shift towards costume and spectacle that was occurring in British cinema towards the end of the war. Unlike the critically despised Gainsborough films, however, it occupied the respectable end of British film culture, being a 'heritage' subject that drew upon Shakespeare for inspiration. An innovative, flamboyant, highly cinematic interpretation of the play, expensively produced in Technicolor and with a cast that reads like a 'who's who' of British stage and screen, *Henry V* was a fusion of heritage culture, propaganda and popular entertainment on an epic scale.

Sue Harper has argued persuasively that 'although there is no direct evidence of government sponsorship, there are plenty of suggestions that the film enjoyed official support'.[31] Olivier himself was 'summoned' to see Beddington, who 'asked me to undertake two pictures intended to enhance the British cause'.[32] Those two films were *The Demi-Paradise* (Anthony Asquith, 1943) and *Henry V*. The associate producer of *Henry V* was Dallas Bower, an ex-Films Division employee who had since produced a radio programme, *Into Battle*, which included Olivier reciting Henry's 'Harfleur' and 'Crispin's Day' speeches. Filippo Del Giudice's Two Cities Films produced the film, with further financial support from J. Arthur Rank. At a final cost of £475,000 it was the most expensive British film of the war.

For all its Shakespearean origins, *Henry V* is nothing if not explicit about its propagandist intent. Released in the autumn of 1944, its stirring account of an English army crossing the Channel and defeating a mighty Continental foe had obvious parallels in the aftermath of the Normandy campaign. This much is inscribed in the film itself, which is dedicated 'To the Commandos and Airborne Troops of Great Britain – the spirit of whose

Plate 17   *Henry V* (Laurence Olivier, 1944): an epic fusion of heritage, spectacle and propaganda.

ancestors it has been humbly attempted to recapture in some ensuing scenes'. That the film is so much more than an exercise in jingoistic nationalism is due to the imaginative way the play is opened up for the screen. 'Can this cockpit hold the vasty fields of France?' asks Chorus (Leslie Banks), and the film ingeniously uses the cinema's capacity for illusion and spectacle to gradually break free from the confines of the stage. It begins with a reconstruction of a performance of the play at the Globe Theatre in 1600 as Henry receives the French ambassador. The theatrical background gives way to painted scenery as Henry leaves with his army for France. The scenery is quite basic at first but gradually becomes more detailed, until the film bursts into real exteriors for the Battle of Agincourt (filmed on location in Eire), before returning to a tapestry background for the peace-making sequence and finally back to the Globe for the closing scenes.

Henry V is a complex and sophisticated narrative that works on several levels: as a version of the events of 1415, as a reconstruction of a performance of the play in 1600, and as an allegorical narrative of the invasion of Europe in 1944. It is symmetrical both formally and structurally, with Agincourt as the centrepiece. The battle itself is a stunning set-piece that exhibits the studied application of the montage techniques of Soviet cinema, especially those used for the Battle of the Teutonic Knights in *Alexander Nevsky* (Sergei Eisenstein, 1938). The sequence is built around a juxtaposition of movement and stasis as the mounted French knights bear down on the English archers. Shots of the charging knights are intercut with the English bowmen and close-ups of Henry in armour and on horseback. When Henry's sword falls, the archers unleash their volleys and the French charge is abruptly halted. This stopping of the enemy in all its massive and flamboyant might has an irresistible symbolism: the defeat of the Nazi war machine by the determined 'Few'. In the *mêlée* that follows, a montage of fast close-ups and rapid movement, the camera follows the English flag, keeping it in the centre of the frame above the heads of the combatants. The English victory is confirmed by Henry's defeat of the Constable of France in single combat, emphasising his personal heroism and inspirational leadership.

As impressive as the battle is, Agincourt is not the only important sequence in propagandist terms. Henry's concern for his men, exemplified by his tour of the English camp in mufti the night before the battle, establishes his caring and democratic nature in contrast to the aloof, arrogant, corrupt French aristocracy. And Henry's exhortations to comradeship and unity ('We few, we happy few, we band of brothers/For he today that sheds his blood with me shall be my brother') echo Churchill's inspirational wartime speeches in reflecting the wartime consensus between leaders and led. The image of the nation presented by *Henry V* is one of national unity and social cohesion – hence all omission from the film of those parts of the play which focused on internal dissent.

Henry V was a critical and commercial success both in Britain and in the United States, where it earned over $1 million when it was belatedly released there in 1946, while Olivier received a special Academy Award for his 'Outstanding Production Achievement as Actor, Producer and Director in bringing *Henry V* to the Screen'. It is deservedly regarded as one of the greatest artistic and commercial triumphs for British cinema of the Second World War, as well as being perhaps the first Shakespearean film to reach a mass audience. But it was, first and foremost, a propaganda film, a patriotic, triumphalist epic that was far removed from the sober, unsensational realism that commentators have generally associated with British wartime cinema. Eloquent testimony to its power as propaganda was provided by American critic James Agee, who, after seeing it, declared: 'I am not a Tory, a monarchist, a Catholic, a medievalist, an Englishman, or, despite all the good that it engenders, a lover of war; but the beauty and power of this traditional exercise was such that, watching it, I wished I was, thought I was, and was proud of it.'[33]

By taking *Henry V* as a case study, it is possible to see how the critical and historical paradigms discussed earlier affect the analysis of a particular text. The success of *Henry V* challenges the assumption of the old film historians that documentary-style realism is the sole criterion of effective propaganda. Indeed, it exposes some of the contradictions within that school of criticism, for some of the proponents of the documentary-realist discourse also admired

Henry V. Wright, for example, considered it a 'beautiful and well-nigh fault-less film'.[34] As far as the theorists are concerned, the use of Shakespeare, the writer privileged above all others in discourses on English heritage, might be seen as an attempt by the propagandists to assert their own officially legitimated culture with audiences. The popular success of the film, however, suggests that this was a transaction in which cinema-goers were complicit. Finally, the work of the empiricists in reconstructing the production history of the film and identifying the role of the MOI in originating the project again challenges the myth that the government took no interest in film propaganda. In this sense, *Henry V* perfectly exemplifies the operation of British film propaganda: the representation of the nation at war arising from a consensus between cinema and state.

NOTES

My thanks to Guy Barefoot, Leo Enticknap, Mark Glancy, Stephen Guy, Sue Harper, Vincent Porter and Sarah Street for their comments after the presentation of this paper at the *Cinema, History, Identity Conference* on 10 July 1998.

1 R. Manvell, *Film*, Harmondsworth, Penguin, revised edition, 1946, p. 133.
2 This paper is based on research undertaken for my Ph.D. thesis, 'Official British Film Propaganda during the Second World War' (Lancaster University, 1996). What follows is a digest of themes and issues elaborated in J. Chapman, *The British at War: Cinema, State and Propaganda, 1939–1945*, London, I.B. Tauris, 1998.
3 See, for example, R. Manvell, *Films and the Second World War*, London, J.M. Dent, 1974; P. Rotha, with R. Griffith, *The Film Till Now: A Survey of World Cinema*, London, Vision Press, revised edition, 1949; and B. Wright, *The Long View: A Personal Perspective on World Cinema*, London, Secker and Warburg, 1974.
4 The nature of British film journalism in the 1940s is discussed in J. Ellis, 'The quality film adventure: British critics and the cinema 1942–1948', in A. Higson (ed.) *Dissolving Views: Key Writings on British Cinema*, London, Cassell, 1996, pp. 66–93.
5 R. Manvell, 'The British feature film from 1940 to 1945', in M. Balcon, E. Lindgren, F. Hardy, R. Manvell, *Twenty Years of British Film, 1925–1945*, London, The Falcon Press, 1947, p. 85.
6 As far as I have been able to establish, this phrase originated with John Shearman, in 'Wartime wedding', *Documentary News Letter*, November/December 1946, vol. 6, no. 54, p. 53.
7 Wright, op. cit., p. 177.
8 *Documentary News Letter*, December 1941, vol. 2, no. 12, p. 221.
9 Manvell, *Films and the Second World War*, op. cit., p. 101.
10 See, for example, E. Rhode, *A History of the Cinema from its Origins to 1970*, London, Allen Lane, 1976, pp. 369–84, and K. Thompson and D. Bordwell, *Film History: An Introduction*, New York, McGraw Hill, 1994, pp. 271–3.
11 See, for example, A. Aldgate and J. Richards, *Britain Can Take It: The British Cinema in the Second World War*, Edinburgh, Edinburgh University Press, second edition, 1994; N. Pronay and D.W. Springs (eds) *Propaganda, Politics and Film, 1918–45*, London, Macmillan, 1982; N. Pronay, 'Introduction', to F. Thorpe and N. Pronay, with C. Coultass, *British Official Films in the Second World War: A Descriptive Catalogue*, Oxford, Clio Press, 1980, pp. 1–56; V. Porter and

C. Litewski, 'The Way Ahead: case history of a propaganda film', Sight and Sound, Spring 1981, vol. 50, no. 2, pp. 110–16; P. Taylor (ed.) Britain and the Cinema in the Second World War, London, Macmillan, 1987; and K.R.M. Short (ed.) Film and Radio Propaganda in World War II, London, Croom Helm, 1983.

12 A selection of this research is published in J. Richards and D. Sheridan (eds) Mass-Observation at the Movies, London, Routledge and Kegan Paul, 1987.

13 J. Richards, 'Wartime cinema audiences and the class system: the case of Ships With Wings (1941)', Historical Journal of Film, Radio and Television, 1987, vol. 7, no. 2, pp. 129–41.

14 A. Higson and S. Neale, 'Afterword', in G. Hurd (ed.) National Fictions: World War Two in British Films and Television, London, BFI, 1984, p. 73. Other examples of this school include A. Kuhn, 'Desert Victory and the people's war', Screen, Summer 1981, vol. 22, no. 2, pp. 45–68, and A. Lant, Blackout: Reinventing Women for Wartime British Cinema, Princeton, Princeton University Press, 1991. Less trenchant and more empirically based work by members of the National Fictions school can be found in C. Gledhill and G. Swanson (eds) Nationalising Femininity: Culture, Sexuality and British Cinema in the Second World War, Manchester, Manchester University Press, 1996; and A. Higson, Waving the Flag: Constructing a National Cinema in Britain, Oxford, Clarendon Press, 1995.

15 C. Barr, 'War record', Sight and Sound, Autumn 1989, vol. 48, no. 4, pp. 261–2. Barr himself is a scholar who does not fit easily into the critical and historical paradigms I have identified, straddling as he does the theorist and empiricist schools. While his ideological reading of texts clearly illustrates his affinity with the theorists, he also draws on empiricist research methods and materials. His classic book Ealing Studios (London, Cameron and Tayleur/David and Charles, 1977), which relates the studio's films to wider social and political trends, was also highly influential in the development of the sort of contextual film history practised by the empiricist school.

16 G. Hurd, 'Notes on hegemony, the war and cinema', in Hurd, National Fictions, op. cit., p. 18.

17 See A. Aldgate, 'What a difference a war makes: The Life and Death of Colonel Blimp', in A. Aldgate and J. Richards, Best of British: Cinema and Society from 1930 to the Present, London, I.B. Tauris, revised edition, 1999, pp. 79–93; I. Christie, 'Blimp, Churchill and the state', in I. Christie (ed.) Powell, Pressburger and Others, London, BFI, 1978, pp. 105–20; and N. Pronay and J. Croft, 'British film censorship and propaganda policy during the Second World War', in J. Curran and V. Porter (eds) British Cinema History, London, Weidenfeld and Nicolson, 1983, pp. 144–63. For a comprehensive overview and discussion of the historiography of the Blimp affair, see J. Chapman, 'The Life and Death of Colonel Blimp (1943) reconsidered', Historical Journal of Film, Radio and Television, March 1995, vol. 15, no. 1, pp. 19–54.

18 Documentary News Letter, July 1940, vol. 1, no. 7, p. 3.

19 M. Powell, A Life in Movies: An Autobiography, London, Methuen, 1987, p. 383.

20 Quoted in E. Sussex, The Rise and Fall of British Documentary, Berkeley, University of California Press, 1975, p. 119.

21 Public Record Office (PRO): INF 1/194, 'Ministry of Information Films Division: general plan of operations', paper by Sir Joseph Ball, 25 September 1939.

22 PRO: INF 1/867, Co-ordinating Committee paper no.1, 'Programme for film propaganda', by Sir Kenneth Clark, 29 January 1940; reprinted verbatim as an appendix to Christie, Powell, Pressburger and Others, pp. 121–4.

23 Ibid.

24 Ibid.

25 Rotha, with Griffith, op. cit., p. 314.

26 'Feature films – MOI policy', attached to the minutes of the British Film Producers' Association, 23 March 1943 (documents in private hands).

27 M. Balcon, *Realism or Tinsel*, Brighton, Workers' Film Association, 1944, pp. 10–11.

28 Barr, *Ealing Studios*, p. 35.

29 BFPA minutes, 25 June 1942.

30 BFPA minutes, 27 July 1942.

31 S. Harper, *Picturing the Past: The Rise and Fall of the British Costume Film*, London, BFI, 1994, p. 86.

32 L. Olivier, *Confessions of an Actor*, London, Sceptre, 1987, p. 130.

33 Quoted in H.M. Geduld, *Filmguide to Henry V*, Bloomington, Indiana University Press, 1973, p. 69.

34 Wright, op. cit., p. 198.

14

THIS MODERN AGE AND THE BRITISH NON-FICTION FILM

Leo Enticknap

Short films in the British exhibition marketplace

Why do the cinemagoers of this country have to tolerate such trashy 'second-feature' films? One is attracted to a cinema by quite a good film about which we have read critics' views, and having seen it one has either to walk out or sit through the most amazing rubbish, which, I am sure, no newspaper critic is ever allowed to see. The point is that most of these silly second features are American-made. Does the British film industry really mean to tell us that it cannot replace this muck with good 'shorts'?

(Letter to the *Daily Herald*, 6 August 1946)

One month after this letter was published, the Rank Organisation launched *This Modern Age*, a monthly series of short documentaries. Forty-one films were released between September 1946 and January 1951, each focusing on a specific aspect of politics, international relations or current affairs. Each one was generally around twenty minutes long, a running time that restricted the exhibition opportunities available to the series. In the 1940s, the vast majority of cinemas programmed their films as double features in three-hour slots, which meant that a typical performance consisted of two films, each lasting an hour to ninety minutes. A current newsreel (seven and a half minutes), a selection of advertising films and trailers and a live performance by a band or organist (five to ten minutes in a typical suburban cinema) was usually sufficient to fill the time available. It was only on the rare occasions when both features were unusually short that any additional material could be included in an average performance at a mainstream cinema. It is difficult to know how widely *This Modern Age* was distributed at the time. Writing in 1950, Paul Rotha speculated that 'Mr. Rank controls some 560 theatres in the United Kingdom, in which, presumably, this screen magazine can regularly play'.[1] Unfortunately, I have been unable to unearth any evidence that might confirm these figures.

This Modern Age was an unprecedented venture in the history of the commercial British film industry. Quite apart from the prevailing exhibition
practices, the institutional conditions under which producers operated also
made short films uneconomic. In fact, the only comparable project was the
Central Office of Information's monthly release programme, inherited from a
propaganda campaign started by the Ministry of Information during the war
and financed entirely by the taxpayer (the programme continued until 1952).

The terms on which cinemas hired films from distributors, which were
effectively dictated by the American-owned distribution outlets operating in
the UK, ensured that the vast majority of an exhibitor's rental fees paid for a
main feature, or 'A' picture. Only a tiny percentage was spent on the rest of
the programme. A government report on distribution and exhibition estimated that during the 1947–1948 financial year, £27.5 million was paid in
film rental fees, of which only £2.5 million went to the 'supporting
programme'.[2] It was for such reasons that the practice of double-feature
programming had become firmly established. The 'amazing rubbish'
condemned by the *Daily Herald*'s correspondent was the second features, or
'B' pictures, supplied by distributors at very low rates as part of a package
deal. However unpopular they were among a vocal minority, most cinemas
could not replace the 'B' picture with other supporting material even if they
wanted to, as this would have meant a considerable increase in their rental
outgoings. In 1948, 94 per cent of cinemas programmed double-features,
while only 6 per cent 'invariably showed a single feature picture with a
supporting programme limited to short films'.[3]

If this was not enough to deter the potential short film producer, it is
worth bearing in mind that, despite the complaints from a vocal minority,
double-features met with a considerable degree of public approval. When a
questionnaire was circulated among customers of the Granada cinema chain
in 1946, 46 per cent of respondents (a clear majority) stated that their
preferred programme consisted of 'two features, newsreel and organ solo'.[4]
Interviewed in 1950, the manager of the Odeon Leicester Square pointed out
that cinema customers could not be expected to understand the intricacies of
the financial arrangements made between exhibitors and distributors. His
conclusion was that single-feature programmes were unpopular:

> During the war some cinemas experimented with single-feature
> programmes but the public thought it an indirect form of profi-
> teering, since other cinemas in the same district offered longer
> programmes for the same price of admission. The emphasis, there-
> fore, is on quantity rather than on quality.[5]

Why, then, did a giant industrial combine like the Rank Organisation
decide to invest considerable resources on a regular series of non-fiction
shorts, which could not easily be accommodated into mainstream cinema

programming practice and which stood little chance of ever making a profit? The answer lies in the complex relationship between the commercial film industry, the political establishment and the intellectual film culture of the day.

The March of Time and the British documentary movement

This Modern Age probably has its origins in the British series of its better-known American counterpart, *The March of Time* (*MOT*), which was launched in the UK in the autumn of 1935. *MOT* was a spin-off from the current affairs magazine *Time*, and, like the print version, quickly developed a reputation for polemical editorialising, for a journalistic style that was frequently compared with that of the popular press, and for causing political controversy. The quickly-paced visuals, stentorian commentary and strident music score which characterised *MOT* proved a popular formula: in June 1936 its distributor, Radio Pictures, published an advertisement claiming that *MOT* was being shown in 800 British cinemas, approximately one-fifth of the total exhibition market.[6]

Despite its status as a commercial entertainment product, one surprising aspect of *MOT*'s British operation is that when a production facility was opened in London in August 1936, *MOT*'s European director, Richard de Rochement, immediately employed John Grierson as a consultant.[7] Grierson was the leading figure in the British documentary film movement, who believed that the cinema was unable to perform an educational or public service role in the private sector. During the 1930s they had built up a Government-run film production and distribution infrastructure (the GPO Film Unit and its associated non-theatrical distribution activities), analogous to the Reithian BBC in nature if not in scale. Grierson himself repeatedly and vociferously condemned what he called the 'Woolworth intentions' of the commercial film industry, arguing that the need for films to be financially successful was often culturally disadvantageous.[8] At first sight, therefore, it seems surprising that the producers of a film series designed to popularise current affairs should wish to avail themselves of his services.

What is even more surprising is that Grierson not only worked for *MOT*, in which capacity he enabled a number of documentary movement activists to produce items for the series, but also supported it enthusiastically throughout the remainder of his time in the UK (he emigrated to Canada in 1939). In response to growing criticism of what some documentarists regarded as the ideologically polemical stance of a number of *MOT* releases, Grierson argued that 'in the atmosphere of the cinema, where political discussion is only a curtain-raiser to Garbo, complication is the devil'.[9] In other words, if *MOT* was to be commercially successful, it would have to make compromises in its coverage of political issues. Several revisionist historians have concluded that Grierson's attempts to secure exhibition for the documentary movement's output essentially failed – as Brian Winston elegantly puts it, 'the church refused to fill'.[10] This perhaps explains why Grierson was attracted to a genre of non-fiction film which had the institutional backing of a major Hollywood distributor and which was shown on a significant scale.

In the context of the 1930s, however, Grierson's involvement with, and endorsement of, *MOT* can be seen as an institutional anomaly. *MOT* operated according to a very different agenda from that of the British newsreels, or the producers of commercial 'shorts' or the documentary movement: indeed, Grierson came under fire from some of his colleagues who believed that his work with de Rochement was undermining the movement's ideals. Paul Rotha, for example, believed that *MOT* was 'a very bad influence before the war on a part of British documentary', while an anonymous *World Film News* editorial warned that 'a less sensational atmosphere of presentation must be sought' if *MOT* were to continue to receive the movement's support.[11]

The association between Grierson and *MOT* is important to a full understanding of subsequent developments in that it established the precedent of a company from the private sector seeking to adopt a public service function. The British series of *MOT* established three further precedents that influenced the thinking behind *This Modern Age*. First, Time Inc. and its owner, Henry Luce, conceived *MOT* not in order to make a profit in its own right, but rather as a vehicle for publicising *Time* magazine and their other media interests. Second, the bulk of the rental income generated by *MOT* was from the US. Despite the overheads incurred by the British operation, British exhibitors were thus able to pick up the finished product for a significantly lower price than one that would realistically be needed to recoup production costs ('B' features were distributed on a similar basis). Finally, the material produced by the British operation represented a collaboration between public and private sector film-makers, even if most of the compromising came from Grierson and his associates.

During the course of the Second World War things changed dramatically. The documentary movement had grown in stature and prominence, mainly as a result of their role in the war effort as a key element in the government's propaganda and public information campaigns. Another documentary compromise had achieved commercial success – the 'story documentary' – a formula in which wartime military operations were depicted in fictional narratives but with a cast of non-professional actors and an emphasis on authenticity in the *mise-en-scène*. As Andrew Higson has observed, part of the rationale behind the development of this genre was the need for government propaganda to reach a mass audience.[12] The unprecedented popularity of these films was interpreted in another way by the growing number of press critics and intellectuals who took an interest in film during and immediately after the war. They argued that the documentary movement had promoted the development of a 'realistic' style of film-making within commercial studios, and expressed a preference for this 'quality' British cinema on the grounds that it was closer to 'reality' than what they perceived as Hollywood escapism.

Although this position is rather more complex than the clear-cut moral elitism of Grierson in the 1930s, it still retained a sense of ideological opposition between the notion of documentary (intellectual and with educationalist connotations) and mainstream cinema as a form of mass-produced popular culture. As John Ellis points out in his definitive analysis of the ideological stance taken by these wartime film critics, their celebration of 'quality' cinema often placed them at odds with distributors and exhibitors.[13] Even so, the wartime period saw an increased degree of mainstream acceptance of the documentary movement's ideas and output.

At the same time, *The March of Time* was, by critical consent, in decline. By the end of the war its journalistic style had come to be regarded as a cultural symbol of the 1930s and as such less suited to the current affairs of the day. In 1949, Edgar Anstey reflected the views of many when he commented that 'today, [*MOT*] has become a medium for the editor rather than the director. The shooting is rarely imaginative and the characters are eliminated rather than interpreted.'[14]

The final significant wartime change relevant to this discussion is the emergence of Joseph Arthur Rank as the most powerful film industry executive in Britain in the 1940s.[15] By 1944, Rank owned or directly controlled approximately one-third of Britain's cinemas and two-thirds of the production, post-production and distribution infrastructure. This was an unprecedented degree of vertical integration (comparable only to the emergence of Gaumont-British following the 1927 Cinematograph Act) and attracted intense and sustained criticism from Rank's political opponents. They accused him of monopolistic and anti-competitive practices and in 1943 the Board of Trade initiated a public inquiry which resulted in a highly critical report, *Tendencies to Monopoly in the Cinematograph Films Industry* (known as the Palache Report, after the inquiry's chairman). Published the following year, it left no one in doubt as to the committee's main area of interest: one columnist described the report as 'really an account of Mr. Rank's recent business activities'.[16]

The organisation and production of *This Modern Age*

It was about this time that the idea for *This Modern Age* (*TMA*) began to take shape. From the evidence available as to who worked on the series, the range of subjects it covered, the ways in which it approached them and the production values it offered, it is possible to see *TMA* very much as a product of its institutional background. Reflected in the operation and output of this series are the commercial precedents established by *MOT*, the cultural agenda promoted by the documentary movement and an attempt to address the political issues raised by the establishment of the Rank Organisation as a large industrial conglomerate.

TMA was put together by a separate production unit within the Rank Organisation, an arrangement that was very much in line with Rank's policy of operating several autonomous companies, with all the shares deposited in a single holding company.[17] By 1949, the permanent staff of *TMA* numbered forty-four.[18] The producer and director in charge of the unit was Sergei Nolbandov, a Russian lawyer who had emigrated to Britain in the late 1920s and entered the film industry. By the outbreak of the war he was working for Ealing, where he produced and directed a number of propaganda features, before briefly joining the Films Division of the Ministry of Information. At the end of the war he was employed by Rank to begin preparatory work on *TMA*.[19] Nolbandov's work at Ealing offers an important clue as to what his priorities for the series were likely to be. The first feature he directed, *Ships With Wings* (1941), told the story of an aircraft carrier pilot who, having compromised himself as the result of an affair with a married woman, subsequently sacrifices his life in order to ensure the success of a mission. The film was criticised by press commentators and documentary movement writers for being overly melodramatic and not 'realistic' enough and for trivialising the 'why-we-fight' agenda that represented the film's apparent propaganda objective. As Jeffrey Richards' analysis of the Mass Observation study into the reception of this film shows, however, the combination of documentary authenticity and a romantic melodrama was immensely successful with audiences.[20] Nolbandov evidently had the ability to make realism popular, to implement the same sort of ideological compromise which enabled the success of the *March of Time* British series and the wartime story documentaries. It is tempting to speculate that this was what brought him to Rank's attention when *TMA* was in the planning stage.

The other key *TMA* personnel consisted of writers and directors drawn from a literary or journalistic background, and technicians taken from the periphery of the feature film industry. With the exception of assistant music director John Hollingsworth,[21] none of the regular *TMA* production staff had any significant connection with the documentary movement.[22] Immediately below Nolbandov, with the title of 'associate producer and literary editor', was George Ivan Smith, an Australian radio journalist and former head of the BBC Pacific Service. Others who worked on the research and script development for the series included the novelist and playwright James Lansdale Hodson, whose only significant film work before *TMA* was writing the commentary script for *Desert Victory* (Roy Boulting, 1943), and Robert Waithman, former diplomatic correspondent of the *News Chronicle*. The commentators included Bernard Miles and Robert Harris, the technical staff featured cameramen Ted Moore and Clifford Hornby, and the music director was Muir Mathieson, the internationally known composer and conductor of feature film scores who, in John Huntley's words, 'put British movie music on the map'.[23]

What is striking about this list of personnel is that members of the documentary movement were virtually excluded from the production of *TMA*. Why should this have been the case? There is evidence to suggest that its leading figures believed that the series did not live up to their expectations. Interviewed in 1977, Pat Jackson wrote it off as 'rather a poor imitation' of *MOT*, implying that a magazine film format inherently limited the scope for debate, which was the documentary movement's ideal, and that the popular screen journalism of *MOT* was its only feasible application.[24] Edgar Anstey had expressed similar sentiments in a contemporary article, noting that 'I am likely to be more conscious of aim than of achievement'.[25]

Even if Jackson and his colleagues were simply not interested in *TMA*, another possibility is that Rank's motivation for initiating the project was to appease his critics. Both the documentary movement and left-wing elements within the pre-1945 coalition government had taken an anti-Rank position in the monopoly debate. In particular, the Palache Report noted the limited opportunities available to producers without access to Rank-owned studio space and exhibition outlets. By capitalising on the cultural kudos of the British 'realist' cinema and offering a forum for political and social debates in a mainstream setting, Rank could claim to be practising responsible capitalism by fulfilling a public service obligation. The political film-maker Jill Craigie (whose B-feature documentary *The Way We Live* (1946) was also underwritten by Rank) expressed the situation rather less discreetly when she described *TMA* as 'a sop to the socialists'.[26]

Although *TMA* did not have any institutional connection with the documentary movement, the stated objectives of the series will seem familiar to anyone conversant with Grierson's writings. These objectives stressed that the series offered an impartial account of the issues covered, that it was intended to educate the viewer, and that it offered a deeper understanding of the subjects under discussion than anything available in the newsreels or popular press. A catalogue issued to cinemas in 1950 by General Film Distributors (GFD, the distribution arm of the Rank Organisation) claimed that:

> Just as a comparison can be made between a newsreel and the news page of a daily paper, so can *This Modern Age* be regarded as the film equivalent of the feature page, which provides the public with a clear idea of what it is that makes the news. *This Modern Age* is not biased in any way. It tackles the problems of nations and peoples who are playing important parts in the political and economic structures of the post-war world. Their difficulties are boldly explained and all possible solutions are given a hearing. *This Modern*

Age can be relied upon to give a complete and clear-sighted picture of every situation with which it deals. It is this quality which has lifted its reputation above that of any other feature and given it first place in the minds of cinema-goers.[27]

Rank's and Nolbandov's aims thus had much in common with those of the documentary movement at the end of the war. *TMA* was to be international in scale, it emphasised impartiality, and, crucially, it linked these attributes to the notion of 'quality'. This was all very similar to the arguments being put forward by their state sector counterparts. Basil Wright, for example, wrote in 1947 that 'it is in the international field that his [the documentarist's] major contribution is to be made', while *TMA*'s emphasis on discursivity is certainly consistent with Grierson's educationalist ethos.[28] But the political function Rank had in mind for *TMA* was to defuse the criticism of his dominant economic position, much of which originated from within the documentary movement. Thus it is hardly surprising that Rank sought to appropriate the movement's ideas but not its members.

This Modern Age: style and content

Stylistically, *TMA* resembled a conventional newsreel, although the production values were notably higher. The bulk of each twenty-minute film consisted of mute actuality footage in black and white, accompanied by a voice-over commentary and incidental music. Sometimes issues were dealt with in a fictionalised narrative format, but documentary exposition or debate were more common organisational models. Interviews with live sound were used more frequently than in most newsreels, and the music was specially composed or arranged, rather than adapted from library material. This was probably due to the higher budgets and longer production schedules available to the series. One aspect that clearly distinguished *TMA* from most other newsreels and documentaries dealing with current affairs was that all footage was originated on studio-quality 35mm stock, even if this meant transporting large quantities of heavy equipment over long distances. As one newsreel cameraman observed, '*TMA* looked beautiful, but it was like cracking a nut with a sledgehammer'.[29] Indeed, even today, some of the issues seem remarkable for their aesthetic quality, notably the cinematography in 'Antarctic Whale Hunt' (issue 12, October 1947) and the clarity of the sound recording in a sequence of tribal dancing from 'Challenge in Nigeria' (issue 19, June 1948).

Although there is a certain amount of overlap, the subjects covered by *TMA* can be broadly divided into four categories: those dealing with domestic political issues (ten films); those dealing with domestic social issues (eleven films); those dealing with international affairs (twenty films); and those eight of the films dealing with international affairs which discussed the forthcoming or putative independence of British Empire colonies and protectorates. Notable stylistic differences can be found between the films in these categories.

Probably the closest to the 'filmed debate' model described by GFD's press release were the issues dealing with the Empire, of which the first, 'Palestine' (issue 6, April 1947) is a representative example. The film examines in turn Jewish and Arab claims to the territory, before covering the more recent events that the narrator argues had precipitated the immediate crisis. Prominent among these were the bombing of the King David Hotel in Jerusalem by Jewish terrorists in July 1946, and links between senior Arab officials and the Nazis. The commentary of the film and the text of the press release issued by GFD stress that the Jewish and Arab cases are treated with scrupulous even-handedness. Extremists from both sides are condemned 'with equal force', and it is argued that Britain was struggling to maintain order in the territory under a League of Nations mandate with little or no help from the wider international community.[30]

Set against the emphasis on impartiality with which the Jewish and Arab cases are presented, there is a less prominent but equally discernible anti-American undercurrent to the film. Thus in the sequence dealing with the King David Hotel bombing, the commentary states that the Jewish

Plate 18   Filmed debate: a scene from 'Palestine' (1947), the sixth issue of *This Modern Age*.

terrorists justify their actions on the grounds of American demands that Britain should immediately admit 100,000 Holocaust refugees. In the closing section we are told that, 'The USA has conflicting interests, which led to support for anti-British Jews at home and appeasement of Arabs for new American oil concessions in Saudi-Arabia.'[31] These sentiments are certainly consistent with the British Government's claims that the USA was hindering its attempts at reducing political tension in Palestine, which stemmed in part from the British Foreign Secretary's alleged 'pathological bitterness' toward President Truman.[32] All this tends to support the view that *TMA* represented a concession on Rank's part toward the Labour Government of the time, as did the numerous *TMA* issues dealing with domestic politics which broadly supported government policy. In a review of one issue, Joan Lester suspected that 'some of Mr. Rank's Tory friends were shocked at the most telling tributes the Labour Government has ever had'.[33]

Although these political undercurrents were an important element in several *TMA* issues, it was the emphasis on even-handedness that captured the attention of the majority of reviewers and critics. An anonymous *Documentary News Letter* reviewer spoke for many in concluding that 'the balance struck leaves each side equally deserving, each equally blameworthy'.[34] The same approach and critical reception can be found to some degree with all the *TMA* issues on international affairs and are strongly apparent in those dealing with Empire countries. For example, in 'Sudan Dispute' (issue 8, April 1947), the Sudanese arguments for independence are contrasted with concerns that an independent Sudan would threaten Egyptian security and destabilise international relations within the region. 'Challenge in Nigeria' (issue 19, June 1948) describes the abolition of slavery and the evolution of a democratic system of administration under British rule. It then warns that 'it will not be enough to hand the Government over to an educated minority, or to return the people to the lordship of traditional rulers'.[35]

In the *TMA* films concerned with domestic political and social issues, the structure of each film was less rigid and the producers evidently did not feel the need to be quite as circumspect in their arguments. Overt support for government initiatives can be found in many of the releases in the political category. 'Homes for All' (issue 1, September 1946) strongly advocates town planning and the government's programme for rebuilding the blitzed inner cities. 'Coal Crisis' (issue 7, April 1947) defended the nationalisation of the coal industry to such an extent that it is alleged that Rank was reluctant to release it.[36] 'Development Areas' (issue 9, May 1947) describes Britain's industrial heritage as 'shot through with the tragedy of unemployment' and then explains how the Ministry of Works is attempting to promote industrial regeneration by subsidising development in the worst hit regions.[37] 'Education for Living' (issue 27, April 1948) describes the improvements in primary and secondary schools brought about by the 1948 Education Act.

'Fight for a Fuller Life' (issue 30, September 1949) does the same for further and higher education.

In terms of their filmic style, the most variable category of *TMA* issues was that dealing with social affairs. A greater degree of aesthetic and technical experimentation is evident in this group of films, while the arguments they put forward tended to be less complex. 'Scotland Yard' (issue 2, October 1946) uses the investigation of a petty crime as the basis for a miniature story documentary, into which is slotted some quickly paced action, a tightly constructed but detailed commentary, nuanced cinematography and intricate editing. A tense atmosphere is created by the total absence of diegetic or ambient sound and a bare minimum of music, while the commentary alternates between a third-person narrative and direct address to the spectator ('if you have ever been convicted, you are indexed here, under your name and every one of your aliases').[38] The message of the film is notably unsubtle, arguing that the purchase of illicit goods from black marketeers, or 'spivs', indirectly supports far more serious organised crime (the film was re-released the following year as part of a police campaign against the black market).[39] But the overall impression given by the film is of aesthetic innovation rather than social commentary.

The less formal approach that characterised this component of *TMA*'s output sometimes appears naïve and overly simplistic. Viewed today, the most entertaining issue in the whole series is probably 'The British – Are They Artistic?' (issue 16, February 1948). Just as press critics espoused 'quality' cinema, the commentary of this film makes a crude distinction between 'high' and 'low' culture. The film-makers cut between Myra Hess giving a concert in the National Gallery and a dance band in a nightclub, and between bookshop shelves containing monographs on art history and volumes entitled *Virgins from Hell* and *Bed for Beginners: Being a Gentleman's Guide to Scientific Seduction in Eight Easy Lessons*.[40] The film culminates in an interview with Robert Donat, who distinguishes between 'good' and 'bad' films according to the degree to which they reflect a populist or elitist culture. Interestingly, the film also includes a strong condemnation of entertainment tax, which was vehemently opposed by the Rank Organisation at that time.[41]

Conclusion

If we accept the argument that *TMA* was regarded by Rank in part as a political bargaining chip in his dealings with the Attlee Government, then the financial crisis within the Rank Organisation which precipitated its end reflected the wider collapse of that relationship. On 6 August 1947 the Board of Trade imposed a 75 per cent *ad valorem* tax on box-office receipts from all imported films as a result of failed trade negotiations with the Americans. In response Hollywood placed a blanket embargo on all exports to the UK. The Rank Organisation was the only British company with any realistic hope of producing a sufficient volume of films to prevent cinema closures, and Rank agreed to underwrite a huge production drive of mass-produced, low-budget feature films. The tax, and subsequently the American embargo, was lifted the following spring just as the first batch of films was ready for release. These films stood little chance of competing at the box office against a nine-month backlog of Hollywood 'A' features. The extent to which Rank felt aggrieved at the government's U-turn is a matter for debate, but what is a matter of record is that the Rank Organisation sustained pre-tax losses of £16,286,521 between the imposition of the tax and the annual shareholders' meeting in September 1949.[42] At that meeting, Rank stated that 'Even if all our films had been of the quality that we had hoped, the unusually strong competition would have made it difficult to achieve satisfactory results'.[43] During the following year the production side of the Rank Organisation underwent major retrenchment. *This Modern Age*, as a politically motivated loss leader, was one of the first victims. On 15 December 1949 a Rank spokesman told a press conference that the series would be terminated once the twelve issues currently in production were complete.[44]

Although the immediate events leading to the closure of *This Modern Age* were specific to the Rank Organisation, it echoed a general trend of contraction for the British non-fiction film. Another consequence of the Rank restructuring was that the production facilities of the two newsreels it owned, Gaumont-British and Universal, were merged in 1949, after which the only difference between the two was in celebrity commentators. The agreement between the Cinema Exhibitors' Association and the Central Office of Information (COI) allowing for the exhibition of government information films came under pressure towards the end of 1949. The Crown Film Unit was subsequently closed down by the incoming Conservative Government in 1952; with it went the COI monthly releases. Meanwhile television current affairs was beginning to make its presence felt: the BBC Television Newsreel was launched in January 1948, expanded to three editions per week in 1950 and relaunched as a daily programme, *News and Newsreel*, in July 1954.

This Modern Age was very much a product of its time. The approaches it used to tackle political and ideological issues had their cinematic precedents in *The March of Time*, the work of the documentary movement before and during the war and in Nolbandov's background in what Grierson might have called 'the commercial treatment of actuality'. There was little commercial justification for *TMA*, as the prevailing distribution and exhibition practices prevented the series from earning any significant revenue. In the absence of such justification, *TMA* was also designed to fulfil a political objective for the Rank Organisation; when it became clear that the series was no longer achieving that objective then the writing was already on the wall, as it was for a number of other political institutions. The range of themes and subjects covered by *TMA*, and the unique ways in which its producers tried to make documentaries with entertainment value, reflect these factors very closely. It is no coincidence that the dates of the series almost exactly mirror those of the 1945–1951 Labour Governments.

NOTES

Thanks to Justine Ashby, Alan Burton, Nicholas Cull, Andrew Higson, Vincent Porter and Jeffrey Richards for comments on earlier versions of this paper.

1 *Public Opinion*, 8 December 1950.
2 Board of Trade, *Distribution and Exhibition of Cinematograph Films* (Cmd. 7837), 23 November 1949, para. 41, p. 19.
3 Ibid., para. 10, p. 7.
4 *The Bernstein Film Questionnaire Report, 1947* (copy in BFI library), p. 16.
5 'The cinema programme in Great Britain', in R. Manvell (ed.) *The Cinema, 1951*, Harmondsworth, Pelican, 1951, p. 186.
6 *World Film News*, June 1936, vol. 1, no. 3, inside front cover.
7 See J. Beveridge, *John Grierson: Film Master*, New York, Macmillan, 1978, pp. 112–17.
8 J. Grierson, 'First principles of documentary', in H.F. Hardy (ed.) *Grierson on Documentary*, London, Collins, 1946, p. 80.
9 J. Grierson, 'Pity the journalist', *World Film News*, October 1936, vol. 1, no. 7, pp. 6–7.
10 B. Winston, *Claiming the Real: The Documentary Film Revisited*, London, BFI, 1995, p. 63.
11 P. Rotha, 'Afterword (1972)', in Ian Aitken (ed.) *The Documentary Film Movement*, Edinburgh, Edinburgh University Press, 1998, p. 161; *World Film News*, April 1936, vol. 1, no. 2, p. 3.
12 A. Higson, *Waving the Flag: Constructing a National Cinema in Britain*, Oxford, Clarendon Press, 1995, pp. 203–4.
13 J. Ellis, 'The quality film adventure: British critics and the cinema, 1942–48', in A. Higson (ed.) *Dissolving Views: Key Writings on British Cinema*, London, Cassell, 1996, p. 67.
14 E. Anstey, 'The magazine film', *Penguin Film Review*, May 1949, no. 9, p. 21.
15 See A. Wood, *Mr. Rank*, London, Hodder and Stoughton, 1952; and G. Macnab, *J. Arthur Rank and the British Film Industry*, London, Routledge, 1993.
16 *New Statesman and Nation*, 12 August 1944.
17 On the financial structure of the Rank Organisation, see Wood, op. cit., pp. 106–202, and Macnab, op. cit., pp. 17–34.
18 Press release issued by This Modern Age Ltd. (copy in BFI library microfiche).
19 On Nolbandov, see C. Barr, *Ealing Studios*, 2nd edn, London, Studio Vista, 1993, pp. 13–38; and C. Moorehead, *Sidney Bernstein: A Biography*, London, Jonathan Cape, 1984, p. 164.
20 J. Richards, 'Wartime British audiences and the class system: The case of *Ships With Wings*', *Historical Journal of Film, Radio and Television*, 1987, vol. 7, no. 2, pp. 130–1.
21 While with the RAF Symphony Orchestra, he had arranged and conducted the music for several documentaries, including *Target for Tonight* (Harry Watt, 1941).

22 *TMA*, issue 7, 'Coal Crisis' (released in April 1947) was jointly produced by Nolbandov and Edgar Anstey, who had been involved in the documentary movement before the war.
23 J. Huntley, *British Film Music*, London, Skelton Robinson, 1947, p. 37.
24 E. Sussex, *The Rise and Fall of British Documentary*, Berkeley, University of California Press, 1977, p. 166.
25 Anstey, op. cit., p. 17.
26 Macnab, op. cit., p. 136.
27 GFD release catalogue, 1950: copy in 'General Film Distributors' subject file, BFI Library.
28 B. Wright, 'Documentary today', *Penguin Film Review*, January 1947, no. 2, p. 43.
29 J. Ballantyne (ed.) *Researcher's Guide to British Newsreels, vol. 2*, London, British Universities' Film and Video Council, 1988, p. 33.
30 GFD press release for 'Palestine' (*This Modern Age* microfiche, BFI Library).
31 'Palestine'. Source: NFTVA, print no. 2029715B, reel 2, 868–899ft.
32 D. Leitch, 'Explosion at the King David Hotel' in Michael Sissons and Philip French (eds) *Age of Austerity, 1945–51*, 2nd edn, Oxford, Oxford University Press, 1986, p. 64.
33 *Reynolds News*, 19 September 1948 (microfiche in BFI Library).
34 *Documentary News Letter*, 1947, vol. 6, no. 56, p. 89.
35 'Challenge in Nigeria'. Source: NFTVA, print no. 2034874B, reel 2, 701–728ft.
36 Sussex, op. cit., p. 166.
37 'Development Areas'. Source: NFTVA, print no. 43289A, reel 1, 67–91ft.
38 'Scotland Yard'. Source: NFTVA, print no. 2030208B, reel 1, 544–570ft.
39 *London Evening Standard*, 16 September 1947 (microfiche in BFI Library).
40 'The British – Are They Artistic?'. Source: NFTVA, print no. 47519A, reel 1, 752–759ft.
41 Ibid., reel 2, 63–90ft.
42 J. Arthur Rank's statement to shareholders, September 1949 (copy in 'Rank Organisation' subject file, BFI Library).
43 Ibid.
44 *Daily Mail,* 16 December 1949 (microfiche in BFI Library).

15

'UNDER-THE-SKIN HORRORS'

Social realism and classlessness in *Peeping Tom* and the British New Wave

Adam Lowenstein

The challenge issued to audiences of *Peeping Tom* on its original release in 1960 proved so threatening that the response of an outraged British press remains a 'landmark in British cinema'.[1] At the time, critics simply could not stomach Michael Powell's disturbing horror film, with its story of a troubled young man whose childhood subjection to his father's cruel psychological experiments leads him to murder the women he films. Today, with *Peeping Tom* firmly established as one of the towering achievements of British film-making, many scholars delight in reproducing their favourite quotations from among the critics' original declarations of seething hatred. But as Ian Christie warns, simply to dismiss these reviews as hysterical or dim-witted is to 'run the risk of incorporating [the film] into a cultish nostalgia'.[2] Unfortunately, much of the scholarship on *Peeping Tom* that has avoided revelling in such 'cultish nostalgia' has also tended to remove the film from its social and historical context. Such scholarship refers to *Peeping Tom* as the ultimate 'film-about-film', what Peter Wollen calls a cold, intellectualised 'aestheticization of death' and a film so neatly prescient of 1970s psychoanalytic film theory that 'psychoanalytic criticism is not simply imposed externally, but justified internally'.[3] Laura Mulvey goes so far as to say, '*Peeping Tom* offers realistic images that relate to the cinema and *nothing more*. It creates a magic space for its fiction somewhere between the camera's lens and the projector's beam of light on the screen.'[4]

In this chapter, I will push *Peeping Tom* beyond the 'magic space' between lens and projector, into the historical realm of contemporary social crisis. I will argue that Powell's film exacerbates anxieties of 'classlessness' precipitated by an ascendant mass culture in late 1950s and early 1960s Britain, while the concurrent films of the British New Wave soothe these same anxieties. By juxtaposing *Peeping Tom* with a key New Wave film, Jack Clayton's *Room at the Top* (1959), I hope not only to return the former to British film history, but also to illuminate contemporary critical discourses regarding realism and taste that suggest the political significance of *Peeping Tom* at a flashpoint in British social history.

Refiguring *Peeping Tom*'s reception

Isabel Quigly, film critic for *The Spectator*, had disposed of Georges Franju's French horror film *Eyes Without a Face* (1959) in February of 1960 by calling it 'the sickest film since I started film criticism'.[5] But in April, with the release of *Peeping Tom*, she revised her earlier judgement. Rather than undertake a broad survey of contemporary reviews, I want to quote Quigly at some length and analyse her review in close detail since she is simultaneously quite representative of the British press's verdict and unusually suggestive in her detraction:

> [*Peeping Tom*] turns out to be the sickest and filthiest film I remember seeing. Some weeks ago we had *Eyes Without a Face*, which I thought set a record for highbrow horrors. It was perhaps more directly ghastly – there were worse visual horrors (the operating scenes) – but it didn't involve you, it made little attempt at direct emotional realism, as *Peeping Tom* does; you had the creeps, but remotely, and often with amusement. *Peeping Tom* didn't make me want to streak out of the cinema shrieking, as Franju's film did at times; it gives me the creeps in retrospect, in my heart and mind more than in my eyes. We have had glossy horrors before ... but never such insinuating, under-the-skin horrors, and never quite such a bland effort to make it look as if this isn't for nuts but for normal homely filmgoers like you and me.[6]

Quigly's distinction between the remote, amusing thrills of *Eyes Without a Face* and the direct, confrontational insinuations of *Peeping Tom* does not rest on the presence of graphic gore. How then, in her view, does Powell get under the skin of his audience without following Franju in literally peeling away the skin of his onscreen victims?

For Quigly, the charged term that differentiates *Peeping Tom* is 'direct emotional realism'. She feels directly addressed by a film she believes *should* have been speaking to the 'nuts' in the crowd rather than to the 'normal homely filmgoers'. She responds to an unnerving sense of inclusion, of collapsed boundaries between herself and an imagined audience of pathologised others. *Peeping Tom*'s 'realism' blurs distinctions of intended audience address – indeed, the film's status as 'the sickest and filthiest' in memory lends it the air of a communicable disease. The jolt which accompanies this new kind of realism results from its painful demand that 'normal' viewers recognise *themselves* as the 'nuts' they have constructed as their others.

Although Quigly acknowledges *Peeping Tom*'s call for self-recognition from its spectators, she does not accept it.[7] Instead, she erects sharp divisions between certain types of films, audiences, and film-makers in order to underline divergences in maturity, social responsibility, and above all, taste. For example, although she opens the review by asking, 'What *are* we coming to, what sort of people are we in this country, to make, or see, or seem to want (so it gets made) a film like [*Peeping Tom*]?', it is clear by the end of the review that Quigly does not wish to include herself as part of this 'we'.[8] Instead, she safeguards her own privileged access to a moral position completely outside the film's purview, where a tasteful 'us' stands apart from and untainted by a tasteless 'them'. The horror film enthusiasts, the 'nuts', are thus contrasted with 'normal homely filmgoers like you and me'. The distinction also informs Quigly's claim that *Peeping Tom* is beneath the 'remarkable technical gifts' of Powell, 'a man who was once respected' as the director of such esteemed films as *The Red Shoes* (1948). She now relegates Powell to the lowly ranks of purveyors of British horror, who are not considered film-makers at all, but 'children playing "dares"'.[9] Other reviewers shared Quigly's sense of betrayal at the association of Powell's name and artistic reputation with *Peeping Tom*. For example, Leonard Mosley complained, 'Mr. Michael Powell (who once made such outstanding films as *Black Narcissus* [1946] and *A Matter of Life and Death* [1946]) produced and directed *Peeping Tom* and I think he ought to be ashamed of himself.'[10] Dilys Powell added, 'It is made by a director of skill and sensibility ... The same stylist's view it is which now and then makes the torturer's stuff of the new film look like the true imaginative thing ... instead of the vulgar squalor it really is.'[11] These reviews express outrage over a lack of taste – explicitly attributed to Michael Powell, but also implicitly directed toward the kind of viewers who would 'see or seem to want' a film like *Peeping Tom*.

Pierre Bourdieu reminds us of the political significance of taste by observing that taste 'fulfill[s] a social function of legitimating social differences'. Taste defines and divides classes by virtue of its negative essence: taste always takes shape in contradistinction to other tastes. In this sense, 'tastes are perhaps first and foremost distastes, disgust provoked by horror of visceral intolerance ("sick-making") of the tastes of others'.[12] With Bourdieu's formulation in mind, the affinities between Quigly's apprehensive review of *Peeping Tom* and Richard Hoggart's contemporaneous, pathbreaking sociological study of British mass culture, *The Uses of Literacy* (1957), become especially striking. In Hoggart's analysis of postwar British society, 'the great majority of us are being merged into one class'.[13] For Hoggart, an emergent mass culture is erasing traditional class-specific cultures (particularly those belonging to the working class) and creating a 'faceless' and 'classless' mass society that he considers to be 'less healthy' than the one it is replacing.[14] British anxieties concerning 'the masses' at this particular historical moment are also evoked (and critiqued) by Raymond Williams, in his conclusion to *Culture and Society* (1958): 'The masses are always the others, whom we don't know, and can't know. Yet now, in our kind of society, we see these others regularly, in their myriad variations; stand, physically, beside them. They are here, and we are here with them.'[15] Although Prime Minister Harold Macmillan could point to Britain's economic growth in the late 1950s and confidently announce that 'the class war is over and we have won',[16] the notion of 'classlessness' evoked by Williams and Hoggart implies an inability to maintain the usual distinctions that allowed the bourgeoisie to differentiate themselves from the working class.

Given these factors, perhaps we might best understand Quigly's review of *Peeping Tom* in terms of the perceived threat presented to the middle class by the ascendance of a 'classless' mass culture. *Peeping Tom*, itself an example of mass cultural entertainment, is also saturated with images portraying the very manifestations of an 'unhealthy' mass culture mentioned by Hoggart, including movies, pornographic pin-ups and the commodification of sensational violence. What finally comprises the film's 'insinuating, under-the-skin horrors' is its capability not only to inhabit mass culture in a confrontational manner, but also to draw resistant viewers into a recognition of their own reflection within this mass culture. An acknowledgement of this kind suggests, as Quigly herself points out, the recognition of a new type of cinematic realism.

Conflicting realisms

What, then, does *Peeping Tom*'s 'realism' have to do with the 'kitchen sink' realism characteristic of the films of the British New Wave? Powell's first choice for the role of *Peeping Tom*'s killer, Mark Lewis (Carl Boehm), was Laurence Harvey, star of one of the most definitive and successful films of the New Wave, *Room at the Top*.[17] But this is not the only connection between the two films. Critical reactions to *Room at the Top* echo the concern with realism present in Quigly's review of *Peeping Tom*, though to a very different end. In a typical example from the *Daily Express*, Leonard Mosley states that

> *Room at the Top* was the real eye-opener for me – the real proof that something had happened in the cinema. For here was a British film which, at long last, got its teeth into those subjects which have always been part and parcel of our lives, but have hitherto been taboo subjects on the prissy British screen ... It is savagely frank and brutally truthful.[18]

Quigly herself heralded *Room at the Top* by proclaiming, 'At last, at long, long last, a British film that talks about life here today ... slap in the middle of the dissolving and reforming social patterns of our time and place'.[19] Even *Room at the Top*'s X certificate from the British Board of Film Censors, a rating then evoking an 'aura of disreputability' associated with horror and exploitation fare,[20] could not dampen critical enthusiasm for the film. Derek Monsey in the *Sunday Express* claimed that *Room at the Top* had 'earned' its rating, 'not for meretricious horror or peek-hole sex: but for sheer, blatant honesty ... In this case at least, and at last, the X certificate looks like a badge of honour'.[21] The realism of *Room at the Top*, though 'savage' and 'brutal', clearly managed to sway the critics in a way *Peeping Tom* could not.

In *Room at the Top*, a working-class clerk, Joe Lampton (Laurence Harvey), leaves the depressed industrial town of Dufton for the more prosperous Warnley and resolves to procure there all the trappings of a more privileged lifestyle: the right car, the right home, and most important, the right woman. He sets his sights on Susan Brown (Heather Sears), the daughter of his employer, who is one of Warnley's wealthiest men. He wins her, but along the way, he falls in love with the older, married, and penniless Alice Aisgill (Simone Signoret). Susan becomes pregnant by Joe, and he agrees to marry her in a bargain with her father that avoids the humiliation of Susan having a child out of wedlock in exchange for Joe's promotion to a comfortable position in the company. As part of the arrangement, Joe must also abandon Alice. Alice reacts by committing suicide, and Joe's wedding is poisoned by regret over a life passed up, and dread of the life to come.

The jumble of elements comprising social realism in *Room at the Top* reflects the somewhat complex prehistory of the New Wave.[22] In one sense, the New Wave grew out of 'The Movement', a literary circle of the early and mid-1950s that included Philip Larkin and Kingsley Amis. J.D. Scott coined the term 'The Movement' in a 1954 column, where he characterised it as 'anti-phoney ... sceptical, robust, ironic, prepared to be as comfortable as possible in a wicked, commercial, threatened world', and a vital component of 'that tide which is pulling us through the Fifties and towards the Sixties'.[23] The Movement gained a mythical dimension with the addition of the Angry Young Man, a figure brought to life in such plays as John Osborne's *Look Back In Anger* (first performed in 1956, then filmed in 1959 by Tony Richardson) and in literature like John Braine's novel *Room at the Top*, published in 1957.

In another sense, the New Wave drew on Free Cinema, a documentary film movement represented by an important series of screenings at the National Film Theatre in London between 1956 and 1959 and led by Lindsay Anderson, Karel Reisz and Tony Richardson – all of whom went on to direct key New Wave films. The New Wave's gritty, spare aesthetic of kitchen sink realism is heavily indebted to the documentary style of Free Cinema, which focused on depictions of the English working class. The 'realist' impulse behind Free Cinema, later imported to the New Wave, is outlined by Lindsay Anderson:

> The number of British films that have ever made a genuine try at a story in a popular milieu, with working-class characters all through, can be counted on the fingers of one hand. This virtual rejection of three-quarters of the population of this country represents more than a ridiculous impoverishment of the cinema. It is characteristic of a flight from contemporary reality.[24]

The New Wave broke into the commercial mainstream by combining aspects of the Movement and Free Cinema with the character of the Angry Young Man. But just what kind of 'contemporary reality' (to use Anderson's term) did these films finally represent, especially with regard to their engagement of bourgeois anxieties about mass culture?

Peeping Tom and *Room at the Top*

A comparison of the openings of *Room at the Top* and *Peeping Tom* reveals a telling insistence on maintaining spatialised class boundaries in the former, and a tendency to violate such boundaries in the latter. *Room at the Top* begins with a journey that quite literally provides viewers with a well-marked road map to Joe Lampton's working-class identity. Joe sits and smokes in a railway carriage, with his shoeless feet elevated. He reads a newspaper which features 'Nottingham' in its front page headline, verifying the locale of the bleak industrial landscape passing outside the window. In a heavily symbolic gesture, Joe dons a new pair of shoes in preparation for his arrival at Warnley. Once reaching the Warnley station, he takes a taxi to the town hall, catches the eye of every secretary in the outer office of the treasurer's department, and finally meets privately with his boss. The sequence ends with Joe's first hungry glimpse of an obviously wealthy Susan Brown, whom he spies in the street from an office window. Joe's colleague, Charles Soames (Donald Houston), follows his gaze and cautions, 'That's not for you, lad.' Joe responds, 'That's what I'm going to have.'

The sequence carefully defines Joe's class status by contrasting his comfort and sense of belonging in certain spaces (the train as it passes through the industrial environs; the outer office while the secretaries ogle him) with his awkward exclusion from others (the private office, where he cringes at his boss's suggestion that the people of Warnley are more 'civilised' than those of Dufton; the affluent world conveyed by Susan's clothing, car and boyfriend). This meticulous spatialisation of Joe's working-class identity produces a peculiar spectator position characteristic of the New Wave films, which John Hill (partially paraphrasing Andrew Higson) describes as a viewpoint ' "outside and above", marking a separation between spectator and subject, [where] the pleasures delivered may well rely less on recognition than the very sensation of class difference'.[25] Joe Lampton may signify the arrival of a new kind of character on the British screen, but the film's inscription of the viewer's relation to him resembles the ethnographic stance of an observer re-creating an unusual species in exacting 'authentic' detail. Reviewer praise for the 'accuracy' of Harvey's performance as Joe attests to the pleasure possible in understanding him as an ethnographic specimen.[26] The bourgeoisie watch an impeccably 'realistic' representation of a working-class character, but the film's insistence on the viewer's distance from him (and from the 'working-class' spaces he inhabits) bypasses any sort of meaningful social recognition of working-class subjects. Instead, the dominant sensation surrounding the middle-class encounter with Joe is closer to what Higson calls 'cultural tourism', where a 'self-conscious aestheticization ... erases the danger, the traces of the otherness, rendering [the] exotic and spectacular ... like so [much else] with which "we" are familiar'.[27]

The opening of *Peeping Tom*, on the other hand, disorients viewers as thoroughly as *Room at the Top*'s introduction reassures and guides them. The film begins with a close-up of a closed eye, which opens with the sound of a camera shutter click. Already Powell has set in motion the questions that will lead viewers to approach the film with a profound sense of unease, and not a little distrust. Whose eye is this? Is it wide-eyed with fright or excitement? Does it open *because* it is being photographed, or is the camera click inseparable from the physical functioning of the eye itself, as involuntary as blinking? Is this the gaze of the film-maker, looking out at the spectators, or a reflection of the audience's own gaze, as they open their eyes to begin watching the film?

The next shot relieves viewers of these disconcerting questions of motivation and agency by establishing a concrete setting: an empty street at night, the uneven glow of street lamps, a woman standing outside a shop window, a man whistling as he approaches her. On the surface, this is exactly the kind of 'realistic' setting so fetishised by the New Wave – contemporary, gritty (or 'working class'), evocative of social issues (here, of course, prostitution). Yet the aura of unease introduced by the film's first shot lingers. For this is not the 'authentic' location shot of the New Wave – it is clearly a self-consciously 'cinematic' phantasmagoria, a studio set with garish lighting and shadowy scenery. As if to confirm an impression of artificial constructedness, the next shot is a close-up of a movie camera cradled inside a jacket lapel, whirring quietly as it is switched on. The camera approaches the spectator directly, blurring out of focus as it draws too close – to the screen, to the audience, to the film-maker filming the film-maker. The camera's unforgiving inspection of the body, clothing, and apartment interior of the prostitute-victim Dora (Brenda Bruce) seems just as invasive as the most weakly motivated working-class location or character study in a New Wave film, but there are key differences in *Peeping Tom*. The audience's initial investigation of Dora comes through the cross hairs of Mark's viewfinder, and spectators immediately re-experience their deliberate participation in

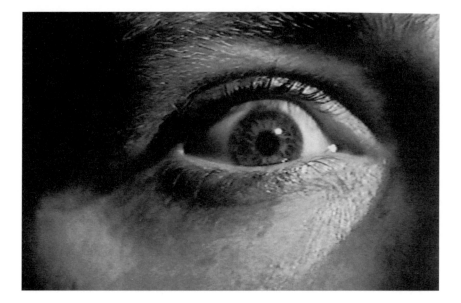

Plate 19   In the eye of the beholder: the under-the-skin horrors of mass consumer culture are reflected back at *Peeping Tom*'s (Michael Powell, 1959) middle-class audience.

this spectacle as they watch Mark (still faceless, just another anonymous film-goer) watching his black-and-white footage of the murder that has just taken place.

The sequence lays bare the potential violence inherent in the social realism so unproblematically adopted by the New Wave. Not only is the camera's subject explicitly rendered as a vulnerable target, but the black-and-white film itself (a stylistic hallmark of every New Wave production) is revealed as an artificial construction of 'reality' with no privileged claim on any social truth. Even Mark's private screening does not reproduce all the images glimpsed only seconds before in colour during the 'live' encounter. The insistent implication of viewer and film-maker in this sequence concludes, appropriately enough, with the credit 'Directed by Michael Powell' superimposed over Mark's projector. Here, then, is a model for the 'direct emotional realism' that strikes Quigly as so 'insinuating', a realism that locates the viewer squarely in the field of the other, not somehow 'outside and above' it. Quigly can praise *Room at the Top* for a brand of social realism that captures 'life here today' amid the 'dissolving and reforming social patterns of our time and place' because the film removes the threat of involvement with these changes, and allows instead for distant, painless contemplation. *Peeping Tom*'s 'under-the-skin' realism, on the other hand, shows that these shifting social currents are shot through with anxieties that include viewers 'like you and me' as agonised participants in 'life here today'.

Beyond 'magic spaces'

I have argued for an assessment of *Peeping Tom* that looks beyond the metafilmic 'magic space' between lens and projector and reinserts the film in its cultural context. By way of conclusion, I will turn to a scene in the film that reaches the heights of cinematic self-reflexivity, but simultaneously registers the film's determination to confront the viewer with contemporary social crisis. The scene occurs later in the film, as Mark's private screening of his murder of the actress Vivian (Moira Shearer) is interrupted by his downstairs neighbour, the blind, drunken Mrs Stephens (Maxine Audley). Mark has been dating Mrs Stephens's daughter, Helen (Anna Massey). The interaction between Mark and Mrs Stephens is measured and distant at first, but then becomes increasingly tactile, as well as sexually suggestive.[28] They perform a sort of dance composed of tentative lunges and parries, without ever making physical contact. At one point, Mark withdraws from her and switches on the projector. She draws closer, reaching out to feel the film reel itself. Finally, Mark touches her, violently at first, as he restrains her arm, but then gently, as he steadies and guides her. 'Take me to your cinema,' she says, and Mark obliges by leading her ever closer to the screen itself, which reflects the image of the murdered Vivian's face (itself growing larger in tighter and tighter close-up). Mark loses bodily contact with Mrs Stephens as he moves ahead of her, completely enraptured in Vivian's image. Mrs Stephens reaches forward to Mark, and then upwards as if to touch the projector beam. Powell accentuates the motion of her hand by following its movement through a cut that reveals the most striking composition of the film. From foreground to background, we see the following: the hand of Mrs Stephens, striving to catch the projector beam; Mark's back, arching in anticipation; and the screen with Vivian's image. But that is not all. As the close-up of Vivian tightens, her ghostly refracted image on Mark's back forms a death's-head shadow.

In notes for a book on film aesthetics that would much later become *Theory of Film: The Redemption of Physical Reality* (1960), Siegfried Kracauer states: 'The face counts for nothing in film unless it includes the death's-head beneath.'[29] Kracauer is referring to film's potential for shock, its threat to 'the viewer's sense of identity, stability, and control'.[30] For Kracauer, 'the representation of horror in film is legitimate because film has the capability and therefore the obligation to reveal the material dimension in its utmost limits'.[31] Kracauer's 'death's-head', as Miriam Hansen explains, 'deflate[s] the image of the sovereign individual' and turns toward an historical materiality that reveals 'the actual state of disorder and crisis'.[32] In this sense, Kracauer follows Walter Benjamin, who claims the death's-head represents 'everything about history that, from the very beginning, has been untimely, sorrowful, unsuccessful'.[33]

The death's-head of *Peeping Tom*, in the tenor of horror suggested by Kracauer and Benjamin, crystallises the film's confrontational engagement with social crisis. This scene is a remarkably unsettling actualisation of Hoggart's fear that 'the great majority of us are being merged into one class' in a 'faceless' mass society – a multiplicity of human bodies, both 'physical' and 'spectral', converging and blending under the sign of cinema. The scene also accesses the long history of associations between mass culture and a femininity coded as passive and consuming.[34] Rarely has the British cinema offered a more disturbing depiction of the infectious, 'feminising' threat of mass culture than a female victim, seemingly safely contained within the mass cultural medium of film, breaking those bounds and assuming a new 'material' form. Perhaps it is not too outlandish to suggest that here, in *Peeping Tom*, we have the beginnings of a discourse which counters Hoggart's narrative of upstanding working-class mothers being replaced by 'flighty, careless and inane' teenage girls passively enslaved to mass culture.[35] Against all expectation, *Peeping Tom* thus shares a certain kinship with Carolyn Steedman's eloquent history/biography *Landscape for a Good Woman* (1986), which represents a landmark in the development of such a counter-discourse. I believe *Peeping Tom*'s transgression of self-reflexive 'magic spaces' and insistence on 'direct emotional realism' can ultimately shock viewers into a position in which they feel truly implicated in social upheaval. A similar sense of implication animates Steedman's desire to remove 'passivity from the figures in Hoggart's … landscape, [and to suggest] what desperations may lie behind the doors of the terraced houses'.[36] In the end, *Peeping Tom*'s notion of social realism depends on presenting these desperations as our own, while *Room at the Top* and many other British New Wave films reassure us that 'realism' hinges on displacing desperation to others. As Michael Powell has so aptly remarked: 'No wonder that when [the critics] got me alone and out on a limb with *Peeping Tom*, they gleefully sawed off the limb and jumped up and down on the corpse.'[37]

NOTES

For their encouragement and helpful criticism on various versions of this essay, I would like to thank Justine Ashby, Lauren Berlant, Ian Christie, Tom Gunning, Miriam Hansen, Andrew Higson, James Lastra, William Paul, Allison Smith, and William Veeder.

1 I. Christie, 'The scandal of *Peeping Tom*', in I. Christie (ed.) *Powell, Pressburger and Others*, London, BFI, 1978, p. 53. Christie's article surveys a cross-section of British criticism of the film during its original release and provides an important backdrop for this chapter.
2 I. Christie, *Arrows of Desire: The Films of Michael Powell and Emeric Pressburger*, London and Boston, Faber and Faber, 1994, p. 94.

3 P. Wollen, 'Dying for art', *Sight and Sound*, December 1994, vol. 4, no. 12, pp. 20, 21. I am not dismissing psychoanalytically-informed readings of *Peeping Tom*, merely pointing out how they have structured critical discussion of the film.

4 L. Mulvey, *Peeping Tom* laserdisc liner notes, New York, Voyager Company, 1994. My emphasis.

5 I. Quigly, 'The small savages', *The Spectator*, 5 February 1960, p. 182.

6 I. Quigly, 'Filthy pictures', *The Spectator*, 15 April 1960, p. 544.

7 The following reading of Quigly's review is informed by Michel Foucault's concept of a 'fellowship of discourse'. See M. Foucault, 'The discourse on language', in *The Archaeology of Knowledge and the Discourse on Language*, trans. A.M. Sheridan Smith, New York, Pantheon, 1972, pp. 215–37; esp. 225–6.

8 Quigly, 'Filthy pictures', op. cit., p. 544.

9 Ibid.

10 L. Mosley, 'Let's not peddle sex that suits this Peeping Tom', *Daily Express*, 18 April 1960, p. 12.

11 D. Powell, 'Focus-pocus and worse', *Sunday Times* magazine, 10 April 1960, p. 25.

12 P. Bourdieu, *Distinction: A Social Critique of the Judgement of Taste*, trans. R. Nice, Cambridge, MA, Harvard University Press, 1994, pp. 7, 56.

13 R. Hoggart, *The Uses of Literacy: Changing Patterns in English Mass Culture*, Fair Lawn, NJ, Essential Books, 1957, pp. 279, 280, 24.

14 Ibid.

15 R. Williams, *Culture and Society 1780–1950*, New York, Columbia University Press, 1983, pp. 299–300. For a broader contextualisation of Williams and Hoggart in relation to the emergence of cultural studies, see D. Hebdige, *Subculture: The Meaning of Style*, London and New York, Methuen, 1979, pp. 5–19; on their place within a British sociological tradition examining working-class culture, see C. Critcher, 'Sociology, cultural studies and the post-war working class', in J. Clarke, C. Critcher and R. Johnson (eds) *Working-Class Culture*, New York, St. Martin's, 1979, pp. 13–40.

16 Quoted in J. Hill, *Sex, Class and Realism: British Cinema 1956–1963*, London, BFI, 1986, p. 6.

17 For accounts of *Room at the Top*'s contemporary significance, see P. Houston, 'Room at the top?', *Sight and Sound*, Spring 1959, vol. 28, no. 2, pp. 56–9; and R. Murphy, *Sixties British Cinema*, London, BFI, 1992, pp. 11–15.

18 Quoted in Hill, op. cit., p. 191.

19 I. Quigly, 'On the make', *The Spectator*, 30 January 1959, p. 144.

20 Murphy, op. cit., p. 15.

21 Quoted in Hill, op. cit., p. 191.

22 The following account of the New Wave draws on Hill, op. cit., pp. 5–34, 127–44; and Murphy, op. cit., pp. 10–33.

23 J.D. Scott, 'In the movement', *The Spectator*, 1 October 1954, p. 400. See also B. Morrison, *The Movement: English Poetry and Fiction of the 1950s*, Oxford, Oxford University Press, 1980.

24 Quoted in Hill, op. cit., pp. 127–8.

25 Hill, op. cit., p. 136. The interior quotation is from A. Higson, 'Space, place, spectacle: landscape and townscape in the "kitchen sink" film', in A. Higson (ed.) *Dissolving Views: Key Writings on British Cinema*, London, Cassell, 1996, p. 145.

26 See, for example, Quigly, 'On the make', op. cit., p. 145.

27 Higson, op. cit., pp. 149, 143. In Higson's essay, this quotation addresses the function of landscape in the films of the New Wave, but his observations are equally pertinent to the treatment of character. For a related discussion, see also

R.B. Palmer, 'What was new in the British new wave?: Re-viewing *Room at the Top*', *Journal of Popular Film and Television*, Fall 1986, vol. 14, no. 3, pp. 125–35.

28 My reading here is informed by the analysis of *Peeping Tom* in L. Stern, *The Scorsese Connection*, Bloomington, Indiana University Press, 1995, pp. 67–8.

29 Quoted in M. Hansen, '"With skin and hair": Kracauer's theory of film, Marseille 1940', *Critical Inquiry*, Spring 1993, no. 19, pp. 437–69; p. 447. Hansen's essay reconstructs the genesis of Kracauer's *Theory of Film* project, drawing on unpublished notebooks written by Kracauer while in exile in Vichy France.

30 Hansen, op. cit., p. 450.

31 Quoted in Hansen, op. cit., pp. 457–8.

32 Hansen, op. cit., pp. 447 and 457.

33 W. Benjamin, *The Origin of German Tragic Drama*, trans. J. Osborne, London, Verso, 1996, p. 166. I am indebted to Tom Gunning for calling this passage to my attention.

34 Space does not permit a detailed discussion of mass culture's long-standing association with the feminine. See, for example, A. Huyssen, 'Mass culture as woman: modernism's other', in *After the Great Divide: Modernism, Mass Culture, Postmodernism*, Bloomington, Indiana University Press, 1986, pp. 44–62.

35 Hoggart, op. cit., p. 45. One should note that Hoggart's description of these teenagers is ultimately tempered by observations about 'why matters are not always as bad as they at first appear' (p. 45), but the overall sense of degeneration remains.

36 C.K. Steedman, *Landscape for a Good Woman: A Story of Two Lives*, New Brunswick, NJ, Rutgers University Press, 1994, p. 102.

37 M. Powell, *Million Dollar Movie*, New York, Random House, 1992, p. 146.

16

TRAVEL AND MOBILITY
Femininity and national identity in Swinging London films

Moya Luckett

From the New Wave to Swinging London

Analyses of 1960s British cinema often constellate around the respective merits of two critically constructed categories: the New Wave and Swinging London films. Both cycles were short lived. The New Wave flourished between approximately 1959 and 1963, while the 'handful of films which might be regarded as genuine Swinging London films ... had already been made and in most cases released by the spring of 1966'.[1] Swinging London films pivot around single young women (and sometimes men), defying convention as they try to fulfil their ambitions and find romance in a modern and uniquely unconventional London. Many of the films are structured around the story of a single girl who arrives in London, a city that comes to represent a site of pleasure and autonomy. This theme can be found in *Darling* (John Schlesinger, 1965), *The Knack* (Richard Lester, 1965), *Repulsion* (Roman Polanski, 1965), *Smashing Time* (Desmond Davis, 1967) and the television play, *Cathy Come Home* (Kenneth Loach, 1965).

The narratives of these films heralded a new feminine perspective marked by the importance of sexual expression to self-identity; the centrality of individualised forms of glamour to a more female-oriented public life, and London's structural role in enabling and authorising this glamour and agency. Like the beauty and fashion spreads in women's magazines, this glamour has a feminine address, foregrounding its role in the creation of a new and powerful self. This feminine archetype contrasts with the New Wave's masculine-oriented dismissal of the false pleasures of mass culture.[2] Yet Swinging London films do not simply celebrate freedom, superficiality, popular culture and affluence, but instead fuse optimism with a keen and often self-reflexive social criticism.[3] Many films from the cycle – such as *Nothing but the Best* (Clive Donner, 1964), *Darling*, *The Knack*, *Georgy Girl* (Silvio Narizzano, 1966), *Alfie* (Lewis Gilbert, 1966), *Smashing Time* and *Joanna* (Mike Sarne, 1968) – have a bitter-sweet quality, while others are more avowedly pessimistic. For example, *Repulsion*'s modernist traumas conjure up a particularly bleak vision of the Swinging London zeitgeist, mirroring and inverting the cycle from within its own parameters.

If the New Wave is most often represented as a long overdue aesthetic and political transformation, Swinging London is evoked as its antithesis – a triumph of crass commercialisation, another re-Americanisation of British film.[4] Critical dismissals of Swinging London films centre on their lack of relevancy, yet ironically these youth-oriented films owe their precise authenticity to their relationship with popular culture. Unlike the New Wave's nostalgic yet critical examination of working-class life (reminiscent of Richard Hoggart's *The Uses of Literacy*),[5] Swinging London's intersections with youth culture facilitate a range of social critiques and formal innovations that express a very *un*-Hollywood self-reflexivity. In sequences that expose film and television's political and cultural proclivities, for instance, *The Knack*, *Darling* and *Smashing Time* display media interest in the antics of youth through news-style reportage that harks back to 1930s documentaries, the Mass Observation movement and Reith's BBC.[6] Swinging London's eclectic formal innovations also manifest the new youthful perspective of contemporary British popular culture as seen in *The Knack*'s surreal black-and-white cinematography, *Smashing Time*'s 'mod' colours, *Repulsion*'s modernist hallucinations and *Darling*'s disjunction between image and sound. As Alan Lovell has suggested, these films are indebted to an art school surrealism that similarly influenced the era's popular music.[7] Surrealism's aspirations to a greater realist discourse should not be forgotten, and it is this precise *sur*-realism that is embedded within Swinging London.[8]

Swinging London's location shooting parallels the New Wave's characteristic 'Shot(s) of Our Town from That Hill', using unnarrativised space to comment on culture and society.[9] Through the exploration by Swinging London's heroines of both its known and unknown sites, the capital is associated with mobility and cultural diversity in contrast to the landscape of the New Wave, which testifies to (masculine) stasis and confinement. The latter films evoke Hoggart's observation that mobility is a threat to the 'group-sense' that binds and defines Northern England's working-class communities.[10] New Wave films also foreground travel as a commodity that many cannot afford (Hoggart, for instance, observes that '1 in 4 of those in the middle-classes had made a journey out of Derby in 1962, but only 1 in 10 of those in the working-classes (day or two day trips were excluded)').[11]

Both Swinging London and New Wave films contrast young women's mobility to stasis of young men, suggesting that travel and mobility play a pivotal role in the period's discourse on sexuality, power and gender. During the 1960s, the commodification of travel opened up unprecedented opportunities for young single women to journey on their own. Promises of unprecedented freedom positioned travel as central to the period's single girl mythology. Thus magazines like *Cosmopolitan* and *Honey* focused on new package holidays for skiing and sunbathing, while their teenage counterparts, for example *Seventeen*, *Teen*, *Ingenue* and *Mademoiselle*, stressed travel's importance for education and self-development, linking mobility with subjectivity. Associations with education positioned travel as the positive side of independence, while the sexual implications of package holidays simultaneously suggested a more threatening alliance with sexual awakening.[12] Furthermore, voluntary travel implies a certain affluence – from paid vacations to independent wealth – that marks the travelling single girl as somewhat privileged. During the 1960s, as Christine Geraghty has pointed out, such affluence was also associated with greater sexual freedom: '[Michael] Schofield's [1965] research suggested that "it does appear that the higher up a girl is on the social scale, the more sexual experience she is likely to have".'[13]

This chapter will analyse how travel and mobility foreground the role of gender in the production of new images of national identity. Through their diverse regional origins, the heroines of the Swinging London films symbolically unify the nation via their journeys to the capital. In the process, they relegate local rivalries (like the North/South divide) to a now redundant male-controlled past, while consigning the rest of the UK to the margins of the national imaginary. London is represented as the seat of feminine power, while masculine rule is consigned to history – a dynamic explored critically in *Darling* and celebrated in *The Knack*.

Versions of travel

Inderpal Grewal and Caren Kaplan, among others, have pointed out that travel (particularly in its mass forms) is a product of modernity – like the nation itself.[14] It consequently has two faces, being associated with both imperialism and its 'subsequent de-colonizations'.[15] It liberates as boundaries are crossed in search of pleasure, while its choices suggest agency. Travellers generally choose their destinations with the dual goals of maximising pleasure and gaining as much experience as possible on a budget. Leaving behind the conventions of home, they often refuse to be bound by the restrictions of the cultures they visit. In *Darling*, for instance, Diana (Julie Christie) first sees Capri as a place of licence, where she and Malcolm (Roland Curram) can take turns sleeping with the island's most beautiful and sexually ambiguous young men. Living in Italy, as she soon discovers, is quite different, requiring adherence to patriarchy and the Church.

Exile, nomadism, immigration and repatriation represent travel's other side – one marked by poverty, forced movement and loss, all of which further strip the woman of her agency, glamour and sexual identity. Travel therefore indicates the tensions of modernity, highlighting the diverse power relationships and subject positions produced by post-industrial capitalism. It articulates workers' increased rights through the subject's greater economic and political power exemplified in the paid vacation. It also testifies to imperialism, exile and the mass exportation of jobs as companies seek greater profits in a global marketplace, regardless of human cost. Tourism and voluntary migration draw together paid leisure and increased individual mobility in fantasies of affluence. Exile and repatriation, on the other hand, demonstrate that agency and freedom of movement are not available to all. As such, travel demonstrates the costs of freedom and subjectivity.

All forms of travel call up specific relationships between self and space. Tourism celebrates the pleasure of motion while acknowledging the space that defines self is elsewhere. Exile produces a total disarticulation of self and space. In both cases, the desire to unify self and space is haunted by impossibility, a lack that foregrounds the presence of desire. The tourist is not at home and were s/he to relocate, her relationship to this new space would be transformed since it would no longer be determined by the pleasurable condition of *not* belonging, or the anticipation of returning home. The exile, on the other hand, has no home, and this pain moulds her relationship to her environment. This exilic form of travel is represented in *Darling* and *Repulsion*, the former film indicating the difficulty of separating diverse experiences of power and their radically different subject positions in the travel narratives of the Swinging London films. As Kaplan observes,

> The commonsense definitions of exile and tourism suggest that they occupy opposite poles in the modern experience of displacement. Exile implies coercion; tourism celebrates choice. Exile connotes the estrangement of the individual from an original community; tourism claims community on a global scale ... Culturally, exile is implicated in modernist high art formations while tourism signifies the very obverse position as the mark of everything commercial and superficial.[16]

Furthermore, pleasure is implicated in the very existence of tourism while exile pivots around its erasure. While distinctions between tourist, immigrant and exile suggest different orientations towards (changed) space, there are however commonalities between these categories, none of which are resolutely hermetic, and thus can slip over into each other at any time.[17]

Phenomenology has linked mobility to subjectivity, suggesting that only the fully mobile body possesses full agency.[18] But, as post-colonial critiques of travel demonstrate, without control over the directions of one's own movement, this assumption only masks disenfranchisement and fails to allow for the resistive powers of stasis. Hence mobility is not in itself sufficient grounds for subjectivity: even unified actions where all parts of the body move together fluidly, in tandem, do not necessarily suggest agency if the body is being forced to move, to travel. When one is forced to move to a place where one does not wish to be, or when one is compelled to move in a way that is embedded with the very cultural values one opposes, stasis might in fact be the more radical gesture, more a sign of subjectivity than movement or travel. 1960s British films explore this dichotomy, with the New Wave often acknowledging the nobility of inertia while regretfully acknowledging its failure for a 'swinging' society where mobility is *the* trope of modernity.

Immobile men

The first episode of the BBC 1 series, *Adam Adamant Lives!* (Moira Armstrong, Laurence Bourne, 1966–1967), foregrounds the intersection of gender, modernity and movement in 1960s popular culture. Its eponymous Edwardian hero (Gerald Harper) awakes in Swinging London after a beautiful woman working with his arch-enemy knocks him off guard, sending him into a sixty-four year long drug-induced sleep. His awakening is marked by expressionist camerawork that highlights the speed of the city, foregrounding London's extreme modernity with canted shots of tall buildings, images of the crowded Underground and blinding floods of electric lights – all seen from Adam's perspective. As his senses are overwhelmed, he staggers around out of control, his inability to recognise his home town passed onto viewers in a visual style associated with silent film. He is unable to make sense of this space until he is rescued by Georgina (Juliet Harmer), a fan of his anthologised exploits who moves around the city with ease. Viewers recognise London despite the elaborate camera tricks because we can identify landmarks like the London Transport icon, linking our knowledge to that of the female lead and privileging her perspective, despite the subjective camera used to narrate Adam's trauma. Although Adam misrecognises Georgina at first, taking her for a boy because she moves fast and is clad in trousers and a cap, he is able to understand that this alienating, overwhelming city is a female space. The first figure to approach him is a prostitute and the halls of the Underground are draped with posters, mostly featuring women. Throughout the show's run, Georgina runs around accompanying Adam and often saving him with her translations of the idioms and customs of modern life while he stays resolutely Edwardian.

While *Adam Adamant* explores the feminisation of the city and physical movement in fairly uncritical terms, the tactical use of masculine immobility as social criticism is at the centre of the New Wave film, *The Loneliness of the Long Distance Runner* (Tony Richardson, 1962). Following a life of crime, Colin Smith (Tom Courtenay) is clearly going nowhere. When his Borstal governor (Michael Redgrave) discovers his talent for long-distance running, he immediately orders special training, anticipating victory in the annual race against the local public school. Although he realises his governor is only interested in institutional pride, Colin follows orders and runs. These scenes segue into flashbacks that suggest Colin's running is directionless because he is consumed by the past, by memories of crimes that went unpunished and by the frustrations of a fragmented society slipping out of male control. When his father dies after a lifetime spent down the mines, his mother is more interested in spending the insurance money on consumer goods (including a television and clothes) than mourning, leaving Colin the sole repository of his father's memory. Protesting his hatred of affluence and its concomitant destruction of community, Colin burns one of the pound notes that his mother gave him after his father's funeral.[19] Similarly, he throws the film's climactic race, stopping just shy of the finishing ribbon so as to let the public school runner win, both gestures highlighting the futility of his decision to resist rather than fight for social change.

Mobile women

The Loneliness of the Long Distance Runner envisions the future as feminine, presenting women's mobility at men's cost. Both the local girls who dream of moving to London and Colin's mother, flourishing amid her new consumer goods, demonstrate how female agency and desire for glamour essentially destroy local communities. *The Knack* similarly grants its protagonist, Nancy (Rita Tushingham), increased mobility, sexual desire and desirability at Tolen's (Ray Brooks) expense, but it optimistically reorients this equation to foreground its progressive social consequences. As the film cuts between Nancy's exploration of London and the boys' arguments about the house, it inverts traditional gendered binaries of public and private space. An itinerant Nancy arrives in London and finds herself truly lost. While exploring the city in a fruitless search for the YWCA, she finds time to buy clothes, suggesting that her travels are not entirely unpleasurable. Indeed, she inadvertently crosses through many of the major sights, acting as a vehicle for the viewers' own tourist gaze.[20] Her tourist status is emphasised when she has a passport-style photo taken shortly after her arrival at Victoria coach station, suggesting her entry into the city and granting her the right to cross its boundaries. But Nancy does not simply enter this new space as a tourist: she conquers it. As the image of her reading *Honey* on the coach into London suggests, she trusts in a feminine image of public space and carries this with her into the city.

Nancy is not the only woman in *The Knack* to embody feminine mobility and power. Although the mannequin-like fantasy women who wait outside Tolen's door in the stylised opening shots initially appear as static objects of male desire, this image is fractured as one woman sprays her ankle with perfume. Her fluid movements combined with her subtle yet sexual gesture reinscribe power, sexuality and agency as feminine prerogatives. As the lyrics for the theme song (not included in the final cut) suggest, 'the knack' is ultimately not about male desire, but women's desire for men.[21] Consequently, Nancy's charges of rape strip Tolen of 'the knack' as they not only imply coercion but also suggest that women may not want him. By the end of the film, Tolen loses both the knack and control over his own movements as he stumbles unrecognised outside his girlfriend reunion at the Albert Hall while hordes of similarly dressed, attractive girlfriends queue up to seduce his co-host Rory Moore.

Through travel, Swinging London films imbue women with the power to draw boundaries and demarcate space. The men in *Darling*, *Alfie*, *The Knack* and *Repulsion* are Londoners, while the female characters have travelled to the capital – from distances as diverse as Sussex, the North of England, Belgium and the United States. This does not suggest that London is a masculine space, but rather places men in a predominantly domestic relationship to the city. In *The Knack*, for instance, Colin (Michael Crawford), Tom (Donal Donnelly) and Tolen are primarily associated with their house. Tom is forced to move from his original accommodation and immediately seizes the next alternative space, claiming ownership by painting his room white. *Billy Liar* (John Schlesinger, 1963) also dramatises the more restricted space occupied by men as dreams constitute Billy's (Tom Courtenay) only escape. When these threaten to come true after Liz (Julie Christie), his essentially itinerant true love, invites him to run away to London with her, he loses his nerve and is left on the station platform, clutching a carton of milk. Instead of experiencing pleasure, love, and urban adventures, domestic pressures trap Billy within his home, preventing him from reaching maturity. As women escape to London – represented for instance in the trainload of brightly dressed young girls swarming onto the platforms of St Pancras at the start of *Smashing Time* – public space threatens to become more feminine as men are confined within their homes and hometowns.

None the less, this itinerant lifestyle has the capacity to destabilise identity as well as to facilitate self-invention. This dialectic is explored in *Georgy Girl*, one of the rare Swinging London films to feature a heroine who is not affiliated with the media or the profession of creating images. (The heroine in *Repulsion* is a manicurist and in *Darling* a model and actress; the heroines of *Smashing Time* are a singer and a model.) Georgy (Lynn Redgrave) principally travels between her Maida Vale apartment and her rooms in the more suburban Leamington mansion which also serve as her work place (she runs a small kindergarten). Although she attempts to preserve an identity across these spaces, she is subjected to different pressures and expectations from others, eroding her low self-esteem. Her mobility foregrounds her ambivalent social status: while she was raised in a mansion, it was as the child of servants; while she received private schooling, it was only because it was paid for by James (James Mason), her parents' employer. Her social uncertainty marks her domestic life as an adult: she replays her parent's servitude in her relationship with her autocratic flatmate, Meredith (Charlotte Rampling), even though she pays for everything, just like James. *Georgy Girl* foregrounds how travel questions the nature of home and with it, problematises the nature of identity, self-esteem and social position. Georgy's uncertainty is neither entirely pleasurable nor liberating, as contemporary reviewers noted: *Mademoiselle* described it as 'a sad-glad flicker, very Now ... as wryly funny [and] as fraught with tears as its all-heart heroine'.[22]

Like *Georgy Girl*, *Darling* and *Cathy Come Home* illustrate the limits on feminine control of space in a modern Britain defined through movement and consumer culture. *Darling* simultaneously advances and inverts metaphors of travel and mobility, revealing the limits of tourism and the extent to which women can traverse through and manipulate consumer culture before it rejects them. Diana Scott is defined by her mobility, passing through international borders with ease, mocking customs officials while betraying the trust of her lovers. None the less, her ventures into Europe are precarious and suggest that she cannot cross Continental space as freely as she moves across London and the rest of England. She leaves Sussex in the middle of the night, stifled by suburbia, wearing a coat over her night-dress, but she cannot be as spontaneous when travelling overseas. On her first trip to Paris, her lover, Robert (Dirk Bogarde), acts as her guide while they cuckold their spouses with fake phone calls – each pretending to be the overseas operator for the other. On her second trip to France with her new lover, Miles (Lawrence Harvey), she repeats the phone trick, revealing that she is neither clever nor careful enough to engage in international subterfuge. She is also confronted with a threatening environment for the first time as Miles shows her another side to Paris. Attending a party with undertones of sexual depravity, she is mocked and abandoned but manages to humiliate Miles and regain her status.

After several trips with Miles, her carelessness and inability to understand the rudiments of international travel catch up with her. Robert finds her passport and tickets on their bed, checks the dates, unmasks her lies, confronts her and they separate, prompting Diana to flee to Capri. After a depressing return home, she moves to Italy and marries a much older prince, only to find herself trapped in his castle. Fleeing back to London and Robert, she finally loses all control over her movements and space. After spending a night with her, Robert books her on the next plane to Rome, tells her he is leaving for America, drives a sobbing Diana to the airport and forces her to fly out to exile. Diana's agency is ultimately erased by men, who reassert their authority over her movements and separate her from her home. In her study of travel narratives, Kaplan notes that exile discourse adopts modernist forms to reveal its subject's dislocation from space and community.[23] As an exile, Diana can now only be at home in her memories, by journeying back in time rather than horizontally through space.[24] This principle structures the film's flashback narrative, with its impossible disjunctions between Diana's nostalgic voice and Schlesinger's highly contemporary images, its unreliable verbal registers matched with equally contradictory and self-aware visuals.

Plate 20   Julie Christie, a key icon of female mobility in 1960s Britain, with Dirk
Bogarde in *Darling* (John Schlesinger, 1965).

Diana's exile emphasises that feminine power has a contingent relationship to space. As with tourism, Diana's mobility is only liberating because it
sets up a dialectic between home and travel that suggests its own completion. *Darling* studies this exile from outside, exploring space in relation to
the creation of a female self. In contrast, *Repulsion* focuses on exile as existential crisis through the figure of a Belgian manicurist, Carol Ledoux
(Catherine Deneuve), who has followed her sister, Helen (Yvonne Furneaux),
to London. While Helen enjoys the city in classic single girl fashion and
enters into an affair with a married man, Carol becomes depressed and alienated. Carol's disturbance is initially revealed in her dislocation from public
space as she wanders through the city in a seeming trance, oblivious to her

surroundings. The film dramatises the plight of the exile, as she repeatedly physically and psychologically *'retreats from* the alien space, rather than embracing it'.[25] Crucially, the space that Carol shuns is precisely that of Swinging London, with its eligible men, urban pop culture and lack of moral constraints, but as she walks through the city, she appears blind to the very sights that thrill other girls. Her condition declines after her sister leaves for a holiday with her lover, and Carol withdraws from the outside world, moving into smaller and more confined spaces until she barricades herself inside her apartment. Her immobility and her hallucinations suggest her loss of normal subjectivity while they demonstrate that Carol sees space as a primary threat, linking it to untrammelled violent sexuality. Her flat becomes uncanny, *unheimlich*, appearing to shelter a rapist while its walls spontaneously crack, become soft and grow hands, demonstrating the simultaneous depth of her isolation and her need for home.

The other side of female mobility is also explored in BBC 1's *Wednesday Play*, *Cathy Come Home*. Cathy (Carol White) is initially presented as a typical upwardly-mobile, freedom-seeking, Swinging London heroine, and we first see her hitching to London. At first the city conforms to her dreams as she falls in love, accumulates consumer goods and enjoys the nightlife before marrying and renting a modern flat. Her initial swinging mobility inverts into homelessness after an accident and a pregnancy rob the couple of their home and livelihoods. While the play preserves Swinging London's associations between femininity, mobility, agency and modernity, it focuses on homelessness as the other side of this equation. As such, it uses its feminine perspective to stress that unbounded public space is not necessarily liberated and, further, to illustrate that women cannot exist on the margins that consumer culture inevitably produces and abandons.

Indeed, many Swinging London films suggest that travel operates dialectically, requiring a fixed home to be truly liberating. Cathy's homelessness shows how the two concepts of home – as domestic space and home country – are linked, as the social services finally 'give up' on her, effectively taking away her citizenship. Domestic space has been central to the modern concept of nation since the nineteenth century with Victorian formations linking female domesticity and purity to the health of the state. Social problem narratives like *Cathy Come Home* and even *Darling* suggest a continued investment in this ideology, albeit without its implicit sexual purity. Women's primary symbolic link to the nation is thus rearticulated in terms of a greater participation in public space, expressed through the trope of travel and its changed model of sexuality.

None the less, the dialectical nature of travel suggests that the greatest pleasure occurs precisely when female protagonists are at their most nomadic, linking feminine subjectivity with public space. This further underscores Kaplan's observation about the sexually liberating aspects of travel.[26] The journey to the capital undertaken by many of the Swinging

London heroines is linked to their discovery of sexual pleasure, although this sometimes implies that a certain puritanism marks the rest of the nation. While *Billy Liar*, *Cathy Come Home*, *The Knack* and *Darling* all suggest that women cannot find satisfaction and fulfilment outside the metropolis, their pleasure is often essentially ephemeral. In some cases (*The Knack*, *Georgy Girl*), London metonymically represents Harold Wilson's new, updated state, ironically taming its women by allowing them to find sexual pleasure, preparing them for marriage and motherhood. Those who cannot be tamed, the resolutely non-conformist girls, are cast into exile (*Darling*). But, as Geraghty has suggested, the more conservative narrative closures of these films cannot erase their pleasures, associated with character and star, sexuality and place.[27] Indeed, the popularity of Julie Christie's star image both transcends the pessimism of *Darling*'s narrative closure and creates a series of associations between viewers (especially with one of the film's target audiences – single women) and out-of-the-ordinary girls like Christie herself or the character she plays, Diana. Christie's position on the cover of the April 1964 edition of *Honey* magazine further underscores this point: this kind of glamour, this kind of mobile, public, active lifestyle can also be co-opted into more everyday incarnations of modern femininity.

Conclusion

In contrast to modernist and scientific travel narratives that promote the traveller as male, then, Swinging London films highlight the feminine experience of travel and its capacity to transform space and gender relations.[28] As Grewal notes, the image of the traveller ultimately represents a powerful understanding of national identity:

> Whether travel is a metaphor of exile, mobility, difference, modernity, or hybridity, it suggests the particular ways in which knowledge of a Self, society, and nation was, and is, within European and North American culture, to be understood and obtained.[29]

Swinging London films not only produce images of a (transient) ideal of feminine citizenship, but also participate in a larger project of reinventing national identity. This occurs at the level of both form and content. Together with its new youthful, swinging (and often single) girl protagonists, Swinging London films like *The Knack*, *Darling*, *Alfie* and *Smashing Time* often favour tracking cameras and fast-paced editing, creating a visual energy that participates in this project of national reinvention. Rather than adopting Hollywood forms of escapism, these films recentred British national cinema around both space *and* time, maintaining their links to the national heritage while imagining a present and a future that might be dialectically related to tradition but not subsumed within it. In exploring this quintessentially non-American city through the ultra-modern girl's eyes, then, these films recast Britain as the global centre of popular culture, rather than yoking national identity exclusively to heritage and tradition.

NOTES

1 R. Murphy, *Sixties British Cinema*, London, BFI, 1992, p. 140.
2 Throughout *The Uses of Literacy*, New Brunswick, NJ, Transaction Publishers, 1992 (reprint of 1957 original), Richard Hoggart presents mass culture as feminine, even dubbing television 'the Great Mother' (p. 143).
3 Murphy, op. cit., p. 4, notes the 'disturbing undertones' of many Swinging London films.
4 Ibid., p. 2. Murphy comments that 'the balance of [contemporary] critical opinion was in favour of the "Kitchen Sink" films ... "Swinging London" films ... have fared particularly badly ... represent[ing] all that was worst about mass culture'.
5 Hoggart, op. cit.
6 A. Higson, ' "Britain's outstanding contribution to the film": The documentary-realist tradition', in C. Barr (ed.) *All Our Yesterdays: 90 Years of British Cinema*, London, BFI, 1986, pp. 72–97.
7 A. Lovell, 'British cinema: The known cinema?' in R. Murphy (ed.) *The British Cinema Book*, London, BFI, 1997, p. 242, note 7.
8 G. Bataille, *Visions of Excess: Selected Writings, 1927–1939*, Minneapolis, University of Minnesota Press, 1985, p. 39.
9 A. Higson, 'Space, place, spectacle: landscape and townscape in "kitchen sink" films', in A. Higson (ed.) *Dissolving Views: Key Writings on British Cinema*, London, Cassell, 1996, pp. 133–56.
10 Hoggart, op. cit., p. 54.
11 Ibid., p. 273.
12 C. Geraghty states, '[contemporary] findings ... may also reveal young women taking a degree of control over sexual behaviour which chimes with [sociologist Michael] Schofield's comments that sexually experienced girls were strongly associated with "a desire for freedom and independence"'. 'Women and sixties British cinema: The development of the "Darling" girl', in Murphy, *The British Cinema Book*, op. cit., p. 155.
13 Ibid., p. 157.
14 C. Kaplan, *Questions of Travel: Postmodern Discourses of Displacement*, Durham, NC, Duke University Press, 1996, pp. 8–64; I. Grewal, *Home and Harem: Nation, Gender, Empire, and the Cultures of Travel*, Durham, NC, Duke University Press, 1996, pp. 14, 135; E. Hobsbawm, *Nations and Nationalities Since 1780: Programme, Myth, Reality*, Cambridge, Cambridge University Press, 1992, 2nd edn, p. 14.
15 Kaplan, op. cit., p. 1.
16 Ibid., p. 27.
17 Ibid., pp. 4–6.
18 I.M. Young, *Throwing Like a Girl and Other Essays in Feminist Philosophy and Social Theory*, Bloomington, Indiana University Press, 1990, pp. 145–50.
19 J. Hill, *Sex, Class and Realism: British Cinema 1956–1963*, London, BFI, 1986, pp. 153–4.
20 Similarly, *Smashing Time* shows London through Brenda and Yvonne's eyes.

21 The full song with lyrics is included on *The Knack ... and How to Get It: Original MGM Motion Picture Soundtrack* (Ryko, 1998).

22 L. Lerman, 'Catch up with ... *Georgy Girl*', *Mademoiselle*, November 1966, vol. 64, no. 1, p. 60.

23 Kaplan, op. cit., p. 27.

24 Ibid., p. 29.

25 Ibid., p. 28.

26 Ibid., p. 45.

27 Geraghty notes that: 'Christie's image and performance call the narrative into question by suggesting that feminine discourses of beauty and fashion are not the property of the Establishment but a way of claiming a feminine identity which can be used as a mode of self-expression, particularly around sexuality.' Op. cit., pp. 159–60.

28 Kaplan, op. cit.; Grewal, op. cit., p. 1.

29 Grewal, op. cit., p. 4.

Part VI

CONTEMPORARY CINEMA 1
Britain's other communities

Introduction

The contributors to this section examine contemporary British cinema's potential to represent and explore the socio-political landscape of post-industrial Britain. Each chapter, to some degree, assesses the legacy of the 1980s, the impact of Thatcherite policies on British cinema and the culture at large, and the ways in which they inform and resonate in Britain under New Labour. Thus John Hill discusses a range of realist films from the 1980s and 1990s depicting the polarisation of British society and the fragmentation of a traditional working class. Claire Monk considers *Trainspotting* (Danny Boyle, 1996), *Brassed Off* (Mark Herman, 1996), *The Full Monty* (Peter Cattaneo, 1997) and other films set in the world of the disenfranchised underclass. Julia Hallam discusses a similar range of films to Monk, but emphasises how these films, both textually and contextually, can be linked to entrepreneurial initiatives to regenerate depressed working-class locales. Finally, Michael Walsh charts the various attempts to represent the Troubles in Northern Ireland. He maps out a burgeoning cycle of films made recently in Ireland, but focuses primarily on British cinema's response to the conflict. Exploring in detail two British films made during the 1980s, John MacKenzie's *The Long Good Friday* (1980) and Alan Clarke's *Elephant* (1988), Walsh argues that British cinema continues to struggle to come to terms with and find adequate ways of representing Northern Ireland.

Aside from a shared concern with political questions, other common themes link the chapters in this section. All the contributors, whether implicitly or explicitly, situate their discussions within the context of a realist British cinema. Hill pursues this line of analysis most systematically, engaging in the critical debates about realism as well as identifying how the work of such contemporary film-makers as Mike Leigh, Ken Loach and Alan

Clarke inflects and departs from the realist conventions of the British New Wave. On the theme of gender, both Hill and Monk draw attention to films that represent working-class males in the 1980s and 1990s as emasculated by unemployment and disempowered by the loss of a collective political voice. Finally, there are also some significant and useful overlaps in the range of films and film-makers discussed in this section. Not only do Monk and Hallam consider the same cycle of underclass films, but also both Hill and Walsh discuss the work of two highly influential film-makers, Alan Clarke and Mike Leigh.

17

FROM THE NEW WAVE TO 'BRIT-GRIT'

Continuity and difference in working-class realism

John Hill

In an article devoted to recent trends in British film-making, the journalist Vanessa Thorpe announced the revival of what she described as 'Brit-grit': a return 'to the hard-bitten tradition of social realism ... launched on the back of pictures such as *Saturday Night, Sunday Morning* [sic; Karel Reisz, 1960], *A Kind of Loving* [John Schlesinger, 1962] and *This Sporting Life* [Lindsay Anderson, 1963]'.[1] The central focus of Thorpe's article is recent British films such as Shane Meadows' *TwentyFourSeven* (1997), Gary Oldman's *Nil by Mouth* (1997) and Tim Roth's *The War Zone* (1999). But she also suggests that such film-makers as Ken Loach, Alan Clarke and Mike Leigh have maintained a tradition of 'gritty realism' since the 1960s by influencing or directly encouraging this new breed of British directors. While Thorpe is clearly right to suggest lines of continuity between the realism of the 1960s and subsequent British film-making, she is also too eager to identify this as a relatively unbroken tradition and to run together differing forms of film-making practice. In the discussion that follows, I will consider the broad continuities but also the changes that have occurred within this tradition. Taking the work of Loach, Clarke and Leigh as my main examples, I will also assess some of the consequences of these developments.

As Thorpe's article indicates, the idea of 'realism' continues to enjoy considerable currency. In reviews and other popular discourses, films are routinely praised for their 'realistic' qualities, or disparaged for their lack of them. Despite this, the concept of realism remains notoriously difficult to define. This is because of the discrepancy between the idea and the practice of realism. The idea of realism implies a privileged relationship between an artwork and an external reality, however defined. Actual realist practices, however, depend upon the employment of conventions which audiences are prepared to accept (by whatever standards) as 'realistic'. The capacity to signify 'realism', therefore, is not intrinsic to any particular set of conventions but is relative to the social and artistic circumstances in which they are employed. Consequently, the conventions associated with realism do not remain fixed and are subject to historical variation and change. These changes in conventions involve two main kinds of representational shifts. The first involves what may loosely be described as content, or subject matter, and has a primarily social dimension. This affects the kinds of people, experiences and issues that are seen as most properly the domain of realism. The second shift relates to formal and stylistic features, the aesthetic means whereby such people and experiences are represented.

The social

As Raymond Williams has argued, innovations perceived as realist have typically involved a 'movement towards social extension', increasing the attention devoted to hitherto under-represented or marginalised groups.[2] Within the British cinematic tradition, this has generally involved the representation of the working class. In so far as the working class is neither more nor less 'real' than other social groups, the idea that realism is linked to the representation of the working class derives in part from context, and specifically the perceived absence of (adequate) representations of this group within the dominant discursive regimes. British realist cinema has thus typically been counterposed to both Hollywood and to commercial British cinema, types of film-making that proponents of realism have perceived as shying away from the lives of 'ordinary' people in the assumed interests of 'entertainment'. In the 1950s and 1960s, for instance, British social realism was defined in opposition to the middle-class comedies and backward-looking war films of the period. More recently, 'Brit-grit' has derived much of its cachet from the alternative that it has provided to heritage films like *A Room with a View* (James Ivory, 1986) and *Sense and Sensibility* (Ang Lee, 1995), or the upper-class comedy, *Four Weddings and a Funeral* (Mike Newell, 1994).

Accordingly, the impulse towards 'social extension' (and the representation of the working class) evident in the history of British cinema is not the result of any coherent epistemological interest in the 'real'. Rather it has derived from a variety of cultural and political assumptions about the workings of society and the role within society that cinema should play.[3] In this respect, a resurgence of realism is rarely a specifically aesthetic matter but is characteristically bound up with a more general social vocabulary, or mode of perceiving social realities. Thus, the British New Wave of the late 1950s and early 1960s did not simply 'represent' the working class but did so from a particular social perspective. Films such as *Room at the Top* (Jack Clayton, 1959), *Saturday Night and Sunday Morning* and *A Kind of Loving* portray the working class at a key moment of economic and social change. They reveal an anxiety about the demise of the 'traditional' working class, associated with work, community and an attachment to place, in the face of consumerism, mass culture and suburbanisation. In so far as these changes are also associated with a certain 'feminisation' of the working class, so these films also extend a degree of sympathy towards the virile, working-class male who seeks to resist the pressures towards embourgeoisement and social conformity (including domesticity).[4]

This has a further consequence for the way in which the working class has been represented. According to Andrew Higson, 'the history of British realism' reveals a 'changing conceptualisation of the relation between the public and the private' and 'the political and the personal'.[5] The concern of the New Wave films with culture (and its expression through patterns of leisure) meant that there was relatively little emphasis upon work while the focus on the discontented male hero involved a certain downplaying of collective conditions and actions in favour of the individual and personal. This is a trend that has become even more pronounced in realist films of the 1980s and 1990s, in which a further narrowing down of social space is evident and the working class is increasingly identified in domestic and familial terms.

This is partly to do with the perception that the 'decline' of the traditional working class identified in the earlier New Wave films has reached a certain terminus. In so far as this 'decline' is linked to both economic success and failure, there are two – apparently contradictory – aspects to this. On the one hand, the C2s, or skilled working class, associated with the rise of Thatcherism and its values of economic self-interest and cultural philistinism, seem to have inherited the mantle of the 'new working class' of the 1950s and 1960s, identified with affluence, consumption and leisure. This social type was given eloquent expression within popular culture in the form of the comedian Harry Enfield's character 'Loadsamoney', who featured in Channel Four's *Friday Night Live* in the late 1980s. It also became a feature of the cinema of Mike Leigh in which, as in *High Hopes* (1988), the upwardly mobile ambitions of the working class are associated with materialism and a lack of good taste. The 'rise of the C2s' is also given a perverse twist in Alan Clarke's semi-allegorical tale of well-to-do football hooligans, *The Firm*, made for television in 1988.

But there is another aspect to the 'decline' of the traditional working class. While the work identified above reveals a concern with the 'beneficiaries' of Thatcherism, British films of the 1980s and 1990s have more commonly focused on the working class as the victims of harsh economic conditions, identified as responsible for yet further erosion of working-class traditions. The idea of the traditional working class celebrated in the earlier films rested upon the strong sense of culture and community that grew out of shared employment and geographical location. In such films as *Letter to Brezhnev* (Chris Bernard, 1985) and *Rita, Sue and Bob Too* (Alan Clarke, 1986), the 'decline' of this working-class 'way of life' is identified not with affluence or upward mobility but with the collapse of traditional heavy industries (especially in the North) and the associated experiences of unemployment and poverty. This in turn is linked to a certain weakening of those ideologies of masculinity that have traditionally underpinned manual work and working-class politics as well as the self-confident forms of (sexual) activity associated with a working-class 'playboy' such as Arthur Seaton in *Saturday Night and Sunday Morning*.

There is, in this respect, a certain reconfiguring of public and private spaces. Terry Lovell, for example, has noted how 'the economy of interior and exterior space' in working-class realism of the 1960s often corresponds to a sexual division of labour.[6] While women are strongly associated with domestic space, the men in these films command exterior space (and actively resist 'confinement' to the domestic sphere). In later films, these distinctions become much less clear cut. In such films as *Letter to Brezhnev, Rita, Sue and Bob Too* and *Road* (Alan Clarke, 1987), female characters often take over public space (such as the street, the estate and the club) and display traditionally 'masculine' characteristics in the way that they embark upon various encounters (including sexual encounters).[7] At the same time, male characters – forced to adjust to unemployment and lack of income – become increasingly associated with domestic space and intra-familial tensions. Thus, in *Nil by Mouth*, the men – seated in the front room, drinking and telling stories – are seen to overwhelm domestic space, confining women to the margins or excluding them altogether.

This is a trend also revealed in Loach's work in the 1990s as it grimly maps out what it identifies as the shrunken actualities of working-class life. In Loach's early work, for example *The Big Flame* (1969), which deals with a workers' take-over of the Liverpool docks, and *Days of Hope* (1975), in the episode concerning the General Strike of 1926, there was still a vivid sense of the strength and possibilities of collective industrial action. In his 1990s films, however, the political prospects for change have diminished radically, and it is on the terrain of domestic and family relations that social conflicts are typically worked out. In *Raining Stones* (1993), the central character struggles to find the money to pay for his daughter's communion dress; in *My Name is Joe* (1998) the main character gets caught up in the financial problems of his nephew; in *Ladybird Ladybird* (1994) a mother simply fights to retain custody of her children. In this way, Loach's films have increasingly adopted features of the family melodrama, foregrounding domestic tensions and highlighting the divided loyalties and unbearably difficult choices that characters face.[8] While familial tensions have always been a feature of Loach's work (as in *Cathy Come Home,* 1966), the growing concentration on the domestic has nevertheless had the effect of encouraging an increasing sense of political impotence and passivity, both in the films' main characters and in their spectators.

The emphasis upon the frailty of the family also continues another strand of the working-class films of the 1960s in which the weakness or absence of fathers signalled the demise of traditional working-class culture.[9] While it is still possible to find evidence of the virtues of the old 'respectable' working-class family in a film such as *Room at the Top*, this is much less so of many recent films, for instance *Rita, Sue and Bob Too*, *Ladybird Ladybird*, *My Name is Joe* and *Nil by Mouth*, in which the family is increasingly marked by breakdown and dysfunction. This, in turn, is commonly linked to changing gender roles in so far as male characters, unable to adjust to their new 'post-patriarchal' circumstances, are increasingly identified with petty criminality, alcoholism and domestic violence. In a sense, the logic of 'social extension' and 'authenticity' (where this is identified with the most extreme of social conditions) has encouraged a gravitation towards the poorest and most disadvantaged sections of the 'rough' working class. In Loach's films, there is none the less a concern to show that familial conflicts are not simply the result of personal and moral shortcomings (or psychic frustrations) but also derive from the pressure of external social and economic circumstance. As working-class drama increasingly occupies the terrain of the domestic and familial, however, there is also a certain severing of the connections with a larger social context. While much of the power of *Nil by Mouth* derives from the claustrophobic involvement it encourages with the central family, for instance, this is only achieved by excluding the wider patterns of social life (neighbourhood, work, politics) that were once seen to shape and define working-class experience.

Plate 21   Foregrounding domestic tensions in contemporary 'Brit-grit' films: the struggle to keep the family together in Loach's *Ladybird Ladybird* (1994).

The alternative side of the same coin may be found in the films of Mike Leigh. In his films, characters generally have jobs although they are rarely manual workers: Andy (Jim Broadbent) in *Life is Sweet* (1990), for example, is a chef, while Maurice (Timothy Spall) in *Secrets and Lies* (1996) is a photographer. Such characters typically come from working-class backgrounds and it is the interface between the working classes and the lower middle classes that Leigh's work characteristically explores. As in other films, there is also a certain shift of attention away from the public towards the private. Thus, in a film like *Life is Sweet*, the bulk of the action takes place within the family home where most of the important events in the characters' lives occur. This is, of course, a double-edged phenomenon. As Williams has argued in relation to theatrical history, the emergence of 'the private domestic room' registered an important shift in the way that the significance of human action was understood by the middle classes.[10] It is also the centrality of the private, domestic room in Leigh's films – and its extension beyond the traditional middle classes – that provides them with some of their realist credentials. For in these rooms, and in related domestic spaces such as the garden, relatively little happens. As in *Life is Sweet*, characters eat, joke, argue with each other and make up.

The Royle Family (BBC, 1998), a television comedy series praised for its 'realist ambitions', pursues this representational logic even more ruthlessly.[11] The first episode, for example, takes place completely within the confines of the front room and kitchen where the characters talk inconsequentially, watch a television which is never switched off and flick through a catalogue. By finding interest (and humour) in the apparently everyday and trivial, such films and television series are thus able to invest 'ordinary' people and 'ordinary' events with a dramatic significance (and value) that they might otherwise lack.

On the other hand, by making the domestic so central to the way that characters' lives are explored, these films also restrict their apparent sphere of action to the home and family. Thus, while inter-connection and mutual support are characteristic concerns of Leigh's work, this rarely extends beyond the boundaries of family (and close friends). Geoff Eley suggests that, in *Life is Sweet*, 'politics is nonetheless inserted ... via the vituperative feminism and leftism of the bulimic daughter's incoherent rage'.[12] This, however, underestimates the way in which Nicola's (Jane Horrocks) political sloganeering is shown both to stand at odds with the practical human concern provided by her family and to fail so completely to chime with her true needs and desires (as political ideologies generally do in Leigh's films). While this may be linked to a failing confidence in the 'grand narratives' of political progress and social improvement, it also entails a diminishing sense of the political and public sphere.[13] In this respect, the films of Leigh, like some of the bleaker portraits of working-class life, seem to demonstrate what Williams, in a different context, has described as 'retreating privatisation', where the 'small-unit entity' of 'you and your relatives, your lovers, your friends, your children' becomes 'the only really significant social entity'.[14]

The formal

In his discussion of 1960s British realism, Peter Wollen questions the appropriateness of the New Wave label. He thus chides these films for their absence of distinctive authorial signatures, their reliance on literature and theatre and their subservience to a realist aesthetic which prevents any rapprochement with modernism.[15] The implication is that these features are inter-connected and that the adoption of a realist aesthetic inhibited the emergence of genuine *auteurs*. What is striking about the contemporary period, however, is not only the resilience of 'realism' but how it is routinely associated (as in Thorpe's article) with such *'auteurs'* as Clarke, Leigh and Loach. To some extent, this is a matter of context. Whereas the British New Wave still operated within a broadly commercial system in which directorial 'authorship' was not a particular selling point, British films since the 1980s have increasingly depended upon a system of production and distribution characterised by state or television support and more international and specialised 'arthouse' exhibition. Such a system has placed an increasing emphasis on the definition and promotion of British cinema in terms of its directors, with the result that '[e]ven realist filmmakers, like Ken Loach,' as Higson puts it, 'are treated as auteurs'.[16]

This is not necessarily as contradictory as it might at first appear. For, as has been noted, the functioning of realism in the cinema is always relational – not just to the external reality (or knowledge of it) to which reference is made but to other works which are regarded as 'realistic'. David Bordwell and Kristin Thompson, for example, identify four main kinds of 'motivation' underpinning the use of a particular device in a film – compositional, realistic, transtextual and artistic – and indicate how each of these may emerge as a dominant organising principle.[17] Thompson's formulation of 'realistic motivation' also reveals the difficulty of clearly distinguishing 'realistic' motivation, understood as relying on appeals 'to notions from the real world', from 'transtextual' motivation, which derives from the 'conventions of other artworks'.[18] For as Thompson indicates, the perception of realism depends on not only 'our knowledge of everyday life' but also 'our awareness of prevailing aesthetic canons of realism'.[19] In this respect, the realism of a film-maker like Loach (and, indeed, 'Brit-grit' more generally) necessarily depends upon a capacity to distinguish itself from prevailing norms and, in so doing, to signal a degree of difference.

As Loach's films show, this also means that the use of 'realistic' devices is generally apparent to the spectator. Thompson identifies a number of features related to subject matter, narrative structure and style that cue realistic motivation.[20] In such films as *Riff-Raff* (1990), *Raining Stones* and *Ladybird*

Ladybird, the impression of realism is thus generated in part by subject matter (the representation of the day-to-day struggles of 'ordinary' working-class people). But it is also cued by the approach to narrative (a certain loosening of the cause-effect chain associated with 'classical' narration) and by the employment of particular stylistic traits (such as an emphasis upon actual locations and the use of non-professional actors). The most striking feature of Loach's cinema is its partial adoption of visual techniques adapted from traditional documentary (such as unbroken takes, long shots and apparently 'natural' sound and light). Thus, in a scene such as that in *Raining Stones* when the van is stolen, the film achieves its effects by the camera holding back from the action, letting the scene unfold at its own pace and permitting other – dramatically insignificant – characters to enter the frame as if by coincidence and engage in seemingly irrelevant and barely audible conversation.

The point about this style is that it achieves much of its 'realistic' quality from being noticed. This is not of course true of all realist discourses. In a series of influential articles written in the 1970s, Colin MacCabe and others defined the narrational form of the typical Hollywood film as 'classic realism'.[21] One of the key points of this argument was that such films were formally transparent. That is to say, the formal means by which these films articulated or enunciated their vision were rendered invisible to the spectator. This argument consequently identified as realist films that would not commonly be regarded as such. MacCabe was thus able to deem *The Sound of Music* (Robert Wise, 1965) as much a work of 'realism' as *The Grapes of Wrath* (John Ford, 1940).[22] If 'classic realism' is then characterised by a relative absence of marks that might identify it as 'enunciation', this is not straightforwardly the case in those works of realism which seek to distinguish themselves from Hollywood norms (as most realist movements have characteristically done).

Loach's film-making provides a good example. As Caughie suggests, Loach's method of 'documentary drama' is not properly regarded as 'transparent' in the manner characteristic of classical Hollywood. On the contrary, it involves 'a rhetoric of mediated style which is clearly marked'.[23] This 'marking' functions in two main ways. On the one hand, it serves as a visible form of differentiation from mainstream cinematic conventions. On the other hand, it uses the association with actuality that 'documentariness' carries to underwrite the claims to 'realism' and 'authenticity' that the films make. In this respect, Loach's films rely less on minimising the spectator's awareness of cinematic technique (as in 'classic realism') than on encouraging the spectator to recognise that a departure from the prevailing norms of narrative cinema and the adoption of documentary modes may enhance their realist credentials. This also helps explain why 'even' a realist film-maker like Loach can be readily identified as an *'auteur'*. Both the relative consistency and distinctiveness of his thematic concerns and the markers of his 'mediated' style allow an authorial reading (such that it is now possible to employ the term 'Loachian' as an adjective). In this case, realism is not so much an obstacle to authorial expression as one of the means by which it is achieved.

It is, of course, the foregrounding of style that has typically marked the presence of the director as *auteur* in 'art cinema'. While art cinema is commonly counterposed to realism, it is worth remembering that both the conceptualisation and the practice of 'art cinema' have typically involved a reliance upon different kinds of 'realism' (as in the case of Italian neo-realism).[24] In the case of the British 'documentary-realist tradition', as Higson suggests, there has always been a tension between aesthetic and social-realist concerns. It is thus possible to identify a play between 'realistic' and 'artistic' motivation as a recurring feature of British 'realist' cinema.[25] Contra Wollen's remarks on 1960s realism, the New Wave conception of realism was in fact intimately bound up with the idea of 'poetry'. Thus, in such films as *The Loneliness of the Long Distance Runner* (Tony Richardson, 1962) and *This Sporting Life*, there is a degree of narrational self-consciousness and visual expressiveness of a kind more commonly associated with (modernist-influenced) art cinema.[26] As realism has become more overtly identified with '*auteurs*', so the degree to which it is reliant upon various forms of aesthetic motivation has also increased.

This is the case with Mike Leigh, for example, whose distinctive (and personal) body of work is in spite of his reputation for realism and 'documentary-inspired verisimilitude'.[27] As with Loach, the realism of his films is cued by various aesthetic devices such as a focus on 'ordinary' people, the use of real locations, loosely structured plots and a visual style characterised by limited camera movement and cutting. In its partial deviation from classical conventions, this visual style indicates not only a degree of 'realism' but also a distinctive authorial signature comparable to that of other, stylistically similar, directors such as Ozu. Unlike Loach, there is also a high degree of stylisation in the way that the acting in Leigh's films, as a consequence of an extended period of improvisation, magnifies physical tics, bodily gestures and patterns of speech and accent. Acting in Leigh's films, in this respect, is much more 'histrionic' than 'verisimilar', drawing attention to its own status as performance and encouraging an awareness of the role of the director and his particular vision.[28]

The work of Alan Clarke exhibits a similar set of characteristics. As with Loach, it is possible to read Clarke's career in terms of a stripping away of artistic devices and a movement towards 'raw naturalism'.[29] This, in turn, may be linked to Clarke's increased use of steadicam, a camera worn by the operator to allow greater mobility. It is common to associate technological innovations such as the emergence of lightweight handheld cameras with the possibility of enhanced 'realism' and similar arguments have been made about the use of steadicam. In works for film and television such as *Rita, Sue and Bob Too* and *Road*, however, the use of steadicam has the opposite effect, drawing attention to itself and functioning as a formal device in its own right.

This is particularly apparent in *Road*. Set in a desolate housing estate in the north of England, it draws on several of the signifiers of northern realism and successfully communicates some of the desperation associated with unemployment and poverty. It does so, however, through a heavily stylised form. Domestic interiors are stripped bare and display the minimum of props, characters speak in an exaggerated manner and directly address the camera, pop songs are used in an often diegetically unmotivated and obtrusive fashion. The film's dominating trademark is its relentless sense of movement and use of unbroken takes. For Bazin, the long take preserved temporal and spatial unities and was associated with realism.[30] By virtue of its elimination of reverse-field cutting and point-of-view shots, it may also carry connotations of documentary. Thus, in *Rita, Sue and Bob Too*, there are a number of scenes in which the camerawork mimics (in a heightened form) the techniques of fly-on-the-wall documentary, for example when we see Sue search the flat for her homework. In *Road*, as in other parts of *Rita*, however, the moving camera works in a way that goes well beyond its conventional attachments to realism and documentary, generating kinetic and rhythmic patterns (particularly in association with the music) that exceed the requirements of both narrative logic and symbolic expression. As such, *Road* is a film in which, in Bordwell's useful phrase, 'the perceptual force of style' is both prominent and dominant.[31]

This is not to deny that these shots continue to carry a semantic dimension, giving expression to the energy and inner resilience of the characters despite the oppressiveness of their environment and the desperation that they feel. As David Thomson argues, the characters 'have not given up on their own naked force' and are 'bursting with words, gesture, movement' which signify their refusal to go under or accept the status quo.[32] It is also significant that the film carries on and develops a long-standing tradition of associating the working class with physicality. It does so in a way that is partly parodic, undermining, in a post-industrial context, the sense of physical grace often associated with the representation of the working-class body involved in manual labour. Inasmuch as the characters are deprived of virtually all save their physical and vocal energy (and the resistance that this can provide), this also involves a further narrowing down of the social.

Conclusion

To some extent, there is a link between the move towards a more artistically motivated, personally marked kind of 'realist' cinema and the paring down of social space identified earlier. Christopher Williams has suggested that, in the 1980s, a British 'social art cinema' emerged which brought together the traditional social concerns of British cinema with the more individualistic and artistically self-conscious interests of European art cinema.[33] While Williams sees this as encouraging a shift in art cinema's concerns with the individual and psychological towards 'the group, the context and the social-diffuse', it has also encouraged a move away from the social towards the more private and personal.[34] It is not surprising, therefore, that the work of Terence Davies has been seen to provide an exemplary case study of this kind of film-making.[35] Thus, in Davies' film *Distant Voices, Still Lives* (1988), recalling working-class life in the 1940s and 1950s, there is a clear combination of subjectively marked, aesthetic stylisation with a semi-autobiographical concentration on the 'micro-social' realities of 'a single street' and 'one particular family'.[36] Accordingly, while Williams identifies the social art cinema with a continuation of interest in social themes alongside a certain abandonment of realism it is also the case that this has involved an attenuation of social features alongside the retention of a number of realist elements.

NOTES

1 V. Thorpe, 'Reality bites (again)', *Observer* ('Screen'), 23 May 1992, p. 2.

2 R. Williams, 'A lecture on realism', *Screen*, 1977, vol. 18, no. 1, p. 63.

3 See J. Hill, 'Ideology, economy and the British cinema', in M. Barrett, P. Corrigan, A. Kuhn and J. Woolf (eds) *Ideology and Cultural Production*, London, Croom Helm, 1979, pp. 126–7; A. Higson, ' "Britain's outstanding contribution to the film": the documentary-realist tradition', in C. Barr (ed.) *All Our Yesterdays: 90 Years of British Cinema*, London, BFI, 1986, pp. 74–5.

4 J. Hill, *Sex, Class and Realism: British Cinema 1956–1963*, London, BFI, 1986, esp. chap. 7.

5 Higson, op. cit., p. 83.

6 T. Lovell, 'Landscapes and stories in 1960s British realism', in A. Higson (ed.) *Dissolving Views: Key Writings on British Cinema*, London, Cassell, 1996, p. 175.

7 See J. Hill, *British Cinema in the 1980s: Issues and Themes*, Oxford, Clarendon Press, 1999, chap. 8.

8 J. Hill, ' "Every fuckin' choice stinks": Ken Loach', *Sight and Sound*, vol. 8, no. 11, 1988, pp. 18–21.

9 See J. Hill, 'Working-class realism and sexual reaction: some theses on the British "new wave" ', in J. Curran and V. Porter (eds) *British Cinema History*, London, Weidenfeld and Nicholson, 1982, pp. 305–9; Lovell, op. cit., p. 367.

10 Williams, op. cit., p. 66.

11 I. Parker, 'They shout "arses" don't they?', *Observer Review*, 20 September 1998, p. 8.

12 G. Eley, '*Distant Voices, Still Lives*: The family is a dangerous place: memory, gender, and the image of the working class', in R.A. Rosenstone (ed.) *Revisioning History: Film and the Construction of a New Past*, Princeton, NJ, Princeton University Press, 1995, p. 220.

13 Cf. J.-F. Lyotard, *The Postmodern Condition: A Report on Knowledge*, trans. G. Bennington and B. Massumi, Minneapolis, University of Minnesota Press, 1984 (orig. 1979).

14 R. Williams, 'Problems of the coming period', *New Left Review*, 1983, no. 140, p. 16.

15 P. Wollen, 'The last new wave: modernism in the British films of the Thatcher era', in L. Friedman (ed.) *British Cinema and Thatcherism: Fires Were Started*, London, UCL Press, 1993, pp. 36–7.

16 A. Higson, 'British cinema', in J. Hill and P. Church Gibson (eds) *The Oxford Guide to Film Studies*, Oxford, Oxford University Press, 1998, p. 504.

17 D. Bordwell, *Narration in the Fiction Film*, London, Methuen, 1985, p. 36; K. Thompson, *Breaking the Glass Armor: Neoformalist Film Analysis*, Princeton, NJ, Princeton University Press, 1988, p. 16.

18 Thompson, op. cit., pp. 16 and 18.

19 Ibid., p. 17.

20 Ibid., p. 205.

21 See in particular, C. MacCabe, 'Realism and the cinema: notes on some Brechtian theses', *Screen*, 1974, vol. 15, no. 2, pp. 7–27; and MacCabe, *'Days of Hope*: a response to Colin McArthur', *Screen*, 1976, vol. 17, no. 1, pp. 98–101.

22 Ibid., p. 12.

23 J. Caughie, 'Progressive television and documentary drama', *Screen*, 1980, vol. 21, no. 3, p. 27.

24 Bordwell, op. cit., chap. 10.

25 Higson, ' "Britain's outstanding contribution to the film" ', op. cit., p. 75.

26 See A. Higson, 'Space, place, spectacle: landscape and townscape in the "kitchen sink" film', in Higson, *Dissolving Views*, op. cit., pp. 133–56; Hill, *Sex, Class and Realism*, op. cit., chap. 6.

27 G.M. Paletz and D.L. Paletz, 'Mike Leigh's "Naked" truth', *Film Criticism*, 1994/5, vol. xix, no. 2, p. 27.

28 R. Pearson, *Eloquent Gestures: The Transformation of Performance Style in the Griffith Biograph Films*, Berkeley and Los Angeles, University of California Press, 1992, chap. 3; Hill, *British Cinema in the 1980s*, op. cit., pp. 194–6.

29 S. Hattenstone, 'Hitting where it hurt', *Guardian* ('Review'), 1 August 1988, p. 4.

30 A. Bazin, *What is Cinema?* (vol. 1), trans. H. Gray, Berkeley, University of California Press, 1967.

31 Bordwell, op. cit., p. 282.

32 D. Thomson, 'Walkers in the world: Alan Clarke', *Film Comment*, May–June 1993, p. 80.

33 C. Williams, 'The social art cinema: a moment in the history of British film and television culture', in C. Williams (ed.) *Cinema: The Beginnings and the Future*, London, University of Westminster Press, 1996, pp. 199. There is a degree of imprecision in how Williams understands 'realism' in this context. He tends to downplay the importance of 'realism' to art cinema and, while drawing a distinction between the 'social' and the 'realist' in British cinema, goes on to define the 'social-diffuse' in terms that include a number of forms of realism – 'observational, cultural and stylistic' – which are not clearly distinguished (ibid., p. 194).

34 Ibid., p. 199.

35 M. Hunt, 'The poetry of the ordinary: Terence Davies and the social art cinema', *Screen*, 1999, vol. 40, no. 1, pp. 1–16.

36 Ibid., p. 3. Eley, op. cit., p. 32, also notes the film's absence of 'public/political referents'.

18

FILM, CLASS AND NATIONAL IDENTITY

Re-imagining communities in the age of
devolution

Julia Hallam

Film-makers in Britain in the mid-1990s showed a renewed interest in
portraying working-class life, projecting images of alienation and crisis
amidst landscapes of industrial recession and economic decline. Such films
as *Raining Stones* (Ken Loach, 1994), *Trainspotting* (Danny Boyle, 1995),
Twin Town (Kevin Allen, 1996), *Brassed Off* (Mark Herman, 1996), *The Full
Monty* (Peter Cattaneo, 1997), *Nil by Mouth* (Gary Oldman, 1997) and
TwentyFourSeven (Shane Meadows, 1997) are shot in locations where the men
of the community traditionally worked in heavy industries such as steel,
shipbuilding, mining and industrial manufacture. These films re-imagine
the 'working-classness' of their characters through their relation to
consumption rather than production, purchasing power rather than labour
power, evoking memories of an earlier cycle of British films with a similar
emphasis on class and regional identity: the New Wave of the 1960s.[1]
Contemporary British films reiterate this approach; working-class identity is
depicted not as the collective political unity of a group in society but as a
site for exploring the personal stagnation, alienation and social marginalisation of their (primarily) white male characters.

   As well as sharing a range of thematic preoccupations, several of these
films interconnect at a number of other levels. Thus Robert Carlyle, who
played Stevie in *Riff-Raff* (Ken Loach, 1991), has major roles in *Trainspotting*
and *The Full Monty*. Ewan McGregor plays Renton in *Trainspotting* and the
romantic interest in *Brassed Off*, while Danny Boyle and Andrew MacDonald
produced both *Trainspotting* and *Twin Town*. Four of the films are based on
stories by writers with strong local connections. *Trainspotting* is adapted from
a cult novel by the Scottish writer Irvine Welsh, the scriptwriters of *The Full
Monty* and *Brassed Off* are both Yorkshiremen, and Kevin Allen, who wrote
and directed *Twin Town*, is a native of South Wales. But beyond these asso-
ciative elements, the films share another less visible aspect; all construct
specific localities and communities, their narratives engaging with situations

and events that are a direct consequence of the socio-economic realities of the places in which they are set. And all owe a debt to these places because projects and schemes created through local regeneration initiatives to attract film and media production to these areas have provided financial support for these productions.

While it is too early to know if these thematic preoccupations are merely a short-term cycle or indicative of longer-term trends, they deserve our attention. In this chapter, I will explore the relationship between film content, local production initiatives and recent changes in film and moving image cultural policies, and especially the influence of these policies on the kinds of films that are being made in Britain today. Significantly for my argument here, a number of recent British films are set in localities where urban regeneration schemes are in operation: *The Full Monty* and its popular forerunner *Brassed Off* are based in an area of Yorkshire that received European structural funds to aid redevelopment; *Trainspotting* and *Twin Town* are similarly located on the outer fringes of Edinburgh and Swansea. In areas hit by the severe loss of employment in traditional manufacturing industries, innovative schemes focused on the cultural industries – including film and television production – have played an important role in economic development and restructuring since the mid-1980s, often in partnership with local authorities seeking to attract entrepreneurial skills and inward investment to their regions. This has stimulated new kinds of business activity and renewed identifications with place.[2] At the local level, the challenge is to ensure that the benefits from these projects feed into training, education and access schemes that attempt to ensure that any benefits gained from these new industries are equally spread and redistributed throughout the area.

Policies initiated in the late 1980s to promote the development of small independent production companies have been central to this process, particularly in areas where the average standard of living is significantly below that for the European Union as a whole. Crucially for this discussion, a number of recent British films (including the most successful film of recent times, *The Full Monty*) are set in localities that provide financial incentives for film production assisted by various forms of European and regional funding. *Brassed Off* benefited from production funding channelled through the Yorkshire Media Production Agency, *The Full Monty* was assisted by the Yorkshire Screen Commission, and *Twin Town* was aided by the Welsh Film Commission and Sgrîn.[3] *Trainspotting* indirectly benefited from the Glasgow Film Fund's successful support for Boyle and MacDonald's first film, *Shallow Grave* (1994).

For local authorities, the issue of re-imagining their communities reaches far beyond the glossy publicity campaigns that heralded the renaissance of cities like Glasgow in the 1980s (which was epitomised by the catchphrase, 'Glasgow's Miles Better'). The development of image- and communication-based industries plays an important role in modernising the post-industrial infrastructure of cities and their hinterlands where manufacturing no longer provides a sufficient means of employment for the majority of the working population. Modernisation is increasingly seen as dependent upon local technical skills and a production base that has direct links with global markets and businesses, a route that emphasises connections with Europe and downplays the metropolitan centre. This disaffiliation from the Anglo-centric axis of British national life is finding a political focus in the newly established parliaments of Scotland, Wales and Northern Ireland (and potentially in England, through the development of Regional Assemblies).[4] Arguably, it is also finding a cultural focus through media production schemes that enable film and media producers to emphasise the specificity of place, projecting national and regional identities which question and contest stereotypical constructions of 'Britishness'.

The devolution of film production

National and regional initiatives to decentralise British film production are taking place in a market for moving image products increasingly dominated by a small number of multinational companies whose operations transcend national boundaries. Globalisation creates economic and structural constraints on the sale and distribution of moving image products that some commentators believe are now beyond the control of any single nation state's cultural policies.[5] The British Film Institute (BFI) seems unquestioningly to support this view, commentating in its yearbook that 'filmmaking these days is an international business where the question of national origin is of increasingly marginal interest'.[6] Such a stance tends to side-step the growing role of the cultural industries at the regional level in post-industrial societies throughout Europe which are seeking to develop their own urban regeneration policies and initiatives. In spite of the homogenising tendencies of the global image market, it is not possible to eradicate or transcend difference at the national and regional level. The case for the local or regional economy as the key unit of production within the global network has been forcefully made by the 'flexible specialisation' thesis, which stresses the importance of localised production complexes. Kevin Robins argues that crucial to the success of local production initiatives are strong local institutions and infrastructures; relations of trust based on face to face contact; a 'productive' community historically rooted in a particular place; and a strong sense of local attachment and pride.[7] But analysts like Robins are wary of idealising the local, which, he maintains, is a structurally relational and therefore relative concept. If the local and regional once had significance in relation to the national sphere, that meaning and significance is now being recast in the context of globalisation. The 'flexible specialisation' thesis is not straightforwardly about the renaissance of local cultures; these are overshadowed by an emergent world culture and by the resilience of national and nationalist cultures.[8]

Against this background of global incorporation, many European countries are seeking to retain a measure of control over their cultural industries by developing initiatives that aim to reap economic benefits at the national and regional level. In the UK, for example, arguments for the devolution of political power to the national centres of Scotland, Northern Ireland and Wales were augmented throughout the1980s by demands for the devolution of funding and responsibility for cultural activities. Following the publication of the Wilding Report in 1989, the Arts Council of Great Britain was disbanded. In its place, the Arts Council of Wales and the Arts Council of Scotland were established as autonomous bodies funded respectively by the Welsh and Scottish Offices, while the Arts Council of England devolved many of its financial responsibilities to ten Regional Arts Boards (RABs). Within this context, the BFI became increasingly dissatisfied with the low priority given to the development of national and regional film and video culture on the Arts Council and RAB agendas. Many RABs remained committed to developing and expanding experimental forms of image production in the interests of sustaining a diverse film, video and electronic media culture, but the BFI adopted a more pragmatic approach that increasingly sought to build partnerships with broadcasters and the mainstream film industry.

By the early 1990s, the BFI was attempting to set up a network of media development agencies that would not only deliver the BFI's cultural remit, but also expand the economic base of the media industries outside London. But in some areas blighted by recession and economic decline enterprising local authorities (and some RABs) had already seized the initiative, based on their own analysis of cities and regions hit by similar problems in Europe and the United States. Part of their project was to change the international image of such cities as Sheffield, Liverpool and Glasgow from associations with dereliction and decay to vibrant, modern environments offering new industrial provision and all the cultural benefits of living in a major city. Following the North American example, enterprising local authorities established film liaison offices to encourage location filming in their areas, based on the dictum that 'there's no finer publicity than that generated by a major motion picture'.[9]

The rationale behind this initiative was to boost tourism and stimulate demand for production skills. The hope was that this would stem the drain of skilled technicians from the area by providing employment opportunities for those shed from regional broadcasting organisations, as well as providing additional income for the service industries. For local authorities and their partners, the issue is not one of producing local programmes for local audiences, but of developing a viable media industry that can sell its products in the global marketplace to national and international distributors and exhibitors.[10]

In Liverpool, for example, a film liaison office was established at the end of the 1980s jointly funded by Mersey Television and the City Council.[11] This was followed in 1992 by the setting up of the Moving Image Development Agency (MIDA), which has limited funds to stimulate script development and offer completion incentives to producers. Similar projects were initiated in Glasgow and in Yorkshire with the help of European structural funds.[12] The success of these commercially orientated production schemes, followed by eligibility of support for film production finance from the National Lottery since 1995, has strengthened the strong commercial orientation of national and regional initiatives.

Steve McIntyre provides a succinct overview of these developments, pointing out that the independent cultural (as opposed to industrial) production sector in the late 1980s became preoccupied with issues of training, in part attempting to open up opportunities for those denied access to the means of film production. But this shift in emphasis was also funding led, particularly in areas where considerable sums of public money were available via European structural funds for training initiatives. The casualisation of the broadcasting industry, accompanied by a collapse in the training infrastructure, has increasingly allied these small independent companies to the broadcasting industries. This effectively completes what McIntyre sees as the long march from the radical political manifestos that initially characterised the film and video workshop movement in the 1970s and early 1980s to their industrial and commercial incorporation.[13]

The challenge for media development agencies is to maintain a commitment to access and diversity and to ensure that the benefits accrued from commercial production initiatives are redistributed through training, education and access projects, thus enabling a range of people to participate in the financial and cultural benefits of these schemes.[14] These agencies operate in a climate governed by competition and commercial constraints. It is therefore interesting to note that one consequence of these strategies in the mid-1990s was the creation of a distinctive body of popular films that offer a sustained critique of contemporary British life, albeit primarily from a white male perspective.[15] There is of course no *necessary* relationship between the kinds of images seen on the screen and where and how they are produced. Even so, these new opportunities for film-making stimulated film-makers to create a body of films with a well-defined sense of place that address the relationship between class and consumption in terms that resonated not only with British audiences but also internationally.

Re-imagined communities

The success of such films as *Trainspotting*, *Twin Town*, *Brassed Off* and *The Full Monty* beyond the international festival circuit has added to the substantial reputation of British films abroad established by film-makers like Ken

Loach, Stephen Frears and Mike Leigh. These productions share a similar range of thematic preoccupations, projecting critical images of contemporary life in post-Thatcherite Britain to international audiences.[16] The films reflect the increasing eclecticism of British film style as it evolved during the 1980s, drawing on a range of codes and conventions associated with European and American independent traditions, television drama, documentary practice, art cinema, advertising and music video, as well as home-grown and Hollywood genres.[17] Although formally and aesthetically diverse, these films all foreground a sense of place in their use of location shooting and vernacular dialogue. They also deal with themes of masculine anxiety and alienation through the economic disenfranchisement and consequent social impotence of their male characters. The issue of unemployment and its effects is, however, treated very differently from film to film.

In some ways, the characters in these films have little in common other than their masculine gender and a shared sense of powerlessness. Working-class identity is depicted as fractured and split by new alliances between workers and owners in *Brassed Off*, by drug taking as a form of shared camaraderie in *Trainspotting*, by crime and revenge in *Twin Town*, and by the changing economic relations between men and women in *The Full Monty*. The style of these films is also very different: the most successful film at the box office, *The Full Monty*, has the nostalgic flavour of an Ealing comedy. It is about a group of men pulling together in times of trouble to overcome adversity, appealing to a rather stereotyped image of working-class life that was common in the 1940s: people laughing and joking together through hard times. *Brassed Off* similarly combines a political message within a romantic-comedy format, evoking an affectionate if somewhat sentimental image of a community disintegrating as the privatisation programme at the local coal mine creates mass redundancy among the workforce.

In spite of their address to contemporary issues, at the heart of the appeal of both films is a somewhat nostalgic sentimentality. *The Full Monty* begins with a promotional documentary for Sheffield that depicts it as an early 1970s boomtown. The colliery band at the narrative centre of *Brassed Off* only survives in the real world with the help of an Arts Council grant. In the film, keeping the band together and making sure it continues to play symbolises a rather desperate attempt to maintain the collective dignity of the community and keep its values intact. These sympathetic portrayals of working-class men as physically redundant in the workplace and emotionally retarded in the home create an image of masculinity in crisis that emphasises the non-aggressive, non-threatening aspirations of the group. In spite of the failure of trade unions and political institutions to maintain a sense of unity and self-worth, male camaraderie and togetherness are given positive values: both films have up-beat, 'feel-good' endings based on the abilities of the group to perform collectively, not as workers but as entertainers.[18]

Plate 22   From factory floor to dance floor: finding new uses for industrial spaces in
The Full Monty (Peter Cattaneo, 1997).

This nostalgic construction of working-class values is a reminder of the
kind of British films that were popular at the box office when the UK had a
more robust home-grown commercial film industry. A hankering for the
spirit of Ealing ghosts both these bittersweet comedies, the Ealing of that
brief postwar period when a focus on whimsical characters in small communities pulling together for the common good projected an idealised image of
a nation united by adversity. The characters in *The Full Monty* seem to yearn
for the stability of that imagined postwar world: for secure employment, the
weekly pay packet, Saturday night at the working-men's club and most of
all, perhaps, for a clearer demarcation of gender roles between men and
women. Their response to adversity is a reluctant acceptance of interdependence, a value traditionally associated with respectable working-class
identity. Beneath the humour and the rather predictable plot structure, *The
Full Monty*, like some of the other films in this cycle, scores a political point
but here the message is blunted by nostalgia rather than sharpened by satire.

Trainspotting and *Twin Town* are rather different kinds of film – and less
like each other than at first seems apparent. They are anarchic, nihilistic
comedies that both thematically and formally seek to overturn rather than
recycle stereotypes. The social-realist style traditionally associated with
images of working-class identity is eschewed in favour of heightened visu-
ality which, in the case of *Twin Town*, caricatures its characters in the
interest of demolishing the hackneyed images of what English speaking

Welsh film-makers call the Welsh nationalist 'Taffia'.[19] The opening monologue to *Twin Town* is a declaration of this intent: 'Rugby. Tom Jones. Male voice choirs. Shirley Bassey. Snowdonia. Prince of Wales. Daffodils. Sheep shaggers. Coal. Now if that's your idea of Welsh culture, you can't blame us for trying to liven the place up can you?'[20]

Set in Swansea, the South Wales city immortalised by Dylan Thomas as an 'ugly, lovely town', the film irreverently replaces his phrase with one of its own – 'pretty shitty city'. In its use of caricature and satire, the film pays homage to contemporary American independent film-makers like the Coen Brothers. In placing the severed head of a favourite pet dog in the bed of the corrupt local club owner and drug dealer, it creates a pastiche of *The Godfather* (Francis Ford Coppola, 1972). But for all its anarchic posturing, at its heart *Twin Town* is a genre piece, a tale of warring families, corrupt policemen, drugs, murder and revenge.

Trainspotting shows a similar preoccupation with the destruction of stereotypical representations of Scottish identity. Surreal images and a sporadically frenetic editing style married to a fast-paced soundtrack construct a fantasy world of heroin addiction.[21] The episodic narration creates a contemporary picaresque based around the drug-taking habits of Renton and his friends, who career from the hedonistic pleasures of heroin to the agonies of withdrawal. But within this frantic journey, the film takes time to comment acidly on what it means to be Scottish, white and working class in the 1990s. A key scene in the film is a trip to the countryside instigated by Renton's friend Tommy, who is drug free at this point in the narrative. The train drops the four friends in an isolated spot of peat bog and distant mountains, an image of Scotland promoted by the tourist board in glossy magazines aimed at the middle classes. Filmed as grotesque, the picture postcard setting inspires fear and loathing in Renton, Spud and Sick Boy. It also provokes Renton into giving voice to his feelings on his Scottish identity:

> The English are just wankers. We're colonised by wankers. Effete arseholes. What does that make us? The lowest of the fuckin' low, the scum of the earth. Ah don't hate the English. They just git oan wi' the shite thuv got. Ah hate the Scots.

What unites *Trainspotting*, *Twin Town*, *Brassed Off* and *The Full Monty* is their re-articulation of working-class identity through its relation to national and regional stereotypes and geographical marginalisation. The changing landscape of working-class poverty and economic decline is most visibly apparent in *The Full Monty*; Gaz and his friends steal from the empty factories where once they worked, while their wives work full-time, one of them in the new hypermarket. In *Brassed Off*, local businesses close as the new pit owners lay off increasing numbers of the workforce and poverty bites into the reserves of the local population. In *Twin Town* and *Trainspotting*, the relationship between work (or the lack of it) and consumption is posed somewhat differently. The market in jobs and drugs created by a culture of chronic unemployment provides the hook for a narrative of vengeance in *Twin Town*. The Lewis brothers, aimless drifters on probation who spend their time joyriding and taking drugs, live in a caravan site on the edge of Swansea. Employed by a corrupt local club owner and drug dealer to repair a roof, their father falls and breaks his leg. The twins demand recompense, but in the 'black' economy there are no insurance or compensation schemes to cushion the effects of injury.

The relationship between work and consumption is posed most starkly in *Trainspotting*. Renton stakes out the choices in the now famous soliloquy at the beginning of the film:

> Choose life. Choose a job, choose a career, choose a family. Choose a fucking big television, choose washing machines, cars, compact disc players, electrical can openers ... But why would I want to do a thing like that? I chose not to choose life, I chose somethin' else. And the reasons? There are no reasons. Who needs reasons when you've got heroin?[22]

In a society where identity is based not on who you are or where you come from but on what you consume, heroin is the ultimate consumer product. If what you consume is the hallmark of your identity, socially sanctioned goods and objects become a sign of social conformity; taking drugs is one way of demonstrating personal alienation and a rejection of establishment values.

Contrasting views

The success of these films and the attendant publicity that followed in their wake unmasks conflicts of interest between media development agencies and other local initiatives. In Wales, for example, *Twin Town* packed local cinemas but created an outcry from those concerned with projecting more traditional images of Wales. Dave Berry, the Welsh cinema historian, argues that *Twin Town* demeans Wales and its people because it suggests that 'traditions such as community loyalty, decency and camaraderie, a shared love of culture, music and rugby are all redundant in an avaricious world'.[23] For Berry, the film is riddled with negative attitudes towards the Welsh and their preoccupations, a position denied by the director and screenwriter Kevin Allen who claims that the film is 'an acid love-letter to my home town'.[24] In his defence of the film, he argues that it could be set in any contemporary British city – drugs and crime happen everywhere. The film uses a rich amalgam of South Wales dialect, Welsh language phrases and familiar swear words combined with the irreverent treatment of distinctively

Welsh signifiers, such as a rugby ball stuffed with bags of cocaine and the vandalising of the rugby pitch by the Lewis twins. Even so, if other local signifiers replaced the details of language and imagery, they would still produce the same meaning. *Twin Town*, like *Trainspotting*, treats images of national identity as impoverished signifiers of a bankrupt culture that has difficulty adjusting to forces of modernisation and change.

The film caused some concern at the Welsh Tourist Board, where an internal memorandum was circulated to key personnel advising them to 'avoid whingeing' about *Twin Town*; as far as any one knew, *Trainspotting* had not been detrimental to the tourist trade in Edinburgh. In spite of the nega-tive projection of Wales, it may actually boost trade.[25] In Sheffield, a similar conflict emerged as a number of councillors and influential local business groups publicly criticised the image of Sheffield as a city in decline in *The Full Monty*. Asserting that the city has much to be proud of, they pointed out that Sheffield produces 70 per cent of the country's engineering and specialist steels, unemployment has fallen below 9 per cent, it has a lively cultural quarter and would soon be home to the National Museum for Popular Music. They accused the film-makers of replaying old myths and stereotypes about the North, preferring the '*Room at the Top*' image of dirt, grime and economic depression, rather than the city's modern science parks, data processing complexes, clean rivers, smokeless air and new, brick-built houses.[26] (In fact, there is a glimpse of this world in *The Full Monty* – Gaz's ex-wife lives with her new partner in a modern, brick-built detached house on a private housing estate. It is depicted as a rather cold and cheerless place, a dormitory suburb with no sense of community.)

In their analysis of cultural policy and urban regeneration schemes in western Europe, Franco Bianchini and Michael Parkinson point out that the experience of cultural policy-led regeneration strategies, particularly when focused on city centre prestige projects, can lead to increased tensions between inner and outer areas, tourists and residents.[27] The effects of making films in impoverished communities can be equally divisive; Grimethorpe, for example, the site of the fictional Grimley in *Brassed Off*, has seen few benefits. The once thriving community is blighted by unem-ployment, while drug-related crime, arson, theft and teenage pregnancy are all on the increase in spite of every form of text-book partnership between local people, government and industry.[28] Irvine Welsh, the author of the novel on which *Trainspotting* is based, points to a similar situation in Edinburgh where more than twenty years of booming tourism have failed to improve conditions of life on the 'schemies' – the city's outer housing estates.[29]

The working-class films of the mid-1990s occupy an ambiguous cultural terrain. They celebrate locality, yet at the same time they commodify the cultural identities of economically marginalised communities, re-packaging their experiences for sale in the global marketplace. Will those who live in these places reap any benefits from these production initiatives in the longer term? As Steve McIntyre has pointed out, the beneficiary of these schemes appears to be the broadcaster or film distributor rather than the local community. Blairite cultural policy has continued this trend, emphasising the commercial aspects of film production and largely ignoring cultural issues such as access and diversity.[30] The influx of money from the lottery poses McIntyre's question even more starkly: to what extent should public money be used to subsidise already wealthy industries?[31] But the various media development agencies are in no doubt about their function, and have undeniably played a part in 'post-modernising' the cultural landscapes of such cities as Sheffield, Liverpool and Glasgow. These areas provide new talent and (occasionally) innovative products for the voracious appetites of the film and media industries. Whether these policies will create new opportunities of sustainable employment for those who bear the brunt of economic change will only become apparent once European funding ends. And whether the devolution of film production can contribute in the longer term to the development of a diverse film and media culture that projects the experiences of Britain's multifarious communities remains a challenge to policy makers, media development agencies and the film-makers which they support.

NOTES

1   For an analysis of working-class identity in New Wave films, see J. Hill, *Sex, Class and Realism: British Cinema 1956–1963*, London, BFI, 1986.

2   For a theoretical overview of these developments, see S. Hall, 'The question of cultural identity', in S. Hall, D. David and T. McGrew (eds) *Modernity and Its Futures*, Oxford, Polity Press, 1992.

3   Ffilm Cymru was established in 1989 to enable the production of low-budget feature films; it was followed by the Welsh Film Council (Cyngor Ffilm Cymru) in 1992. Sigrîn was formally constituted in April 1997. Funded by the Arts Council of Wales, the BFI, BBC Wales, Cardiff Bay Development Corporation, S4C, TAC and the Welsh Development Agency, it is responsible for 'the formulation of a strategic vision for the development of the industrial and cultural aspects of [film, television and new media] to their full potential'. Sigrîn publicity material, 1999, p. 2.

4   Initiatives to establish nine Regional Development Agencies began during New Labour's first year in government (1997): it is envisaged that these institutions will contribute to the formation of Regional Assemblies in England. See P. Lynch, 'New Labour and the English Regional Development Agencies: devolution as evolution', in *Regional Studies*, 1999, vol. 33, no. 1, pp. 73–8.

5   For an overview of these developments, see K. Robins and D. Morley, *Spaces of Identity: Global Media, Electronic Landscapes and Cultural Boundaries*, London, Routledge, 1995, pp. 105–24.

6   *BFI Yearbook*, London, BFI Publishing, 1998, p. 23.

7   K. Robins, 'Tradition and translation: national culture in its global context', in J. Corner and S. Harvey (eds) *Enterprise and Heritage: Crosscurrents of National Culture*, London, Routledge, 1991, pp. 28–31.

8   Robins and Morley, op. cit., pp. 117–18.

9 'Justifying a Film Commission's existence', *Locations*, Fall 1992, p. 14. Quoted by T. Brown in 'Everytown, Nowhere City: Location Filming and the British City', unpublished MA dissertation, British Film Institute (undated). The British Tourist Authority now publishes an official 'movie map' that aims to 'combine two thriving industries and the leisure pursuits of the cinema and days out ... to lure visitors away from the "honeypot" tourist centres to less explored areas of Britain'. See J. Meikle, 'Movies redraw the tourist map', *Guardian,* 16 June 1999, p. 12.

10 For a full discussion of this point, see K. Robins and J. Cornford, 'Not the London Broadcasting Corporation? The BBC and the new regionalism', in S. Harvey and K. Robins (eds) *The Regions, the Nations and the BBC*, BBC Charter Review Series, London, BFI Publishing, 1993, pp. 16–17.

11 According to local estimates, Liverpool's Film Liaison Office attracted sixty-seven film and television productions to the city in 1994, generating six million pounds in revenue and creating an estimated 150 jobs; the figures do not include any income generated from accommodating production crews and actors. See R. Gilbey, 'Cut and print: tales of the celluloid city', *Independent* ('Metro' section), 19 April 1995, p. 20.

12 Like Liverpool, these areas were granted 'Objective One' status by the European Commission, which is based on an average standard of living 75 per cent below that of the European Union as a whole.

13 S. McIntyre, 'Art and industry: regional film and video policy in the UK', in A. Moran (ed.) *Film Policy: International, National and Regional Perspectives*, Routledge, London, 1996, pp. 215–34.

14 Shane Meadows ensured that £40,000 would be invested in local projects when he signed a production contract following the success of *TwentyFourSeven*. See N. Spencer, 'Interview: Shane Meadows', *Observer Review*, 29 March 1998, p. 7.

15 See Paul Bucknor's comments on the 'whiteness' of *The Full Monty* in M. Baker, 'The missing Monty', *black filmmaker*, 1998, vol. 1, no. 2, pp. 14–15.

16 Wim Wenders, for example, states 'I don't see any other national cinema that manages to make very popular stories which are also deeply rooted in social life, in certain realities and experiences', in *The Art of Seeing: Essays and Conversations*, Faber and Faber, London, 1997, p. 31.

17 For a more detailed discussion see the chapter 'Space, place and identity: revisioning social realism', in J. Hallam with M. Marshment, *Realism and Popular Cinema*, Manchester, Manchester University Press, 2000.

18 Claire Monk argues that these films pose solutions to their problems through homosocial bonding, offering emotional catharsis and reassurance for a 1990s male audience. 'Underbelly UK: the underclass film and the 1990s British cinema revival', paper presented at *Cinema, Identity, History: An International Conference on British Cinema*, University of East Anglia, July 1998. See this volume, Chapter 19, for a revised version of this paper.

19 M. Wroe, 'Sprawling, joy-riding, hot-bed of mediocrity', *Observer*, 13 April 1997, p. 16.

20 The wording is taken from the advertising campaign; it appeared primarily on posters.

21 Will Self is particularly critical of this expressionistic technique, claiming that it misrepresents the effects of heroin, which provokes no visions, no fantasies of surreal bliss and surrender. 'Carry on up the hypodermic', *Observer Review*, 17 February 1996, p. 6.

22 The wording is taken from the poster.

23 *Ffocws*, 1997, vol. 4, no. 1, p. 3.
24 Wroe, op. cit., p. 16.
25 Ibid.
26 See, for example, C. Pepinster, 'Sheffield's really a post-industrial paradise: many in the city are cross at its bleak portrayal in *The Full Monty*', *Independent*, 7 December 1997, p. 5.
27 F. Bianchini and M. Parkinson, *Cultural Policy and Urban Regeneration: The Western European Experience*, Manchester, Manchester University Press, 1993, p. 168.
28 D. McKie, 'Muck and brass but precious little money', *Guardian*, 18 September 1997, p. 19.
29 I. Welsh, 'City tripper', *Guardian* ('G2' section), 16 February 1996, p. 4.
30 See *A Bigger Picture*, a government report on the British Film Industry compiled by the Film Policy Review Group, Department for Culture, Media and Sport, DCMSJO285NJ, March 1998.
31 McIntyre, op. cit., pp. 231–3.

19

UNDERBELLY UK

The 1990s underclass film, masculinity and the ideologies of 'new' Britain

Claire Monk

The 1990s saw a notable cycle of British films that drew their subject or subtext from the problems of unemployment and social exclusion faced by a social stratum identified by some social and political commentators as an 'underclass'. The cycle is loose-knit, spanning a range of genres (and, in keeping with wider trends of the 1990s, often mixing different genres), and including films aimed at both minority and mainstream audiences. The use of the term 'underclass' by its best-known populariser, the conservative American academic Charles Murray,[1] and in the bulk of subsequent debate, has been condemnatory, portraying a class seen as parasitically dependent and work-shy rather than merely work-less. By contrast, my use of the term is descriptive, denoting a 'subordinate social class'.[2] In common with Murray's critics on the liberal centre and neo-Marxist left,[3] my discussion takes the 'underclass' to be a *post-working* class that owes its existence to the economic and social damage wrought by globalisation, local industrial decline, the restructuring of the labour market and other legacies of the Thatcher era. In what follows, I shall examine the cycle of underclass films in terms of what they say about gender, class and national identity in the context of the culture and politics of contemporary Britain.

Underclass films and the British social-realist tradition

The first 'underclass' films of the 1990s were Ken Loach's politically committed comic dramas *Riff-Raff* (1992) and *Raining Stones* (1993), and Mike Leigh's existential, despairing art film *Naked* (1993). These were in the tradition of cultural film-making aimed at minority audiences and were generally exhibited in an art-house context. In keeping with the 1990s drift away from cultural film-making and towards a British cinema increasingly commercial in its aspirations,[4] the latter half of the 1990s saw a concentration of British films with underclass themes or subtexts, aimed squarely at one or other of the decade's fragmented mainstream audiences. The cycle included crime and conspiracy thrillers, such as the modestly successful *Face* (Antonia Bird, 1997) and the unsuccessful *The Innocent Sleep* (Scott Michell, 1995); low-budget social comedies of underclass petty crime, such as *Small Time* (Shane Meadows, 1996)[5] and *Twin Town* (Kevin Allen, 1997); the generically hybrid *Trainspotting* (Danny Boyle, 1996); the gangland comedy *Lock, Stock and Two Smoking Barrels* (Guy Ritchie, 1998); and the social-realist comedies *Brassed Off* (Mark Herman, 1996) and *The Full Monty* (Peter Cattaneo, 1997). For the purposes of my argument, the mainstream or commercial underclass films can usefully be divided into two broad cross-genre categories. The 'youth' underclass films, such as *Trainspotting*, *Twin Town* and *Lock, Stock and Two Smoking Barrels*, were aimed primarily at the young 'core' cinema-going audience of 18–25 year olds, implicitly treated by the industry as predominantly male, and certainly addressed as if they were by film marketeers and the mainstream film consumer media.[6] *Brassed Off* and *The Full Monty*, by contrast, sought and attracted a non-niche mainstream audience broader in terms of age and, ostensibly, gender.

The underclass films of the 1990s of course have their antecedents in a long tradition of British social-realist film-making. In particular, as John Hill notes, 'the debilitating, and sometimes brutalising, consequences of unemployment and poverty' were also the subject of British films of the 1980s, from *Letter to Brezhnev* (Chris Bernard, 1985) to *Rita, Sue and Bob Too* (Alan Clarke, 1987).[7] The relationship of the underclass films to the social-realist tradition is, however, neither straightforward nor unproblematic. Hill argues that significant changes took place in the socially aware British cinema in the 1980s in terms of both aesthetic strategies and thematic concerns which meant that it was no longer possible to describe it as 'working-class realism'. Aesthetically, he notes the emergence of 'an implicit dissatisfaction with straightforward "realism"'.[8] Thus an increasing number of British films of the 1980s committed to exploring 'realist' subjects rejected 'straight' verisimilitude in favour of stylisation, fantasy and a more diverse and hybrid range of aesthetic approaches.[9] More directly relevant to my argument in this chapter are the thematic shifts that Hill identifies. In keeping with the displacement of class politics by identity politics in the 1980s, British cinema was characterised by a loss of 'concern with working-class culture', which was 'no longer seen as a source of either "authentic" values or popular resistance'.[10] One corollary of this loss was that British films of the 1980s offered 'virtually no representation of "community" [and] very few images of collective action'.[11] Another was that a central focus on white, working-class masculinity became an increasing rarity.[12]

The underclass films of the 1990s advance some of the trends of the 1980s identified by Hill while reversing others. The success of *Brassed Off* and *The Full Monty* appeared superficially – but deceptively, I will argue – to mark the return with a vengeance of the class-consciousness and sense of collectivity and community repressed in the 1980s. More pertinent in my view is the fact that the most commercially and critically successful films in the underclass cycle share an obsessive focus on white, non-working masculinity. Aesthetically, the youth underclass films continued, and in some cases extended, the 1980s anti-realist trend noted by Hill. This is most evident in *Trainspotting*'s depiction of junkie life on Edinburgh's fringe housing estates, with its combination of a highly choreographed heightened realism and surreal fantasy. (The sequences in which Renton [Ewan McGregor] struggles to retrieve two lost heroin suppositories from 'the worst toilet in Scotland' and later hallucinates his way through withdrawal are the two most notable examples of the latter.) *Brassed Off* and *The Full Monty*, by contrast, displayed an anonymous naturalism and lack of stylistic self-awareness that reversed the anti-realist trajectory. (Indeed, the most memorable element stylistically in *The Full Monty* is its title sequence.)

'Traditionally,' Hill writes, 'social realism within Britain has been associated with the *making visible* of the working class.'[13] In this chapter, I will argue that, far from signalling straightforward social or economic concern, the 'making visible' of a non-working underclass in British films of the 1990s had wider ideological implications. I will focus on those commercial underclass films that attracted a cross-demographic audience, especially *Brassed Off* and *The Full Monty* (which on its release was the most profitable British box-office success of all time in both home and export markets). My interest in these films derives from the anachronism at the heart of their success, namely their transformation of underclass material into an appealing, profitable and exportable commodity. *The Full Monty*'s transformation of feel-bad subject matter (redundancy, economic desperation, divorce, despair, impotence, loss of family, loss of self-esteem) into feel-good comedy is the quintessential example of this process. In elevating underclass life into a *lifestyle*, films like *Trainspotting* enact an equivalent commodification for a younger market.

Befitting the 1990s film industry's preoccupation with the youth market, films from both strands were packaged and marketed to audiences via strategies devised to suggest an affinity with young British style and creative culture. Examples range from youth-orientated pre-publicity and clever poster, graphic and/or title design (in the cases of *Face* and *The Full Monty*), to the association with cutting-edge cool that was achieved via the post-*Trainspotting* casting of Ewan McGregor and Robert Carlyle in the more staid *Brassed Off* and *The Full Monty* respectively. Thus both strands of commercial underclass film became very much implicated in the rhetoric of a British cultural and cinematic 'revival' in the 1990s. The international success of *Trainspotting*, *The Full Monty* and (more modestly) *Brassed Off* – and their consequent high profile as projections of contemporary British identity – also implicated them in the wider 're-branding' of Britain taking place in the late 1990s, both at home and for the benefit of export 'markets'.

A superficial content analysis might suggest that the ideological role performed by films like *Brassed Off* and *The Full Monty* is, almost by definition, positive and 'progressive'. The market-driven cultural and political context in which the underclass films were conceived and circulated necessitates a more detailed scrutiny of the films, however. For example, through what mechanisms are the underclass films – most notably, *The Full Monty* – able to produce the 'euphoric'[14] effects and 'sense of exhilaration'[15] for audiences noted by critics? Who are these films addressing, and what messages might be drawn from them by their audiences?

In exploring these questions, my central contention will be that the commodification of the underclass in these films was symptomatic of the abandonment of the project of a socially committed British cinema rather than the reverse. My discussion will focus on two main issues. First, I will argue that the preoccupation of both strands of the cycle with a *male* under-class performs a symbolic displacement, functioning as a conduit through which a wider, more diffuse set of male emotions, anxieties and resentments around gender as much as economic disempowerment are articulated and soothed. Hill has noted that Loach's *Riff-Raff* marked a return to class poli-tics, but in a very masculinist form.[16] I would add that, far from enacting an authentic reversion to 'old', pre-1980s class politics, those underclass films of the 1990s that deployed a patina of old class politics often did so to masculinist ends.

Second, I will comment further on the underclass cycle's contribution to the wider re-branding of Britain in the late 1990s. The success and high profile of films with underclass concerns at the close of eighteen years of Conservative rule seemed to symbolise – however fleetingly and spuriously – a shift in the favoured projection of British identity. I will argue, however, that the close association of this re-branding with the inherently market-driven 'modernising' project adopted by Tony Blair's New Labour Govern-ment, elected in May 1997, made the role of the underclass films in this respect a paradoxical one at best.

Men, women and work in the underclass films

Both strands of commercial underclass film of the later 1990s exhibit traits that support the analysis sketched above. From *Brassed Off* to *Trainspotting*, they typically acknowledge economic and political causes only as taken-for-granted backdrop, if at all. With the arguable exception of *Brassed Off*, they are also resignedly post-industrial in their outlook. There are substantial differences between the labour politics of *Brassed Off* and *The Full Monty* that should not be effaced. *Brassed Off*'s Old Labour collectivism, for instance, is antithetical to *The Full Monty*'s Blairite gospel of entrepreneurial self-help, labour flexibility and the sublimation of old industrial antagonisms in the interests of enterprise. Despite this distinction, however, the central narra-tive problem that both films address is not so much unemployment *per se* as its psychic and emotional effects. *Brassed Off*, for example, appears sincere in its outrage over pit closures and its lucid stance on some (if not all) of the industrial and political issues surrounding them. It nevertheless milks the emotions of its protagonists' struggles to an extent that insists that its audience too should respond emotionally, leaving understanding and the desire to take action optional.

Whether these films are preoccupied with underclass problems (*Brassed Off*, *The Full Monty*) or subcultures (*Trainspotting*, *Twin Town*), it is noticeable that the most commercially successful of them implicitly define the underclass as *male*. (One of the few films with claims to underclass status that breaks this gender rule is Michael Winterbottom's *Butterfly Kiss* [1994].) At the level of narrative, theme and the patterns of identification they invite, both *The Full Monty* and *Brassed Off* are expressly concerned with the impact of long-term joblessness, poverty and social exclusion not on the community at large, but on *men*. The subcultural worlds of *Trainspotting* and *Lock, Stock and Two Smoking Barrels* are likewise inherently homosocial.

The youth and cross-demographic strands of the cycle, however, differ markedly in their attitudes to male disempowerment and in the forms of reassurance which they offer male audiences. The youth underclass films present joblessness and social exclusion as an accepted state. The young male underclass of *Trainspotting* or *Twin Town* is emphatically not framed as a 'social problem' requiring a 'solution' but, with a certain knowing detachment, as a subculture. Rather than seeking to provoke social anger, the films encourage an empathetic complicity between their audience and the two films' jobless young male inhabitants, respectively heroin users and petty criminals. The lives led by the protagonists are thus framed as a lifestyle with certain attractions for a young, post-political male audience, although irony is never absent from this framing.

In *Lock, Stock and Two Smoking Barrels*, this appeal to young men is achieved by the virtual absenting of girls and women from the frame: the only female characters of note are a card dealer and a comatose stoned girl who, at one point in the plot, literally functions as furniture. The more interesting portrayals of young women in *Trainspotting* and *Twin Town* suggest a society in which traditional gender roles have been inverted. Crucially, however, neither film expresses resentment of female empowerment or of the male loss of the 'right to work'. Through the figures of Adie (Rachel Scorgie), working sister of *Twin Town*'s delinquent male protagonists, and *Trainspotting*'s teenage schoolgirl Diane (Kelly Macdonald), paid work and study are coded as 'female' activities. Girls and women nevertheless remain peripheral in both films, suggesting that the female pursuit of work and qualifications is marginal, located outside the young male's sphere of interest and hardly worthy of emulation or respect. This reading is supported by *Trainspotting*'s treatment of Diane's self-assurance as a scary excess, and *Twin Town*'s contemptuous revelation that Adie's job as a massage-parlour 'receptionist' is less respectable than she claims. The youth underclass films thus address the possible gender anxieties of their young male viewers by portraying the underclass as a reassuring subculture of dissent and escape from the demands of adulthood, women and work.

By contrast with this nonchalance, *Brassed Off* and *The Full Monty* are explicitly preoccupied with male disempowerment as a *problem*. Both films pointedly equate the loss of working-class male labour power with the loss of male *gender* power – in the case of *Brassed Off*, with obtrusive misogyny. The explicit links drawn in both films between the closure of heavy industries and the weakening of ideologies of traditional masculinity have led Hill to describe them as ' "delayed" 1980s films'.[17] In their consistent expression of the problems of the post-industrial male as problems of gender, however, *Brassed Off* and *The Full Monty* are very much films of the 1990s.

Plate 23   Commodifying the underclass: the youth-orientated marketing of *Trainspotting* (Danny Boyle, 1996), like the film itself, framed underclass life as a lifestyle.

279

In the 1990s, British cinema, and popular culture more generally, has addressed male anxieties relating to perceived shifts in workplace and gender power via three main strategies. The first involves addressing these anxieties on what might be termed a rational level: via direct acknowledgement, discussion and the search for some kind of (re)solution. The second strategy is masculinist reaction. This has primarily taken the form of the re-admission into the media and film culture of a degree of sexism and misogyny, which gained a new acceptability in some quarters provided they were cloaked in postmodern irony or humour. (The media-invented figure of the 'new lad', and much of the content of the men's magazines that competed to address him after the launch of the influential men's monthly *loaded* in 1994, epitomise this trend.) This strategy can be viewed as both an attempted retrenchment of male power and a mechanism of escapist denial. The third strategy is a retreat into nostalgia for old patriarchal hierarchies, whether in the workplace or in male–female relations. This may take the form of the production of new cultural goods that gratify this nostalgia or the excavation of old ones. An illustration of the latter is the 1990s nostalgia for the British gangster films of the 1960s and 1970s (reassuring because of their sexism and patriarchal organisational hierarchies). Examples include the 1990s celebration of Michael Caine in such men's magazines as *loaded* and *GQ*, the re-release of one of his star vehicles, *Get Carter* (Mike Hodges, 1971), in British cinemas in 1999 and *Empire* magazine's canonisation of the gangster thriller *The Long Good Friday* (John Mackenzie, 1979) as the best British film of all time.[18]

Between them, *Brassed Off* and *The Full Monty* deploy all three strategies. Of particular significance, however, is their nostalgia. This nostalgia arouses audience emotions not so much around stable employment and the old industries in themselves as around the lost homosocial communities they engendered and the powerful emotional bonds associated with them. It is this arousing of emotion around the idea of men as a community under threat, I would argue, that explains the widespread appeal of these films for a 1990s male audience, while also contributing to their empathetic appeal to women. It particularly seems to explain the films' ability to appeal to an international male audience far broader and more affluent than the 'under-class' depicted, with little personal investment in post-industrial traumas, and with no knowledge of the film's northern English cultural and industrial setting.

Neither *Brassed Off* nor *The Full Monty* can offer their protagonists or their audiences a return to the days of secure male employment or the restoration of lost male power: historical knowledge makes such a narrative resolution untenable. *Brassed Off*'s unresolved ending acknowledges this, leaving the members of the Yorkshire colliery band at the centre of the film triumphant in a national brass band competition, yet defeated in that their protests against the closure of the pit where they worked have failed. *The*

Full Monty's upbeat ending, on the other hand, encourages us to believe that a successful new career as male strippers lies ahead for the film's unemployed ex-steelworkers. It is significant, however, that the film ends by freezing its action in mid-striptease. If the resolution we require is a solution to the protagonists' unemployment and poverty, *The Full Monty* can offer only unconvincing closure. The viewer is offered no evidence that the narrative's numerous crises have been resolved: for all we know, the film's flawed hero Gaz (Robert Carlyle) and his co-strippers may be about to be arrested for indecency, fail to get paid, or never strip again. We do not even know whether Gaz has earned enough to pay off his maintenance arrears to his ex-wife Mandy (Emily Woof), or whether he will regain access to their son Nathan (William Snape), whom Gaz is not allowed to see because of his stripping activities.

What *The Full Monty*'s narrative does resolve beyond doubt is the problem of its male protagonists' loss of confidence and self-esteem. It translates an intractable real-life crisis in male economic and social roles into a more diegetically resolvable crisis in relations between women and men. Thus the predicament faced by Gaz, his desperately insecure friend Dave (Mark Addy) and their co-strippers is overwhelmingly articulated in terms of (real or feared) rejection by their female partners, torments about body image, and so on, rather than economic hardship. The film's emotional highs and lows are orchestrated almost entirely around the men's crises of masculinity, their supportive or destructive relations with women, and above all the growing therapeutic bond between the men.

The primary fear *The Full Monty* addresses and 'resolves' is that women have usurped men's roles and territory. This fear is clearly articulated early in the film when Gaz and Dave observe the raucous women queuing to see the American male strippers, the Chippendales, at a local Sheffield venue at £10 a ticket. The venue is a working man's club – traditionally a homosocial male enclave into which women are admitted only if related to a male member, and then only in limited circumstances. Sneaking in out of curiosity, Gaz hides in the men's toilets; but the traditional male pleasure of voyeurism is transformed into humiliation when he discovers that the toilets are being used by women. Moreover, these are loud, unruly women who talk dirty, drink pints and urinate standing up. Later, Gaz describes them to Dave as 'genetic mutations ... a few years more, and men won't exist ... We're obsolete. Dinosaurs. Yesterday's news'.

Even at this early stage in the film, however, the viewer is aware of what Gaz does *not* tell Dave – that one of the women was Dave's wife Jean. Further, Gaz has missed what Jean was actually saying (as Dave will continue to do throughout the film): she loves Dave, and is determined to stand by him even though his unhappiness is making her bewildered and miserable. *The Full Monty*'s reassuring message (affirmed by its ending, in which even Gaz's disdainful, bourgeoisified ex-wife Mandy turns up to see him strip) is that women *do* need men. The female invasion of male space is not exactly an expression of female domination: as Dave points out: 'Why were them women in working men's club in first place? 'Cos of us. Men.'

The more potent message that *The Full Monty* offers a male audience, however, is that *men* need men, and, in particular, that sons need fathers. A similar message provides the emotional and narrative core of *Brassed Off*: from the opening scenes, we are told that the colliery closure which the film's miners are fighting (the nominal narrative 'problem' to be resolved) is almost certainly a *fait accompli*. It is the possibility that the colliery brass band (and analogously, the masculine emotional community rooted in the workplace) will also die which is presented as the ultimate tragedy.

Yet in both films, the threatened 'community' which must be re-membered and preserved is expressly one which excludes women: women are not normally permitted to play in the colliery band any more than they are allowed to enter the working man's club. In *Brassed Off*, flugel-horn player Gloria (Tara Fitzgerald) – the film's love interest – is allowed to join the colliery band only because she is patriarchally linked with the pit. It is revealed that her dead grandfather was the bandleader Danny's (Pete Postlethwaite) coal-face partner or 'marrer' – an expression from north-east England which denotes a male bond between miners closer than that between husband and wife. *Brassed Off*'s most manipulative plot strand threatens the audience that if the (patriarchal) band does not play on, not one but *two* generations of father–son bonds will be lost. The first bond is between ageing bandleader Danny, battling with a mining-related disease, and his son Phil (Stephen Tompkinson); the second is between the emotionally tattered Phil and the young sons taken away by his absconding wife. Critic Nina Caplan wrote of *The Full Monty* that 'conversation, admission of need and collective action provide the only solutions to these men's situation … they are framed and filmed as a cohesive (if volatile) unit'.[19] She could have added that *The Full Monty*, like *Brassed Off*, is explicit in linking this unit's healing powers with its exclusive maleness.

Both *The Full Monty* and *Brassed Off* play out a drama in which the male social and emotional bonds once associated with the workplace and the working man's club are threatened, mourned, struggled for, and finally restored. Their message – cathartic and powerfully appealing for audiences – is that the 'community' these bonds constitute can live on (and, in *The Full Monty*, be reinvented) even though the industrial base which once provided its justification has gone, probably for good. In proposing that this community is organised around shared male emotions rather than class, *The Full Monty* and *Brassed Off* re-frame the economic oppressions of long-term unemployment as problems of male self-doubt and/or gender oppression by women. The youth underclass films, as already noted, perform an equivalent manoeuvre by rejecting the whole vocabulary of 'problems' and 'solutions'.

The commodification of the underclass and the 're-branding' of Britain

The conclusions both strands of commercial underclass film encourage us to draw about the spirit of 1990s Britain also fit uncannily with the goals of the 'modernised' national identity which Tony Blair's New Labour and others have attempted to promote in the late 1990s. In 1997, the British think-tank Demos published *Britain*^{TM}, a much discussed 'how-to' manual proposing strategies for the global 're-branding' of Britain.[20] The report's structuring contention was that perceptions of Britain across most of the globe remained mired in the past. Despite the 1990s phenomena of Britpop, Brit Art, the media invention of 'Cool Britannia' and the sense of a British creative revival, the report's author, Mark Leonard, suggested that Britain's international image remained twenty to forty years out of date: 'The perception around the world [is] that Britain remains a backward-looking island immersed in its heritage ... bogged down by tradition, riven by class and threatened by industrial disputes.'[21] The re-branding of Britain proposed by Demos – and subsequently in effect adopted as an official project by the New Labour Government – sought to overcome this image problem by promoting 'the reality of Britain as a highly creative and diverse society', innovative, dynamic, non-conformist, forward-looking and optimistic.[22]

The representations of the nation in the commercial underclass cycle clearly contradict the re-branding project in certain respects (*Brassed Off*'s espousal of industrial action, for example). The major paradox of these films, however, is that their focus on the underclass on the whole supports this projection of an optimistic, 'modernised' Britain rather than undermining it. Their energetic cultural confidence, combined with the projection of images apparently antithetical to bourgeois and upper-class 'heritage' Britain, broadcasts a loud message that a quantum shift has taken place in 1990s British culture and identity. This implied shift is, however, more a matter of surface symbolism than substance or deep structure, and its ideological implications are more complex than they initially appear.

At the narrative level, *Trainspotting*, *Brassed Off* and *The Full Monty* project an apparently democratised British identity which is urban and working class or post-working class rather than bourgeois and rural. The films also embrace diverse regional identities (especially northern English and Celtic) rather than privileging the south of England. Above all, they appear to signal a shift away from backward-looking complacency towards national self-criticism, suggesting that 'new' Britain is mature enough to acknowledge the presence of poverty, unemployment, industrial unrest, regional decline and drug addiction within the fabric of the nation.

Such a reading, however, disregards the commercialised, market-driven film and political cultures within which the films were produced and circulated. In this context, it would be a mistake to interpret the underclass cycle as simply the binary antithesis of heritage cinema or as straightforward proof of a wider rejection of heritage values. The 'post-heritage' films of the earlier 1990s, as I have argued elsewhere, had already strategically differentiated or distanced themselves by various means from the aesthetic and ideological conservatism for which heritage cinema had been criticised.[23] By the late 1990s, 'post-heritage' films from the stylistically self-conscious *Elizabeth* (Shekhar Kapur, 1998) to the more conventional *Shakespeare in Love* (John Madden, 1999) were being marketed on their youth appeal and 'cool' contemporaneity – or, in the case of *The Wings of the Dove* (Iain Softley, 1997), on a mixture of style, sexuality and (putative) social relevance. In short, the underclass and post-heritage cycles were increasingly marketed via similar strategies to similar audiences, and contributed to the same trend in British cinema promoting a 'modernised', 'cool' Britannia.

In such a climate, representations of history and contemporary poverty alike become, first and foremost, commodities, capable of serving peculiarly similar economic and ideological objectives. It should be pointed out that the primary objective of the official national re-branding proposed by Demos and taken up by the New Labour Government was not to promote one British cultural identity over another, but to promote a global perception of Britain as a competitive and innovative enterprise economy, thus enhancing its industrial prospects in a global capitalist free market.[24] As Leonard puts it: 'Coherent and attractive national identities have social and political benefits. Above all, they have an economic value.'[25] The composite national identity projected by British cinema in the 1990s might seem at first sight to be incoherent in its rampant hybridity; its coherence, however, lies in its ability to harness this diversity of representations and themes to the needs of the market.

The Full Monty, for instance, supports and promotes the objectives set out in the Demos report with remarkable effectiveness, both as a successful product in the global market, and in terms of how it speaks to its audiences. This effectiveness derives precisely from the use the film makes of its post-industrial, underclass setting. Though debunking and deflationary, its comedy nevertheless cumulatively projects an image of national and regional creativity and chutzpah that is pleasurable to audiences at home and, crucially, abroad. The poverty and initial hopelessness of the characters only serves to heighten the effectiveness of the film's message: if these guys (skinny, fat, middle-aged, unsexy) can succeed as male strippers, it surely follows that Britons (or anyone) can make a success of any enterprise.

Above all, the sheer improbability and cheek of Gaz's business idea (and *The Full Monty*'s concept) serve as a show-stopping advertisement for British entrepreneurial inventiveness, persistence and spirit. What could be more creative – or enterprising – than making a success of an idea which no one believes could possibly work? The fledgling strippers' ups and downs also transmit a host of related optimistic pro-enterprise messages: for example, that business success depends not on innate qualities or qualifications but on self-belief and mutual support, and that even crazy ideas deserve a backer (an idea to which only Gaz's young son Nathan gives credence in the film).

While *The Full Monty*'s narrative serves as an exceptionally lucid vehicle for such ideas, it is far from unique in the underclass cycle in its projection of the creative, non-conformist entrepreneurial values advocated by Britain's would-be re-branders. The drugs and criminal subcultures of *Trainspotting* and *Twin Town*, for example, combine the attractions of a highly marketable culture of youth dissent with the ultimate in maverick, high-risk (although illegal) free enterprise. Despite *Trainspotting*'s caustic opening denouncement of 'straight' (implicitly, capitalist and consumerist) society, it should not be forgotten that the film concludes with Renton (now a London estate agent) and his old associates Spud (Ewen Bremner) and Begbie (Robert Carlyle) making £16,000 on a heroin deal. Although the film's treatment of this reversal is loaded with irony, it addresses a generation of 'Thatcher's children' for whom the conflation of subcultural dissent and entrepreneurial capitalism holds no contradictions.

Whatever the fictional future holds for the characters of *Trainspotting* or *The Full Monty*, the films' denouements at least suggest that the psychological and emotional barriers to business success have been overcome. The optimistic message broadcast by *The Full Monty* is that even a de-industrialised community – or country – with few apparent resources or natural markets can put itself back on its feet. The stance of *Trainspotting* and *Twin Town* is more cynically individualistic; even so, they suggest that the young underclass, far from being victims, are fledgling entrepreneurs in an admittedly amoral free market where the fittest survive to make their own luck.

The political implications of these narratives of underclass enterprise are more than a little dubious, however. In *The Full Monty*, the shifting dynamics between Gaz, Dave and their former foreman Gerald (Tom Wilkinson) suggest that the emerging creative entrepreneurial Britain will be achieved through the effacement of old industrial and class conflicts. In a triumph of capitalist competitive instincts over collective loyalty, *Trainspotting* ends with Renton deciding to keep most of the proceeds of the drug deal for himself and fleeing abroad. Just as the film had earlier equated membership of a heroin subculture with conscious social dissent, so its conclusion implies that leaving the underclass is simply a matter of exercising free choice. (*Twin Town* features an identical 'escape' ending: after a string of thefts and murders, the brothers head for Morocco.) Still more problematic is the fact that *The Full Monty* fantasises a post-industrial Britain in which a flexible former manual workforce can remould themselves, with only temporary pain, into new careers in the creative and entertainment industries so heavily favoured by the nation's image-makers in the late 1990s. To describe the activity of stripping more cynically, the film proposes a career that replaces the sale of labour with the commodification of the body. Even the bittersweet ending of *Brassed Off*, in which the film's miners, by now redundant, vow to fight on via the success of their colliery band, raises hopes – or suspicions – that if a sequel were to be made we would find them forging a new career as full-time entertainers.

These optimistic narratives of underclass resourcefulness, entrepreneurialism, empowerment and self-transformation do at least serve as a pointed riposte to Charles Murray's demonisation of the underclass as passive and work-shy. But the vision or fantasy these films project is also symptomatic of the drift away from social analysis, commitment or action which typified the 1990s. This vision conveniently denies the need for any solution to the problems faced by the underclass other than those offered by 'free' human agency in a 'free' market. Whether or not we believe this solution intellectually, the strength of our desire to accept it within the world of the narrative – in the words of *The Full Monty*'s soundtrack, to 'believe in miracles' – produces a powerful emotional investment and catharsis. It seems likely, however, that the underclass films' exhilarating, uplifting effects and pleasures will be limited to audiences who do not have to test the viability of this particular 'miracle' in their own lives.

NOTES

1 See especially C. Murray, *The Emerging British Underclass*, London, Institute of Economic Affairs Health and Welfare Unit, 1990; and Murray, *Underclass: The Crisis Deepens*, London, Institute of Economic Affairs Health and Welfare Unit, 1994.
2 This is the more neutral definition of 'underclass' offered by the *Oxford Encyclopedic English Dictionary*, Oxford, Oxford University Press, 1991, p. 1570.
3 See, for instance, M. Fitzpatrick, 'Yob culture clash', *Living Marxism*, November 1994, no. 73. (Reproduced at http://www.informinc.co.uk/LM/LM73/LM73_Underclass.webmaster@mail.informinc.co.uk. Page numbers not given.)
4 For a critique of this shift, see N. Roddick, 'Show me the culture!', *Sight and Sound*, December 1998, vol. 8, no. 12, pp. 22–6.
5 Meadows' film is an extreme case in that it was filmed on video on a minuscule budget (reputedly £5,000). It also departs from the mainstream trends discussed in this chapter in its more critical treatment of gender. See C. Monk, 'From underworld to underclass: Crime and British cinema in the 1990s', in S. Chibnall and R. Murphy (eds) *British Crime Cinema*, London, Routledge, 1999, pp. 184–8.
6 For a discussion of the fragmentation, and especially gendering, of the 'mainstream' cinema audience in the UK, see Monk, 'Heritage films and the British cinema audience in the 1990s', *Journal of Popular British Cinema*, 1999, no. 2, pp. 22–38.
7 J. Hill, *British Cinema in the 1980s*, Oxford, Oxford University Press, 1999, p. 167.
8 Ibid., p. 134.
9 Ibid., pp. 135–6.
10 Ibid., p. 166.
11 Ibid.
12 Ibid., p. 135.

13 Ibid. (my italics).
14 N. Caplan, '*The Full Monty*' (review), *Sight and Sound*, September 1997, vol. 7, no. 9, p. 43.
15 P. Kemp, '*Trainspotting*' (review), *Sight and Sound*, March 1996, vol. 6, no. 3, p. 66.
16 J. Hill, 'More sex, class and realism? British cinema in the 1980s and 1990s', paper presented at *Cinema, Identity History: An International Conference on British Cinema*, University of East Anglia, 10–12 July 1998.
17 Hill, *British Cinema in the 1980s*, op. cit., p. 168.
18 See, for example, the front cover and C. Upcher, 'The mark of Caine', *GQ*, September 1992, pp. 103–5; front cover and B. Prince, 'Michael Caine', *GQ*, November 1998 ('Men of the Year' issue), pp. 172–8; front cover, *loaded*, February 1999; and A. Smith, 'I wouldn't get out of bed for *The Italian Job*', *Empire*, November 1997, pp. 120–6.
19 Caplan, op. cit.
20 M. Leonard, *Britain™: Renewing Our Identity*, London, Demos, 1997.
21 Ibid., pp. 15–16.
22 Ibid., p. 10.
23 See C. Monk, 'Sexuality and the heritage', *Sight and Sound*, October 1995, vol. 5, no. 10, pp. 32–4; and (indicatively) A. Higson, 'Re-presenting the national past: nostalgia and pastiche in the heritage film', in L. Friedman (ed.) *British Cinema and Thatcherism*, London, University College Press, 1993, pp. 232–48.
24 Leonard, op. cit., p. 17.
25 Ibid., p. 10.

20

THINKING THE UNTHINKABLE

Coming to terms with Northern Ireland in the 1980s and 1990s

Michael Walsh

Since the 1960s, the United Kingdom has seen a number of social and political developments that have challenged and changed the meanings of the
terms 'Britain' and 'British'. These include resurgent national consciousness
in Scotland and Wales, the new cultures of black and Asian Britishness, and
a continuing discussion of the place of Britain in Europe. In Ireland, by
contrast, the question of what constitutes the United Kingdom and who
counts as British is by no means new. It is instead an issue over which a long
series of low-intensity wars have been fought, with the most recent thirty
years of hostilities beginning in reaction to the Northern Irish movement for
civil rights in the late 1960s. The fact that the relationship between Britain
and Ireland has long been problematic does not mean that the question of
Northern Ireland is unaffected by the new stresses on the concept 'British'.
Yet Ulster still seems to test the British ability to think national questions.
In what follows, I will take this contradiction as the starting-point for an
analysis of some British films about Northern Ireland.

In 1988, John Hill remarked that 'it has been the cinemas of Britain and
the United States which have been responsible for the vast majority of films
about Ireland and the Irish'.[1] Since then, however, with the international
success of films by Neil Jordan and Jim Sheridan, and the appearance during
the 1990s of a significant number of films produced in both the Republic
and the North, the balance has perhaps begun to shift in favour of indigenous producers. Thus the 1980s may mark the end of the long period during
which films about Ireland were directed mainly by non-nationals. The
recent cycle of Irish films about Northern Ireland includes some major
successes such as *The Crying Game* (Neil Jordan, 1992) and *In the Name of the
Father* (Jim Sheridan, 1993), some less successful but still widely-distributed
films such as *Angel* (Neil Jordan, 1982), *Cal* (Pat O'Connor, 1984), *Hush-
A-Bye-Baby* (Margo Harkin, 1984), *December Bride* (Thaddeus O'Sullivan,
1991), *Nothing Personal* (Thaddeus O'Sullivan, 1995) and *Some Mother's Son*
(Terry George, 1996), and some significant films not much seen outside film

festivals such as *High Boot Benny* (Joe Comerford, 1993), *Bogwoman* (Tom Collins, 1997) and *Divorcing Jack* (David Caffrey, 1998).

It would be pleasing to report that these films have broken with the established ideas and images of Northern Ireland. In her contribution to a *Cinéaste* supplement on contemporary Irish cinema, Ruth Barton makes a good case for an emergent awareness of gender issues, citing films set in the North, for instance *The Crying Game*, *December Bride* and *Hush-A-Bye Baby*.[2] In *Shooting to Kill: Filmmaking and the 'Troubles' in Northern Ireland*, Brian McIlroy argues persuasively that Ulster Protestants have been grossly under-represented in films.[3] On this front, again there is some progress, with several recent features focusing principally on Protestants. However, two of these, *Nothing Personal* and *Resurrection Man* (Marc Evans, 1998), depict Loyalist paramilitaries at their most psychotically bloodthirsty, while a third, *Divorcing Jack*, studiously avoids identifying its protagonist's community, even though the source novel suffers from no such squeamishness. Thus, there have been some incremental changes in the cinematic representation of Northern Ireland, but the two most basic habits of thought remain in place. The first is that Northern Ireland continues to be conceived almost exclusively in terms of the Troubles. The rare exceptions to this rule are period pieces such as *December Bride* and *All Things Bright and Beautiful* (Barry Devlin, 1994), though the IRA versus B-Specials is still a significant subplot in the latter. The second is that nationalism/republicanism is more culturally articulate (and therefore more sympathetic) than unionism/loyalism. As McIlroy suggests, nationalism/republicanism must be more articulate, since it is the movement agitating against the *status quo*.[4]

In some ways, then, the new wave of Irish cinema reproduces difficulties familiar from earlier non-indigenous films about Ireland. This suggests that the metropolitan-British imagination of Ireland, while no longer dominant, is still worth studying. In the pages that follow, I will examine a strand of that imagination by looking at two films that confront the question of Northern Ireland made by British directors at either end of the Thatcher years, *The Long Good Friday* (John Mackenzie, 1980) and *Elephant* (Alan Clarke, 1988). *The Long Good Friday*, a relatively conventional feature-length gangster film, treats the IRA in a way that seems particularly symptomatic of metropolitan-British attitudes. *Elephant*, a highly stylised thirty-seven minute drama produced by Danny Boyle for BBC Northern Ireland, has received little critical attention, but is arguably both one of the most powerful films about Northern Ireland as well as one of the most stylistically brilliant of all British films of the 1980s.[5] In their quite different ways, both films construct the war in Northern Ireland as impossible, unthinkable. This 'incomprehensibility' of the Ulster conflict is not a new topic, but nor is it one that has been fully explored by previous scholars. For McIlroy, discussing Irish perceptions of the war in the North, 'a paradigm shift has occurred from the "inexplicable Troubles" of the 1970s to the "overdetermined struggle" of the 1980s and 1990s'.[6] I will argue that as far as British film is concerned, the 'inexplicability' of the Troubles does not find its deepest articulation until the late 1980s and survives into the 1990s.

The modern history of Irish nationalism, from the time of Wolfe Tone's rebellion (1798) to that of Eamonn de Valera's resignation as Prime Minister (1959), can be reductively yet plausibly described as a question of resistance to British rule. However, the current conflict in the north-east of the island is one in which the signifier 'British' is much more vexed, and is deployed in some profoundly contradictory ways. One reason for this is that Republicanism wants to have done with a Britishness it conceives as the colonial vestige of hundreds of years of foreign rule, while Loyalism holds fast precisely to a British identity, though it retreats when pressed to an identification with 'Ulster'. In other words, one party to the dispute secures the meaning 'British', but only by opposing it, while another tries to secure it by identifying with it, yet must to some extent recognise its instability.

This contest of representations is plainly articulated in the outspoken Loyalist who is introduced a few minutes into Mike Leigh's film, *Four Days in July* (1984). Stopped for a vehicle check, Edward McCoy (John Keegan) regales the bemused members of the security forces with his view that they are all descended from an ancient 'race of Ulster people'. His ideological purpose is to discredit the Republican narrative of the seventeenth-century plantation of Ulster by rewriting it as the homecoming of the original people of the province. Although his case is based on the historical fact of a pre-Gaelic population of Ulster, scholars are divided as to whether these people were in fact driven out of Ireland by the Gaels, let alone whether the Scots who arrived in Ulster a millennium later can sensibly be seen as their descendants.[7] The point here is not to re-adjudicate the arguments of the clownish McCoy; it is instead to establish the salience of national-symbolic stories in Northern Irish popular consciousness, and the eagerness of each community rhetorically to outflank the other.

McCoy is of particular interest in so far as his type of argument is more commonly associated with romantic Republicanism; as earlier commentators have suggested, one face of the problem in Northern Ireland is a symbolic deficit on the side of Unionism, exacerbated by the asymbolic status of the entire conflict in the eyes of the English.[8] In giving the first sustained speech in his film to a critic of Republicanism, Mike Leigh is taking for granted that his audience has at least an outline familiarity with the Republican cause. In his very contrariness to expectations, then, McCoy reminds us that international audiences tend to see Irish nationalism as the historical movement of an oppressed people, while construing Ulster Unionism as a politics of defiance and obstruction. In other words, Irish nationalism seems to have all the stories. At the same time, it should be clear that cinema has most commonly fastened upon Republicanism as a dramatic motive for violence. Thus while audiences may be more fully-versed in the mythopoetics of nationalism than in those of unionism, they are hardly fully informed about Ulster.

The partition of Ireland took place as the British state moved away from imperialism and reduced the United Kingdom's Irish territory to the six counties which included Ireland's four most industrialised. Subsequently, Britain has moved almost as decisively away from industrialism, in favour of a systematic stripping of public assets ('privatisation') and a finance and service capitalism focalised around the City of London. The result for Northern Ireland is summarised, grimly but vividly, by Bob Rowthorn as 'a workhouse economy' in which those who are not unemployed 'are chiefly engaged in servicing and controlling each other'.[9] So unless colonialism is understood as the broadest of synonyms for economic subordination, the current British presence in Northern Ireland has less to do with colonialism, and more to do with the capitalist security management of an industrial and proletarian region in decline. This requires substantial subsidies to Ulster, so that a security Keynesianism peculiar to the region has mitigated losses in the linen, shipbuilding and engineering industries that might otherwise have been catastrophic. The new capitalist imaginary of globalised exchange means that national questions, insistent in Ireland but displaced in Britain, have become even more difficult for metropolitans to symbolise. Indeed, as *The Long Good Friday* suggests, it sometimes seems that the question of Northern Ireland impinges on London only to the extent that the IRA threatens the position of the city as the financial capital of Europe.

The Long Good Friday

On the face of it, *The Long Good Friday* is very much a London film, revolving around the docklands redevelopment fantasies of one Harold Shand, an East End crime boss played by the iconic cockney Bob Hoskins. Shand's upward mobility is clear from his stable of flashy cars, his houseboat home and his trophy consort, the socially superior and symbolically named Victoria (Helen Mirren). As this pairing suggests and a second glance confirms, this is a film that more or less consciously intensifies conventional Britishness. Released in the year of Margaret Thatcher's accession to power as Prime Minister, *The Long Good Friday* features a protagonist consciously conceived by screenwriter Barrie Keeffe as a low Tory, a gangster version of the self-made man, with a particularly reactionary variant of a regional and national consciousness.[10] This last is the element that makes the film's connection with Northern Ireland more than just a clever twist.

Thus Harold Shand makes much of his childhood in the East India Dock Road and delivers a prideful speech on the London docks as once the biggest in the world. Thus too, the film is incidentally full of exoticism, with the Arab visitors to Shand's casinos, the 'Indonesian bird' from whom his bent copper once caught the clap and the French chef who raises the eyebrows of

Plate 24   *The Long Good Friday* (John Mackenzie, 1980): Harold Shand (Bob
Hoskins) and friends, would-be rulers of post-industrial London, before
he is unmanned by the inexplicable violence of the IRA.

his henchmen. More to the plot is Shand's visit to Brixton, where he encounters the inhabitants of an Afro-Caribbean street, who speak not with West
Indian but with London and Liverpool accents. The harshness of his treatment of these black Britons is in marked contrast to his delighted
indulgence of the white English children who demand car protection money
from him on the same street. Elsewhere, he gives a promotional speech on
London as the prospective capital of Europe and spends much of the film
trying to win the investment favours of a pair of American Mafiosi. Finally,
he watches as his henchmen are killed and his cars, pubs and casinos are
blown up by a force which for much of the film remains mysterious, but
ultimately proves to be 'Irish', 'political' and 'fanatical'.

Harold Shand treats black Britons with a mixture of contempt and pater-
nalism, and sounds as though he only half-understands his own words on
business in Europe and partnership with America. Yet his dealings with the
legacies of empire and the prospect of a new Atlantic capitalism are for his
own purposes effective; this gangster proletarian takes for granted his supremacy over the members of immigrant communities and encourages Victoria
to play her social status as snootiness in order to conform with a caricature of
Englishness. In other words, Shand's intensification of Englishness is based
on a simple binary of inclusion and exclusion, us and them, within and

without. What first surprises, then mystifies and finally defeats him is the eruption of violence from a quarter which does not fit so clearly either within or without, a quarter legally within the United Kingdom, yet a fraction of whose inhabitants have taken up guerrilla war in pursuit of their desire to be without.

In the world of Harold Shand, insiders are white English men. The list includes Jeff (Shand's brains), Razors (his driver and heavy), Parker (his corrupt policeman), Harris (his corrupt councilman) and Colin (his best mate, with whom he did his National Service in the army). Also insiders are the film's representatives of three familiar types of femininity: Shand's mother, his mistress and the bereaved wife he meets in a graveyard. The limits of Shand's power are clear in his inability to protect these women from the IRA.

Outsiders are foreigners, of whom Shand is reasonably tolerant, and people of colour, whom he treats with undisguised racism. The film's principal Afro-Caribbean is 'Errol from Brixton' (Paul Barber), who is an informer, pimp and drug dealer, all kinds of crime of which Harold Shand is openly contemptuous; his own operation is much more respectable, a criminal version of the capitalism then hegemonic in London, the financing of redevelopment. Errol is associated with the standard racist tropes of nakedness and body odour; driving away from Errol's, Shand deploys the most perennial of images in English racism, speaking of 'dog shit on the doorstep'. In other words, Shand is essentially secure in a world of violence divided between inside and outside, equals and inferiors. He then comes face to face with the violence of those who can be placed with certainty neither inside nor outside, the 'pig-eyed Micks', the 'right hard-looking Paddies', and is unmanned. The film ends with a long take of a seething Shand being driven away, presumably to his death, by the Provisionals, whose triumph is underscored in so far as the camera position corresponds to the point of view of the smirking gunman in the passenger seat.

Brian McIlroy argues that *The Long Good Friday* typifies English incomprehension of Northern Ireland, imagining the IRA as a ruthless, efficient, but inexplicable force.[11] Historians and sociologists of Northern Ireland concur that both communities in the six counties feel in different ways estranged from Britain – Republicans believe that the British presence is the source of all Ireland's woes, while Unionists recognise that their historical alignment with the Conservatives has never translated into authentic popular support in England.[12] Yet this failure of the English to make Ireland meaningful is not an accident; it has historical causes, most obviously the long-settledness of any national question within England. As nearly every commentator in some sense agrees, Ireland is a country in which it has proved particularly difficult to align the various identities of ethnic nationality, nation, state and national territory. Culturally consumed by the national question, it is perhaps the principal misfortune of Ireland to have been historically dominated by a country in which a national question can be said to exist only in displaced, marginal and emergent forms.[13] Long-habituated to national stability, the British have no means of making the Irish question signify and, as Lacan argued from the 1950s onwards, what is excluded from the symbolic returns in the Real, often in shocking and violent ways.[14]

As I have already noted, *The Long Good Friday* is essentially a London film, its *mise-en-scène* of empty docklands, motionless cranes and deserted warehouses speaking eloquently of the development pause between the death of one of London's oldest industries and the city's reorganisation around a new finance capitalism. Yet the very first shot of the film, a long slow fade-up to reveal a white farmhouse in green fields, is a setting we later understand to have been Northern Ireland. Republicanism has strongholds in the countryside, so the rural setting is not anti-naturalistic; however, as the film's only shot of anywhere non-urban, it underscores the film's polarisation of spaces between a post-industrial metropolis and a rural periphery.

This polarisation of regions within the United Kingdom (metropolis restructured around finance and service versus post-colonial and deindustrialised province) can be mapped onto a polarisation of images of Ulster (city centre versus country, especially border country). The latter can be found in many of the recent films on Northern Ireland. Both *Angel* and *The Crying Game* move their protagonists between the country and the city; the *Bogwoman* is so named because she leaves the bogs of Donegal for the Bogside in Belfast; and urban films like *Hidden Agenda* (Ken Loach, 1990), *Divorcing Jack* and *Nothing Personal* all place key sequences in the countryside. The same binary underwrites the Northern Irish work of Alan Clarke, whose pair of grimly structural films for television are *Contact* (1985), set in the hedgerows of South Armagh, and *Elephant*, set in the back streets of Belfast.

Elephant

Elephant is thirty-seven minutes long. It contains 117 shots, divided into eighteen sequences, each of which shows an execution-style killing. The number of shots per sequence varies between three and ten, with the majority clustered at between five and eight shots. Most sequences begin with a long take that serves as an establishing shot and tracks either the killer or the victim onto the killing ground (a municipal baths, a petrol station, a football field, an industrial estate, a fish and chip shop, a car park, a taxicab office). These Steadicam takes are all at least thirty seconds long, with some lasting as long as two and a half minutes, and the locations are always either deserted or actually derelict; we see only killers, victims and occasional victim's friends, who for obvious reasons flee. By contrast, each segment pivots on a flurry of shots lasting less than a second – a medium close-up of the killer, a close-up of the weapon, often a shot of the victim falling, sometimes more shots of the weapon being emptied into the prostrate body. Each segment then concludes with further long takes which follow the killer's departure and return to a merciless inspection of the unmoving body; these shots of corpses last between twenty and thirty-five seconds. Some segments slightly vary the basic regime, but the essential impression is one of a thoroughgoing regularity.

The severe formality of *Elephant* is further underscored in terms of camera style and use of sound. Establishing shots always use a wide-angle lens, often pivoting to follow the progress of the killer or victim; the same lens is used for shots of corpses. Close-ups of killer and weapon are always in profile, and the long looks at dead bodies stir slightly but definitely, indicating use of a hand-held camera. The film's gunfire is dramatised with muzzle flashes, sparks, smoke and overamplified sound, which reverberates in some of the more cavernous industrial interiors. Persistent throughout the film and continuing under the closing credits is the sound of passing traffic. Also notable as a kind of stark chorus in the aftermath of each killing is the sound of dogs barking, birds chirping and, in the case of the taxi office, the dispatcher's radio. With the shooting on the football field as the single semi-audible exception, there is no dialogue anywhere in the film, so that aural attention is sharply focused on car engines, gunfire and walking feet. This last is especially insistent, since killers and victims alike walk very briskly.

Costumes are studiedly ordinary. With just one or two exceptions (characters sporting the youth culture regalia of leather jackets, studded wristbands, earrings and spiked hair), the victims and killers alike wear car coats, parkas, boiler suits, pullovers, jeans, trainers and wellingtons. The forty killers and victims are therefore difficult and sometimes impossible to distinguish; one or two killers produce guns the moment we see them and one or two victims reveal their status by an action like locking a car, but just as often we see one or two people briskly approaching one or two others and we don't know who is who until the shooting starts. Shootings take place either in broad daylight or under cover of darkness. In the latter case, the buildings are brilliantly lit, with harsh white and blue lighting for exteriors and some yellow light for the interiors of houses. The film's characters are all civilians, and all appear to be working class or lower middle class – they are bath attendants, book-keepers, cabdrivers, house painters, shopkeepers, factory workers and managers. They are also all men, with not a single woman appearing even incidentally.

The strictly stylised regularities of *Elephant* are further evident in the frequency of action matches at doorways, the stress on camera distance and the frequency of shots looking into the sun, with blinding light at the top and back of the frame to better emphasise the fisheyed foreground. I have lingered on this description of the film for two reasons. The first is the sheer remorselessness of the film, an impact best conveyed by a pure accounting.

The second is that this film is comparatively difficult for readers to access themselves.

In one sense, *Elephant* looks like a gangster film and nothing intrinsic prevents this understanding. Nothing, that is, other than the film's Northern Ireland production and Belfast setting. Note, however, that the location is never named and must be supplied by a viewer who catches sight of a telltale street name ('Linenhall Street') or knows that the only redbrick industrialised city in Ireland is Belfast. This of course is the very power of the film. *Elephant* is precisely not the standard Northern Ireland news report of a gun battle in the Falls Road, or an incident in which masked men shoot an off-duty RUC officer. In *Elephant*, there is no hint of historical or political significance to any of the killings so tirelessly depicted; instead, the film offers a relentless series of killings of unidentified men by unidentified men. In lieu of conclusion, the film offers one or two even more horrific slayings. In the penultimate sequence, the victim is brought down by a shotgun and is trying desperately to crawl away when he is finished off with a revolver; in the last, after a forced march lasting a full two minutes and twenty-five seconds, the victim is suddenly shot in the back of the head. Thus the film ends with an interminable long take on blood and brains on a dirty white factory wall, with a blue stripe above where some fixture was removed, a red stripe below and the sound of the gunshot echoing through the deserted rooms.

One reading of *Elephant* is that it is a pitiless demonstration of what the conflict in the six counties really amounts to, suggesting that for all the history, politics and ideology of Ireland, the stark reality is that anonymous men drive or walk up to other men's front doors or places of work and shoot them down. On this reading, the film's stylisation is calculated to strip away the justifications of context and motive and to rub the viewers' noses in the very brutality of sudden death in front halls and back alleys. However, another reading might see the film's studied de-emphasis of identity, motive and context as another and more profound registration of the asymbolic status of the Ulster conflict. This 'incomprehensibility' is only underscored by the naturalistic accuracy of dress and demeanour and the stylisation of camera, lens, lighting and sound; indeed, the film represents a kind of terminus for the social realism of British television, faithfully adhering to some of its codes while flagrantly violating others.

At the same time, the very starkness of the *mise-en-scène* of *Elephant* provides a kind of answer to the question the film's action leaves open. Deliberately avoiding the city's landmarks, the film becomes a study of the basic urban textures of Belfast, dramatising the region's deindustrialisation in the very ease with which it finds empty factories and commercial spaces in which to shoot. The frequency of killings at places of work certainly suggests that most of the victims have jobs; yet very commonly the person killed seems to be the only worker left in a substantial building or warehouse. In other cases, the victim is seated alone at the back of a fish restaurant, tends the sales counter in a deserted petrol station, or walks to his car across an otherwise empty parking lot. As a terminus for British social realism, *Elephant* also offers a last word on the focalisation of that tradition around depictions of an industrial working class.

Conclusion

Brian McIlroy places Alan Clarke along with Mike Leigh and Ken Loach in a category of English social-realist directors whose films about Northern Ireland betray a 'soft nationalism'.[15] Though a persuasive argument for the work of Leigh and Loach, it is a scarcely credible way of categorising *Elephant*. McIlroy proposes that sequences focalised around the point-of-view of the killers 'promote an affinity' with them.[16] It seems to me that the focalisation in question is better understood as Clarke's attempt to disturb the viewer – making the audience look through the eyes of the killer is a tactic of disorientation familiar in slasher films from *Psycho* (Alfred Hitchcock, 1960) onwards. In any case, I have concentrated on *Elephant* along with *The Long Good Friday* in order to emphasise another component of the metropolitan-British imagination of Northern Ireland: its 'unthinkability'. What I am suggesting is that the British national imagination is premised on an experience of national stability so historically long as to prevent the war in Ulster from beginning to be really meaningfully thinkable. It is not simply that the British do not understand, not as though all they need is a good seminar on Irish history; it is more nearly the case that some British films come close to 'foreclosing' on this most bitterly-contested of United Kingdom national questions.

Finally, what becomes of the notion of a national cinema in a place in which national identity is (violently) contested? Fiction features about Northern Ireland seem to answer that the cinema in question will be largely preoccupied with the conflict. This in turn suggests that a conflicted national identity may be just as paradigmatic as a stable one. So once again, instead of imagining Ireland as an eccentric or tortured national space that defies reasoned commentary, we should question the historically-conditioned metropolitan-British assumption that national stability is the norm.

NOTES

1 J. Hill, 'Images of violence', in K. Rockett, L. Gibbons and J. Hill, *Cinema and Ireland*, London, Croom Helm, 1997, p. 147. See also J. Hill, 'Filming in the north', *Cinéaste*, 1999, vol. XXIV, nos. 2–3, pp. 26–7.

2 R. Barton, 'Feisty colleens and faithful sons', *Cinéaste*, 1999, vol. XXIV, nos. 2–3, pp. 40–5.

3 B. McIlroy, *Shooting to Kill: Filmmaking and the 'Troubles' in Northern Ireland*, Trowbridge, Flicks Books, 1999.

4 Ibid., p. 146.

5 *Elephant* has been discussed by McIlroy, ibid., pp. 89–90, and by Tim Corrigan (paper presented at *Society for Cinema Studies Conference*, New York, 1995). See also the comments of the film's producer and camera operator in R. Kelly (ed.) *Alan Clarke*, London, Faber and Faber, 1998, pp. 192–9.

6 B. McIlroy, ibid., p. 2.

7 See, for example, B. Graham, 'Ulster: a representation of a place', in P. Shirlow and M. McGovern (eds) *Who Are 'The People'? Unionism, Protestantism, and Loyalism in Northern Ireland*, London, Pluto, 1997, pp. 49–50.

8 See Hill, 'Images of violence', op. cit.; and B. McIlroy, 'The repression of communities: visual representations of Northern Ireland during the Thatcher years', in L. Friedman (ed.) *Fires Were Started: British Cinema and Thatcherism*, Minneapolis, Minnesota University Press, 1993, pp. 92–108.

9 B. Rowthorn and N. Wayne, *Northern Ireland: The Political Economy of Conflict*, Cambridge, Polity, 1988, p. 98.

10 B. Keeffe, 'Haunting Friday', *Sight and Sound*, August 1996, vol. 6, no. 8, pp. 20–1.

11 McIlroy, 'The repression of communities', op. cit., p. 97.

12 A good initial guide to the political and historical literature on Northern Ireland is J. Whyte, *Interpreting Northern Ireland*, Oxford, Oxford University Press, 1990.

13 For a fuller account of this peculiarity of the English, see T. Nairn, *The Enchanted Glass: England and its Monarchy*, London, Vintage, 1990.

14 J. Lacan, *Seminar Book III, The Psychoses*, trans. R. Grigg, London, Routledge, 1993, p. 88.

15 McIlroy, *Shooting to Kill*, op. cit., p. 3.

16 Ibid., p. 90.

Part VII

CONTEMPORARY CINEMA 2
Whose heritage?

Introduction

Heritage drama has become a familiar feature of British cinema and television. It has also generated considerable debate. The contributors to this section take this debate further – although only Amy Sargeant tackles heritage drama head-on. The others explore different traditions of art cinema in the 1980s and 1990s, but in each case contrast them with heritage cinema. As one would expect in such discussions, there is much interest in questions of film style and meaning and an effort to find an adequate means of doing justice to some quite complex and demanding films. But there is an equal commitment to the rather different questions of cultural identity, English heritage and British cinema.

Sargeant is interested in the role film and television costume drama of the 1990s plays in the marketing of Britain's past. As she notes, heritage properties are frequently used as locations, which bodies like the National Trust then use to promote those properties further. While she sees such trends as a democratising of heritage, she also notes tensions in the design of filmed drama between the concern for visual style and the search for historical authenticity. Phil Powrie looks at *Distant Voices, Still Lives* (Terence Davies, 1988), *The Long Day Closes* (Davies, 1995) and *Small Faces* (Gillies MacKinnon, 1995), which he calls 'alternative heritage films'. While they share high production value period detail with the sort of drama Sargeant discusses, their protagonists are lower class, their settings regional, the maternal community is confronted by male violence and they play self-consciously with time, memory and narrative structure. Powrie also analyses the way the films articulate a nostalgic sense of community, identity and place and the implicit challenge they offer to the idea of the national.

John Orr considers the work of two of the most prominent British *auteurs* of the 1980s and 1990s, Derek Jarman and Peter Greenaway. In a richly metaphorical reading, he explores their aesthetic sensibilities and links their films to developments in painting, theatre and European modernist cinema. Again, he interrogates their work in terms of debates about national identity and national cinema. Paul Dave takes on these same themes in his exposition of Patrick Keiller's films, *London* (1993) and *Robinson in Space* (1997), which are firmly rooted in the poetic traditions of avant-garde and art cinema. His concern is with the ways in which Keiller works through questions of capitalism, class, history and nation and he reads the films as anti-heritage critiques, which defamiliarise the landscapes of English heritage culture and the pictorialism of heritage cinema.

21

MAKING AND SELLING HERITAGE CULTURE

Style and authenticity in historical fictions on film and television

Amy Sargeant

It is traditional to distinguish between history proper and the historical novel, a fiction written or located in the past. In filmic terms, there is a parallel distinction between the history film, which reconstructs documented events, and the costume film, which adapts historical or classic novels, but allows lavish and spectacular display to predominate over narrative content. Authors of historical novels and designers of costume films have often looked to writers of history proper as a way of guaranteeing historical authenticity. Although this is by no means the exclusive preserve of what critics in the 1990s have referred to as heritage film and television, it is certainly one of the defining features of such historical costume drama in that period.

Sometimes tacitly, sometimes explicitly, the term 'heritage drama' connects these productions with a particular cultural and entrepreneurial activity: the marketing and consumption of Britain's cultural heritage as a tourist attraction. Links undoubtedly exist between heritage drama and the heritage industry. In the field of Heritage Studies, cinema and broadcasting are widely recognised as effective means of presenting and marketing Britain's past, while the heritage industry increasingly takes film and television as its model (for instance, in the recent trend for museums to use actors, spectacular special effects and interactive technologies in their installations).[1] The reciprocity between cultural heritage and cultural entrepreneurship has also been recognised in the recent debates about the 'branding of Britain' and the acknowledgement of the part played by fine art, the applied arts and design in advertising and marketing such a product.[2] Discussion of the relationship between film and television productions and the classic novels from which they have been adapted is also bound up with the contemporary (but seemingly perennial) arguments about the supposed 'dumbing down' of art by entertainment, perhaps of enchantment by vulgarisation.[3]

In this chapter, I will explore some of the implications of both the distinction between history and fiction, and the symbiosis of cultural practice and marketing as they relate to recent heritage drama. I will map the multifarious ways in which public debate, institutions and cultural practices engage in the visual presentation of heritage. My examples will be drawn from both cinema and television, since there are many similarities in the way they currently approach costume drama. Thus personnel and objects are exchanged between large and small screen, both in front of and behind the camera. Most of the flagship television productions referred to in the chapter were made on film, whether or not they were intended for theatrical release. This has an impact at the level of production, as film is habitually associated with a patina of surface quality and encourages attention to verisimilitude and detail. Most television costume drama is also now available for sale or for hire on video alongside 'higher' status feature films (as well as 'lower' status sit-coms and soaps). A good night in is now worth as much to a film's distributors and television programme's sponsors as a good night out.

The relationship between visual style and historical authenticity is central to my discussion. In what ways does the style of heritage drama, whether on the large or the small screen, fabricate or endorse a sense of authenticity? In what ways do our perceptions of the palpable elements of film (sound, props, script, actors, light) combine with preconceptions of historical and cultural verisimilitude? Should an adaptation of a novel aim to be more faithful to historical context or to the source narrative? Has a sub-antiquarian 'authentick of Olden Days' (as the comedians French and Saunders would have it) become a style of its own, replacing the need to re-negotiate anew questions of style and authenticity with each particular occurrence in the heritage genre? How is authenticity manifested in the cinematic experience, whether at the level of production, distribution or reception?

History and heritage

Early discussions of the heritage film tended to deploy the term negatively. In the 1980s the heritage industries were often criticised for their complicity with a false notion of historical reality and their contribution to a bogus enterprise, the marketing of 'an attractively packaged consumer item'.[4] Heritage films, it was argued, served to promote the cultural worthiness of particular towns, houses and sites, enchanted as they were by the aura of certain 'landscapes, architecture, artefacts [and] values'.[5] 'The key heritage films in the national cinema of the 1980s,' writes Andrew Higson, 'are fascinated by the private property, the culture and values of a particular class.'

> By reproducing these trappings outside of a materialist historical context, they transform the heritage of the upper classes into the national heritage: private interest becomes naturalised as public

interest ... The national past and national identity emerge in these films not only as aristocratic, but also as male-centred, while the nation itself is reduced to the soft pastoral landscape of southern England untainted by the modernity of urbanisation or industrialisation ... In each instance, the quality of the films lends the representation of the past a certain cultural validity and respectability.[6]

Here heritage is defined as something distinct from history proper in the absence of a 'materialist context'. Adaptations from novels are found doubly at fault, for using particular locations and scenography and for bolstering the 'cultural validity and respectability' of certain classic texts. Complaints against the heritage film are complexly interwoven, however, and need to be disentangled. Some criticisms concern questions of history, and the assumed distinction between heritage and the merely historical. Others concern the processes by which literary sources are adapted. Yet others concern visual style. As James Walton has remarked of the BBC's most recent adaptation of *Great Expectations* (1999), it may be customary to adopt heritage film style, but it is by no means a necessary treatment for literary adaptations.[7] Moreover, objections to this style are very often little more than matters of taste. Perhaps it is as false an endeavour to separate history from heritage as it is to confuse one with the other. Perhaps it is vain to pursue any form of absolute authenticity in contemporary representations of the past.

Criticisms of heritage inherit much from earlier writings of the 1980s on the depiction of history, both on screen and in the standard academic syllabus. Some critics, Colin McArthur amongst them, complained that the depiction of history was reduced to the biographies of Great Men.[8] But in the intervening years, the teaching of history has shifted towards the recognition of the hitherto seemingly marginal and inconsequential, as social and cultural historical studies have gained ground from economic and political history: peasants are now considered worthy of study individually as well as *en masse*.

The democratising trend is also visible in the vast growth in amateur local history research and in the acquisition and listing policies of museums and bodies such as English Heritage and the National Trust. The latter, for instance, recently acquired Southwell Workhouse and the eccentric but humble Worksop house of the brothers Straw.[9] In its education and community programmes, the National Trust demonstrates weaving at a working mill (Quarry Bank) and involves its public in learning through such activities as those of the Young National Trust Theatre, as much as in admiring fine objects at a distance. There is also a continuing interest in re-enactments and reconstructions and in the practical 'below stairs' aspects of running a house. The National Gallery's 'Constable's Cornfield' exhibition in 1996 was exemplary in this respect in its citing of personal histories within a shared national heritage and in its acknowledgement of various individual and cultural appropriations of a particular single art work. Elsewhere, the Imperial War Museum ran 'Dig for Victory', 'Forties Fashion' and 'From the Bomb to the Beatles' exhibitions alongside its displays of military paraphernalia, the work of commissioned war artists and its memorial to the Holocaust. Both the Imperial War Museum and the National Trust archive oral histories of ordinary and extraordinary experience.

The positive effect of all this activity is that more voices are heard and a wider range of experiences are acknowledged. Filmed heritage can easily fall into this pattern, showing us social distinctions in dress, situation and occupation, or demonstrating domestic rituals appropriate to men and women and to town and country at different times of year. Filmed heritage, especially on British television, with its guiding public service remit 'to inform, educate and entertain', can be said to perform a didactic function in displaying such visual evidence in its period detail of costumes and customs.

The negative effect of these trends in the presentation of the past may be a return to what E.H. Carr saw as one of the traits of nineteenth-century history writing: the fetishising of documents and facts and the accumulation thereof to the detriment of concrete argument, so that we 'know ... more and more about less and less'.[10] Letters to producers of films and television drama often suggest an obsessive belief on the part of certain audiences that screened history is incorrect in the very details on which it has sought to secure credibility. Critical responses have tended to complain about such details and idiosyncrasies *per se*, advocating instead some Great Theory of History red in tooth and claw.[11] Now that the teaching of history encompasses the study of practical historiography and historical reception, however, certain aspects of its lowly relation 'heritage', the 'attractively packaged consumer item', can be regarded as grist to the mill of legitimate historical study.

One needs to be wary here of an aesthetic prejudice against and dismissiveness of the heritage product. There is a basic adverse reaction in academic and artistic circles to English ghastly good taste in general, and in film culture to 'the stifling daintiness of the Merchant-Ivory canon and the saccharine reworkings of Jane Austen ... what Alan Parker dubbed "the Laura Ashley school of film making"'.[12] A more light-hearted reaction was the 1998 Comic Relief spoof *Rest and Recreation*. With a cast that included Benjamin Whitrow and Alison Steadman from the 1995 BBC adaptation of Jane Austen's *Pride and Prejudice*, it made easy fun of prim gentility: Miranda Richardson plays Miss Bonnet, who sketches a little for her own amusement but whose star turn is to play 'Colonel Bogey' on her armpit and to demonstrate her prowess as the most famous arc-welder in the county.

There is perhaps a more principled objection to the frequency with which certain houses and sites appear on screen and hence appear to corroborate received ideas of cultural value. Prominent examples include Constable's

Suffolk, Thomas Hardy's Dorset, Broughton Castle in *Jane Austen's Emma* (BBC, 1996) and *Shakespeare in Love* (John Madden, 1999), Bath in *Persuasion* (BBC, 1996) and Langor and Lacock in *Pride and Prejudice* (BBC, 1995). But such locations are not unique to heritage drama; nor are heritage films and television programmes alone in their implication in the heritage industry. Visitors are as likely to be familiar with Oxford architecture from *Inspector Morse* (Carlton Television, 1987–present) and with Derbyshire from *Peak Practice* (Central Television, 1993–present), neither of which have period settings. It seems that the boundaries of heritage activity are no longer confined to representations of the past and that the heritage industry increasingly offers its attractions as a 'lived' and everyday experience, often imitating the means of filmic dramatisation.

Historical adaptations from the classics

Many of the recent costume dramas made for cinema and television were adapted from novels, and many of those novels were already established classics, the sorts of texts that are traditionally adopted by school and university examination boards. In the latter half of the 1990s, the novels and short stories of Henry James and Thomas Hardy were in vogue. James adaptations included *Portrait of a Lady* (Jane Campion, 1996), *The Wings of a Dove* (Iain Softley, 1997) and *Turn of the Screw* (Meridian, forthcoming). Hardy films included *Jude* (Michael Winterbottom, 1996), *The Scarlet Tunic* (Stuart St. Paul, 1997) and *The Woodlanders* (Phil Agland, 1997). Previously there was a glut of E.M. Forster and Anthony Trollope, while Dickens and Austen (currently available on BBC Video as a boxed set) are perennially adapted for the screen.

Reaction to this preference for literary source texts is varied. On the one hand, the privileging of the source text as the standard against which adaptations are judged is increasingly challenged in critical discourse. From this perspective, adaptations should be judged as dramas in their own right. On the other hand, the very idea of adaptation – the reliance on another medium – is seen as problematic: film and television programme makers, it is argued, should develop their own material rather than depend on literature. Some object to the frequency with which the works of supposedly serious and classic authors are adapted.[13] But one might also complain of the lack of time and funds for project development, which makes it all too easy for production companies to fall back on known commodities (classic, historical or otherwise) and adapt them to a different medium instead of fostering new purpose-built material. Others have argued that adaptations bolster the classic and approved status of the novels, foisting their conservative values upon a popular audience.[14] This is a partial and tendentious view which disregards the enormous and genuine popularity enjoyed by the works of Charles Dickens, Thomas Hardy, Wilkie Collins and Jane Austen upon their original publication, sometimes in serial rather than novel form (that is to say, before they became incorporated into an official literary heritage).

Another frequent criticism of adaptations, and particularly of supposed classics, is that viewing is a passive activity in which a more strenuous, engaged act of private imagining is substituted by a passive encounter with an external visualisation.[15] It is worth remembering, however, that, on their original publication, many such novels were accompanied by illustrations that mediated the narratives to their readers. Dickens also performed his own work while Wilkie Collins re-worked *The Woman in White* for the stage. Film and television adaptations may similarly invest their source novels with new emotions and meanings.

Reading the book of the film (of the book) is a going concern for publishers of tie-in editions; but books of films and films of books can stimulate an interest in the work of the author in question, which in turn creates a desire for further screen plays. The sales pitch used for recent adaptations and tie-in publications is very interesting. These cultural products are in fact rarely presented as venerable 'classics' by which to be enchanted, or through which one might be initiated into the highbrow canon as a cultural rite of passage. Instead, they are marketed as middlebrow or popular. Michael Winterbottom's *Jude*, for instance, following the example of Roman Polanski's *Tess* (1979), abbreviated its source title. The short title also appears on the cover of the tie-in Penguin edition, with pictures of the stars, Kate Winslet and Christopher Eccleston, the film's poster credits and a Mills and Boon-style gloss on the novel's content: 'A time without pity; a society without mercy; a love without equal.' The typography of the title sequence for the BBC's *Pride and Prejudice* is reproduced on the 1995 Penguin edition of the novel, all but gold-embossed. The title sequence itself, with its luxuriant wanderings over lavishly rouched satin, lace, embroidery and bows, has the air of a Georgette Heyer airport bestseller, announcing the production as 'Pure Romance'. At the time of writing, Robert Louis Stevenson's *St Ives* was being developed for television with the more populist title, *All for Love*, starring Anna Friel and Jean-Marc Barr.

Here and elsewhere the casting strategy seems to have been designed not only in accordance with authentic good looks but also to render the product appealing to a wider and younger audience. Thus Anna Friel (Beth Jordache from Channel 4's soap, *Brookside*) appeared in *Our Mutual Friend* (BBC, 1998), Kathy Burke (Waynetta Slob from the BBC comedy series, *Harry Enfield and Friends*) in *Tom Jones* (BBC, 1998), Andrew Lincoln and Natasha Little (Egg and Rachel from the BBC drama-soap, *This Life*) in *The Woman in White* (BBC, 1997) and *Vanity Fair* (BBC, 1998) respectively, and Angus Deayton (television presenter) and Eric Cantona (celebrity ex-footballer) in *Elizabeth* (Shekhar Kapur, 1998). Further instances of this strategy to attract younger audiences include the trailing of *Vanity Fair* as an example of 'Girl

Plate 25   The cover of the Penguin edition of *Pride and Prejudice*, published to tie in with the 1995 BBC serial, showing the stars in costume and reproducing the typography of the title sequence.

Power' and the publicity for *Elizabeth*, which mimicked the graphics of the thriller, *Se7en* (David Fincher, 1995).

Heritage and tourism

If the past is another country, then we should expect historical tourism to evince some of the features of travel. Some things are comfortingly similar to our own experience; some things are exotic and strange. In such time travel stories as *Orlando* (both Virginia Woolf's novel of 1928, with its authentic typographies, and Sally Potter's film of 1993, with its sometimes authentic locations) the fantasy of living through, of inhabiting or even escaping into history is strong. Historical films may grant sight of places we go to imaginatively and sometimes physically.

Tourism is a major earner of foreign currency for Britain and heritage is vital to the appeal of Britain as a tourist destination. Foreign visitors cite 'visiting historic sites and cities or towns' more frequently as 'a particularly important reason in their decision to visit Britain' than any other activity: 'a powerful attraction is the combination of visible history and beautiful countryside'.[16] It also serves to locate the nation's past in rural Britain. This same combination of visible history and beautiful countryside is also central to the appeal of heritage cinema and television. The success of such high-quality costume drama both at home and abroad in effect affords an excellent means of promoting a particular view of national heritage. The jury is out as to whether this is a good or a bad thing. Some writing of the 1980s and early 1990s, for instance, warned against the contamination of culture in general and film culture in particular by contact with the heritage industry.[17] Correspondence in the press has accused the National Trust of aiding the vulgarisation of serious art in abetting filmed novels:

> Escapism is one thing, but losing sight of the reality of our historical and literary inheritance is another. Instead of protecting this inheritance, the National Trust is in effect creating theme parks: surely a task better left to Disney?[18]

There is also a more positive view of the relationship between enterprise and heritage. The National Trust has gratefully received location fees from film and television productions (for Lacock a tidy £20,000 per day),[19] which then enables the Trust to spend more on the activities it undertakes. The increased visibility of National Trust properties through appearances in heritage drama may encourage a wider variety of people to attend Trust properties or to enrol as members of the Trust. The use of historic locations for screen adaptations may encourage visitors to return to National Trust properties with a renewed purpose (hence the items in seasonal brochures advertised as 'New for 1998' and so on). It may even encourage a more representative agenda for an institution often criticised for being middle class, middle-aged and middle England.

Appearance on screen undeniably attracted visitors to the principal locations for the 1995 BBC production of *Pride and Prejudice*. That year admissions rose by 59 per cent and 42 per cent to Sudbury and Lyme, the interior and exterior of Mr Darcy's Pemberley, and the production received an award for its demonstrable benefit to regional tourism.[20] Pickford's House in Derby took the opportunity to deck out a suitable Regency dinner table. Lyme offers a picturesquely varied walk around the estate in the manner of Mr Darcy.[21] Austen's precise setting of the action of *Persuasion* lends itself to a walking tour of the locations in Bath.[22] Mompesson House gave half price admission to any visitor bearing a Salisbury Odeon cinema ticket stub for *Sense and Sensibility* (Ang Lee, 1995), part of which had been filmed there.[23]

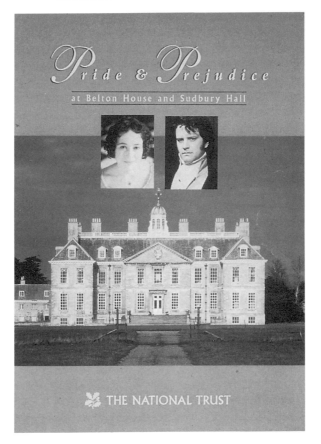

Plate 26   The 1996 National Trust brochure for Belton House and Sudbury Hall, both used as locations in the 1995 BBC serialisation of *Pride and Prejudice.*

Current touristic tie-ins are not unique to historical drama. The East Midlands Film Commission's publication 'On Location' (available free from all good information centres in the area) gives the locations for *Pride and Prejudice* and also for *Peak Practice*, and characters from this production are in turn used to advertise the Peak National Park.[24] Yorkshire has for many years received coachloads of *Emmerdale* (YTV) and *Last of the Summer Wine* (BBC) groupies, along with followers of *The Railway Children* (BBC, 1970). Popular interest shifted last year from *the* lake that Darcy swam through to *that* dole office in *The Full Monty* (Peter Cattaneo, 1998). What interests me here is that the fact of filming at a particular location seems to attract public interest rather more than what was actually filmed. Perhaps location tourism owes as much to the perceived glamour and glory of the activity of making and selling cinema as to any particular film's subject matter. The activity of filming historic reconstruction is further celebrated in such Penguin tie-ins as *The Making of Pride and Prejudice*[25] and *The Making of Jane Austen's Emma*,[26] and coverage by the magazine *Homes and Antiques* of the making of *Vanity Fair*, authenticated by the involvement of the production crew.[27] These detail the lengthy procedures entailed in the reconstruction of period sets, props, costumes and make-up.

Cinema and television are thoroughly embroiled in the culture industry, however much intellectuals may seek to identify a distinct film culture. BBC television, films and radio advertise the spin-off products of BBC enterprises, from books, toys and cassettes to 'The BBC Experience' and the junketing of the Official Archers' Fan Cub. The cinema and broadcasting industries increasingly flaunt their own pasts as tourist and heritage attractions. London's Museum of the Moving Image, the National Museum of Photography, Film and Television in Bradford, the Bill Douglas Centre in Exeter, Granada in Manchester and Blackpool and the BBC *EastEnders* Elstree lot all contribute towards this sense of the media as subject and object of exhibition. The IMAX screen on the South Bank ranks London's tourist facilities alongside those of other European capitals; it contributes somewhat less to British film culture. Pathé and the BBC have marketed their own pasts by releasing archive material on video.

'The BBC Experience' in Portland Place announces itself on the tourist agenda as 'the most innovative interactive exhibition in the West End ...

Plate 27   The publicity leaflet for *The Full Monty* Tour, produced by Sheffield's Tourist Information Centre.

transporting you back to1896'.[28] It now seems incumbent upon any film set in the late nineteenth century to include a scene which re-visits cinema's roots as a slide show or fairground attraction: examples include *Jude* and *Bram Stoker's Dracula* (Francis Ford Coppola, 1992). As Steve Neale once remarked in a different context, 'films are there precisely to exhibit cinema'.[29] This process of exhibition extends beyond the four walls of the cinema itself. Sensational phenomena such as waxwork museums and lantern shows, described by Vanessa Schwartz and others as pre-cinematic, survive alongside their progeny.[30] Museums and heritage centres aim increasingly for a cinematic experience in their presentation: reconstructed, appropriately dressed rooms are populated by mannequins, alive (as at the Black Country Museum and the Museum of the Moving Image) or dead (as in Johnson's birthplace museum in Lichfield). Sometimes there is an accompanying soundtrack (as at Salford Museum's Larkhill Place, where one hears noises typical of a late Victorian street in an industrial town – children playing, a horse-drawn carriage, the knocker-upper). This is the museum as lived, everyday experience rather than a catalogued repository of culturally or artistically significant objects. Philippe de Loutherbourg's sensational, pre-cinematic stage prototype of sublime Derbyshire scenery devised in 1779 is matched by the sound and light phantasmagoria now on offer at Wookey Hole in Somerset.[31] To require film culture to distance itself from such heritage and tourist manifestations would be to require it to deny its own history within a broader cultural context. Cinema emerged from a number of cultural practices and institutions, many of which were received and sold as tourist attractions. These still extant precursors of cinema, museums and scenic displays included, now turn to cinema as their model.

Designing authenticity

Set and costume designers for period films consult museum collections, portraits, inventories, sumptuary regulations, catalogues and journals, as well as secondary scholarship.[32] By way of returning the compliment, the costumes for the BBC production of *Pride and Prejudice* toured National Trust houses and were displayed alongside originals in the Pump Room in Cheltenham. But scholarship sometimes reveals that even National Trust restorations are often a stylised product of their age and cannot be relied upon as an absolute guarantee of historic verisimilitude: they do not bear the authentic stamp of history proper.[33]

However much critical theorists and new historians may declare the pursuit of authenticity a spurious and redundant endeavour, for design practitioners the question remains a vexed one.[34] When a film is adapted from an historical novel, or a novel with what is now a period setting, should the makers strive to be authentic to the source narrative or to the period depicted? My own ambivalence and scruples about the heritage film concern the procedures adopted in response to this quandary as much as the final product. One way or another, the period will have to be indicated and the film designer will have to fabricate the past in a way that does some justice to audience expectations of historical authenticity as well as narrative integrity. For many designers, historical verisimilitude is ideally of less importance than the interpretation of theme and character and the dictates of the practice of design.

Perhaps the filming of history proper and of historical settings should follow the example of history writing and more readily and explicitly acknowledge the subjective, interpretative distance between the record and the event. Anachronisms such as a mobile phone and a classic Chanel suit in Derek Jarman's *Caravaggio* (1986) and *Edward II* (1991) conveyed much about character to the films' audiences. From a design point of view, such theatrical license is one of the admirable aspects of Jarman's historical films.[35] Of course, he follows the precedent of several centuries of performance of Shakespeare and the Ancients in modern dress, a practice revived on the twentieth-century stage and in film adaptations of Shakespeare such as Ian McKellen's *Richard III* (1995). Transpositions of drama and opera are frequent and there has been any number of productions of Shakespeare's histories played out in leather and studs against a backdrop of corrugated iron and graffiti.

Professional constraint often contrives against such boldness in design for the cinema. One might in fact speak of an art of theatre design and a corresponding craft of film. From Ammanati and Buontalenti through Rubens and Rembrandt to Hodgkin and Hockney, academy-trained architects and fine artists have provided backdrops and scenery for spectacles and the stage. Sometimes such artists have worked autonomously, sometimes in collaboration. In the theatre, stage and costume design are often conceived together by an individual, traditionally working in close contact with a small group of colleagues towards a single vision of the final product. Design for television and film, on the other hand, is routinely divided between professions (production design, costume and make-up, lighting and special effects) where attitudes towards the relation of style and authenticity may vary. The heritage film as we know it, 'the attractively packaged consumer item', has in general attempted to efface such differences. *Elizabeth*, for instance, remarkably brought together 'correct' period style costumes with sometimes historically 'incorrect' sets (360-degree camera swings showed off Durham cathedral to great advantage, but there is no evidence whatsoever that Elizabeth I actually stayed there).

From a modernist, purist perspective, production design in particular is compromised by the limitations of its inherited materials and resources. The designer may be constrained by the use of extant locations and interiors courtesy of English Heritage, the National Trust, the National Parks and the Countryside Commission, or may be required to use ready-mades like

Beamish and the Black Country Museum. There may be a requirement to use locations which are not ideal aesthetically, historically or stylistically, but which are in convenient reach of one another and are otherwise amenable. There may also be budgeting pressure to use prefabricated stock elements or whatever props are available from hire companies and antique dealers. In this sense, the activity of the production designer on an historical film is less that of an old-style artist (working on a blank canvas) or a purist designer (form follows function) and more that of an assembler of parts.

Very often, production design is concerned with achieving internal consistency and homogeneous style where each aspect of the design appears to be 'in keeping' with the others. Striving for historical unimpeachability is one means of rendering a uniform 'look' across sound, props, decor, script, actors and lighting. However, design in heritage film and television actually directs as much effort towards maintaining self-effacing congruity and meeting the preconceptions of practitioners and audiences of how historical material ought to look: hence, pre-digital post-production, the acres of peat and cobblemat. Paradoxically, the presence of this received notion of authentic style has contrived against each production being functionally and visually designed anew.

Nevertheless, the design of heritage film and television is consistently recognised by the industry in the form of awards from BAFTA and the American Academy. Often a single heritage production will receive some combination of design awards. For instance, *A Room with a View* (James Ivory, 1986) won Oscars for Costume Design and Art Direction, *Tess* for Costume Design, Art Direction and Cinematography. There is a common feeling that films with more recent settings are not designed at all. Thus Tom Sutcliffe suggested that *Amongst Women* (BBC, 1998), set in rural Ireland in the 1950s, allowed the viewer 'to enjoy a drama without the encumberment of period costume'.[36] In fact the efforts of the designer to achieve authenticity may well be as strenuous and arduous whatever the period. As period reconstruction, Roger Cann's BAFTA design award for the adaptation of Hanif Kureishi's story of 1970s adolescence, *The Buddha of Suburbia* (BBC, 1993), was as well deserved as Ken Adam's Oscar for *The Madness of King George* (Nicholas Hytner, 1994), for which, with the exception of the vast bed which provided an entire interior in its own right, credit seemed largely due to Eton College.

Conclusion

Much early writing on the heritage film objected to the notion of a distinct film culture being infected by its contact with the heritage industry. As I trust I have demonstrated in this chapter, cinema, in its production, distribution and reception, is inextricably bound up with other aspects of the national culture and heritage. This is even true of films that are not historical in style or content. Moreover, the very institutions of cinema and broadcasting are now structurally implicated in the tourism and heritage business. Cinema and television have much to contribute purposefully and positively to public debates around heritage. Design can be a means of rethinking a text or a period for a contemporary audience, liberating it from a timid or slavish imitation of received ideas of the past or from the enchantment of the classic status of the source text. Far from distancing themselves from current representations of history, film and television can renegotiate the relationship between heritage and a variety of historical realities.

NOTES

This chapter is a re-working of material that first appeared in my article 'The Darcy Effect: regional tourism and costume drama', in *International Journal of Heritage Studies*, vol. 4, nos. 3–4, Autumn 1998, © Intellect Ltd (www.intellect books.com).

1 T. Bennett, 'Museums and "the people"', in R. Lumley (ed.) *The Museum Time Machine*, London, Comedia/Routledge, 1988, p. 74.
2 See, for example, M. Leonard, *Britain^{TM}: Renewing Our Identity*, London, Demos, 1997; see also Millennium Products, an initiative launched by the Design Council in 1997, involving a nation-wide search for innovative new products and services.
3 I am adopting terms used by M. Horkheimer and T. Adorno, but do not concur with the pessimism with which they regarded the divide between them: see *The Dialectic of Enlightenment*, trans. J. Cumming, New York, Herder and Herder, 1972.
4 R. Hewison, *The Heritage Industry*, London, Methuen, 1987, p. 144.
5 J. Corner and S. Harvey, 'Mediating tradition and modernity: the heritage/enterprise couplet', in Corner and Harvey (eds) *Enterprise and Heritage: Crosscurrents of National Culture*, London, Routledge, 1991, p. 51.
6 A. Higson, 'Re-presenting the national past: nostalgia and pastiche in the heritage film', in L. Friedman (ed.) *British Cinema and Thatcherism*, London, UCL Press, 1993, p. 114.
7 J. Walton, 'Television review', *Daily Telegraph*, 14 April 1999, p. 42.
8 See, for instance, C. McArthur, *Television and History*, London, BFI, 1980, p. 9.
9 See A. Lambert, 'Signs of the times', *National Trust Magazine*, Summer 1998, no. 84, pp. 26–31.
10 E.H. Carr, *What is History?*, London, Macmillan, 1962, p. 9.
11 See, for instance, C. McArthur, *Television and History*, London, BFI, 1980.
12 S. Bruzzi, *Undressing Cinema*, London, Routledge, 1997, p. 35.
13 See, for instance, J. Hill, *British Cinema in the 1980s*, Oxford, Clarendon Press, 1999, p. 78.
14 See, for instance, A. Higson, 'The heritage film and British cinema', in Higson (ed.) *Dissolving Views: Key Writings on British Cinema*, London, Cassell, 1996, p. 233; also Higson, 'Re-presenting the national past', op. cit., pp. 114–15 ff.
15 For one version of this argument, see the exchange between Natasha and Mark Darcy in H. Fielding, *Bridget Jones's Diary*, London, Picador, 1996, pp. 101–2.
16 P. Fowler, *The Past in Contemporary Society*, London, Routledge, 1992, p. 6.
17 See Hewison, op. cit., p. 146; and Corner and Harvey, 'Mediating tradition and modernity', op. cit., p. 46.

18 K. Stevenson, letters page, *The Times*, 25 January 1996, p. 19.
19 Dan Glaister, 'Film locations make most of period charm', *Guardian*, 21 May 1996, p. 11.
20 *Nationwide*, BBC Radio 5, 12 March 1996.
21 J. Nuttall and A. Nuttall, 'A slice of Lyme', *Manchester Evening News* ('Go' section), 14 December 1996, p. 22.
22 'A ... Walking Tour ... Jane Austen and Bath in Film and Literature', Bath Parade Guides, Bath TIC, 1998.
23 The National Trust, *Wessex Region News*, 21 February 1996, p. 1.
24 'Summertime '98, a guide to tourism, leisure and shopping in Derbyshire', produced by Amber Valley Tourist Board, shows Gary Mavers (Dr Andrew Attwood) and Adrian Lukis (Dr David Shearer) gazing into the distant yonder with copies of the Amber Valley guidebook.
25 S. Birtwistle and S. Conklin, Penguin, Harmondsworth, 1995.
26 S. Birtwistle and S. Conklin, Penguin, Harmondsworth, 1996.
27 S. Fokschaner, 'Vanity flair', *Homes and Antiques*, issue 71, Dec. 1998, pp. 52–8.
28 'BBC Experience', publicity leaflet, 1998.
29 S. Neale, *Genre*, London, BFI, 1980, p. 34.
30 See V. Schwartz, 'Cinematic spectatorship before the apparatus: the public taste for reality in *fin de siècle* Paris', in V. Schwartz and L. Charney (eds) *Cinema and the Invention of Modern Life*, Berkeley, University of California Press, 1995, pp. 297–319.
31 See S. Rosenfeld, *Georgian Scene Painters and Scene Painting*, Cambridge, Cambridge University Press, 1981, p. 33.
32 For example, I. Bristow, *Interior House-Painting Colours and Technology, 1615–1840*, Newhaven, Yale University Press, 1996; and P. Thornton *Authentic Décor*, London, Weidenfeld and Nicholson, 1984.
33 See, for example, J. Cornforth's discussion of J. Fowler's interiors for the National Trust, including Claydon, Petworth and Sudbury, in *The Inspiration of the Past*, Harmondsworth, Viking, 1985.
34 See H. White, 'The modernist event' (and discussion of this in subsequent chapters), in V. Sobchak (ed.) *The Persistence of History*, London, Routledge, 1996, pp. 17–39.
35 For Christopher Hobbs' account of working with Jarman, see his 'Film architecture: the imagination of lies', in F. Penz and M. Thomas (eds) *Cinema and Architecture: Méliès, Mallet-Stevens, Multimedia*, London, BFI, 1997, pp. 166–74.
36 T. Sutcliffe, 'Television review', *Independent*, 15 July 1998, p. 24.

22

ON THE THRESHOLD BETWEEN PAST AND PRESENT

'Alternative heritage'

Phil Powrie

In her book on British cinema, Sarah Street points out that there have been two types of historical film during the 1980s, the heritage film, as defined by Andrew Higson, and the bio-pic.[1] The former include the Merchant-Ivory films, for example *A Room with a View* (James Ivory, 1986) and *Howards End* (James Ivory, 1992); the latter include such films as *Dance with a Stranger* (Mike Newell, 1985), *Sid and Nancy* (Alex Cox, 1986) and *Scandal* (Michael Caton-Jones, 1989). There is, in my view, a third category of historical film, the rite of passage film set in the past, focusing on child or adolescent protagonists, most of which appeared in the 1980s. Like the heritage film, 'they engage with the idea of the national past in a national context',[2] but they do so through the eyes of a single child protagonist. In that respect they are also like the bio-pic, showing 'a fascination with diffi-cult moments in the national past which indicate contemporary fears'.[3] After suggesting a taxonomy for the rite of passage films, I shall look more closely at a small selection of them which help to define what I propose to call an 'alternative heritage' film.

A number of the rite of passage films have girls as their protagonists: *The Country Girls* (Desmond Davis, 1983), set in County Clare in the mid-1950s; *Those Glory Glory Days* (Philip Saville, 1983), set in London; *Secret Places* (Zelda Barron, 1984), set in an English girls' school during the Second World War; *Wish You Were Here* (David Leland, 1987), set in a seaside town during the 1950s. These films tend towards a cosy nostalgia, however, and, more often than not, combine an obsession with sexuality and whimsy, if not comedy. This is particularly the case with *Wish You Were Here*, for example, with its memorably excessive song 'I Like Willies' sung by the sexually precocious Lynda (Emily Lloyd) in the staid seaside tea-rooms. In the 1990s, however, such films have shown a darker side. *Blue Black Permanent* (Margaret Tait, 1992), set in present-day Edinburgh with flashbacks to a 1950s childhood in the Orkneys, and *An Awfully Big Adventure* (Mike

Newell, 1994), set in Liverpool during the 1940s, have none of the whimsy of the 1980s films.

The majority of the rite of passage films are boy-centred, however.[4] Like those with girl protagonists, they tend, with the exception of *Hope and Glory*, to be set somewhere other than London: *Hope and Glory* (John Boorman, 1984; London during the Blitz); *The Innocent* (John MacKenzie, 1984; Yorkshire in the 1930s); *The Kitchen Toto* (Harry Hook, 1987; the Kenyan struggle for freedom in the 1950s); *Distant Voices, Still Lives* (Terence Davies, 1988; Liverpool in the 1950s);[5] *Burning Secret* (Andrew Birkin, 1988; Vienna in 1919); *Venus Peter* (Ian Sellar, 1989; Orkney in the 1940s); *The Long Day Closes* (Terence Davies, 1992; Liverpool in the 1950s); *Small Faces* (Gillies MacKinnon, 1995; Glasgow in the 1960s). In what follows, I have selected three of these films, *Distant Voices, Still Lives*, *The Long Day Closes* and *Small Faces*, which seem to me to be exemplary of a sub-genre within the rite of passage genre, which I would like to call 'alternative heritage'.

These three films are heritage films because they have high production value period detail in common with what Andrew Higson calls 'bourgeois heritage'. But they are not 'versions of heritage', as Higson would have it.[6] They are, rather, distinctly 'alternative', because, like the majority of the boy-centred rite of passage films, they focus on and frequently aestheticise the working class or the lower middle class rather than the upper middle class of 'bourgeois heritage'. What also characterises the three films I have selected is self-reflexivity, by which I mean that they encourage spectators to question their status (both the status of the films, and the status of the spectators themselves). They push the rite of passage narrative to its limits, and in so doing, allow us to reconsider the notion of heritage, ultimately pointing to an 'alternative heritage' sub-genre. *Distant Voices, Still Lives*, and *The Long Day Closes* are both about a young boy's childhood in Liverpool (Tony in the first film, Bud in the second). The first film centres on family occasions such as weddings, baptisms and Christmas, and is dominated by a psychotic father. In the second film, which is lighter in tone, the father is absent, but what was only implied in the first film, the young boy's homosexuality, is made more explicit, and he suffers taunts from his peers at school. *Small Faces*, set in Glasgow, is about three young brothers who become involved in gang violence.

'Alternative heritage' and self-reflexivity

Unlike the more standard narrative structure of many of the rite of passage films, these three films are constructed on the principles of ellipsis and fragment, rather than coherent narrative linearity. They are often made up of aleatory 'occasions' that struggle towards the sense of a story or a history. This raises the question of how they manage to sustain spectator identification, given their fragmentary nature. Arguably, the fragments function like snapshots. The act of viewing becomes, for the spectator, something like leafing through a photograph album, trying to supply a broader context for the personal history of which one sees only isolated 'occasions', or 'events'. This is particularly pronounced in the case of *Distant Voices, Still Lives*, with its articulation around family events such as weddings, baptisms and funerals. Identification occurs as a result of two potentially contradictory actions. First, there is the effort of supplying the broad context for the 'snapshots' which constitute the narrative. Arguably, the effort required could lead to spectator resistance and prevent identification. If this does not happen, it is because of the lack of a context, a lack that gives rise to effort in the first place, since the spectator must supply the context to make sense of the narrative situation. That lack, potentially off-putting, can also be attractive, because it figures the gulf of passing time and generates nostalgia, the pain of having left the 'home' and all that it represents in an unrecoverable past. The spectator therefore maps onto the protagonist who is not simply remembering the past, but re-membering it, putting the bits back together again, recreating the body of the child, reliving (and therefore arguably relieving) the pain of a childhood dispersed and dis(re)membered in the past.

There is a second formal procedure which affects the narrative, and which will support my notion of the 'snapshot', namely 'fixing' (to use a photographic term) through the use of paintings in *Small Faces* and photography or pseudo-photographic shots in *Distant Voices, Still Lives*. The 'painterliness' of the three films is considerably more self-conscious than in the Merchant-Ivory heritage film, despite the possible ironies in the Fauvist painting with which *Howards End* opens. Both types of heritage film deal in aestheticisation, but *Howards End*'s narrative line is on the whole undisturbed by the kind of art-house framing and fixing found in the Davies films, where form tends to overwhelm narrative. In *Distant Voices, Still Lives*, for example, the film opens with a long-held shot of the front door of the family home, followed by a series of shots of the family 'posing' for Eileen's wedding. On the wall behind them, underlining the photographic nature of the family pose, there is a black-and-white photograph of the absent father. *Small Faces* is not particularly slow or elliptically fragmentary like *Distant Voices, Still Lives*; however, its distinct narrative line recounting the three brothers' absorption into gangland warfare is constantly slowed down by *mise-en-scène* which draws attention to itself. These set pieces threaten to 'freeze' the narrative in an excess of spectacle predicated on fetishised objects (the circus clown heads at the fair, Bobby's blood on the ice in the ice-rink) or fetishised cinematography (canted camera). It is as if the films are suggesting that the past can only be recaptured if slowed down, frozen, or magnified in discrete occasions: this is the process that I term 'fixing'.

If the narratives of these three films are distinctively fragmentary, there is also something characteristic about the ways in which they combine their fragmentary narratives with scenes of male violence. Male posturing and violence is a recurrent theme of heritage films. In the 'bourgeois heritage' films, one thinks of Cecil Vyse's pompous foppishness in *Room with a View*, or Charles Wilcox's class hatred in *Howards End*. What is particularly striking about the rite of passage films listed above is that those with girls as protagonists tend to be whimsical if not comical in tone, whereas those with boys as protagonists tend to be associated with violence. This can be because of a war setting, as in *Hope and Glory* and *The Kitchen Toto*, or the films can contain references to war, as in *The Innocent*. Other films simply display male brutality, for example in the shape of the psychotic patriarchal father in *Distant Voices, Still Lives*.

The three films that I have chosen as examples of 'alternative heritage' stand out from the rest where male violence is concerned. First, there is a pronounced contrast between the outside 'bad' community, versus the domestic 'good' community, which is more or less coterminous with an extended family. In *The Long Day Closes* the violent outside is school, where the boys gang up on Bud, taunting him about his homosexuality and beating him up. In *Small Faces* it is the violence of gangland, which results, as the title allusively suggests, in disfigurement, as headbutts and thrown bricks result in expressionistically mutilated faces. Second, the contrast between good and bad, inside and outside, is further emphasised by the use of music, most particularly singing, which is generally associated with female communities and domestic interiors. The songs in *Distant Voices, Still Lives* are usually initiated by women and serve to bind the community together. In *Small Faces*, Lex's mother sings a traditional Scottish song, with a 'family' threatening to fall apart momentarily united in reverent silence around the mother as centre. Singing, as indeed music more generally in these films, functions, much like painting or photography, to compensate for the male-oriented and frequently violent action which disrupts the community, and which is paralleled by the fragmentary nature of the narrative. Thus the father in *Distant Voices, Still Lives* beats his daughter who asks for money to go dancing, upsets the Christmas dinner table, and refuses to join his son in a drink; he does sing, but only when by himself grooming his pony. His anti-social behaviour is countered by communal singing in the pub or at home. These sequences freeze the narrative in moments of remembered unity, or, to use the metaphor above, re-membered community, a community whose members are brought together again, and who function as the context for the re-membering of the protagonist.

In this respect, male violence is what threatens not only the community, but also the remembering of that community. Male violence is traumatic, turning the past into a negative freezing, the freezing of death, rigor mortis. This is achieved literally in *Distant Voices, Still Lives*, which begins with the father's funeral, and flashes back to his slow demise. Music, on the other hand, works to bind the community together (re-membering). It also clearly functions to activate memory (remembering). Davies talks of *Distant Voices, Still Lives* as being a set of ripples, Eileen's wedding being the stone cast into the pool of water: 'It's the day of her wedding, she remembers her dad, that's the pebble dropped in the pool, and then there are these ripples of memory, which is what the film is all about.'[7] Events in these films are sounds sent into the depths of the past. Like the fragment of Vinteuil's music in Proust's *The Remembrance of Things Past*, they stimulate the involuntary memory of earlier events. Events, especially those that focus on music, function quite literally as sounding-lines, or sonars, sent to bounce back echoes from the past.

The threshold

There is a key image in these three films, which allows the past and the future, the inside and the outside to communicate. It is the image of the doorway: the main door of the house in *Distant Voices, Still Lives* and *The Long Day Closes*, and the main door of the flat in *Small Faces*. The metaphorical function of the doorway image is so complex that I shall call it the threshold. That function is in part about framing, which thus complements what I described earlier as fixing. In both *Distant Voices, Still Lives* and *The Long Day Closes*, the threshold is an anchoring image in the sense that it is constantly returned to and dwelt upon. In *Distant Voices, Still Lives* the film opens with the threshold of the family home, which gradually fills with sounds, and eventually music. It also gradually fills with people, the first of whom is the mother collecting the milk, an apparently prosaic image, but given the importance of the maternal in these films, in fact a very significant one. The opening image of the threshold is paralleled by the closing image of Tony's wedding, as he stands on the threshold both literally and figuratively, weeping, before the revellers pour out of the house and wend their way back home. Between these two images, there are several other sequences where the threshold plays a major role, such as Tony's exclusion from the home, or, more important, the extraordinary six-minute tracking shot some ten minutes into the film (actually a composite of several tracking shots). The shot begins with Eileen sobbing in Tony's arms as she longs for her father. It tracks left to a pub exterior, and then Christmas scenes from childhood: the family in church, the father decorating the Christmas tree (from outside, then as an interior shot), the father filling stockings as the children sleep, and finally his psychotic outburst at the dinner table the following day. The threshold is located in the middle of this tracking shot. It acts spatially as the transitional point between the outside and the inside. More importantly for this tracking shot, it also acts temporally, as the gateway from Eileen's present to the children's past, the nostalgic but bittersweet memory ironically emphasised by the sound of the carol, 'In the Bleak Midwinter'.

Plate 28   The protagonists of Terence Davies' *Distant Voices, Still Lives* (1988),
gathered on the threshold of the family home.

A similar tracking shot occurs twice in *The Long Day Closes*, once some
twenty-five minutes into the film, at the end of the first of the film's three
major sections, and again towards the end of the film. The first section of
the film is characterised narratively by optimism and family-centred
sequences, where the mother plays a key role. It has a very full soundtrack of
mainly non-diegetic music, and an important feature of the section is that
there are several sequences where apparently real-time camera-work is
contradicted by temporal ellipses in the narrative events which occur. For
example, Bud pesters his mother to go to the cinema but, in what appears to
be the same time-frame, is said to be at the cinema; Bud then waits at the
doors of the cinema, only to be seen coming out of them as the camera tracks
forward. Another example occurs during the three-minute shot closing this
part of the film. It tracks right from the same threshold as in *Distant Voices,
Still Lives*, to the accompaniment of Mahler's 10th Symphony; it reaches a
street corner where the community dances on New Year's Eve to the accompaniment of an excerpt from the soundtrack of *The Magnificent Ambersons*
(Orson Welles, 1942). The camera cranes up and follows the family's return
to the threshold, an indeterminate time-lapse having occurred in spite of the
continuous real-time camera-work.

The threshold plays an equally important role in the central section of

The Long Day Closes. This begins when Bud changes school, and is considerably darker in tone. Bud is bullied ('who's a fruit?'), caned, and humiliated by having the nurse pronounce his hair full of lice. Whereas the music in the more optimistic first section was mainly non-diegetic, here it is diegetic and infrequent. The central sequence of this section is Bud sitting on the threshold, excluded from his older brother's and sisters' evening revelries.

The final section of *The Long Day Closes* returns to the family focus of the first section, celebrating moments of family closeness such as a picnic on the doorstep of the house. Its central sequence shows Bud again left on the threshold, as this time his siblings go off on a Sunday bike-ride. An overhead camera tracks left as Bud swings on the rails outside the house, then goes to a cinema, to the church, to the school, and back to the threshold, improbably coming in from the right, in a mirrored loop, which echoes the time-lapses earlier in the film.

As in *Distant Voices, Still Lives*, the threshold in *Small Faces* is associated with family interiors and song. Song is here connoted positively with a mother-centred community as Lorna, Lex's mother, sings a traditional song. Attention is drawn to the threshold partly by its colour (backlit yellow and red stained glass), and partly by the fact that after the first appearance which locates it as the passage from familial community inside to violent gang outside, it always appears on significant occasions. The three most important occasions are when the boys return from their narrow escape at the club; when the American Andrew, the possible father-figure, leaves, after brother Bobby's death; and, finally, at the close of the film, after Malkey's death. The final sequence returns to these significant occasions and replays them through Lex's voice-over (the only one of the film). He tells us that his psychotic brother Bobby is now remembered as a wise person, that Andrew, the father-figure, has returned to marry Lorna ('just my luck,' he says, 'the only American to emigrate to Scotland'), and that he himself 'dreamt that I was a man. Luckily when I woke up I was still a boy'. The literal and figurative threshold coalesce in the present of a remembered past.

The threshold therefore acts as a complex metaphor in all three films. It is both the threshold of adulthood, and the no man's land between the domestic space and the public space. It is both developmental and spatial, therefore, its topicality associated with the mother as representative of domestic space and childhood. It is also clearly a temporal metaphor, the location between the past of childhood and the future of adulthood, a kind of precarious present. That precariousness is signalled spatially by narrative events where domestic and public space overlap. In *The Long Day Closes*, for example, the domestic spills out into the public when the family picnic on the doorstep, or the brothers and sisters leave for a night out. Conversely, the public encroaches on the domestic in the form of outsiders, whether the genial Curly or the frightening black stranger in search of Mona in *The Long Day Closes*. This overlap is emphasised in the long tracking shots of the

Davies films, which start and end on the threshold, but visit a variety of usually public locations before they return to the point of departure.

The past, in nostalgia, is very literally the aching for the domestic place, and the three films in question show this particularly well by their strong sense of location, so strong in fact that they threaten to trap the protagonists in a perpetual childhood. Hence Lex's statement in *Small Faces* that 'I dreamt that I was a man. Luckily when I woke up I was still a boy'. Psychological development is sacrificed for something else, a sense of locatedness; much the same could be said of *Distant Voices, Still Lives* and *The Long Day Closes*, which are as rooted in Liverpool as *Small Faces* is in Glasgow. The threshold is the way into not just the specific location of the films in working-class Liverpool or Glasgow, but beyond that, the way into the past. And yet there is clearly a paradox here. Despite their very specific locations and their auto-biographical nature, the films appealed to a wide audience. According to Davies:

> People all over the world have said that they've seen their own childhood on the screen. I'm always astonished that people get so much out of the film because it seems to me to be peculiarly English, and about an England thirty years ago, that doesn't even exist now. Liverpool is not the same, my family is not the same, I'm not the same.[8]

Utopia, metatopia and difference

To explain the appeal of the films, we need to return to the issue of location. One reason for spectators 'over-riding' regional and autobiographical speci-ficities is that the nostalgic structure is simply a way of signifying pastness for most spectators. The spectator 'maps' onto this structure, which explains why, to Davies' surprise, so many people liked *Distant Voices, Still Lives*. The notion of 'mapping' may make identification appear a highly theoretical and abstract process, although I would argue that this is not empirically how we experience it in such films. Rather, the regional factor localises pastness geographically, making the general more specific. Spectators need that speci-ficity because it gives a strong sense of place, and the evocation of the past requires that we be displaced from the present by the pull of a past place, the unrecoverable home. Spectatorial response can therefore be defined as a kind of *metastasis*: we are displaced from the present into a very abstract place, a utopia – literally, a no-place – but we are attracted there by a very specific place, a place whose regional specificity is precisely what makes it attractive. The spectators of a film that generates nostalgia are thus invited to relocate the past place, and relocate themselves within it: 'I wish to be that boy in that place, because I was once (like) that boy in that place. I once also inhabited a very specific place.' We are thus invited to desire sameness while maintaining difference ('I could have been that boy in Liverpool, although in fact I was that/this boy in London').

There is a second reason why the regionalism of the films is a key issue. Regionalism is in effect the geographical fragmentation of the nation into parts. To hold in mind the idea of the nation is to conjure up a utopian image, to conjure up an imaginary wholeness from these parts. The spectator's utopian drive to an individual wholeness lost in the past thus corresponds to this imaginary national wholeness. We might even suggest that the personal re-membering of a childhood traumatised by male violence has its equivalence in this geographical scenario. From this point of view, these films act as an allegorical mapping of the imagined re-membering of the national body politic traumatised over time into geographical fragmentation. National identity assumes a sense of sameness in spite of obvious difference, in spite of the specificity of regional identity. It thus presupposes transparency at the national level: 'I could have been in Liverpool, although in fact I was in London – but it does not matter since they are the same (only different).' 'Transparency' allows both locations to exist as different locations, but also abolishes their differences in the act of 'gazing through', of seeing something other than what is apparently there. Difference, however, requires violence, in the sense that an idealised wholeness which collapses into the fragmentation of difference can only do so if we assume some kind of violence done to the whole. This helps explain why male violence is so prevalent in these films.

This allegory of the nation as a nostalgic yoking together of fragments is powerfully realised in the opening sequence of *Distant Voices, Still Lives*, during which, as I have already pointed out, the camera lingers on the open doorway into the house. I have suggested that this functions as a metaphorical way in to a *place* which is also a *past* for the individual spectator. The metaphor is complicated by the soundtrack, which, among other elements, features the shipping forecast on the radio. This too can be read metaphorically. At one level, the forecast is pure nostalgia, a recitative whose relative meaninglessness enables it to articulate an unfocused yearning for something lost, the mother(land). Part of the nostalgia is the ritualistic nature of the forecast, as Davies himself points out: 'The shipping forecast was like magic because I didn't understand what it meant – I still don't – so it was like a kind of ritual, an incantation. Even now, when I hear it I go cold, because I can just see that parlour and the house gradually waking up.'[9]

The idea of ritual is vital. The forecast is a series of place names which emphasise fragmentation and dispersal; but at the same time the ritualised structure and daily occurrence of the forecast bring together the place names to form an utopia, a magical no-place, to be etymologically exact. The forecast is the emblem of ordered disorder, geographical fragmentation being counterbalanced by the order of ritual. The forecast, then, like the regional element, is on the cusp between an imaginary wholeness and the difference of the real that disrupts that wholeness. In the case of the forecast it is not the actual location of the film's narrative (Liverpool as opposed to my imagined London), but the names of scattered locations which gesture to an imaginary 'nation'. The nation is thus something that, in the imagination at least, resolves separateness, difference, fragmentation; the forecast conjures up the same (place) for 'everyone', wherever and whoever they are (even if, in reality, the ritual is culturally very specific).

The threshold looks both backwards and forwards in moments of productive tension that map onto each other: childhood/adulthood, family/community, region/nation. The threshold does not therefore signify a no-place or utopia that might reunite the fragments, the differences, the conflicts. It is not a metaphorical union, but a place necessarily formed from fragments and yet beyond specificities. The differences must be evoked, but at the very same moment in which they are evoked, they must also be dissolved, to re-emerge in the moment of dissolution, and so on. In that respect, what I chose to call spectatorial metastasis above, the sense of being displaced into a no-place by the attraction of a very specific place, is paralleled by a *metatopia*, the tension of an idealised 'nation' constantly disrupted by the fragmentation of the regional. What this also tells us, of course, is that the 'nation' is a necessary fiction whose function is to legitimise narrative/s, or history/ies.

Conclusion

In 'bourgeois heritage', finality (strong narrative closure) and regret (reviewing the past as idyll) predominate. I have argued that certain films from the rite of passage genre can function as 'alternative heritage'. They do so because they combine four factors, which we could gather loosely under the heading of 'eccentricity'.

First, they focus on working-class or lower-middle-class protagonists, unlike mainstream heritage, which tends to focus on the upper middle classes. Second, the films are located outside of the 'centre', London, in the 'provinces'. In this instance, 'provincial' is not a term of disparagement but an indication of the ways in which the films question the pernicious fictions of nationalism and de-centre the nation-state. Third, and following on from this, 'alternative heritage' films disrupt the fiction in a different sense, by slowing or freezing narrative, which tends to be centripetal, in that it seeks a finality and/or a closure; the narrative of 'alternative heritage' films, on the other hand, is centrifugal. This draws attention to temporality in ways which mainstream heritage narratives do not. 'Alternative heritage' deflects us away from linear time to cyclical time, forcing us to focus on the production of memory as fiction rather than presenting memory as 'real', as perfected spectacle, as nothing more than a (re)collection of fragments.

Finally, these films are the site of the struggle between extreme and disruptive male violence, and a maternally-centred communal binding.

Violence and a maternal centre could arguably be seen in 'bourgeois heritage'. It is the fact that the violence is extreme, however, and that the binding is effected through heavily foregrounded diegetic as well as non-diegetic music that differentiates the 'alternative heritage' films from 'bourgeois heritage'. There is a tension between the 'eccentric' or centrifugal elements (working-class, provincial, disrupted narrative) and the centripetal maternalism of these films. It is a tension which is never resolved, and that lack of resolution makes the kind of neat closure of 'bourgeois heritage' impossible.

Predicated narratively and cinematographically on difference, these 'alternative heritage' films are sufficiently and multiply different from 'bourgeois heritage' that one can see them as a distinct sub-genre. Located so firmly in difference, the sub-genre radically decentres the idea of the nation, of national identity and of national cinema. At the same time, the films fracture what the rite of passage film is predicated on: the establishment of an unproblematic individual identity.

NOTES

My thanks to Chris Perriam, Justine Ashby and Andrew Higson for their comments on this chapter.

1 S. Street, *British National Cinema*, London, New York, Routledge, 1997; A. Higson, 'The heritage film and British cinema', in A. Higson (ed.) *Dissolving Views: Key Writings on British Cinema*, London, New York, Cassell, 1996, pp. 232–48.
2 Higson, op. cit., p. 236.
3 Street, op. cit., p. 105.
4 Indeed, we could see them forming a sub-set of a wider group of films, both American and British, in which men revisit their youth. Examples of these, which include *The Long Day Closes*, are discussed by Susannah Radstone in terms of regressive nostalgia; see 'Cinema/memory/history', *Screen*, 1995, vol. 36, no. 1, pp. 34–47.
5 This film is arguably more family-centred than boy-centred. I have included it in this list, however, because I feel that the struggle between father and son is more acutely dramatic than the relationship between father and daughters; it is not for nothing that the film closes with Tony's wedding.
6 Higson, op. cit., p. 236.
7 T. Davies, 'A pebble in the pool and ships like magic', *Monthly Film Bulletin*, October 1988, vol. 55, no. 657, p. 295.
8 Ibid., p. 296.
9 Ibid.

23

THE ART OF NATIONAL
IDENTITY

Peter Greenaway and Derek Jarman

John Orr

Englishness and Otherness

While there is much discussion about how cinema can reinforce national identity, it can also very effectively challenge national identity: far from confirming it, film can point out contradictions or the frailties of perception; it can unveil discord or division. As a culture industry, it is not so much a medium of true nationhood, more a *jeu sans frontières*, happily taking money and personnel from wherever it can if that means all the difference between mere intention and final execution. The higher the budget, the more the American market looms, the more this applies. Often it raises the question, to what country does this film belong? For the cause of the true nation there is no comforting rhyme or reason. Some of England's most successful heritage movies have been made by a writer from a Jewish-Polish family living much of her life in India, Ruth Prawer Jhabvala, a producer from that same country, Ismail Merchant, who now lives in New York along with James Ivory, the American director completing the triangle.[1] What is essentially English about any of them? Very little. Yet they are gifted in the art of screening English fiction and Ivory is especially effective in bringing out the best in his English actors.

To stress the point of Otherness we might note that two recent heritage hits *not* by Merchant-Ivory, *Elizabeth* (1998) and *Sense and Sensibility* (1995), have Asian directors, Indian Shekhar Kapur and Taiwanese Ang Lee respectively. If film-makers are from somewhere else, might not the location shoot be a truer guide to nationhood? It is not always so. Michael Winterbottom's *Jude* (1996) has given Thomas Hardy's vision of Christminster, a coded disguise of Oxford, an even thinner disguise by crossing the border to Edinburgh's Old Town. The visuals of historical replication depend on what architecture is left and usable from any century anywhere, never mind what country. Yet even the authentic location can land us back in the arms of the foreign director. London had its first taste of 1960s modernism from

Joseph Losey's *The Servant* (1964), Roman Polanski's *Repulsion* (1965) and Michelangelo Antonioni's *Blow-Up* (1967). The paradox thus remains. It is often film's cosmopolitan voices that give a universal edge to the particular, to the landmarks of time, place and essence.

In analysing the composite nature of British cinema, other nuances come into play. The relative weakness of auteurist film-making in Britain would tend to affirm Adorno's stress upon the impersonal nature of the artwork.[2] This is confirmed by the recent triumph of two genres of British film-making. The first is the bio-pic, which resurrects the notorious 'celebrity' of postwar England. We can think of *Dance with a Stranger* (Mike Newell, 1984), *Ten Rillington Place* (Richard Fleischer, 1971), *Prick up Your Ears* (Stephen Frears, 1987), *Scandal* (Michael Caton-Jones, 1988), *Sid and Nancy* (Alex Cox, 1986) and *Love is the Devil* (John Maybury, 1998), all with dubious heroes or heroines – Ruth Ellis, John Christie, Joe Orton, Christine Keeler, Sid Vicious, Francis Bacon. The second genre is the filmic translation of F.R. Leavis' Great Tradition, the literary film which has seen Austen, Eliot, Dickens, the Brontës, Conrad, James, Hardy, Forster and Lawrence all successfully brought to the screen. While the first genre of reincarnation is vaguely satanic through its notoriety, the second genre is vaguely angelic through its literary pedigree. A director who succeeded in both genres in the 1990s was Iain Softley, first with his Beatles bio-pic set in the early 1960s, *Backbeat* (1993), and then with a bold version of *The Wings of the Dove* (1997), which brings the Jamesian text a decade forward out of the late Victorian age. Points of contact between Stu Sutcliffe and the other members of the band and the complex rituals of courtship in late James would seem slim. But in Softley's versions they are subtly connected, first through a bold reworking of English history in different decades of the century, second through the fine-tuning of a love-triangle doomed in a foreign country and third in a tale of two cities, one English, the other European. *The Wings of the Dove* matches historical London and Venice. *Backbeat* matches industrial Liverpool and Hamburg. Both stage cultural encounters of a transnational kind.

Beyond autobiography: Jarman and Greenaway

This achievement seems impossible without the landmark films of two of the most inventive English directors in the late twentieth century, Derek Jarman and Peter Greenaway. Jarman in *Caravaggio* (1986) and Greenaway in *The Belly of an Architect* (1986) had already created key confrontations between Englishness and Otherness which contained the powerful intimacy of the doomed love-triangle yet were also charged enough to invoke the broader canvas of Europe's cultural heritage. This breadth of vision can be measured not only against the bio-pic, with which both films play in subtle ways, but also against that great strength of Anglo-Scottish filmwork in particular, the autobiographical picture. Three of the National Film School's critically acclaimed directors have defined themselves in this way, Bill Douglas in his 1970s Edinburgh trilogy, Terence Davies in his 1980s Liverpool trilogy and Glaswegian Gillies MacKinnon in his recent film-memoir, *Small Faces* (1995). Jarman and Greenaway by contrast opted to move outside the realm of autobiography, projecting their own experience onto a wider canvas. What they might lose at times in the remembrance of time past, they gain from the imaginative extension of both past and present as objective histories. It is true that Jarman sometimes appears in his own films in order to frame his singular vision. Yet in the work of both directors there is a movement away from the known experience that acts as a powerful spur to filmic innovation. Consequently both film-makers have often been seen as overreachers, keen to explore the very margins of cinematic possibility, and never afraid of idiosyncrasy as a mark of original vision.

Here they have many things in common: a background in London art schools (Jarman at the Slade, Greenaway at Walthamstow College), a concern with the vexed identities of England past and present, a cryptic rivalry for the role of art *auteur* in the British cinema of the 1980s, and a conscious vision of film as outrageous narrative designed to provoke and shock. These provide a necessary template for measuring their differences. Jarman's *mise-en-scène* is often spare and minimalist, Greenaway's usually ornate and baroque. Jarman's roving camera seeks out English city wastelands. In Greenaway, they are conspicuous by their absence. Greenaway has shot standard feature length films in colour and 35mm or 70mm with European funding and co-production, moving to video only in its recent digital phase. Despite faithful support from the British Film Institute, Jarman had a rough time with any kind of collateral funding, insisting with great impatience on mixing different low-budget formats, monochrome and colour, Super 8mm – his preferred format for exteriors – and pre-digital video, and using 35mm blow-up for theatrical distribution. Moreover, Jarman's films raise more clearly the imperatives of standard length that distribution imposes upon contemporary film-makers. In cinema, time and space have their own ironies. Length matters in a way that it does not in either stage drama or fiction. Duration matters in a way that size does not in the painter's canvas. Jarman's predilection for the shorter film, say in *Blue* (1993) or *The Garden* (1990), meant not only a sacrifice of large cinema audiences. Channel Four producers were more attracted to the standard feature lengths of Greenaway and the other talents whom they funded in the 1980s renaissance of British cinema.[3] Here Jarman clearly came off second best.

Pairings of key films can enable us to continue this assessment of sameness within difference, of key variations in adjacent visions of English society. In Jarman's *Jubilee* (1978) and Greenaway's *Drowning by Numbers* (1988), for example, there is a subversive proto-feminist echo of the English music hall tradition which pervades the Ealing and later the *Carry On* comedies. In

Plate 29   Flamboyant imagery and cultural Otherness: Stourley Kracklite (Brian
Dennehy) contemplates an uncertain future in Rome in Peter
Greenaway's *The Belly of an Architect* (1986).

their very different versions of the same Shakespeare text, *The Tempest*
(Jarman, 1979) and *Prospero's Books* (Greenaway, 1991), narrative is dominated less by plot and more by meticulous *mise-en-scène*. Mutual concern with
the politics of 1980s Britain also provides a fascinating contrast. Jarman's
low-budget expressionist assault on the legacy of Thatcher's decade in *The
Last of England* (1987) can be set against Greenaway's allegorical deconstruc-
tion of the same in his baroque *The Cook, the Thief, his Wife and her Lover*
(1989). While the former is a location movie, largely improvised, the latter
is a studio movie, pre-planned in great detail. Outside England, the existence of Italy in *Caravaggio* and *Belly of an Architect* is a source of primal
vision and cultural Otherness, of a strange transcendental release for both in
their quest for artistic origins. Yet here the roles are reversed. Greenaway
shoots ambitiously and flamboyantly on location in Rome while Jarman
shoots within the confines of a London studio set tautly designed by
Christopher Hobbs. For Greenaway's American architect the present of the
eternal city is chained to its past. He cannot escape from the imitation of a
history whose evidence surrounds him. For Jarman the historical enigma of
Caravaggio is chained to his present predicament, the fatal intersection of art
and sexuality. Finally both provide their own variations on the filmic
double, a central theme of *A Zed and Two Noughts* (Greenaway, 1985) and a
passing motif in *The Tempest* and *The Garden*, and both capture different

kinds of English country garden in *The Draughtsman's Contract* (Greenaway, 1982) and *The Garden*. If we wish to celebrate their original vision, we can only do so by stressing that the visual look each has forged in his work is also a shared look, as any film is. On the one hand, Greenaway developed that look with Sacha Vierney, the photographer of *Last Year in Marienbad* (Alain Resnais, 1961), a superb technician equipped to handle his labyrinthine adventures into cool baroque. Jarman, although using different cinematographers through his career, has the look of nearly all his films indelibly stamped with the visual design of Christopher Hobbs, an expert in functional staging and in minimalist form.[4]

The intertextual frame: cinema, painting, theatre

The work of Jarman and Greenaway also illustrates the intertextuality of cultural form. Both respond to the trends and movements in modernist painting which preceded their work in cinema. Jarman, as Michael O'Pray points out, responds critically to the 1960s Pop Art idiom of David Hockney and Peter Blake and their cultural network of which he was briefly a part. Indeed, he was brave enough to attack Hockney, a fellow gay and by then a cult figure, for his embrace of all things American.[5] During the cultural flowering of the New Left in the 1970s, Jarman took a strongly libertarian as opposed to a rigidly Marxist position. Greenaway, as David Pascoe notes, integrated his interest in modernist art directly into his films. Right from the start of his film career he resourced the high modernism of Ralph Kitaj with its conceptual usage of grids and frames which had strongly influenced his pre-filmic painting.[6] Greenaway's flair for abstract and deliberate composition of the filmic frame is above all painterly, and in that respect Kitaj was a more seminal influence than Alain Resnais. In addition, both directors have emerged from the visual force-field of Francis Bacon which had so clearly defined *Performance* (Donald Cammell and Nicolas Roeg, 1970), the one British film of the late 1960s keying into their own work.

Their debt to English theatre should not be ignored either. First, we can point to its dynamic representation of historic legacy in new productions of Renaissance tragedy or Restoration comedy, second to the political renaissance of such forms in the 1970s drama of Edward Bond and Howard Brenton.[7] Bond argued polemically for specific aggro-effects in his radical dramaturgy to augment the use of the Brechtian *gestus* and its alienation effects. This has its parallel in the disruptive power of audio-visual shock that Jarman and Greenaway use, not to heighten narrative in the idiom of Hollywood melodrama, but to disturb it and to interrogate the very nature of its fabric. Jarman's connection with the 1970s English stage is also firmed up by politicising anachronism, rendering it integral to his film aesthetic in *Jubilee*, *Caravaggio* or *Edward II* (1991), just as Bond had made it central to stage aesthetics in *Lear* and Brenton even more so in *The Romans in Britain*. Both plays move gesturally and aggressively in their use of shock tactics from a distant past from which the audience feels safe into an immediate present which is clearly discomforting. Moreover, past and present are brought in tandem by anti-historicist and anti-psychologistic means. Both playwrights thus undermine the methods of naturalist theatre while retaining their themes. Likewise, Jarman undermines the realist cinema while sharing many of its themes. For Greenaway, filmic theatricality draws on the acting idioms of the London stage and on such talented actors as Michael Gambon, Helen Mirren, Joan Plowright, John Gielgud, Janet Suzman and Alan Howard, whose experience in English tragedy became a crucial resource.

While both film-makers absorb theatre into film, they also extend film form by other means. We need here to look more closely at the different ways they use time and space. While both are concerned with history and its present meanings, Jarman's systematic use of anachronism and palimpsest provides a key contrast with Greenaway, who uses them more sparingly and sticks, by and large, to the rigours of narrative continuum. Jarman is largely fascinated by the temporal frame-within-the-frame of film narrative, the leap of epochs acting as a disruptive shock not only to the viewer's sensibilities but to his/her sense of linear history. Greenaway in contrast is more obsessed by the spatial frame-within-the-frame, the viewfinder, the painting, the photograph, even the photocopy. Noel Burch and Pascal Bonitzer have noted the 1960s challenge to the enterprise of film itself, the question of how to signify within the frame the absence of the off-screen presence,[8] that field of the perpetual out-of-frame defining the rectangular limits of film stock and screen projection. Greenaway turns this into an even more self-conscious and cerebral meditation. Recently this concern for the frame has found its most extreme expression in *The Pillow Book* (1995), with its complex multiple screens forcing us to read simultaneous text and images. While for Jarman time cannot be absorbed by film's duration, for Greenaway space cannot be absorbed by its technical projection. In both cases, film is a problematic of multiple worlds that remain unresolved but lead to different emphases.

Following Eisenstein, Jarman gives us montage juxtapositions as forms of temporal shock, but then dissolves the boundaries of time itself. In *Jubilee*, Jenny Runacre is Elizabeth I and all of a sudden the leader of a gang of female punks in 1970s London, the casual assassin of Elizabeth II. In *Edward II*, the historic murder of the homosexual king jumps centuries directly into strident footage of a Gay OutRage demonstration of the 1980s. Likewise *Caravaggio* is both a Renaissance Italy reinvented in a London studio and a random summation of everyday artefacts from the intervening epochs of European history. *The Garden* improvises *ad hoc* the crucifixion of a modern Christ against a mystic, Blakean but familiar South Coast backdrop. Yet at the same time it is an hallucinated vision of Jarman, the film-maker who constantly sleeps and wakes through its errant passage.

The limits of excess: collecting and kitsch

In Greenaway's films, the rectangular screen is a frail aesthetic which sets off contrary movements since its frame is equally a source of fascination and a form of impaired vision. Either its limit is signalled by self-conscious framing like the draughtsman's viewfinder that draws attention to that deficiency, or that limit is obliterated by the richness of content within the frame, a radical compression of layered artefacts into a finite field. Often in a strange override of Simmel's tragedy of culture which laments the dilemmas of accretion,[9] Greenaway crams as much as he can of history's collectible objects into a single deep-focus shot. The artefacts themselves are collected largely from cultures of extravagance and adornment. Ornate or baroque in their original setting, these qualities are amplified by the time they travelled through culture and technology into Greenaway's final cut. Here his European heritage nurtures a strident dualism. The cool spatial framing of his 1960s mentors, Resnais and Antonioni, offsets his mimicking of Fellini's Rabelaisian appetite and Pasolini's sacrificial excesses of the flesh. But while Fellini collects the gross, the kitsch, the sensuous and the grotesque with effortless gusto, Greenaway usually oscillates between excess and refinement, between good taste and its complete negation. Collecting cinematic influences as voraciously as art objects, he often falls between two stools.

Greenaway's framing often has a deceptive simplicity. One thinks in *The Draughtsman's Contract* of the hero's viewfinder centred within the frame of a still camera. Here the landscape and the house that are seen, and meant to be seen, by the viewfinder are filled with the intrigues of intruding figures who are clearly not meant to be there. In terms of the contract they are not meant to be present in the final illustrations yet their significance is vital to the fate of the draughtsman himself. The selective conceits of the pastoral, which Greenaway stresses through the saturated greens of landscape, are followed through in the depopulating images which move humans out of the frame to capture a 'nature' more congenial to posterity. In the dining-room of *The Cook*, Franz Hals' portrait of the Haarlem officers, who stare down from the back wall, mocks the latter-day chevaliers of Albert Spica who sit parodically framed under their portrait doubles in similar sashes, similar saturations of red and black. This self-conscious framing creates multi-layered images whose richness is enhanced by widescreen, by saturated colours and by depth of field. The danger is that this technique can degenerate into well-meaning kitsch.

The opening track in *Prospero's Books* along the Renaissance library of the exiled hero is a visual conceit which tries to turn Prospero's first book, his self-conscious book of Genesis, into Greenaway's first image: 'In the beginning was the Word and the Word was Greenaway. And Greenaway said let there be light, and there was light.' The image springs out of the book in this case, the book of water which leads onto images of water and tempest but never gets out of the library. The dilemma is acute but typical. In making the bookish literal and Prospero his own double, Greenaway is forced back into contrivance. The composite facsimile of the Renaissance library is a crowded museum overpopulated by figures from Renaissance painting and kitsch models from twentieth-century fashion. This anthropomorphic conceit – the figures of paintings coming to life, as in the lovers' chess game, is generically kitsch in Adorno's sense of the word.[10] It is the cue for the educated audience that values its own powers of discrimination to applaud the lifeless facsimile of the Renaissance or Baroque without realising its deathly mistake. Greenaway's kitsch, we might say, is the unconscious dumbing-down of cultural capital. By contrast, the allegorical bite of *The Cook* derives its *mise-en-scène* of conspicuous consumption from clusters of objects that resonate with a corrupt and recognisable present. More than that, consumption in the modern sense of celebrating plenty is restored to its more primitive sense of consuming-as-devouring. The items on the daily menu at *Le Hollandais* exist, it seems, only to be devoured in perpetual travesty of an ancient sacrificial feast. This reaches its nemesis in the beaten and tortured lover's forced devouring of the bookish text on which he chokes to death and then in Spica's unwitting consumption of the sacrificial flesh of his victim. Such clinching images are precisely what *Prospero's Books* lacks. It mistakenly tries to collect the classical and the revered into a single frame yet the clutter of the past becomes devoid of life. The 1990s turn in Greenaway has indeed shown the layering of excess at its most complex, frames within frames within frames, object upon object upon object, and for the spectator the nightmare of a mad Mabuse museum without exit, a labyrinth forcing upon the viewer cultural death through asphyxiation of the senses.

We might say then that Greenaway and Jarman appropriate contrary signs of cultural capital. Greenaway is the manic collector acquiring the refined loot of the European art world before extending his reach to the Orient. Jarman wants to ritualise excess in a different way by obsessively repeating sacred ceremony as a camp gesture. Here ritual becomes an excuse for extravagant fun. Thus one can speculate that Jarman is high camp because he was also in upbringing High Anglican, because he needed the visual surety of sacred spectacle if only to make it profane. His sacrificial unconscious, where thankfully the sacrificial images of his surrogate Christ-figures run deeper than his self-conscious posturing, are flavoured by fetishistic ceremonies of consecration which are often too formless to be taken seriously. Where they are serious and visceral, as in *Caravaggio*, they can be devastating. When they are jokily camped up in a parody of subversive gesture, they degenerate into a peculiar form of kitsch. His English eccentricity pleads to be accepted by being hysterical. He aims at times for the eccentric feel of earlier English film comedy but lacks its formal control. His intellectual concern is really to inflate his subject matter rather than deflate it and for most audiences he draws the sting of tragedy without compensating through humour. Campness can mean that, unlike Pasolini, his images lack genuine sacrilegious power; though when he does forego it, as in *Caravaggio*, he can match Pasolini frame for frame.

His low-budget operation can thus seem like a feverish impatience with form coupled with a naïve delight in instant effect. At times, his improvised Super 8 images can become tedious and repetitive, like a child playing with film stock for the first time. At other times, this format can seem disturbing in its inspired fusion of montage and expressionist gesture where human anguish inhabits a void, where any rational explanation for such anguish is impossible. The more uninhibited or outrageous Jarman becomes, the more one senses something remains unuttered or unutterable, as if freedom merely reveals the depth of repression. The loudest of images can thus have a mute resonance. One thinks of Tilda Swinton's dress tearing at the end of *The Last of England*, a touch overwrought but still impacted with a visual power landscaped by vast unyielding spaces of urban desolation. Here lack of definition in the Super 8 image matched by the presence of twilight conjures a genuine alchemy that elsewhere Jarman sought obsessively but often failed to find. Often sexual display follows the same pattern. His naked male couples are so obviously kitsch and camp that one senses a hidden denial of eros rather than homoerotic celebration. The sharp epiphany of lovemaking between victim and masked SAS terroriser is arguably the most erotic gay sequence Jarman has ever filmed outside of *Caravaggio*. Word has it that in the filmed sequence the masked SAS 'man' was played by a female stand-in, in which case the love that dare finally speak its name finds eros in a reverse transvestism, the erotic woman masquerading as male aggressor. In the artwork, true eros lies in concealment not display, while the *auteur*, one feels, desperately wishes it were the other way around.

Landscapes, cities and interior spaces

Jubilee and *The Last of England* have left a mixed legacy in the filming of London. Many of the features that were to follow in Jarman's wake draw greater power from their neo-naturalist framing and linear narrative. Alan Clarke's *The Firm* (1989), Ken Loach's *Riff-Raff* (1990), Mike Leigh's *Naked* (1993) and Gary Oldman's *Nil by Mouth* (1997) all negate Jarman's aesthetic but often do greater justice to his didactic intent than his own films. Gay director Ron Peck's neglected *Empire State* (1987), set in the changing vista around Canary Wharf, equally asked questions of Jarman's extreme anti-naturalism. The greater 'freedom' which Jarman claimed to find in Super 8 was often his undoing. Greenaway's 35mm landscapes, both garden and shoreline, are more consistently powerful in *The Draughtsman's Contract* and *Drowning by Numbers*. Even allowing for his clear debt to Fellini's *Roma* (1972), no current film-maker has ever systematically reinvented a modern city as Greenaway does with Rome in *The Belly of an Architect*. On the other hand, only *The Cook* rivals the uses of interior space that Jarman had developed in *Caravaggio* and *Edward II*. Despite his own wishes, it is precisely the match of structured setting to semi-structured narrative that has worked best for him. As Colin MacCabe astutely notes, the labyrinthine spaces of Prospero's country house which disorient the eye in *The Tempest* are a perfect visual match for Jarman's serious concern with the surveillance politics of the Elizabethan state.[11] All the history films show the power of stylistic and loose narrative framing to liberate Jarman's filmic imagination. Here their political and sexual politics are a fluid and labile interior space, a space of conspiratorial epochs which creates its frisson of Machiavellian intrigue. It contrasts favourably with the library or museum interiors, which can sometimes be oppressive in the later Greenaway films. They are mausoleum interiors reminding us just as much of death's presence as Greenaway's exhibited corpses.

The danger facing Greenaway is often the greater presence of the corpse over the living actor who is sometimes reduced to an item in a curator's collection. Indeed his compulsion to collect is sometimes so obsessive it goes beyond any credible claim to be a new aesthetic. While Jarman's high-camp extravagances often give the viewer the sense of a liberated boy scout troop attempting a nativity play, Greenaway's obsessions display a mania for refinement which has its pedigree in good English breeding and taste. But once the camera starts to whirr it goes awry. The anxieties of collecting and exhibiting dominate the narrative until it becomes a constipated clutter, an unconscious parody perhaps of the still life in Dutch painting. Only when they are reflexive as in Stourley Kracklite's stage exhibitions in *The Belly of an Architect* or destructively wasteful as in Spica's predatory feasting in *The Cook* do they have the right kind of impact. When Greenaway pointedly deconstructs his own devices in creating them, he shows a powerful and controlled intelligence. Otherwise the compulsion to collect merely arouses suspicions of the director's own monomania which leads at times, it must be said, to an intellectual dead-end. More recently, the desire to be a new Darwin, to adopt the Victorian genius of natural selection as his own double and as a metaphor of omnipotent film-making, seems like muddled self-indulgence. For in the various library tableaux of Greenaway's television documentary, *Darwin* (1992), Charles Darwin seems to elide the roles of curator and creator, framed like a Victorian patriarch at the centre of his facsimiles of natural selection. In the same way the 'natural selection' in Greenaway's narrative, which charts decay, decomposition and death, is patently not that of nature but that of Greenaway, the contrivance of his imaginary narratives. At its best, Greenaway's work does not need

Darwinian framing in any way at all. It is most compelling when his male paranoiacs are tragic victims, when Neville (the draughtsman in *The Draughtsman's Contract*), Kracklite and Spica appear as victims of the complex interface between culture, politics and their flawed egos, victims of the world and of themselves.

The end of Englishness?

The mythic 'necessity' of Darwin is an oblique version of Englishness that shows the tenuousness of the very term, a vain search for roots which founders on excess. Another oblique version of this excess is Jarman's love-hate relationship toward the British Army uniforms of the twentieth century, a fetish source of fear and attraction he may well have inherited from his childhood in the domestic quarters of an army barracks he thought of more as prison than as home.[12] The more he rails against the uniform, the more he demonstrates his unspoken love for it. The stilted awkwardness of characterisation that comes from this cultural enclave brings to mind that other middle-class Englishman whom Jarman so admired, Michael Powell. The irony is that Powell's conservative vision of the end of colonial Britain is followed by the radical Jarman's apocalyptic vision of the end of England *per se*. Yet England has not ended. The Greenwich wastelands which featured in Jarman's films as images of decay are now host to the Millennium Dome, a project more suited to Greenaway, who one suspects would have clear ideas on how to fill every available inch.

It is a suitable moment at which to pause and take stock. At the turn of the century we are now in a position to assess the legacy of both directors. They show us that film as art is not only about national identities but also about their transcendence. Only among a host of other compulsions do they meditate on a sense of Englishness as an acquired heritage to love and hate, to construct and deconstruct, to worship and to lampoon as myth. We should end too with a brief meditation on the very fragility of nationhood and identity in the transnational world of the information age. It should be remembered that Jarman's army officer of a father was actually a New Zealander while Greenaway was born not in England but in Wales. England is more than ever a country full of people from somewhere else. At a time when essentialism is coming back into fashion, hybridity appears to have the last laugh.

NOTES

1 For analysis of recent British heritage films, including Merchant-Ivory productions, see A. Higson, 'Re-presenting the national past: nostalgia and pastiche in the heritage film', in L. Friedman (ed.) *British Cinema and Thatcherism: Fires Were Started*, London, UCL Press, 1996, pp. 109–30.

2 Adorno theorises the impersonal nature of the artwork in *Aesthetic Theory*, trans. C. Lenhardt, London, Routledge, 1984, pp. 251–68.

3 Details of Channel Four commissioning and transmission, including the films of Greenaway and Jarman, can be found in J. Pym, *Film on Four: A Survey, 1982/1991*, London, BFI, 1992.

4 Hobbs discusses his ingenious techniques for cut-price design in 'Film architecture: the imagination of lies', in F. Penz and M. Thomas (eds) *Cinema and Architecture: Méliès, Mallet-Stevens, Multimedia*, London, BFI, 1997, pp. 166–74.

5 See M. O'Pray, *Derek Jarman: Dreams of England*, London, BFI, 1996, pp. 42–6.

6 D. Pascoe, *Peter Greenaway: Museums and Moving Images*, London, Reaktion Books, 1997, pp. 42–6.

7 Bond's dramaturgy is analysed in J. Shaw, *Dramatic Strategies in the Plays of Edward Bond*, Cambridge, Cambridge University Press, 1992.

8 On the contributions of Burch and Bonitzer to the discourse of spatial framing, see J. Aumont, *The Image*, London, BFI, 1997, pp. 99–111, 160–73.

9 See his key essay, 'The concept and tragedy of culture', in D. Frisby and M. Featherstone (eds) *Simmel on Culture*, London, Sage, 1997, pp. 55–75.

10 Adorno, op. cit., pp. 337–41.

11 C. MacCabe, 'A post-national European cinema: Derek Jarman's *The Tempest* and *Edward II*', in D. Petrie (ed.) *Screening Europe*, London, BFI, 1992, pp. 12–14.

12 Jarman discusses these aspects of his childhood in *Kicking the Pricks*, London, Vintage, 1996, pp. 107–9, 115–22.

24

REPRESENTATIONS OF CAPITALISM, HISTORY AND NATION IN THE WORK OF PATRICK KEILLER

Paul Dave

The field of English experimental film since the late 1970s has been perceived as increasingly complex and hybridised in terms of the classic distinctions between avant-gardism and more mainstream types of film practice such as those found in art cinema. A.L. Rees, for instance, has said that the 'current state of experimental film ... defies summary'.[1] In this context, two films by Patrick Keiller stand out: *London* (1993) and *Robinson in Space* (1997). They are perhaps best described as fictionalised documentaries, blending the picaresque narrative, the documentary portrait and the filmed essay. Both films work through their themes with a wry, ironic, often surreal sense of humour and an avant-garde commitment to aesthetic experimentation. Equally, they adopt a self-consciously literary, personal and poetic sensibility with affinities to art cinema. The style of the films is very specific, with their long-held and enigmatically framed still images and their unexpected juxtapositions between sound and image and between one image and the next.

In *London*, the unnamed narrator and his partner Robinson, whom we never see, embark on a series of journeys across London. In *Robinson in Space*, the same two *flâneurs* undertake seven picaresque trips around England, recalling Daniel Defoe's literary tour of the country. In both films, the narrator relates their quotidian adventures in voice-over, interspersing his account with a series of philosophical and historical observations about place, politics, Englishness, literature and the past. It is a strategy that de-familiarises the landscapes and cityscapes of modern England.

Keiller's films are at one level poetic and enigmatic. The carefully assembled collage of sounds and images and the often densely informative voice-over narration insists that we also see them as political essays investigating England's past, present and future. I want to examine this aspect of the films, and in particular Keiller's exploration of capitalism, class and history and his critique of some influential commentaries on the state of the nation. In so doing, I will necessarily be going against a particular view of his films – one that confines them within the overlapping discourses of English empiricism and whimsy.

Keiller originally trained as an architect and practised until 1979, at which time he enrolled as a student in the Department of Environmental Media at the Royal College of Art. At the College he began to make films influenced by such avant-garde groups as the surrealists and the Russian formalists. In particular, he was interested in a project shared by these movements – that of refining creative methods to transform our experience of everyday life. He began with techniques based in fine art practices such as architectural photography, but eventually moved on to experiment with film forms such as the documentary. Keiller would take journeys and record documentary-style images of landscape and townscape. He would later assemble a soundtrack that consisted of a first-person narrator and fragments of music and text. This soundtrack provided the edited images with fictional contexts that lent them a sense of strangeness. The resulting short films shot on 16mm include *Stonebridge Park* (1981), *Norwood* (1983), *The End* (1986), *Valtos* (1987) and *The Clouds* (1989).

London and *Robinson in Space*, his first two 35mm feature-length films, continue the concerns of his short films. Thus Robinson's sensibility is one shaped by the culture of European modernism, and in both films this sensibility is contrasted with an English culture that appears inhospitable to it. Robinson's lifestyle imitates a tradition of urban wandering in pursuit of transforming illuminations of the quotidian that stretches back to Baudelaire and Rimbaud, and includes surrealists like Louis Aragon and situationists such as Raoul Vaneigem.

These films include a wide range of references to history, philosophy, art, economics and politics. Keiller has also written theoretical pieces on film and has produced a book that glosses both the script and selected stills from *Robinson in Space*.[2] It is therefore unsurprising that his work has been described as 'intellectual film-making'.[3] What is surprising is that this perceived intellectualism has not generally been viewed with hostility.[4] However, this general tolerance may well be linked to what appears to be a commonly held belief that, despite the intellectualism, Keiller is deeply, 'quintessentially' English in his dry humour and 'eccentric' interests and knowledge.[5] His work is insistently read through the discourse of English empiricism and whimsical observation, the implication being that it has no other coherence. One reviewer described *Robinson in Space* as 'revealing in its nonsensicality', but exactly what it revealed was left unspecified.[6] Another critic claimed *London* had 'no definite point to make'.[7] There is no doubt that both films delight in the use of non sequiturs and contain apparently bizarre and humorous observations. However, this should not prevent us from recognising that there is a consistency, coherence and unity to the representations of class, history and nation in the two films. Indeed, it seems that the characteristics of humour, eccentricity and useless fact – what for some viewers make the films 'very English' – might be valued precisely because they are perceived as warding off the danger of this more politicised coherence.[8]

Thus despite general bafflement, reviews for both films were mainly enthusiastic in a wide range of publications – from the mainstream press to avant-garde film journals. The enthusiasm had waned a little by the time of the release of *Robinson in Space*, however, with, for instance, Jonathan Romney in the *Guardian* calling it 'boring'.[9] One reason for this may be that the film subjects some of the presuppositions about English culture, class and history found in the first film to greater scrutiny. As it is these presuppositions that this chapter will attempt to render explicit, my comments will concentrate on *Robinson in Space*.

In considering representations of culture, class and history this essay will necessarily be concerned with ideas of 'heritage'. What is the relationship of the Robinson films to heritage culture and to what has been called the heritage film? It is clearly felt that there is a link. For instance, one reviewer claimed confidently that *Robinson in Space* is a 'devastating riposte to Heritage Cinema'.[10] The term heritage cinema has been used to refer to such recent British costume dramas and literary adaptations as *A Passage to India* (Lean, 1984), *A Room with a View* (James Ivory, 1986), *Howards End* (James Ivory, 1991) and *Sense and Sensibility* (Ang Lee, 1995). Many of the characteristic features of the heritage film appear in the Robinson films – for example, the focus on representations of archaic, elite English institutions, the countryside and country houses, the aristocracy and the monarchy. The significance of these representations in heritage films is the subject of a complex and ongoing debate within Film Studies.[11] For some, Keiller's films signal a regressive and reactionary nostalgia for a unified English national identity.[12] Such arguments overlap with similar criticisms of a wider heritage culture developed by anti-heritage critics in which the anachronisms of English culture condemn Britain to the past and bar it from a modern future.[13] *Robinson in Space* explores these arguments. Keiller's response to heritage culture is mediated through an exploration of anti-heritage discourses. In giving an account of the Robinson films it is these discourses that we must attempt to open out more fully.

The cultural critique and the bourgeois paradigm

In the 1960s, several commentators linked an archaic English culture, rooted in a peculiar class structure, to national economic backwardness and decline. W.D. Rubinstein associates this habit with such cultural critics and historians as Anthony Sampson, Perry Anderson, Tom Nairn, Martin J. Wiener and Corelli Barnett.[14] These writers do not all share the same

political perspectives or belong to the same intellectual formations; nevertheless they argue that the relationship between a dominant, landed aristocracy and a subordinate bourgeoisie has been critical in shaping contemporary Britain. Rubinstein, who is quoted by the narrator in *Robinson in Space*, designates such arguments in the work of Wiener, Sampson and Barnett, the 'cultural critique' of British economic decline.[15]

Some of the key terms of the 'cultural critique' can be seen in the following extract from Wiener's *English Culture and the Decline of the Industrial Spirit 1850–1980*:

> Over the past century ... high among the internal checks upon British economic growth has been a pattern of industrial behavior suspicious of change, reluctant to innovate, energetic only in maintaining the status quo. This pattern of behavior traces back in large measure to the cultural absorption of the middle classes into a quasi-aristocratic elite, which nurtured both the rustic and nostalgic myth of an 'English way of life' and the transfer of interest and energies away from the creation of wealth.[16]

What are the assumptions about the nature of and relationships between class, history and capitalism here? The bourgeoisie is identified as the capitalist class, the aristocracy as a pre-capitalist class. There is an implied historical progression running from the aristocracy with its regressive 'rustic and nostalgic myths' of Englishness to the 'innovation', 'change' and 'energy' of a modern bourgeoisie. Also, capitalism is seen as a purely creative force that produces 'wealth' but only in circumstances in which it remains unhindered by 'checks' such as those provided by the longevity of the culture of the 'status quo'.

This 'cultural critique' is evident in Keiller's Robinson films. The examination of public space in *London*, for instance, is influenced by the idea that the energies of the bourgeoisie have historically been contained by an aristocratic hegemony. These energies conventionally include the values of modern urbanism that the narrator remarks are absent in London, whose public places are 'either void or the stage sets for the spectacles of nineteenth century reaction endlessly re-enacted for television'. Examples provided of this archaic 'heritage' spectacle in the film, such as the Lord Mayor's Show and Trooping the Colour, are linked to the *ancien régime* – here the Corporation of London and the Monarchy respectively. For Perry Anderson, whose 'theses' on the course of English history have clearly influenced Wiener, the historical explanation for the perceived failings of the national culture lies in the fact that the English Revolution was the 'least pure bourgeois revolution of any European country'.[17] In other words, because the aristocracy was not ultimately displaced the revolution failed to modernise the social structure and the political system. Again, this line of argument is reproduced in Keiller's films. As Robinson bleakly puts it in *London*: 'The failure of the English Revolution is all around us.'

Representations of the English 'class system' in both films often concentrate their venom on the aristocracy. In *Robinson in Space*, for instance, a shot of West Green House, accompanied by the narrator's voice-over, informs us of the house's links to the Hanoverians and the bloody process of British state formation. The house was built by General Henry 'Hangman' Hawley, reputedly the illegitimate son of George I and the commander of the English cavalry at Culloden. In recent times the house has been associated with the Conservative Party (Lord McAlpine was both recent tenant and former Tory treasurer). Anti-modernist architect Quinlan Terry, whose work, we are informed by the narrator, carries an inscription celebrating Lord McAlpine's avoidance of 'tax gatherers', constructed the gateposts and obelisk which dominate the composition of the shot. This country-seat links the past and the present under the sign of an enduring and rapacious elite.

As well as linking representations of the national class structure with problems of national historical development, *Robinson in Space* raises the question of what it is that constitutes a 'modern economy' and in so doing raises the issue of the nature of capitalism. In recent years the British economy's apparent distance from the successful manufacturing industries of Europe appears to have confirmed the 1960s perception of its economic backwardness.[18] These issues are central to *Robinson in Space*, which originated partly in a critique of 'gentlemanly capitalism' (as the narrator puts it in the film, 'the capitalism of land, finance and commercial services centred on the City of London').[19] The 'cultural critique' holds that the historical connections between the City, the government and the aristocracy are crucial in producing English economic failure. According to this argument, capitalism in this country is cavalier towards the domestic industrial economy because it has always principally operated internationally through the City. British capitalism, it is felt, has failed to take a modern form and has been deflected by a 'gentlemanly' English manifestation. As the narrator puts it early on in the film, 'The narrative of Britain since Defoe's time is the result of a particularly English kind of capitalism.'

These interlocking assumptions concerning the role of class, national history and capitalism in defining the nature of modern England constitute what Ellen Wood calls the 'dominant paradigm of progress and historical change'.[20] Her critique of this 'bourgeois paradigm' overturns received ideas about class, capitalism and modernity. First, she views capitalism dialectically. The capitalist system may be dynamic but it also involves exploitation, cruelty, poverty and coercion. It is not associated with any simple logic of modernity and progress. Second, Wood does not see the bourgeoisie as necessarily synonymous with the capitalist class. Drawing on the work of Marxist historians, in particular Edward Thompson and Robert Brenner, she argues that the revolutionary bourgeoisie of France was not capitalist whereas England's early modern aristocracy was capitalist.[21] Finally, she refuses to contrast European modernity with English backwardness. The invention of capitalism took place in that apparent heartland of archaism, the English countryside, and produced a general culture of 'improvement' that is as inventive today as it was when it first appeared.[22] The 'culture of improvement' is summed up by Wood as 'the improvement of property, the ethic – indeed the science – of productivity and profit, the commitment to increasing the productivity of labour, the ethic of enclosure and dispossession'.[23]

How do these paradoxical insights about history, class, capitalism and modernity affect our understanding of Keiller's Robinson films? I want to argue that these films adopt first, a dialectical model of capitalism, second, a contested definition of modernity and third, an understanding of class unrestricted by preconceived ideas about the historical roles of specific classes.

Capitalism and modernity

For the proponents of the 'cultural critique', the plight of the north of England signifies the tragic failure of capitalist modernity while the south represents the continuing dominance of 'gentlemanly' commercial and landed capital.[24] The complex mappings of the economy in *Robinson in Space* (the seven journeys of exploration around England) dismantle this opposition between north and south. The journeys to the north reveal a successful manufacturing economy through the conventional iconography of industrial landscape. For instance, the shots of the steelworks at Redcar and the chemical production site at Wilton feature the familiar northern skyline silhouettes of chimneys and storage tanks under slow moving smoke clouds, while at the same time the narrator informs us of the buoyancy of these industries. However, the objective does not seem to be simply to invert established representations of the national economy in which such images of the northern industrial landscape often signify economic obsolescence and decline. The more significant discovery is that a successful economy can produce social and urban decay. Thus while the narrator briskly stacks up the abstract indices of economic success, he also reminds us of the conditions and effects of that success. These include high levels of unemployment in industries with automated plant; unregulated labour markets; the highest prison population in Europe and urban dilapidation. Furthermore, these circumstances are not restricted to the north-east. Urban dilapidation, for instance, is also visible in the images provided of the north-west (Liverpool) and the south (Reading).

What begins to come into focus in Robinson's journeys around England is an understanding of capitalism that involves social relationships and effects far beyond the narrowly 'economic'. In this respect, the sequence showing the Queen gliding into the north-west to give her blessing to its economic 'regeneration' by opening the Samsung plant at Wynyard Park is instructive. It is edited in such a way that the announcement of her arrival anticipates her actual appearance and is relayed instead over a shot of local prison construction. Prisons – their privatisation and construction – form a motif in the film. Reminders of their omnipresence help to embed the abstract facts and figures of economic activity researched by Robinson and the narrator into a wider context of social relations marked by conflict and struggle.

A similar emphasis on struggle is to be found in the film's representations of science and technology. Robinson's obsession with the buckminster-fullerene focuses these issues. This carbon molecule was discovered partly by British scientists working unsupported by state or industry and, as the narrator informs us, the patents for its exploitation are all held abroad. The fate of the molecule seems then to epitomise the anatomy of anti-industrial British backwardness suggested by the 'cultural critique'. But this sense of blocked economic glory promoted by the 'cultural critique' tends to restrict our understanding of the dynamic of capitalism. On one side are the scientists battling against the short-sightedness of state and industry; on the other is the Promised Land of a thriving capitalist economy. This scenario presents technological change as an autonomous scientific and technical process and disguises the struggles that inseparably accompany technological development. Keiller brings these struggles to our attention in the film through the reproduction of the spherical, geodesic form of the buckminsterfullerene molecule in various objects featured in the landscape throughout the journeys. Take for instance the shape of the camp set up by the ecological group 'The Land is Ours' that is featured following the first mention of buckminsterfullerenes.[25] These protesters are squatting on land near the site of the Diggers' occupation of the commons in 1649. They therefore establish a link with those who struggled to resist the capitalist enclosure of the commons and the spread of the exclusive rights of private property during the English revolution. Technological futures, the ones glimpsed through the new molecule, are bound together through this visual figure with a tradition of struggle that is far from exhausted.

Keiller also tries to find a filmic means of handling the opposition, central to the 'bourgeois paradigm', between the urban market place as the authentic site of capitalist modernity and the rural as the site of the feudal past. In the representations of the rural scene in *Robinson in Space* single shots often combine an agricultural or pastoral landscape with an unfamiliar industrial one. A shot of the Knauf factory at Ridham, for example, has as its foreground a pastoral landscape while the background is dominated by the futuristic structures of the factory. Conversely, a shot of the village Leigh-upon-Mendip has a foreground that is dominated by the vertiginously sliced hillsides that form the Halecombe quarry. The village is in the background, but because of the compression of the perception of depth in the shot, it appears to be perched on top of the quarry itself.

In this film the country house and park pastoral is situated in a complex rural landscape, which is, in the context of the presumptions of the 'bourgeois paradigm', unfamiliarly 'modern'. Among the images of stately homes and pastoral landscapes Keiller shows us 'the windowless sheds of the *logistics* industry – new prisons, agribusiness, UK and US military bases, mysterious research and training centres', the 'proliferation of new fencing of various types', 'cameras' and 'security guards'.[26] These images create the unified impression of, as Keiller puts it, a culture of 'cruelty'.[27] The prominence given to shots featuring fences, walls and gates helps to elicit the impression of surveillance and aggressive exclusion. They also help to locate this new, rural space in a continuous tradition – that of the 'culture of improvement'.

Originating in the seventeenth century, this culture was born in the English countryside as the discourse and practice of capitalist profitability. Created out of the activities of 'improving' landowners it involved extinguishing the customary claims of the landless to the commons. A new definition of property was being elaborated as these landlords claimed the commons through enclosure. Property was not just private but for the exclusive use of the owner. The sense of 'making better' carried by the word 'improvement' could not be separated then from the effect of making the lives of the dispossessed worse.[28]

The history of this dispossession is the memory space that Keiller supplies for the cruel, 'new space' of the contemporary rural scene.[29] For example, in the Charborough Park sequence a shot shows a picturesque parkland, a drive and surrounding statuary which cast long shadows in the afternoon light. However, the commentary alerts us to the connection between the estate and the wealth generated from the slave trade. (The culture of improvement flourished in the colonies also.) The following shot and the narrator's commentary recall the transported Tolpuddle Martyrs and remind us of the connection between the Enclosure Acts in Dorset and the 'degradation and starvation' of the proletariat of which George Loveless spoke. (The process of enclosure prevented the rural proletariat from supplementing their starvation wages with the resources of the commons.) Thus this sequence offers a contextualisation of the iconography of English pastoralism. Images of the pastoral picturesque do not signify a timeless Old England. Neither are such images indexes of 'pastoral retreatism' as they are in the 'cultural critique'.[30] Rather, we might view them as the effacement of the scars of a very busy history. As the narrator puts it, quoting Sherlock Holmes, a 'dreadful record of sin' is concealed by the 'smiling and beautiful countryside'.

To summarise, if we consider these representations of the rural and urban together, it becomes apparent that the 'oldness' of England, a central perception of the 'cultural critique', is misleading. 'Oldness' in the sense of urban dilapidation and decay is actually the result of a thriving capitalist economy – it is not the index of the incompletion of the inherently regenerative

Plate 30   Charborough Park in Patrick Keiller's *Robinson in Space* (1997): the
'improved' landscape of enchanted old England – simultaneously
'smiling', picturesque and sinister.

effects of capitalist modernity. 'Oldness' in the sense of archaism is equally
misleading. The English countryside is indeed marked by the effects of a
long tradition. But this tradition is not that of the immemorial English
rustic spirit guarded by an aristocratic culture but that of the capitalist
culture of 'improvement'. The new ruthlessly assaulting the old is the origi-
nary moment of this culture. Keiller shows it to be as vigorously active
today as it was in the past. The contemporary signs of surveillance, confinement, punishment and concealed sweated labour in the film are echoed then
by the historical references scattered throughout that link the countryside to
dispossession, exploitation and judicial persecution.

Class

The 'bourgeois paradigm' projects a narrative of history in which the aristocracy and the bourgeoisie have predetermined roles to play in the grand
march of capitalism. The aristocracy is unsuited to carry capitalism into
modernity and is therefore destined to be supplanted by the bourgeoisie –
a class equipped for the task. The 'cultural critique' adds an English inflec-
tion to this meta-narrative. The dominance in England of the culture of the

aristocracy leads to the persistence of pre-capitalist forms of hierarchy and the obsession with the differences of style, language and 'cultural separatism' that has become known as the 'class system'.[31] Class reproduces a frozen world of status. It is what stops things happening.

Within contemporary Film Studies, discussions of the heritage film have made the influence of these conceptions of class apparent. Andrew Higson argues that films like the Merchant-Ivory adaptations of E.M. Forster's novels manufacture 'images of permanence' of an elite English upper class.[32] While the narratives of these films are often concerned to subject aristocratic values to a moral critique, the images re-ground these values with alluring heritage spectacle. This latter includes the lifestyles, institutions and property of the upper classes – the precise cultural formation isolated as culpable in the 'cultural critique'.

Keiller manages to transfigure this apparently static world through the use of aesthetic practices inspired by traditions of modernism, in particular practices of de-familiarisation. He acknowledges the influence of Russian formalism and surrealism and their shared objective of constructing representations that transform our experience of the world by 'revealing strangeness'.[33] For instance, *London* and *Robinson in Space* adapt and de-familiarise a pictorialist camera style that is common to heritage films. In the latter this style is self-consciously 'artistic' and uses 'studied compositions', long shots and long takes with elegant, stately camera movements to show off heritage spectacle.[34] Higson has argued that such shots exceed the narrative requirements of the depiction of character point of view and that they establish a public gaze which has heritage spectacle as its object.[35] The construction of such a gaze fits the phenomenon noted by anti-heritage critics in heritage culture generally, whereby the private property of an elite class becomes the pseudo-public, national 'treasure' of everyone.[36]

By contrast, Keiller's fictional witnesses establish an ambiguous viewing position around his carefully composed long shots and long takes of pastoral and urban heritage. Our awareness of the unseen narrator and his companion, Robinson, endows each image with the potential to act as a point-of-view shot – framings often include obstructions that are consistent with the type of fictional look being suggested. These shots imply that we are surveying private not public property, from a space that is specifically inhabited and vulnerable. In this way the secure, taken for granted public space that acts as the precondition of a public gaze acquires an unfamiliar presence – that of a contested space only brought into existence by the efforts of invisible trespassers. These implied situations of clandestine observation and the enforcement and maintenance of private property activate off-screen space and generate the insistent sensation of narrative suspense. Something might happen at any moment to Robinson and the narrator. Heritage spectacle, the very landscape of the immobile 'class system', becomes then a living site of struggle rather than the encrustation of anachronism.

How do these effects bring us closer to alternative representations of class? It is necessary here to return to Ellen Wood's accounts of class and capitalism and in particular her discussion of Edward Thompson's work.[37] Thompson encourages us to distinguish between achieved class formations and class struggle. The former involves classes that have consolidated a collective identity – it is these visible class formations that have become frozen as ideal types by the English 'class system'. Class struggle, however, is anterior to achieved class formation or the 'class system'. Classes presuppose the experience of conflict and struggle issuing from the social relations of production in which those possessing the means of production exploit those who possess nothing but their own labour power which they must sell to survive. The 'class system' for Wood is an ideology that works to 'contain' the conflict inherent in capitalism's social relations by fixing attention on images of an unchanging social world in which the classes have little to do with one another.[38] The English, it transpires, are not obsessed with class but with what conceals class struggle.

Keiller's representations of class reveal class struggle. For instance, both films feature conflicts between Robinson and his employers that culminate in his sacking. *Robinson in Space* thematises the relentless hostility of state and employers towards trade unions. However, class struggle cannot be restricted to conflict between workers and employers over wages and conditions. It is at the heart of an encompassing or 'totalising' social process that 'shapes and limits all social relations' under capitalism.[39] The film explores the diffuse, intricate variety of experiences generated within these social relations. An example is the visit Robinson and the narrator make to Britain's first American-style 'boot camp' for young offenders and to its first KinderCare nursery in Warrington. The juxtaposition of these two sites generates a complex series of associations and connections. The legitimation of the aggressive subordination of the young offender and the accompanying moral judgements it implies become, through the contiguity created in the edited images and the calm continuity of the voice-over, the context for the consideration of nursery provision.

Such an analogy (infants are 'young offenders' requiring punishment) in turn might remind us of the Tory Government's attempts to legitimise child beating – indeed, Keiller's gloss in the book prompts us to make this connection.[40] Equally, we might recall the thematisation of the privatisation of prisons and detention camps in the film (Campsfield House, Blakenhurst and Doncaster, for example) along with their reputations for violence and neglect. The sadism and aggression in the culture, affecting so many different groups (here infants, youths, asylum-seekers and prisoners), are thus linked to neo-liberal capitalism's unregulated markets and the withdrawal of the state from welfare functions. Again Keiller's own commentary makes this determinative pressure of capitalism on diverse areas of social life clear. He suggests that we might consider sexual repression in the same context as neo-liberal capitalism. Thus the repression of homosexuality by the Tory Party 'cannot be put down simply to the influence of the public schools'; rather, he argues, it seems relevant to link this repression to unregulated markets which like repression inflict 'pain and suffering'.[41]

In conclusion, the 'problem' of England that Robinson is asked to investigate in *Robinson in Space* is not, as he at first presumes and as the 'cultural critique' understands it, the *failure* of English capitalism but rather its *success*. Instead of a weak economy caused by an anachronistic culture, we have a vigorous capitalism that conceals its destructive effects under the cloak of oldness. It is with this discovery that Keiller's work seems to connect most clearly with larger contemporary political and cultural concerns. Anti-heritage discourses such as the 'cultural critique' currently intersect with certain political discourses. Simply put, if it is an anachronistic culture that is to blame for the irreducible problems generated by capitalism then a modern culture will do the magic trick of reversing these problems. This is exactly what 're-branding' exercises such as New Labour's Cool Britannia project promise. Keiller's films cannot but help make us sceptical of such promises.

NOTES

I would like to thank Justine Ashby, Andrew Higson, Patrick Keiller, Maria Kilcoyne, Mike O'Pray and Julia Monk for the help they have given me in writing this chapter.

1 A.L. Rees, *A History of Experimental Film and Video*, London, BFI, 1999, p. 119.
2 P. Keiller, *Robinson in Space*, London, Reaktion Books, 1999.
3 A. Kossoff, 'A metaphysical mirror', *Vertigo*, Winter 1994/5, p. 46.
4 Although there have been exceptions, for example Mike Phillips calling *London* 'pretentious crap'. M. Phillips, 'No time for contradiction', *Vertigo*, Winter 1994/5, p. 45.
5 N. Norman, '*Robinson in Space*', *Evening Standard*, 9 January 1997, p. 27.
6 N. Andrews, *Financial Times*, 9 January 1997, p. 21 (title of article missing from *Robinson in Space* microfiche, British Film Institute Library).
7 J. Romney, 'Music for unknown ears', *New Statesman and Society*, 17 June 1994, p. 33.
8 G. Andrew, '*Robinson in Space*', *Time Out*, 8–15 January 1997, p. 69.
9 J. Romney, '*Robinson in Space*', *Guardian*, Section 2, 11 January 1997, p. 7.
10 J. Romney, '*Beyond the Clouds*; *Robinson in Space*', *New Statesman and Society*, 10 January, 1997, p. 40.
11 See J. Hill, *British Cinema in the 1980s*, Oxford, Oxford University Press, 1999, pp. 73–98.
12 See A. Higson, 'Re-presenting the national past: nostalgia and pastiche in the heritage film', in L. Friedman (ed.) *British Cinema and Thatcherism: Fires Were Started*, London, UCL Press, 1993, pp. 109–29.
13 See R. Samuel, *Theatres of Memory*, London, Verso, 1994, pp. 264–5.
14 W.D. Rubinstein, *Capitalism, Culture and Decline in Britain: 1750–1990*, London, Routledge, 1993.
15 Ibid., pp. 1–3.

16 Martin J. Wiener, *English Culture and the Decline of the Industrial Spirit 1850–1980*, Harmondsworth, Pelican, 1987, p. 154.
17 P. Anderson, *English Questions*, London, Verso, 1992, p. 17.
18 Keiller, op. cit., p. 225.
19 Ibid., p. 223.
20 E. Wood, *The Pristine Culture of Capitalism: A Historical Essay in Old Regimes and Modern States*, London, Verso, 1991, p. 3.
21 Ibid., pp. 2–11.
22 E. Wood, 'Modernity, postmodernity, or capitalism?', *Monthly Review*, July/August 1996, p. 33.
23 Ibid., p. 33.
24 See Wiener, op. cit., p. 42.
25 Keiller, op. cit., p. 14.
26 Ibid., p. 211.
27 Ibid.
28 E. Wood, *The Origin of Capitalism*, New York, Monthly Review Press, 1999, pp. 80–92.
29 Keiller, op. cit., p. 228.
30 Wiener, op. cit., p. 52.
31 Wood, *The Pristine Culture*, op. cit., pp. 36–38.
32 Higson, op. cit., p. 119.
33 Keiller interviewed by A. Price, *Artifice 1*, 1994, p. 32.
34 Hill, op. cit., p. 81.
35 Higson, op. cit., p. 117.
36 Hill, op. cit., pp. 77–8.
37 E. Wood, *Democracy Against Capitalism: Renewing Historical Materialism*, Cambridge, Cambridge University Press, 1995, pp. 76–107.
38 Wood, *The Pristine Culture*, op. cit., p. 38.
39 C. Barker, 'Reflections on two books by Ellen Wood', *Historical Materialism*, Autumn 1997, no. 1, p. 46.
40 Keiller, op. cit., p. 211.
41 Ibid.

SELECT BIBLIOGRAPHY

British cinema 1930–2000

Compiled by Jane Bryan

Contents

Reference/source books

The British Film Institute (BFI), *BFI Film and Television Handbook*, London, BFI (annual, from 1983).

The British Film and Video Council, *The Researcher's Guide to British Film and TV Collections*, London, British Film and Video Council, 1997.

Burrows, E., Moat, J., Sharp, D. and Wood, L., *The British Cinema Source Book: BFI Archive Viewing Copies and Library Materials*, London, BFI, 1995.

Burton, A. (ed.) *The British Co-operative Movement Film Catalogue*, Trowbridge, Flicks Books, 1997.

Caughie, J., with Rockett, K., *The Companion to British and Irish Cinema*, London, Cassell, 1996.

Gifford, D., *The British Film Catalogue, 1895–1970: A Guide to Entertainment Films*, Newton Abbott, David and Charles, 1973.

—— *The Illustrated Who's Who in British Films*, London, B.T. Batsford, 1978.

Palmer, S., *A Who's Who of British Film Actors*, Metuchen, N.J./London, The Scarecrow Press, 1981.

—— *British Film Actors' Credits, 1895–1987*, Jefferson, N.C./London, McFarland and Co., 1988.

Quinlan, D., *British Sound Films: The Studio Years, 1928–1959*, London, B.T. Batsford, 1984.

General histories of British cinema and film culture

Aldgate, A. and Richards, J., *Best of British: Cinema and Society from 1930 to the Present*, London, I.B. Tauris, 1999 (revised edition).

Armes, R., *A Critical History of British Cinema*, London, Secker and Warburg, 1978.

Barr, C. (ed.) *All Our Yesterdays: 90 Years of British Cinema*, London, BFI, 1986.

Betts, C., *The Film Business: A History of British Cinema, 1896–1972*, London, Allen and Unwin, 1973.

Curran, J. and Porter, V. (eds) *British Cinema History*, London, Weidenfeld and Nicholson, 1983.

Dick, E. (ed.) *From Limelight to Satellite: A Scottish Film Book*, London, BFI/Scottish Film Council, 1990.

Dixon, W.W., *Re-Viewing British Cinema, 1900–1992: Essays and Interviews*, New York, State University of New York Press, 1994.

Higson, A., *Waving the Flag: Constructing a National Cinema in Britain*, Oxford, Clarendon Press, 1995.

—— (ed.) *Dissolving Views: Key Writings on British Cinema*, London, Cassell, 1996.

—— 'British cinema', in J. Hill and P. Church-Gibson (eds) *The Oxford Guide to Film Studies*, Oxford, Oxford University Press, 1998, pp. 501–9.

Landy, M., *British Genres: Cinema and Society 1930–1960*, Princeton, N.J./Oxford, Princeton University Press, 1991.

Murphy, R. (ed.) *The British Cinema Book*, London, BFI, 1997.

Richards, J., *Films and British National Identity: From Dickens to Dad's Army*, Manchester, Manchester University Press, 1997.

Rockett, K., Gibbons, L. and Hill, J., *Cinema and Ireland*, London, Croom Helm, 1987.

Street, S., *British National Cinema*, London, Routledge, 1997.

British cinema in the 1930s and 1940s

Aldgate, A. and Richards, J., *Britain Can Take It: The British Cinema in the Second World War*, Edinburgh, Edinburgh University Press, 1994 (2nd edition).

Aspinall, S. and Murphy, R. (eds) *BFI Dossier 18: Gainsborough Melodrama*, London, BFI, 1983.

Chapman, J., *The British at War: Cinema, State and Propaganda, 1939–1945*, London, I.B. Tauris, 1998.

Coultass, C., *Images for Battle: British Film and the Second World War, 1939–1945*, London, Associated University Presses, 1989.

Drazin, C., *The Finest Years: British Cinema of the 1940s*, London, Andre Deutsch, 1998.

Dyer, R., *Brief Encounter*, London, BFI, 1993.

Ellis, J., 'The quality film adventure: British critics and the cinema, 1942–1948', in A. Higson (ed.) *Dissolving Views: Key Writings on British Cinema*, London, Cassell, 1996, pp. 66–93.

Gledhill, C. and Swanson, G. (eds) *Nationalising Femininity: Culture, Sexuality and British Cinema in the Second World War*, Manchester, Manchester University Press, 1996.

Higson, A., *Waving the Flag: Constructing a National Cinema in Britain*, Oxford, Clarendon Press, 1995.

Hogenkamp, B., *Deadly Parallels: Film and the Left in Britain, 1929–1939*, London, Lawrence and Wishart, 1986.

Houston, P., *Went the Day Well?*, London, BFI, 1992.

Hurd, G. (ed.) *National Fictions: World War Two in British Films and Television*, London, BFI, 1984.

Kennedy, A.L., *The Life and Death of Colonel Blimp*, London, BFI, 1997.

Landy, M., *British Genres: Cinema and Society, 1930–1960*, Princeton, N.J./Oxford, Princeton University Press, 1991.

—— 'Melodrama and femininity in World War Two British cinema', in R. Murphy (ed.) *The British Cinema Book*, London, BFI, 1997, pp. 79–89.

Lant, A., *Blackout: Reinventing Women for Wartime British Cinema*, Princeton, N.J./Oxford, Princeton University Press, 1991.

Low, R., *The History of the British Film, 1929–1939: Documentary and Educational Films of the 1930s*, London, Allen and Unwin/BFI, 1979; London, Routledge, 1997.

—— *The History of the British Film, 1929–1939: Films of Comment and Persuasion of the 1930s*, London, Allen and Unwin/BFI, 1979; London, Routledge, 1997.

—— *Film-Making in 1930s Britain*, London, Allen and Unwin/BFI, 1985; London, Routledge, 1997.

Macpherson, D. (ed.) *Traditions of Independence: British Cinema in the Thirties*, London, BFI, 1980.

Murphy, R., *Realism and Tinsel: Cinema and Society in Britain, 1939–49*, London, Routledge, 1989.

Napper, L., 'A despicable tradition? Quota quickies in the 1930s', in R. Murphy (ed.) *The British Cinema Book*, London, BFI, 1997, pp. 37–47.

Richards, J., *The Age of the Dream Palace: Cinema and Society in Britain, 1930–1939*, London, Routledge and Kegan Paul, 1984.

—— '"Patriotism with profit": British imperial cinema in the 1930s', in J. Curran and V. Porter (eds) *British Cinema History*, London, Weidenfeld and Nicholson, 1983, pp. 245–56.

—— (ed.) *The Unknown 1930s: An Alternative History of the British Cinema, 1929–1939*, London, I.B. Tauris, 1998.

Richards, J. and Sheridan, D. (eds) *Mass-Observation at the Movies*, London, Routledge and Kegan Paul, 1987.

Ryall, T., *Blackmail*, London, BFI, 1993.

Shafer, S.C., *British Popular Films, 1929–1939: The Cinema of Reassurance*, London, Routledge, 1997.

Street, S., 'British film and the national interest, 1927–1939', in R. Murphy (ed.) *The British Cinema Book*, London, BFI, 1997, pp. 17–26.

Taylor, P.M. (ed.) *Britain and the Cinema in the Second World War*, London, Macmillan, 1988.

Vaughan, D., *Odd Man Out*, London, BFI, 1995.

Wood, L., 'Low-budget British films in the 1930s', in R. Murphy (ed.) *The British Cinema Book*, London, BFI, 1997, pp. 48–57.

British cinema in the 1950s, 1960s and 1970s

Aldgate, A., *Censorship and the Permissive Society: British Cinema and Theatre 1955–1965*, Oxford, Clarendon Press, 1995.

Cook, P., '*Mandy*: daughter of transition', in C. Barr (ed.) *All Our Yesterdays: 90 Years of British Cinema*, London, BFI, 1986, pp. 355–61.

Durgnat, R., *A Mirror for England: British Movies from Austerity to Affluence*, London, Faber and Faber, 1970.

Geraghty, C., 'Women and sixties British cinema: the development of the "Darling" girl', in R. Murphy (ed.) *The British Cinema Book*, London, BFI, 1997, pp. 155–63.

Harper, S., 'Bonnie Prince Charlie revisited: British costume film in the 1950s', in R. Murphy (ed.) *The British Cinema Book*, London, BFI, 1997, pp. 133–43.

Harper, S. and Porter, V., 'Cinema audience tastes in 1950s Britain', *Journal of Popular British Cinema*, 1999, no. 2, pp. 66–82.

Higson, A., 'A diversity of film practices: renewing British cinema in the 1970s', in B. Moore-Gilbert (ed.) *Catastrophe Culture? The Challenge of the Arts in the 1970s*, London, Routledge, 1994, pp. 216–39.

—— 'Space, place, spectacle: landscape and townscape in the "kitchen sink" film', in A. Higson (ed.) *Dissolving Views: Key Writings on British Cinema*, London, Cassell, 1996, pp. 133–56.

Hill, J., 'Working class realism and sexual reaction: some theses on the British "New Wave"', in J. Curran and V. Porter (eds) *British Cinema History*, London, Weidenfeld and Nicholson, 1983, pp. 303–11.

—— *Sex, Class and Realism: British Cinema 1956–1963*, London, BFI, 1986.

Hunt, L., *British Low Culture: From Safari Suits to Sexploitations*, London, Routledge, 1998.

Hutchings, P., *Hammer and Beyond: The British Horror Film*, Manchester, Manchester University Press, 1994.

Jordan, M., 'Carry On … follow that stereotype', in J. Curran and V. Porter (eds) *British Cinema History*, London, Weidenfeld and Nicholson, 1983, pp. 312–27.

Landy, M., *British Genres: Cinema and Society, 1930–1960*, Princeton, N.J./Oxford, Princeton University Press, 1991.

Lovell, T., 'Landscapes and stories in 1960s British realism', in A. Higson (ed.) *Dissolving Views: Key Writings on British Cinema*, London, Cassell, 1996, pp. 157–77.

MacCabe, C., *Performance*, London, BFI, 1998.

Murphy, R., *Sixties British Cinema*, London, BFI, 1992.

Rattigan, N., 'The last gasp of the middle class: British wartime films of the 1950s', in W.W. Dixon (ed.) *Re-Viewing British Cinema, 1900–1992: Essays and Interviews*, New York, State University of New York Press, 1994, pp. 143–54.

Tarr, C., '*Sapphire, Darling* and the boundaries of permitted pleasure', *Screen*, 1985, vol. 26, no.1, pp. 60–5.

Walker, A., *Hollywood England: The British Film Industry in the Sixties*, London, Harrap, 1986.

British cinema in the 1980s and 1990s

Auty, M. and Roddick, N. (eds) *British Cinema Now*, London, BFI, 1985.

Bersani, L. and Dutoit, U., *Caravaggio*, London, BFI, 1999.

British Film Institute (BFI), *BFI Film and Television Handbook*, London, BFI (annual, from 1983).

Finney, A., *The Egos Have Landed: The Rise and Fall of Palace Pictures*, London, Heinemann, 1996.

Friedman, L. (ed.) *British Cinema and Thatcherism: Fires Were Started*, London, UCL Press, 1993.

Giles, J., *The Crying Game*, London, BFI, 1997.

Hill, J., *British Cinema in the 1980s: Issues and Themes*, Oxford, Clarendon Press, 1999.

Hill, J. and McLoone, M. (eds) *Big Picture, Small Screen: The Relations Between Film and Television*, Luton, University of Luton Press/John Libbey Media, 1996.

Hill, J., McLoone, M. and Hainsworth, P. (eds) *Border Crossing: Film in Ireland, Britain and Europe*, Belfast, IIS/BFI, 1994.

Malik, S., 'Beyond "the cinema of duty"? The pleasures of hybridity: Black British film of the 1980s and 1990s', in A. Higson (ed.) *Dissolving Views: Key Writings on British Cinema*, London, Cassell, 1996, pp. 202–15.

Monk, C., 'Heritage films and the British cinema audience in the 1990s', *Journal of Popular British Cinema*, 1999, no. 2, pp. 22–38.

Murphy, R. (ed.) *British Cinema of the 90s*, London, BFI, 2000.

Park, J., *Learning to Dream: The New British Cinema*, London, Faber and Faber, 1984.

Petrie, D., *Creativity and Constraint: Contemporary British Cinema*, London, Macmillan, 1990.

—— (ed.) *New Questions of British Cinema*, London, BFI, 1992.

Quart, L., 'The politics of irony: the Frears-Kureishi films', in W.W. Dixon (ed.) *Re-Viewing British Cinema, 1900–1992: Essays and Interviews*, New York, State University of New York Press, 1994, pp. 241–8.

Street, S., *British National Cinema*, London, Routledge, 1997.

Walker, A., *National Heroes: British Cinema in the Seventies and Eighties*, London, Harrap, 1985.

Walker, J., *The Once and Future Film: British Cinema in the Seventies and Eighties*, London, Methuen, 1985.

Williamson, J., *Deadline at Dawn*, London, Marion Boyars, 1993.

Wood, R., *The Wings of the Dove*, London, BFI, 1999.

Film-makers and production workers

Atkins, T.R. (ed.) *Ken Russell*, New York, Monarch Press, 1976.

Balcon, M., *Michael Balcon Presents ... A Lifetime of Films*, London, Hutchinson, 1969.

Barr, C., 'Desperate yearnings: Victor Saville and Gainsborough', in P. Cook (ed.) *Gainsborough Pictures*, London, Cassell, 1997, pp. 47–59.

—— *English Hitchcock*, Moffat, Cameron and Hollis, 1999.

Bergfelder, T., 'The production designer and the *Gesamtkunstwerk*: German film technicians in the British film industry of the 1930s', in A. Higson (ed.) *Dissolving Views: Key Writings on British Cinema*, London, Cassell, 1996, pp. 20–37.

Box, M., *Odd Woman Out*, London, Leslie Frewin, 1974.

Brown, G., *Launder and Gilliat*, London, BFI, 1977.

Brown, G. and Kardish, L., *Michael Balcon: The Pursuit of British Cinema*, New York, Museum of Modern Art, 1984.

Brownlow, K., *David Lean*, London, Richard Cohen Books, 1996.

Burton, A., O'Sullivan, T. and Wells, P. (eds) *Liberal Directions: Basil Dearden and Postwar British Film Culture*, Trowbridge, Flicks Books, 1997.

Burton, A., O'Sullivan, T. and Wells, P. (eds) *The Family Way: The Boulting Brothers and British Film Culture*, Trowbridge, Flicks Books, 1999.

Christie, I., *Powell, Pressburger and Others*, London, BFI, 1978.

—— *Arrows of Desire: The Films of Michael Powell and Emeric Pressburger*, London, Waterstone, 1985; London, Faber and Faber, 1994.

Coveney, M., *The World According to Mike Leigh*, London, Harper Collins, 1996.

Dick, E., Noble, A. and Petrie, D. (eds) *Bill Douglas: A Lanternist's Account*, London, BFI, 1993.

Dixon, W.W., *The Charming Evil: The Life and Films of Terence Fisher*, Metuchen, N.J./London, The Scarecrow Press, 1991.

—— *The Films of Freddie Francis*, Metuchen N.J./London, The Scarecrow Press, 1991.

—— 'An interview with Wendy Toye', in W.W. Dixon (ed.) *Re-Viewing British Cinema, 1900–1992: Essays and Interviews*, New York, State University of New York Press, 1994, pp. 133–42.

Elliott, B. and Purdy, A., *Peter Greenaway: Architecture and Allegory*, London, Academy Editions, 1997.

Friedman, L., and Stewart, S., 'Keeping his own voice: an interview with Stephen Frears', in W.W. Dixon (ed.) *Re-Viewing British Cinema, 1900–1992: Essays and Interviews*, New York, State University of New York Press, 1994, pp. 221–40.

Gottlieb, S., *Hitchcock on Hitchcock: Selected Writings and Interviews*, London, Faber and Faber, 1995.

Gough-Yates, K., *Michael Powell in Collaboration with Emeric Pressburger*, London, BFI, 1971.

—— 'Berthold Viertel at Gaumont-British', in J. Richards (ed.) *The Unknown 1930s: An Alternative History of the British Cinema, 1929–1939*, London, I.B. Tauris, 1998, pp. 201–17.

Grant, B.K., 'The body politic: Ken Russell in the 1980s', in L. Friedman (ed.) *British Cinema and Thatcherism: Fires Were Started*, London, UCL Press, 1993, pp. 188–203.

Hacker, J. and Price, D., *Take Ten: Contemporary British Film Directors*, Oxford, Clarendon Press, 1991.

Hanke, K., *Ken Russell's Films*, Metuchen, N.J./London, The Scarecrow Press, 1984.

Hedling, E., 'Lindsay Anderson and the development of British art cinema', in R. Murphy (ed.) *The British Cinema Book*, London, BFI, 1997, pp. 178–86.

—— *Lindsay Anderson: Maverick Film-maker*, London, Cassell, 1998.

Hill, J., '"Every fuckin' choice stinks": Ken Loach', *Sight and Sound*, November 1998, vol. 8, no. 11, pp. 18–21.

Jennings, M., *Humphrey Jennings: Film-maker, Painter, Poet*, London, BFI in association with Riverside Studios, 1982.

Johnson, L. (ed.) *Talking Pictures: Interviews with Contemporary British Film-makers*, London, BFI, 1997.

Kemp, P., *Lethal Innocence: The Cinema of Alexander Mackendrick*, London, Methuen, 1991.

Kulik, K., *Alexander Korda*, London, W.H. Allen, 1975.

Lawrence, A., *The Films of Peter Greenaway*, Cambridge, Cambridge University Press, 1997.

Leach, J., '"Everyone's an American now": Thatcherist ideology in the films of Nicholas Roeg', in L. Friedman (ed.) *British Cinema and Thatcherism: Fires Were Started*, London, UCL Press, 1993, pp. 204–20.

Lippard C. (ed.) *By Angels Driven: The Films of Derek Jarman*, Trowbridge, Flicks Books, 1996.

Lippard C. and Johnson, G., 'Private practice, public health: the politics of sickness and the films of Derek Jarman', in L. Friedman (ed.) *British Cinema and Thatcherism: Fires Were Started*, London, UCL Press, 1993, pp. 278–93.

Loach, K., *Loach on Loach*, London, Faber and Faber, 1998.

Macdonald, K., *Emeric Pressburger: The Life and Death of a Screenwriter*, London, Faber and Faber, 1994.

McFarlane, B. (ed.) *Sixty Voices: Celebrities Recall the Golden Age of British Cinema*, London, BFI, 1992.

—— 'Lance Comfort, Lawrence Huntington, and the British program feature film', in W.W. Dixon (ed.) *Re-Viewing British Cinema, 1900–1992: Essays and Interviews*, New York, State University of New York Press, 1994, pp. 53–66.

—— *An Autobiography of British Cinema by the Actors and Filmmakers Who Made It*, London, Methuen, 1997.

—— 'Jack of all trades: Robert Stephenson', in J. Richards (ed.) *The Unknown 1930s: An Alternative History of the British Cinema*, London, I.B. Tauris, 1998, pp. 161–79.

McIlroy, B., 'British filmmaking in the 1930s and 1940s: the example of Brian Desmond Hurst', in W.W. Dixon (ed.) *Re-Viewing British Cinema, 1900–1992: Essays and Interviews*, New York, State University of New York Press, 1994, pp. 25–40.

McKnight, G. (ed.) *Agent of Challenge and Defiance: The Films of Ken Loach*, Trowbridge, Flicks Books, 1997.

Merz, C., 'The tension of genre: Wendy Toye and Muriel Box', in W.W. Dixon (ed.) *Re-Viewing British Cinema, 1900–1992: Essays and Interviews*, New York, State University of New York Press, 1994, pp. 121–31.

Minney, R.J., *The Films of Anthony Asquith*, South Brunswick, A.S. Barnes, 1976.

Nowell-Smith, G., 'Humphrey Jennings: surrealist observer', in C. Barr (ed.) *All Our Yesterdays: 90 Years of British Cinema*, London, BFI, 1986, pp. 321–33.

O'Pray, M., *Derek Jarman: Dreams of England*, London, BFI, 1996.

Pascoe, D., *Peter Greenaway: Museums and Moving Images*, London, Reaktion Books, 1997.

Petrie, D., *The British Cinematographer*, London, BFI, 1996.

—— (ed.) *Inside Stories: Diaries of British Filmmakers at Work*, London, BFI, 1996.

Phillips, G.D., *Ken Russell*, Boston, Twayne Publishers, 1979.

Richards, J., *Thorold Dickinson and the British Cinema*, Lanham M.D./London, The Scarecrow Press, 1997.

Ryall, T., *Alfred Hitchcock and the British Cinema*, London, Croom Helm, 1986; London, Athlone, 1996.

Silver, A. and Ursini, J., *David Lean and his Films*, London, Leslie Frewin, 1974.

Sussex, E., *Lindsay Anderson*, London, Studio Vista, 1969.

Truffaut, F., *Hitchcock*, London, Secker and Warburg, 1968.

Vaughan, D., *Portrait of an Invisible Man: The Working Life of Stewart McAllister, Film Editor*, London, BFI, 1983.

Walsh, M., 'Allegories of Thatcherism: the films of Peter Greenaway', in L. Friedman (ed.) *British Cinema and Thatcherism: Fires Were Started*, London, UCL Press, 1993, pp. 255–77.

Williams, T., 'The masochistic fix: gender oppression in the films of Terence Davies', in L. Friedman (ed.) *British Cinema and Thatcherism: Fires Were Started*, London, UCL Press, 1993, pp. 237–54.

Wood, R., *Hitchcock's Films Revisited*, London, Faber and Faber, 1989.

Yacowar, M., *Hitchcock's British Films*, Hamden, Connecticut, Archon, 1977.

Yule, A., *Enigma: David Puttnam, the Story So Far*, London, Sphere Books, 1989.

Stars and other actors

Geraghty, C., 'Diana Dors', in C. Barr (ed.) *All Our Yesterdays: 90 Years of British Cinema*, London, BFI, 1986, pp. 341–5.

—— 'Albert Finney: a working-class hero', in P. Kirkham and J. Thumin (eds) *Me Jane: Masculinity, Movies and Women*, London, Lawrence and Wishart, 1995, pp. 62–72.

—— 'Women and sixties British cinema: the development of the "Darling" girl', in R. Murphy (ed.) *The British Cinema Book*, London, BFI, 1997, pp. 155–63.

Lockwood, M., *Lucky Star*, London, Odhams, 1955.

McFarlane, B. (ed.) *Sixty Voices: Celebrities Recall the Golden Age of British Cinema*, London, BFI, 1992.

—— *An Autobiography of British Cinema, by the Actors and Filmmakers Who Made It*, London, Methuen, 1997.

Macnab, G., *Searching for Stars: Stardom and Screen Acting in British Cinema*, London, Cassell, 1999.

Mason, J., *Before I Forget*, London, Hamilton, 1981.

Medhurst, A., 'Can chaps be pin-ups? The British male film star in the 1950s', *Ten-8*, February 1985, no. 17, pp. 3–8.

—— 'Dirk Bogarde', in C. Barr (ed.) *All Our Yesterdays: 90 Years of British Cinema*, London, BFI, 1986, pp. 346–54.

Morley, S., *Odd Man Out: James Mason*, London, Weidenfeld and Nicholson, 1989.

O'Pray, M., 'A body of political work: Tilda Swinton in interview', in P. Cook and P. Dodd (eds) *Women and Film: A Sight and Sound Reader*, London, Scarlett Press, 1993.

Petley, J., 'Reaching for the stars', in M. Auty and N. Roddick (eds) *British Cinema Now*, London, BFI, 1985, pp. 111–22.

Richards, J., *The Age of the Dream Palace: Cinema and Society in Britain, 1930–1939*, London, Routledge and Kegan Paul, 1984.

Sedgwick, J., 'The comparative popularity of stars in mid-30s Britain', *Journal of Popular British Cinema*, 1999, no. 2, pp. 121–7.

Spicer, A., 'Male stars, masculinity and British cinema, 1945–1960', in R. Murphy (ed.) *The British Cinema Book*, London, BFI, 1997, pp. 144–53.

Walker, A., 'Random thoughts on the Englishness (or otherwise) of English film actors', in A. Walker, *'It's Only a Movie, Ingrid'*, London, Headline, 1988, pp. 207–81.

Mainstream genres

Aldgate, T., 'Comedy, class and containment: the British domestic cinema of the 1930s', J. Curran and V. Porter (eds) *British Cinema History*, London, Weidenfeld and Nicholson, 1983, pp. 257–71.

—— 'Loose ends, hidden gems and the moment of "melodramatic emotionality"', in J. Richards (ed.) *The Unknown 1930s: An Alternative History of the British Cinema, 1929–1939*, London, I.B. Tauris, 1998, pp. 219–36.

Aspinall, S. and Murphy, R. (eds) *BFI Dossier 18: Gainsborough Melodrama*, London, BFI, 1983.

Brown, G., 'Paradise found and lost: the course of British realism', in R. Murphy (ed.) *The British Cinema Book*, London, BFI, 1997, pp. 187–97.

Burton, A. and Petley, J. (eds) *Journal of Popular British Cinema* (special issue on 'Genre and British cinema'), 1998, no. 1.

Chapman, J., 'Celluloid shockers', in J. Richards (ed.) *The Unknown 1930s: An Alternative History of the British Cinema, 1929–1939*, London, I.B. Tauris, 1998, pp. 75–97.

—— *Licensed to Thrill: A Cultural History of the James Bond Films*, London, I.B. Tauris, 1999.

Chibnall, S. and Murphy, R. (eds) *British Crime Cinema*, London, Routledge, 1999.

Conrich, I., 'Traditions of the British horror film', in R. Murphy (ed.) *The British Cinema Book*, London, BFI, 1997, pp. 226–34.

Cook, P., 'Neither here nor there: national identity in Gainsborough costume drama', in A. Higson (ed.) *Dissolving Views: Key Writings on British Cinema*, London, Cassell, 1996, pp. 51–65.

—— (ed.) *Gainsborough Pictures*, London, Cassell, 1997.

Dacre, R., 'Traditions of British comedy', in R. Murphy (ed.) *The British Cinema Book*, London, BFI, 1997, pp. 198–206.

Dave, P., 'The bourgeois paradigm and heritage cinema', *New Left Review*, July–August 1997, no. 224, pp. 111–26.

Durgnat, R., 'Some lines of inquiry into post-war British crimes', in R. Murphy (ed.) *The British Cinema Book*, London, BFI, 1997, pp. 90–103.

Gray, F., 'Certain liberties have been taken with Cleopatra: female performance in the *Carry On* films', in S. Wagg (ed.) *Because I Tell a Joke or Two*, London, Routledge, 1998, pp. 94–110.

Green, I., 'Ealing: in the comedy frame', in J. Curran and V. Porter (eds) *British Cinema History*, London, Weidenfeld and Nicholson, 1983, pp. 294–302.

Guy, S., 'Calling all stars: musical films in a musical decade', in J. Richards (ed.) *The Unknown 1930s: An Alternative History of the British Cinema, 1929–1939*, London, I.B. Tauris, 1998, pp. 99–118.

Harper, S., 'Historical pleasures: Gainsborough costume melodrama', in C. Gledhill (ed.) *Home is Where the Heart is: Studies in Melodrama and the Woman's Film*, London, BFI, 1987.

—— *Picturing the Past: The Rise and Fall of the British Costume Film*, London, BFI, 1994.

—— 'Bonnie Prince Charlie revisited: British costume film in the 1950s', in R. Murphy (ed.) *The British Cinema Book*, London, BFI, 1997, pp. 133–43.

Higson, A., '"Britain's outstanding contribution to the film": the documentary-realist tradition', in C. Barr (ed.) *All Our Yesterdays: 90 Years of British Cinema*, London, BFI, 1986, pp. 72–97.

—— 'Re-presenting the national past: nostalgia and pastiche in the heritage film', in L. Friedman (ed.) *British Cinema and Thatcherism: Fires Were Started*, London, UCL Press, 1993, pp. 109–29.

—— 'The heritage film and British cinema', in A. Higson (ed.) *Dissolving Views: Key Writings on British Cinema*, London, Cassell, 1996, pp. 232–48.

Hutchings, P., *Hammer and Beyond*, Manchester, Manchester University Press, 1993.

Jordan, M., 'Carry On … follow that stereotype', in J. Curran and V. Porter (eds) *British Cinema History*, London, Weidenfeld and Nicholson, 1983, pp. 312–27.

Landy, M., *British Genres: Cinema and Society, 1930–1960*, Princeton, N.J./Oxford, Princeton University Press, 1991.

Medhurst, A., 'Music hall and British cinema', in C. Barr (ed.) *All Our Yesterdays: 90 Years of British Cinema*, London, BFI, 1986, pp. 168–88.

—— 'Carry on camp', *Sight and Sound*, August 1992, vol. 2, no. 4, pp. 16–19.

Miller, L., 'Evidence for a British film noir cycle', in W.W. Dixon (ed.) *Re-Viewing British Cinema, 1900–1992: Essays and Interviews*, New York, State University of New York Press, 1994, pp. 155–64.

Monk, C., 'Heritage films and the British cinema audience in the 1990s', *Journal of Popular British Cinema*, 1999, no. 2, pp. 22–38.

Murphy, R., 'Riff-raff: British cinema and the underworld', in C. Barr (ed.) *All Our Yesterdays: 90 Years of British Cinema*, London, BFI, 1986, pp. 286–305.

Pirie, D., *A Heritage of Horror: The English Gothic Cinema, 1946–72*, London, Gordon Fraser, 1973.

Ross, R., *The Carry On Companion*, London, B.T. Batsford, 1996.

Sanjek, D., 'Twilight of the monsters: the English horror film 1968–1975', in W.W. Dixon (ed.) *Re-Viewing British Cinema, 1900–1992: Essays and Interviews*, New York, State University of New York Press, 1994, pp. 195–209.

Williams, C., 'The social art cinema: a moment in the history of British film and television culture', in C. Williams (ed.) *Cinema: The Beginnings and the Future*, London, University of Westminster Press, 1996, pp. 190–200.

Wollen, T., 'Over our shoulders: nostalgic screen fictions for the eighties', in J. Corner and S. Harvey (eds) *Enterprise and Heritage: Crosscurrents of National Culture*, London, Routledge, 1991, pp. 178–93.

Documentary and non-fiction film

Aitken, I., *Film and Reform: John Grierson and the Documentary Film Movement*, London, Routledge, 1990.

Aldgate, A., *Cinema and History: British Newsreels and the Spanish Civil War*, London, Scolar Press, 1979.

Ballantyne, J. (ed.) *Researcher's Guide to British Newsreels*, London, British Universities' Film and Video Council, 1983; also vol. 2, 1988 and vol. 3, 1993.

Brown, G., 'Paradise found and lost: the course of British realism', in R. Murphy (ed.) *The British Cinema Book*, London, BFI, 1997, pp. 187–97.

Dodd, K. and Dodd, P., 'Engendering the nation: British documentary film, 1930–1939', in A. Higson (ed.) *Dissolving Views: Key Writings on British Cinema*, London, Cassell, 1996, pp. 38–50.

Hardy, F. (ed.) *Grierson on Documentary*, London, Faber and Faber, 1966.

—— (ed.) *Grierson on the Movies*, London, Faber and Faber, 1981.

Higson, A., ' "Britain's outstanding contribution to the film": the documentary-realist tradition', in C. Barr (ed.) *All Our Yesterdays: 90 Years of British Cinema*, London, BFI, 1986, pp. 72–97.

Hood, S., 'John Grierson and the documentary film movement', in J. Curran and V. Porter (eds) *British Cinema History*, London, Weidenfeld and Nicholson, 1983, pp. 99–112.

Jones, S., *The British Labour Movement and Film, 1918–1939*, London, Routledge and Kegan Paul, 1987.

Lovell, A. and Hillier, J., *Studies in Documentary*, London, Secker and Warburg/BFI, 1972.

Low, R., *The History of the British Film: Documentary and Educational Films of the 1930s*, Allen and Unwin/BFI, 1979; London, Routledge, 1997.

McKernan, L., *Topical Budget: The Great British News Film*, London, BFI, 1992.

Sussex, E. (ed.) *The Rise and Fall of British Documentary*, Berkeley, University of California Press, 1975.

Swann, P., *The British Documentary Film Movement 1926–1946*, Cambridge, Cambridge University Press, 1989.

Avant-garde cinema, art cinema and independent cinema

Blanchard, S. and Harvey, S., 'The post-war independent cinema – structure and organisation', in J. Curran and V. Porter (eds) *British Cinema History*, London, Weidenfeld and Nicholson, 1983, pp. 226–41.

Curtiss, D. and Dusinberre, D. (eds) *A Perspective on English Avant-Garde Film*, London, Arts Council, 1978.

Dickinson, M., *Rogue Reels: Oppositional Film in Britain 1945–90*, London, BFI, 1999.

Friedman, L. and Stewart, S., 'The tradition of independence: an interview with Lindsay Anderson', in W.W. Dixon (ed.) *Re-Viewing British Cinema, 1900–1992: Essays and Interviews*, New York, State University of New York Press, 1994, pp. 165–76.

Harvey, S., 'The "other" cinema in Britain: unfinished business in oppositional and independent film, 1929–1984', in C. Barr (ed.) *All Our Yesterdays: 90 Years of British Cinema*, London, BFI, 1986, pp. 225–51.

Hedling, E., 'Lindsay Anderson and the development of British art cinema', in R. Murphy (ed.) *The British Cinema Book*, London, BFI, 1997, pp. 178–86.

Hunt, M., 'The poetry of the ordinary: Terence Davies and the social art cinema', *Screen*, Spring 1999, vol. 40, no. 1, pp. 1–16.

Lant, A., 'Women's independent cinema: the case of Leeds Animation Workshop', in Friedman, L. (ed.) *British Cinema and Thatcherism: Fires Were Started*, London, UCL Press, 1993, pp. 161–87.

O'Pray, M. (ed.) *The British Avant-Garde Film, 1926–1995: An Anthology of Writings*, Luton, University of Luton Press/The Arts Council of England, 1996.

—— 'The British avant-garde and art cinema from the 1970s to the 1990s', in A. Higson (ed.) *Dissolving Views: Key Writings on British Cinema*, London, Cassell, 1996, pp. 178–90.

Rees, A.L., *A History of Experimental Film and Video*, London, BFI, 1999.

Whitaker, S., 'Declarations of independence', in M. Auty and N. Roddick (eds) *British Cinema Now*, London, BFI, 1985, pp. 83–98.

Wollen, P., 'The last New Wave: modernism in the British films of the Thatcher era', in L. Friedman (ed.) *British Cinema and Thatcherism: Fires Were Started*, London, UCL Press, 1993, pp. 35–51.

Representation and identity

Aspinall, S., 'Women, realism and reality in British films, 1943–53', in J. Curran and V. Porter (eds) *British Cinema History*, London, Weidenfeld and Nicholson, 1983, pp. 272–93.

Barber, S.T., 'Insurmountable difficulties and moments of ecstasy: crossing class, ethnic, and sexual barriers in the films of Stephen Frears', in L. Friedman (ed.) *British Cinema and Thatcherism: Fires Were Started*, London, UCL Press, 1993, pp. 221–36.

Barr, C., 'Broadcasting and cinema: 2: screens within screens', in C. Barr (ed.) *All Our Yesterdays: 90 Years of British Cinema*, London, BFI, 1986, pp. 206–24.

Berry, D., *Wales and Cinema: The First Hundred Years*, Cardiff, University of Wales Press in co-operation with the Wales Film Council and the BFI, 1994.

Bourne, S., *Brief Encounters: Lesbians and Gays in British Cinema, 1930–1977*, London, Cassell, 1996.

—— *Black in the British Frame: Black People in British Film and Television, 1896–1996*, London, Cassell, 1998.

Bruce, D., *Scotland the Movie*, Edinburgh, Polygon, 1996.

Cleary, J., '"Fork-tongued on the border bit": partition and the politics of form in contemporary narratives of the Northern Irish conflict', *South Atlantic Quarterly*, Winter 1996, vol. 95, no. 1, pp. 227–76.

Cook, P., '*Mandy*: Daughter of transition', in C. Barr (ed.) *All Our Yesterdays: 90 Years of British Cinema*, London, BFI, 1986, pp. 355–61.

Cook, P., *Fashioning the Nation: Costume and Identity in British Cinema*, London, BFI, 1996.

Desjardins, M., 'Free from the apron strings: representations of mothers in the maternal British state', in L. Friedman (ed.) *British Cinema and Thatcherism: Fires Were Started*, London, UCL Press, 1993, pp. 130–44.

Diawara, M., 'Power and territory: the emergence of black British film collectives', in Friedman, L. (ed.) *British Cinema and Thatcherism: Fires Were Started*, London, UCL Press, 1993, pp. 147–60.

Dyer, R., *The Matter of Images: Essays on Representations*, London, Routledge, 1993.

Eley, G., '*Distant Voices, Still Lives*, the family is a dangerous place: memory, gender and the image of the working class', in R.A. Rosenstone (ed.) *Revisioning History: Film and the Construction of a New Past*, Princeton, Princeton University Press, 1995.

Geraghty, C., 'Women and sixties British cinema: the development of the "Darling" girl', in R. Murphy (ed.) *The British Cinema Book*, London, BFI, 1997, pp. 155–63.

Harper, S., 'From *Holiday Camp* to high camp: women in British feature films, 1945–1951', in A. Higson (ed.) *Dissolving Views: Key Writings on British Cinema*, London, Cassell, 1996, pp. 94–116.

Hill, J., *Sex, Class and Realism: British Cinema 1956–1963*, London, BFI, 1986.

Hill, J., 'British cinema as national cinema: production, audience and representation', in R. Murphy (ed.) *The British Cinema Book*, London, BFI, 1997, pp. 244–54.

Hill, J. and McLoone, M. (eds) *Border Crossing: Film in Ireland, Britain and Europe*, Belfast, IIS/BFI, 1994.

King, J., 'Crossing thresholds: the contemporary British woman's film', in A. Higson (ed.) *Dissolving Views: Key Writings on British Cinema*, London, Cassell, 1996, pp. 216–31.

Kureishi, H., *My Beautiful Launderette and The Rainbow Sign*, London, Faber and Faber, 1986.

McArthur, C. (ed.) *Scotch Reels: Scotland in Cinema and Television*, London, BFI, 1982.

McIlroy, B., 'The repression of communities: visual representations of Northern Ireland during the Thatcher years', in L. Friedman (ed.) *British Cinema and Thatcherism: Fires Were Started*, London, UCL Press, 1993, pp. 92–108.

—— *Shooting to Kill: Filmmaking and the 'Troubles' in Northern Ireland*, Trowbridge, Flicks Books, 1999.

Malik, S., 'Beyond "the cinema of duty"? The pleasures of hybridity: black British film of the 1980s and 1990s', in A. Higson (ed.) *Dissolving Views: Key Writings on British Cinema*, London, Cassell, 1996, pp. 202–15.

Medhurst, A., 'That special thrill: *Brief Encounter*, homosexuality and authorship', *Screen*, Summer 1991, vol. 32, no. 2, pp. 197–208.

—— '*Victim*: text as context', in A. Higson (ed.) *Dissolving Views: Key Writings on British Cinema*, London, Cassell, 1996, pp. 117–32.

Mercer, K. (ed.) *Black Film, British Cinema*, London, ICA, 1988.

Michie, A., 'Scotland: strategies of centralisation', in C. Barr (ed.) *All Our Yesterdays: 90 Years of British Cinema*, London, BFI, 1986, pp. 252–71.

Petley, J., 'The lost continent', in C. Barr (ed.) *All Our Yesterdays: 90 Years of British Cinema*, London, BFI, 1986, pp. 98–119.

Petrie, D. (ed.) *Screening Europe: Image and Identity in Contemporary European Cinema*, London, BFI, 1992.

Pines, J., 'British cinema and black representation', in R. Murphy (ed.) *The British Cinema Book*, London, BFI, 1997, pp. 207–16.

Spicer, A., 'Male stars, masculinity and British cinema, 1945–1960', in R. Murphy (ed.) *The British Cinema Book*, London, BFI, 1997, pp. 144–53.

Stead, P., *The Working Class and Film*, London, Routledge, 1989.

Thumin, J., *Celluloid Sisters: Women and Popular Cinema*, London, Macmillan, 1992.

Various authors, 'Contemporary Irish cinema supplement', *Cineaste*, 1999, vol. XXIV, nos. 2–3, pp. 23–76.

Young, L., *Fear of the Dark: 'Race', Gender and Sexuality in the Cinema*, London, Routledge, 1996.

Studios and film production

Aspinall, S. and Murphy, R. (eds) *Gainsborough Melodrama*, London, BFI, 1983.

Barr, C., *Ealing Studios*, London, Cameron and Tayleur/David and Charles, 1977.

Cook, P., *Gainsborough Pictures*, London, Cassell, 1997.

Eberts, J. and Ilott, T., *My Indecision is Final: The Rise and Fall of Goldcrest Films*, London, Faber and Faber, 1990.

Eyles, A., Adkinson, R. and Fry, N. (eds) *The House of Horror: The Complete Story of Hammer Films*, London, Lorrimer, 1984.

Falk, Q., *The Golden Gong: Fifty Years of the Rank Organisation, Its Films and Its Stars*, London, Columbus Books, 1987.

Finney, A., *The Egos Have Landed: The Rise and Fall of Palace Pictures*, London, Heinemann, 1996.

Hearn, M. and Barnes, A., *The Hammer Story*, London, Titan Books, 1997.

Hunter, J., (ed.) *House of Horror: The Complete Hammer Films Story*, London, Creation Books, 1996.

Hutchings, P., *Hammer and Beyond: The British Horror Film*, Manchester/New York, Manchester University Press, 1993.

Johnson, T. and Del Vecchio, D., *Hammer Films: An Exhaustive Filmography*, Jefferson N.J./London, McFarland and Company, 1996.

Macnab, J., *J. Arthur Rank and the British Film Industry*, London, Routledge, 1993.

Meikle, D., *A History of Horrors: The Rise and Fall of the House of Hammer*, Lanham, M.D./London, The Scarecrow Press, 1996.

Petrie, D., *Creativity and Constraint in the British Film Industry*, London, Macmillan, 1991.

Porter, V., 'The context of creativity: Ealing Studios and Hammer Films', in J. Curran and V. Porter (eds) *British Cinema History*, London, Weidenfeld and Nicholson, 1983, pp. 179–207.

—— *On Cinema*, London, Pluto Press, 1985.

—— 'Methodism versus the market-place: the Rank Organisation and British cinema', in R. Murphy, *The British Cinema Book*, London, BFI, 1997, pp. 122–32.

Pulleine, T., 'A song and dance at the local: thoughts on Ealing', in R. Murphy (ed.) *The British Cinema Book*, London, BFI, 1997, pp. 114–21.

Ryall, T., 'A British studio system: The Associated British Picture Corporation and the Gaumont-British Picture Corporation in the 1930s', in R. Murphy (ed.) *The British Cinema Book*, London, BFI, 1997, pp. 27–36.

Threadgall, D., *Shepperton Studios*, London, BFI, 1994.

Warren, P., *Elstree: The British Hollywood*, London, Elm Tree Books, 1983.

—— *British Film Studios: An Illustrated History*, London, B.T. Batsford, 1995.

Wood, L., 'Julius Hagen and Twickenham Film Studios', in J. Richards (ed.) *The Unknown 1930s: An Alternative History of the British Cinema, 1929–1939*, London, I.B. Tauris, 1998, pp. 37–55.

Woollacott, J., 'The James Bond films: Conditions of production', in J. Curran and V. Porter (eds) *British Cinema History*, London, Weidenfeld and Nicholson, 1983, pp. 208–25.

Audiences, exhibition and reception

Atwell, D., *Cathedrals of the Movies: A History of British Cinemas and their Audiences*, London, Architectural Press, 1980.

Corrigan, P., 'Film entertainment as ideology and pleasure: towards a history of audiences', in J. Curran and V. Porter (eds) *British Cinema History*, London, Weidenfeld and Nicholson, 1983, pp. 24–35.

Docherty, D., Morrison, D. and Tracey, M., *The Last Picture Show? Britain's Changing Film Audience*, London, BFI, 1987.

Eyles, A., *ABC, The First Name in Entertainment*, London, BFI, 1993.

—— *Gaumont British Cinemas*, London, BFI, 1996.

—— 'Exhibition and the cinemagoing experience', in R. Murphy (ed.) *The British Cinema Book*, London, BFI, 1997, pp. 217–25.

Field, A., *Picture Palace: A Social History of the Cinema*, London, Gentry Books, 1974.

Halliwell, L., *Seats in All Parts*, London, Granada, 1985.

Kuhn, A. and Street, S. (eds) *Journal of Popular British Cinema* (special issue on 'Audiences and reception in Britain'), 1999, no. 2.

Mayer, J.P., *British Cinemas and their Audiences: Sociological Studies*, London, Dobson, 1948.

Morgan, G., *Red Roses Every Night: An Account of London's Cinemas Under Fire*, London, Quality Press, 1948.

Moss, L. and Box, K., *The Cinema Audience: An Inquiry Made by the Wartime Social Survey for the Ministry of Information*, London, Ministry of Information, 1943.

O'Brien, M. and Eyles, A. (eds) *Enter the Dream-House: Memories of Cinemas in South London from the Twenties to the Sixties*, London, Museum of the Moving Image/BFI, 1985.

Richards, J., *The Age of the Dream Palace: Cinema and Society in Britain 1930–1939*, London, Routledge and Kegan Paul, 1984.

Richards, J. and Sheridan, D. (eds) *Mass Observation at the Movies*, London, Routledge and Kegan Paul, 1987.

Roddick, N., 'New audiences, new films', in M. Auty and N. Roddick (eds) *British Cinema Now*, London, BFI, 1985, pp. 19–30.

Samson, J., 'The film society, 1925–1939', in C. Barr (ed.) *All Our Yesterdays: 90 Years of British Cinema*, London, BFI, 1986, pp. 306–13.

Sedgwick, J., 'Cinemagoing preferences in Britain in the 1930s', in J. Richards (ed.) *The Unknown 1930s*, London, I.B. Tauris, 1998, pp. 1–36.

Sedgwick, J., 'Film "hits" and "misses" in mid-1930s Britain', *Historical Journal of Film, Radio and Television*, August 1998, vol. 18, pp. 333–51.

Sharp, D., *The Picture Palace and Other Buildings for the Movies*, London, Hugh Evelyn, 1969.

Stacey, J., *Star Gazing: Hollywood Cinema and Female Spectatorship*, London, Routledge, 1994.

Staples, T., *All Pals Together: The Story of Children's Cinema*, Edinburgh, Edinburgh University Press, 1997.

Thumin, J., *Celluloid Sisters: Women and Popular Cinema*, London, Macmillan, 1992.

The British film industry and the international market

Jarvie, I., *Hollywood's Overseas Campaign: The North Atlantic Movie Trade, 1920–1950*, Cambridge, Cambridge University Press, 1992.

Dale, M., *The Movie Game: The Film Industry in Britain, Europe and America*, London, Cassell, 1997.

Higson, A. and Maltby, R. (eds) *'Film Europe' and 'Film America': Cinema, Commerce and Cultural Exchange, 1920–1939*, Exeter, University of Exeter Press, 1999.

Murphy, R., 'Rank's attempt on the American market', in J. Curran and V. Porter (eds) *British Cinema History*, London, Weidenfeld and Nicholson, 1983.

—— 'Under the shadow of Hollywood', in C. Barr (ed.) *All Our Yesterdays: 90 Years of British Cinema*, London, BFI, 1986, pp. 47–71.

Puttnam, D. with Watson, N., *The Undeclared War: The Struggle for Control of the World's Film Industry*, London, Harper Collins, 1997.

Thompson, K., *Exporting Entertainment: America in the World Film Market, 1907–34*, London, BFI, 1985.

British cinema and the state (censorship, policy, regulation)

Aldgate, A., *Censorship and the Permissive Society: British Cinema and Theatre, 1955–1965*, Oxford, Clarendon Press, 1995.

Caughie, J., 'Broadcasting and cinema: 1: converging histories', in C. Barr (ed.) *All Our Yesterdays: 90 Years of British Cinema*, London, BFI, 1986, pp. 189–205.

Dickinson, M., 'The state and the consolidation of monopoly', in J. Curran and V. Porter (eds) *British Cinema History*, London, Weidenfeld and Nicholson, 1983, pp. 74–95.

Dickinson, M., and Street, S., *Cinema and State: The Film Industry and the British Government, 1927–84*, London, BFI, 1985.

Ferman, J. and Phelps, G., *A Student's Guide to Film Classification and Censorship in Britain*, London, BBFC, 1993.

Hartog, S., 'State protection of a beleaguered industry', in J. Curran and V. Porter (eds) *British Cinema History*, London, Weidenfeld and Nicholson, 1983, pp. 59–73.

Hill, J., 'British film policy', in A. Moran (ed.) *Film Policy: International, National and Regional Perspectives*, London, Routledge, 1996, pp. 101–13.

Journal of Popular British Cinema (special issue on censorship), 2000, no. 3.

Petley, J., 'Cinema and state', in C. Barr (ed.) *All Our Yesterdays: 90 Years of British Cinema*, London, BFI, 1986, pp. 31–46.

Pronay, N. and Croft, J. 'British film censorship and propaganda policy during the Second World War', in J. Curran and V. Porter (eds) *British Cinema History*, London, Weidenfeld and Nicholson, 1983, pp. 144–63.

Richards, J., *The Age of the Dream Palace: Cinema and Society in Britain, 1930–1939*, London, Routledge and Kegan Paul, 1984.

—— 'British film censorship', in R. Murphy (ed.) *The British Cinema Book*, London, BFI, 1997, pp. 167–77.

Robertson, J.C., *The British Board of Film Censors, 1896–1956*, London, Croom Helm, 1985.

—— *The Hidden Cinema: British Film Censorship in Action, 1913–1975*, New York, Routledge, 1989.

Slide, A., *Banned in the USA: British Films in the United States and their Censorship, 1933–60*, London, I.B. Tauris, 1998.

Street, S., 'The Hays Office and the defence of the British market in the 1930s', *Historical Journal of Film, Radio and Television*, 1985, vol. 5, no. 1, pp. 143–60.

—— 'British film and the national interest, 1927–1939', in R. Murphy (ed.) *The British Cinema Book*, London, BFI, 1997, pp. 17–26.

INDEX